# Power: a reader

MANCHESTER
UNIVERSITY PRESS

# POWER:
# A READER

*Edited by*
MARK HAUGAARD

**Manchester University Press**

Manchester and New York

*distributed exclusively in the USA by Palgrave*

Editorial matter Copyright © Mark Haugaard 2002
All other material Copyright © as acknowledged

The right of Mark Haugaard to be identified as the author
of this work has been asserted by him in accordance
with the Copyright, Designs and Patents Act 1988.

*Published by* Manchester University Press
Oxford Road, Manchester M13 9NR, UK
*and* Room 400, 175 Fifth Avenue, New York, NY 10010, USA
www.manchesteruniversitypress.co.uk

*Distributed exclusively in the USA by*
Palgrave, 175 Fifth Avenue, New York,
NY 10010, USA

*Distributed exclusively in Canada by*
UBC Press, University of British Columbia, 2029 West Mall,
Vancouver, BC, Canada V6T 1Z2

*British Library Cataloguing-in-Publication Data*
A catalogue record for this book is available from the British Library

*Library of Congress Cataloging-in-Publication Data applied for*


ISBN 0 7190 5728 0   *hardback*
     0 7190 5729 9   *paperback*


First published 2002

10 09 08 07 06 05 04 03 02   10 9 8 7 6 5 4 3 2 1
Typeset in Stone Serif
by SNP Best-set Typesetter Ltd., Hong Kong
Printed in Great Britain
by Biddles Ltd, Guildford and King's Lynn

# Contents

# Acknowledgements

I would like to thank the SSRC NUI, Galway for its assistance and Mary Silke for her typing. Thanks to Pete Morriss for his insightful comments and to Ricca Edmondson for her encouragement. I would also like to acknowledge the patience and flexibility of my editors at MUP.

I dedicate this book to my friends and colleagues in the IPSA Research Committee on Political Power (RC 36) with whom, over many meetings and social occasions, I have analysed the concept of political power. These include, in particular, Erkki Berndtson, Stewart Clegg, Phil Cerny, Henri Goverde and Howard Lentner.

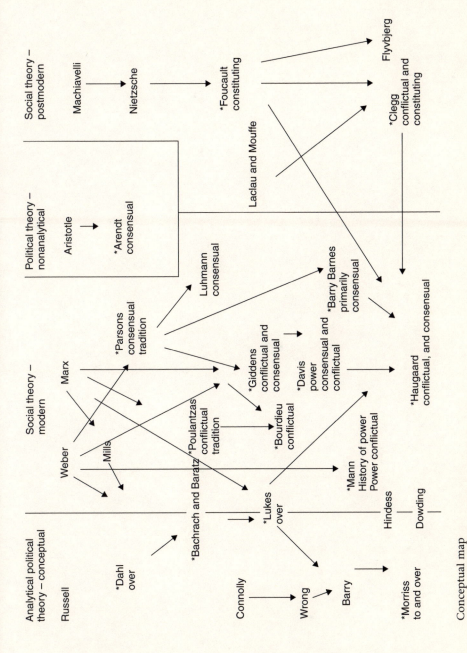

Conceptual map
Note: * indicates people discussed in this book.

# Introduction

This annotated reader is intended as an introductory guide to some of the most significant perspectives on power within social and political theory. Each article or extract has been provided with its own introduction which places the work in context. In some instances the introductions are longer than others. This does not indicate some form of prioritization but, rather, reflects the level of complexity of introducing the material in question – introducing thinkers such as Giddens, Bourdieu and Foucault necessitates more ink than, for instance, Bachrach and Baratz.

In writing the introductions, I was confronted by the choice of writing either a few bland paragraphs with which no one could disagree or, alternatively, writing short, but theoretically substantive, statements which draw upon my reflections on power over the past years. I opted for the latter course of action because it has the advantage of providing the reader with substantive theoretical tools with which to make sense of the thinkers in question.

With regard to choice of readings, it was invariably a question of compromise. Some thinkers have to be included at the expense of others. There is also the choice between length and readability, and finally there is the problem of copyright. When I first undertook this project, I had no idea how difficult it is to obtain permission from copyright holders. In fact, in certain instances it proved impossible to track them down. Copyright determined many choices. However, despite these constraints, the result has worked out as I originally intended: the book which you hold is an excellent point of departure for understanding more about social and political power. It may be used as a course text for undergraduates, as an initial point of orientation for postgraduate or academic researchers and last, but not least, it may be tackled by the non-academic reader with an interest in understanding power.

To the uninitiated, the array of power perspectives may appear bewildering (see conceptual map, p. vii). The lack of unity is, in part, a reflection of the nature of power as a concept. Power is, what the philosopher Wittgenstein terms, a 'family resemblance' concept. This entails that when we use the concept in different contexts its meaning changes sufficiently so that there is no single definition of power which covers all usage. In order to understand this idea,

1

imagine the members of a family each of whom resembles the other but as a group have no one set of characteristics in common – Mary has the same hair as her mother, and has her father's chin, whereas John has his mother's nose and his father's ears. The example which Wittgenstein used to illustrate the concept of a family resemblance concept was the word 'game'. If we compare cards and football, we might think that winning and losing are central to defining a game but then, on the other hand, if we observe a child engaged in a solitary game of bouncing a ball against a wall there is no winning or losing (Wittgenstein 1967, p. 32 §67). Again we may find some characteristic which these three games have in common but, invariably, a different game will turn up which does not share this characteristic (and so on and so forth). While the family resemblance nature of the concept 'game' may be a considerable inconvenience to compilers of dictionaries, it does not, in the vast majority of circumstances, cause any problems in communication. The reason is that the meaning of words is relationally constituted by context, and the human mind is incredibly fast and efficient at grasping which usage is the pertinent one (many puns are based upon fooling us into imagining the wrong context or family relative).

In everyday usage there exists power as in 'horse power' and power as in 'political power' – while these 'powers' share similarities, are possibly even second cousins, they are far from the same. While such obviously different contexts entail family resemblance, the uninitiated might be forgiven for thinking that all instances of political power, or social power, may be reducible to one concept but, unfortunately, this is not the case either. There will never be a single concept of either political or social power because each usage takes place within local, tacit or explicit, theoretical systems. Any theory which we construct (or take for granted) is almost like a sub-language within the greater language. To use another felicitous term coined by Wittgenstein, each theory is a local 'language game'. Words should not be viewed as essences but, rather, as conceptual tools. They are devices which enable us to create things – ideas and theoretical systems. Just as plumbers, carpenters and mechanics each have their particular tool boxes with special pliers, spanners, grips, cutting devices, cramps and those 'handy home-made thingamajigs', so, too, sociologists, political scientists and social and political theorists fill their conceptual tool chests with exactly the conceptual tools which they need to get their job done. There is nothing intrinsically unsatisfactory with this arrangement but it does entail that the search for a single concept of power is intrinsically illusory. There will always be specific usages which are particularly suitable to certain theoretical projects.

Broadly speaking, there are four general language games within which the power debate has taken place: normative political theory of the analytical conceptual variety, political theory building of non-conceptual variety, and social theory of modern and postmodern orientations. This division is, of course, an ideal type classification: theorists frequently do not fall neatly into one category or the other. In fact, one of the main protagonists, Lukes, falls between categories and even an obviously social thinker such as Giddens has moments when he moves from one category to another.

Moving between language games is not intrinsically a problem if the author in question is aware that power has altered meaning as a result of changing language game. However, it can cause confusion when the author is unaware of what is going on. To cite one instance among the many that have bedevilled power analysis, Lukes conceptualizes power in the third dimension as the unintended structural effects of actions ('the bias of the system is not sustained simply by a series of individually chosen acts, but also, most importantly, by the socially structured and culturally patterned behaviour of groups . . .' (Lukes 1974, p. 22)) and, entirely inconsistently with this, asserts that Poulantzas was mistaken in thinking that power could be structural (Lukes 1974, p. 55) because, by definition, power entails fixing responsibility (Lukes 1974, p. 56). This obvious inconsistency (in a short book) is a consequence of using power as a social theory concept in the first instance while, in the second usage, considering power within the language game of analytical normative political theory.

The analytical tradition seeks to clarify concepts as part of a process of building logically consistent normative theory. In this spirit we find, for instance, Dahl wishing to distinguish power from power resources and Morriss maintaining that power should not be confused with influence.

Those whom I term 'social theorists' construct empirical models of how society works and, depending upon their theory, define power in a manner which best suits their model. This sometimes means that their concept of power is highly specific. There is nothing inherently wrong with this except if the theorist in question (or reader) is unaware that what they are calling power may be substantially narrower and different from the way other people use the term. For instance, Parsons constructed a systems theory model of society in which power is a consensual circulating medium while, in contrast, Poulantzas built a Marxist social theory where power is conceptualized in terms of the ability of a class to realize its objective interests. These perceptions of power are virtual opposites. As a consequence, when using their work it has to be born in mind that they are not writing about power in general but using power as a local conceptual tool within a specific language game.

Social theory is, in turn, divided between modern and postmodern social perspectives. At the most general level, modernists are those thinkers who still hold with the Enlightenment idea that reason can deliver knowledge which is true until proven false whereas postmodernists view all knowledge as strategic.

The final general class is political theory operating from a nonanalytical perspective. There is only one theorist in this class included in this book. Rather than clarify concepts, Arendt builds a model of how society should be constituted based upon her knowledge of phenomenology and theoretical observations on totalitarianism. As with the social theorists, her conceptualization of power is a tool made for a highly specific task and, as such, is slightly esoteric (in the non-pejorative sense of the word).

Within these groups there are certain generalized perceptions of power which seem to dominate. These include: power 'over' and power 'to' (analytic), 'conflictual power' and 'consensual power' (social theory of the modern variety), and power as constitutive of reality (postmodern social theory). Power 'over' entails the ability of one actor to prevail over another despite resistance whereas power 'to' is power as a generalized capacity as in 'A has power to make x happen'. To an extent, conflictual and consensual power mirror power 'over' and power 'to' respectively but, because they are couched within an empirically based theoretical system, the objective is not so much to clarify what we mean by power 'over' or 'to' but to characterize the general nature of social life and, as a consequence, I consider conflictual and consensual power are more appropriate terms. Arendt's view of power is also linked to a general theory of social order, hence it is a form of consensual power.

Within postmodern social theory, power is frequently perceived of as constituting reality; this view has a certain affinity with the consensual view of power but is sufficiently different, due to the theoretical context, to deserve a separate term. Constitutive power is sometimes referred to as 'positive' power which has the potential to cause misunderstanding if, mistakenly, interpreted in the normative sense.

In order to provide an overview of the terrain, I have drawn a general conceptual map of the various schools and interpretations. The arrows indicate conceptual affinities rather than substantive claims of direct influence. I have had to be sparing with the use of arrows in order to draw a diagram which is not too complex to be useful. In reality, the influences and affinities are greater than indicated. Some authors, whose work does not feature in this reader, are, nevertheless, of theoretical significance and an asterisk has been used to indicate that a theorist has been included.

From practical experience of using overheads in lectures, I am aware that people think in different ways. People who think visually find diagrams more useful than those who learn orally or kinetically. If you find the diagram more of a hindrance than a help, skip it for now and come back to it when you have finished the book. For those who learn visually, the diagram is like geographical map: it is a plan of an exciting theoretical terrain which will, hopefully, hold you spellbound. Like a geographical map, it shows only the mountain peaks, a few contours and the main roads; the trees, great outcrops of rock, beautiful valleys and tumbling waterfalls are for you to discover by yourself – between you and the printed page.

# 1  Dahl

*[handwritten: Polyarchy ⟶ government by a plurality of interacting elites. (& non-hierarchical)]*

## Introduction

The article 'Power', which appeared in 1968 as an entry in the *International Encyclopaedia of Social Science*, is in many respects a summation of Dahl's views on power as they developed during the 1950s and 1960s.

Dahl entered the power debate in response to criticisms of the workings of American democracy. Community power theorists, most notably Hunter (1953), analysed power at a local level and concluded that it was highly unequal in its distribution. Despite the existence of democratic institutions, local politics were run by economic notables and associated unaccountable figures who worked behind the scenes. The methodology used by the community power theorists was largely 'reputational'. They asked locals 'in the know' to make lists of those who, in their opinion, ran the community. These lists were compared and the names that appeared repeatedly were taken to constitute the local power elite. *[handwritten: local elites]*

Another critic of American democracy was C. Wright Mills – one of the chief exponents of left-wing sociology in the States at that time and author of, what is now considered, one of the classic introductions to sociology, *The Sociological Imagination* (1959). In *The Power Elite* Mills analysed who held power in the US at a national level. He concluded that power was essentially pyramidal in shape, comprising an elite of approximately four hundred who either made or influenced the 'big decisions' – the decisions that really matter. Below the top elite were smaller pyramids, again of four hundred, comprising the local elite. Echoing the ideas of Max Weber and, to some extent, Robert Michels, Mills conceived of these elites as coming from mutual and dependent bureaucracies (economic, military and political), constituted by an internal bureaucratic logic that set the agenda of political power. It is not that there was a conspiracy but, rather, that the economic, military and political organizations had mutual dependent needs which created a shared agenda. Furthermore, he also showed that these bureaucracies were led by individuals who had shared life experiences and, as a consequence, were likely to share common perceptions of the world – an elite culture did indeed exist. *[handwritten: hierarchies of elites]*

Dahl defended American democracy by developing a sophisticated vocabulary of power, which is still influential. Building upon Weber's definition of power 'as the probability that one actor within a social relationship will be in a position to carry out his will despite resistance, regardless of the basis on which this probability rests' (Weber 1978, p. 53), within Dahl's framework A has power over B to the extent to which A can get B to do something which B would not otherwise do (in the article which follows, Dahl uses C and R in place of A and B but, for whatever reason, A and B are current usage in debates on power).

This definition fitted within Dahl's view of democracy as a set of institutional procedures for ensuring equality in decision-making. Within this vision democracy is not conceived of as a wider emancipatory project but concerns political decisions which matter in the running of the state political structures. Within this paradigm, power is highly specific in its meaning. It is about prevailing in decision-making and is not to be equated with power resources, which are only potential power. Importantly for Dahl, resources may or may not be mobilized in decision-making. One wealthy person may choose to collect paintings while another collects politicians, both may have equal resources but only the latter is powerful. Not only are resources potential power but they also have different scopes, where the scope of power concerns the specific issues which can be affected. Both a university professor and the local traffic police may have power over the students at Yale but their powers are of entirely different scope: the professor can influence how they study and the police where they park their cars. However, neither the professor nor the police have generalized power over the students. Furthermore, it is hard to imagine how they could combine their resources to constitute a power elite with regard to students.

Armed with a sophisticated conceptual vocabulary, Dahl argued that all Mills had managed to prove was that resources (potential power) were unequal but not that these resources were activated by a monolithic elite. The community power theorists had not even managed to prove an unequal distribution of resources but, rather, an unequal distribution of reputations for power.

Using these and other conceptual distinctions Dahl undertook his own community power study in New Haven – the city where Yale is situated. In *Who Governs?* (1961) Dahl analysed who initiated and who vetoed decisions in key issue areas. The chosen areas were political nominations (self-evidently a key), public education (the biggest item on the city budget) and urban renewal (New Haven was undergoing massive urban renewal at that time). This focus upon decisions avoided the error of equating actual power with either resources or reputations.

In his study, Dahl found that while there was an unequal distribution of resources, there was not a single elite which exercised power in all three areas. The only person who had power in more than one issue area was the democratically elected Mayor. From this he concluded that there was not one elite in New Haven but a plurality of elites. In place of a single pyramid of power he argued that there was a multiplicity of competing power pyramids, none of which was dominant. Building on Schumpeter's model of democracy (Schumpeter 1976), Dahl argued that modern democracies delivered democratic outcomes through competition between elites. While people are not equal in power resources, as in some forms of participatory democracy, the US could be considered a pluralist democracy through a process whereby the unintended consequence of competition resulted in democratic outcomes. Reminiscent of Aristotle's classification of forms of government, Dahl termed this form of government polyarchy.

*[handwritten margin note: pluralistic democracy ↓ polyarchy]*

Dahl's model of power was criticized by many, including Bachrach and Baratz (see chapter 2) and Lukes (see chapter 3). Both argued that his concept of power was unduly narrow. This is a critique which, in his writings on democracy, Dahl has largely come to accept. In the 1980s, Dahl reworked his analysis of polyarchy to include substantial levels of citizen participation in the economic realm (1985) and in the everyday running of the business of state through the use of electronic mass media. While Dahl has not found it necessary to redefine the concept of power, he has argued that in order for polyarchy to deliver genuinely democratic outcomes, democracy should not be thought of solely in terms of equality in the arena where decisions are made but, significantly, should also include the wider economic and educational context which shapes people's ability to articulate their interests. Polyarchy entails the empowerment of the people. It is a vision of democracy which receives its most powerful articulation in *Democracy and Its Critics* (1989).

## Further reading

The background reading in this area is truly extensive. For those who are interested in 'classic' sociological background, Weber's analysis of power and domination should be read. This includes *Economy and Society*, vol. I (Weber 1978): his definition of power is on p. 53, his analysis of forms of domination is the first half of chapter 3 (pp. 212–54). This is also available as *The Theory of Social and Economic Organization* (Weber 1947, [1964 and many reprints] p. 152 and pp. 324–72). In *Economy and Society*, vol. 2 he returns to these themes on pp. 910–65. Max Weber (1948 – many reprints) may be more convenient and contains useful extracts from *Economy and Society*. Most selections or readers of classic sociology include some of the relevant extracts (for instance McIntosh 1997) and Lukes (1986) also contains a short extract from Weber on power. Robert Michels *Political Parties* (1913 – some reprints) is a 'classic' but, by now, is possibly only of more specialist interest.

Good starting points for the general debate include Mills *The Power Elite* (1956 – reissued), Dahl *Who Governs?* (1961 – reissued), Dahl (1957 – also in Scott 1994) and Polsby (1963, 2nd edn 1980). I would recommend Hunter (1953) only to the enthusiast. The three-volume collection *Power* (Scott 1994) reproduces many useful specialist articles concerning the analytic and normative approaches to power. For those who wish to look at Dahl's more recent analysis of pluralist democracy, I would recommend *Democracy and Its Critics* (Dahl 1989) – it is also an excellent general introduction to democratic theory.

# 'POWER'
## Robert A. Dahl
(1968)

In approaching the study of politics through the analysis of power, one assumes, at a minimum, that relations of power are among the significant aspects of a political system. This assumption, and therefore the analysis of power, can be applied to any kind of political system, international, national, or local, to associations and groups of various kinds, such as the family, the hospital, and the business firm, and to historical developments.

At one extreme, an analysis of power may simply postulate that power relations are one feature of politics among a number of others – but nonetheless a sufficiently important feature to need emphasis and description. At the other extreme, an analyst may hold that power distinguishes 'politics' from other human activity; to analysts of this view 'political science, as an empirical discipline, is the study of the shaping and sharing of power' (Lasswell & Kaplan 1950, p. xiv).

In either case, the analyst takes it for granted that differences between political systems, or profound changes in the same society, can often be interpreted as differences in the way power is distributed among individuals, groups, or other units. Power may be relatively concentrated or diffused; and the share of power held by different individuals, strata, classes, professional groups, ethnic, racial, or religious groups, etc., may be relatively great or small. The analysis of power is often concerned, therefore, with the identification of elites and leadership, the discovery of the ways in which power is allocated to different strata, relations among leaders and between leaders and non-leaders, and so forth.

Although the approach to politics through the study of power relations is sometimes thought to postulate that everyone seeks power as the highest value, analysts of power generally reject this assumption as psychologically untenable; the analysis of power does not logically imply any particular psychological assumptions. Sometimes critics also regard the analysis of power as implying that the pursuit of power is morally good or at any rate that it should not be condemned. But an analysis of power may be neutral as to values; or the analyst may be concerned with power, not to glorify it, but in order to modify the place it holds in human relations and to increase the opportunities for dignity, respect, freedom, or other values (Jouvenel 1945; Lasswell & Kaplan 1950; Oppenheim 1961, chapters 8, 9).

Indeed, it would be difficult to explain the extent to which political theorists for the past 25 centuries have been concerned with relations of power

Reprinted by kind permission of The Gale Group from the *International Encyclopedia of the Social Sciences*, ed. David L. Sills, vol. 12 (pp. 405–15). Copyright © 1968, Crowell Collier and Macmillan, Inc.

and authority were it not for the moral and practical significance of power to any person interested in political life, whether as observer or activist. Some understanding of power is usually thought to be indispensable for moral or ethical appraisals of political systems. From a very early time – certainly since Socrates, and probably before – men have been inclined to judge the relative desirability of different types of political systems by, among other characteristics, the relations of power and authority in these systems. In addition, intelligent *action* to bring about a result of some kind in a political system, such as a change in a law or a policy, a revolution, or a settlement of an international dispute, requires knowledge of how to produce or 'cause' these results. In political action, as in other spheres of life, we try to produce the results we want by acting appropriately on the relevant causes. As we shall see, power relations can be viewed as causal relations of a particular kind.

It therefore seems most unlikely that the analysis of power will disappear as an approach to the study of politics. However, the fact that this approach is important and relevant does not shield it from some serious difficulties. These have become particularly manifest as the approach has been more earnestly and systematically employed.

## Origins

The attempt to study and explain politics by analyzing relations of power is, in a loose sense, ancient. To Aristotle, differences in the location of power, authority, or rule among the citizens of a political society served as one criterion for differentiating among actual constitutions, and it entered into his distinction between good constitutions and bad ones. With few exceptions (most notably Thomas Hobbes) political theorists did not press their investigations very far into certain aspects of power that have seemed important to social scientists in the twentieth century. For example, most political theorists took it for granted, as did Aristotle, that key terms like *power*, *influence*, *authority*, and *rule* (let us call them 'power terms') needed no great elaboration, presumably because the meaning of these words was clear to men of common sense. Even Machiavelli, who marks a decisive turning point from classical–normative to modern–empirical theory, did not consider political terms in general as particularly technical. Moreover, he strongly preferred the concrete to the abstract. In his treatment of power relations Machiavelli frequently described a specific event as an example of a general principle; but often the general principle was only implied or barely alluded to; and he used a variety of undefined terms such as *imperio*, *forza*, *potente*, and *autorità*.

From Aristotle to Hobbes political theorists were mainly concerned with power relations within a given community. But external relations even more than internal ones force attention to questions of relative power. The rise of the modern nation-state therefore compelled political theorists to recognize the saliency of power in politics, and particularly, of course, in international politics (Meinecke 1924).

Thus political 'realists' found it useful to define, distinguish, and interpret the state in terms of its power. Max Weber both reflected this tradition of 'realism' and opened the way for new developments in the analysis of power. '"Power" (*Macht*) is the probability that one actor within a social relationship will be in a position to carry out his own will despite resistance, regardless of the basis on which this probability rests' (Weber [1922] 1957, p. 152). This definition permitted Weber to conclude that 'the concept of power is highly comprehensive from the point of view of sociology. All conceivable . . . combinations of circumstances may put him [the actor] in a position to impose his will in a given situation' (p. 153). It follows that the state is not distinguishable from other associations merely because it employs a special and peculiarly important kind of power – force. In a famous and highly influential definition, Weber characterized the state as follows: 'A compulsory political association with continuous organization (*politischer Anstaltsbetrieb*) will be called a "state" if and in so far as its administrative staff successfully upholds a claim to the *monopoly* of the *legitimate* use of physical force in the enforcement of its order' (p. 154).

In his well-known typologies and his analyses of political systems, however, Weber was less concerned with power in general than with a special kind that he held to be unusually important – legitimate power, or authority.

Later theorists, practically all of whom were directly or indirectly influenced by Weber, expanded their objectives to include a fuller range of power relations. In the United States attempts to suggest or develop systematic and comprehensive theories of politics centering about power relations appeared in books by Catlin (1927; 1930), an important essay by Goldhamer and Shils (1939), and numerous works of the Chicago school – principally Merriam (1934), Lasswell (1936), and, in international politics, Morgenthau (1948). In the decade after World War II the ideas of the Chicago school were rapidly diffused throughout American political science.

### Elements in the analysis of power

Power terms evidently cover a very broad category of human relations. Considerable effort and ingenuity have gone into schemes for classifying these relations into various types, labeled power, influence, authority, persuasion, dissuasion, inducement, coercion, compulsion, force, and so on, all of which we shall subsume under the collective label power terms. The great variety and heterogeneity of these relations may, in fact, make it impossible – or at any rate not very fruitful – to develop general theories of power intended to cover them all.

At the most general level, power terms in modern social science refer to *subsets of relations among social units such that the behaviors of one or more units* (the responsive units, *R*) *depend in some circumstances on the behavior of other units* (the controlling units, *C*). (In the following discussion, *R* will always symbolize the responsive or dependent unit, *C* the controlling unit. These symbols will be used throughout and will be substituted even in direct quotations where the authors themselves have used different letters.) By this broad definition, then, power terms in the social sciences exclude relations with inanimate or even nonhuman objects; the control of a dog by his master or the power of a scientist over 'nature' provided by a nuclear reactor would fall, by definition, in a different realm of discourse. On the other hand the definition could include the power of one nation to affect the actions of another by threatening to use a nuclear reactor as a bomb or by offering to transfer it by gift or sale.

If power-terms include *all* relations of the kind just defined, then they spread very widely over the whole domain of human relations. In practice, analysts of power usually confine their attention to smaller subsets. One such subset consists, for example, of relations in which 'severe sanctions . . . are expected to be used or are in fact applied to sustain a policy against opposition' – a subset that Lasswell and Kaplan call power (1950, pp. 74–5). However, there is no agreement on the common characteristics of the various subsets covered by power terms, nor are different labels applied with the same meaning by different analysts.

Despite disagreement on how the general concept is to be defined and limited, the variety of smaller subsets that different writers find interesting or important, and the total lack of a standardized classification scheme and nomenclature, there is nonetheless some underlying unity in the various approaches to the analysis of power. In describing and explaining patterns of power, different writers employ rather similar elements (compare Cartwright 1965). What follows is an attempt to clarify these common elements by ignoring many differences in terminology, treatment, and emphasis.

*Some descriptive characteristics*

For purposes of exposition it is convenient to think of the analysis of power in terms of the familiar distinction between dependent and independent variables. The attempt to understand a political system may then be conceived of as an effort to *describe* certain characteristics of the system: the dependent variables; and to *explain* why the system takes on these particular characteristics, by showing the effects on these characteristics of certain other factors: the independent variables. Some of the characteristics of a political system that analysts seek to explain are the *magnitude* of the power of the *C*'s with respect to the *R*'s, how this power is *distributed* in the system, and the *scope*, and *domain*, of control that different individuals or actors have, exercise, or are subject to.

*Magnitude* Political systems are often characterized explicitly or implicitly by the differences in the 'amounts' of power (over the actions of the government or state) exercised by different individuals, groups, or strata. The magnitude of $C$'s power with respect to $R$ is thought of as measurable, in some sense, by at least an ordinal scale; frequently, indeed, a literal reading would imply that power is subject to measurement by an interval scale. How to compare and measure different magnitudes of power poses a major unsolved problem; we shall return to it briefly later on. Meanwhile, we shall accept the assumption of practically every political theorist for several thousand years, that it is possible to speak meaningfully of different amounts of power. Thus a typical question in the analysis of a political system would be: Is control over government highly concentrated or relatively diffused?

*Distribution* An ancient and conventional way of distinguishing among political systems is according to the way control over the government or the state is distributed to individuals or groups in the systems. Aristotle, for example, stated: 'The proper application of the term "democracy" is to a constitution in which the free-born and poor control the government – being at the same time a majority; and similarly the term "oligarchy" is properly applied to a constitution in which the rich and better-born control the government – being at the same time a minority' (*Politics*, Barker ed., p. 164). Control over government may be conceived as analogous to income, wealth, or property; and in the same way that income or wealth may be distributed in different patterns, so too the distribution of power over government may vary from one society or historical period to another. One task of analysis, then, is to classify and describe the most common distributions and to account for the different patterns. Typical questions would be: What are the characteristics of the $C$'s and of the $R$'s? How do the $C$'s and $R$'s compare in numbers? Do $C$'s and $R$'s typically come from different classes, strata, regions, or other groups? What historical changes have occurred in the characteristics of $C$ and $R$?

*Scope* What if $C$'s are sometimes not $C$'s, or $C$'s sometimes $R$'s, or $R$'s sometimes $C$'s? The possibility cannot be ruled out that individuals or groups who are relatively powerful with respect to one kind of activity may be relatively weak with respect to other activities. Power need not be general; it may be specialized. In fact, in the absence of a single world ruler, some specialization is inevitable; in any case, it is so commonplace that analysts of power have frequently insisted that a statement about the power of an individual, group, state, or other actor is practically meaningless unless it specifies the power of actor $C$ with respect to some class of $R$'s activities. Such a class of activities is sometimes called the range (Cartwright 1965) or the scope of $C$'s power (Lasswell & Kaplan 1950, p. 73). There is no generally accepted way of defining and classifying different scopes. However, a typical question about a political system would be: Is power generalized over many scopes, or is it specialized? If it is specialized, what are the characteristics of the $C$'s, the elites, in the different scopes? Is power specialized by individuals in the sense that $C_a$ and $C_b$ exercise power over different scopes, or is it also specialized by classes, social strata, skills, professions, or other categories?

*Domain*   $C$'s power will be limited to certain individuals; the $R$'s over whom $C$ has or exercises control constitute what is sometimes called the 'domain', or 'extension', of $C$'s power (Lasswell & Kaplan 1950, p. 73; Harsanyi 1962*a*, p. 67). Typical questions thus might be: Who are the $R$'s over whom $C$ has control? What are their characteristics? How numerous are they? How do they differ in numbers or characteristics from the $R$'s not under $C$'s control?

Given the absence of any standard unit of measure for amounts, distributions, scopes, domains, and other aspects of power, and the variety of ways of describing these characteristics, it is not at all surprising that there is an abundance of schemes for classifying political systems according to some characteristic of power. Most such schemes use, implicitly or explicitly, the idea of a *distribution of power over the behavior of government*. The oldest, most famous, and most enduring of these is the distinction made by the Greeks between rule by one, the few, and the many (*see* Aristotle, *Politics*, Barker ed., pp. 110 ff.). Some variant of this scheme frequently reappears in modern analyses of power (e.g., Lasswell & Kaplan 1950, p. 218). Often, as with Aristotle himself, the distribution of power is combined with one or more other dimensions (e.g., Dahl 1963, p. 38). Rough dichotomous schemes are common. One based on 'the degree of autonomy and interdependence of the several power holders' distinguishes two polar types, called autocracy and constitutionalism (Loewenstein 1957, p. 29). American community studies have in recent years called attention to differences between 'pluralistic' systems and unified or highly stratified 'power structures'. In one study that compares four communities the authors developed a more complex typology of power structures by combining a dimension of 'distribution of political power among citizens' with the degree of convergence or divergence in the ideology of leaders: the four types of power structures produced by dichotomizing these two dimensions are in turn distinguished from regimes (Agger et al. 1964, pp. 73 ff.).

*Some explanatory characteristics*

Given the different types of political systems, how are the differences among them to be explained? If, for example, control over government is sometimes distributed to the many, often to the few, and occasionally to one dominant leader, how can we account for the differences? Obviously these are ancient, enduring, and highly complex problems; and there is slight agreement on the answers. However, some factors that are often emphasized in modern analysis can be distinguished.

*Resources* Differences in patterns or structures of power may be attributed primarily, mainly, or partly to the way in which 'resources', or 'base values', are distributed among the individuals, strata, classes, and groups in different communities, countries, societies, and historical periods. This is an ancient, distinguished, widespread, and persuasive mode of explanation, used by Aristotle in Greece in the fourth century B.C., by James Harrington in seventeenth-century England, by the fathers of the American constitution in the late eighteenth century, by Marx and Engels in the nineteenth century, and by a great many social scientists in the twentieth century. A central hypothesis in most of these theories is that the greater one's resources, the greater one's power. Although explanations of this kind do not always go beyond tautology (by defining power in terms of resources), logical circularity is certainly not inherent in this mode of explanation. However, there is no accepted way of classifying resources or bases. Harold Lasswell has constructed a comprehensive scheme of eight base values which, although not necessarily exhaustive, are certainly inclusive; these are power (which can serve as a base for more power), respect, rectitude or moral standing, affection, well-being, wealth, skill, and enlightenment (Lasswell & Kaplan 1950, p. 87). Other writers choose more familiar categories to classify resources: for example, in trying to account for the patterns of influence in one community, the author described the patterns of social standing; the distribution of cash, credit, and wealth; access to legality, popularity, and control over jobs; and control over sources of information (Dahl 1961, pp. 229 ff.).

*Skill* Two individuals with access to approximately the same resources may not exercise the same degree of power (over, let us say, government decisions). Indeed, it is a common observation that individuals of approximately equal wealth or social status may differ greatly in power. To be sure, this might be accounted for by differences in access to other resources, such as the greater legality, bureaucratic knowledge, and public affection that fall to any individual who is chosen, say, to be prime minister of Britain or president of the United States. Another factor, however, one given particular prominence by Machiavelli, is political skill. Formally, skill could be treated as another resource. Nonetheless, it is generally thought to be of critical importance in explaining differences in the power of different leaders – different presidents, for example, as in Neustadt's comparison of presidents Roosevelt, Truman, and Eisenhower (1960, pp. 152 ff.). However, despite many attempts at analysis, from Machiavelli to the present day, political skill has remained among the more elusive aspects in the analysis of power.

*Motivations*  Two individuals with access to the same resources may exercise different degrees of power (with respect to some scope) because of different motivations: the one may use his resources to increase his power; the other may not. Moreover, since power is a relationship between *C*'s and *R*'s, the motivations not only of the *C*'s but also of the *R*'s are important. One person may worship authority, while another may defy it. A number of writers have explored various aspects of motivations involved in power relations (e.g., Lasswell 1930; Rogow & Lasswell 1963; Cartwright 1959).

*Costs*  Motivations can be related to resources by way of the economists' language of cost – a factor introduced into the analysis of power by a mathematical economist (Harsanyi 1962*a*; 1962*b*). In order to control *R*, *C* may have to use some of his resources. Thus *C*'s supply of resources is likely to have a bearing on how far he is willing to go in trying to control *R*. And variations in *C*'s resources are likely to produce variations in *C*'s power. *C*'s *opportunity costs* in controlling *R* – that is, what *C* must forgo or give up in other opportunities as a result of using some of his resources to control *R* – are less (other things being equal) if he is rich in resources than if he is poor in resources. In concrete terms, to a rich man the sacrifice involved in a campaign contribution of $100 is negligible; to a poor man the sacrifice entailed in a contribution of $100 is heavy. *C*'s willingness to use his resources to control *R* will also depend on the value to *C* of *R*'s response; the value of *R*'s response is, in turn, dependent in part on *C*'s motivations. The relationship may also be examined from *R*'s point of view. *R*'s opportunity costs consist of what he is then unable to do if he complies with *C*. In *R*'s case, as in *C*'s, his supply of resources and his motivations help determine his opportunity costs. Thus a power relation, can be interpreted as a sort of transaction between *C* and *R*.

*[handwritten margin note: Harsanyi ↓ transaction cost]*

## Problems of research

Like all other approaches to an understanding of complex social phenomena, the analysis of power is beset with problems. At a very general level, attempts to analyze power share with many – perhaps most – other strategies of inquiry in the social sciences the familiar dilemma of rigor versus relevance, and the dilemma has led to familiar results. Attempts to meet high standards of logical rigor or empirical verification have produced some intriguing experiments and a good deal of effort to clarify concepts and logical relationships but not rounded and well-verified explanations of complex political systems in the real world. Conversely, attempts to arrive at a better understanding of the more concrete phenomena of political life and institutions often sacrifice a good deal in rigor of logic and verification in order to provide more useful and reliable guides to the real world.

There are, however, a number of more specific problems in the analysis of power, many of which have only been identified in the last few decades.

Relevant work is quite recent and seeks (1) to clarify the central concepts, partly by expanding on the analogy between power relations and causal relations, (2) to specify particular subsets that are most interesting for social analysis, (3) to develop methods of measurement, and (4) to undertake empirical investigations of concrete political phenomena.

*Power and cause*

The closest equivalent to the power relation is the causal relation. For the assertion '*C* has power over *R*', one can substitute the assertion, '*C*'s behavior causes *R*'s behavior'. If one can define the causal relation, one can define influence, power, or authority, and vice versa (Simon [1947–56] 1957, p. 5).

Since the language of cause is no longer common in the formal theoretical language of the natural sciences, it might be argued that social scientists should also dispense with that language and that insofar as power is merely a term for a causal relation involving human beings, power-terms should simultaneously be dispensed with. But it seems rather unlikely that social scientists will, in fact, reject causal language. For the language of cause, like the language of power, is used to interpret situations in which there is the possibility that some event will intervene to change the order of other events. In medical research it is natural and meaningful to ask, Does cigarette smoking cause lung cancer and heart disease? In social situations the notion of cause is equally or even more appropriate. What makes causal analysis important to us is our desire to act on causes in the real world in order to bring about effects – reducing death rates from lung cancer, passing a civil-rights bill through Congress, or preventing the outbreak of war.

To interpret the terms *power, influence, authority*, etc., as instances of causal relations means, however, that the attempt to detect true rather than spurious power relations must run into the same difficulties that have beset efforts to distinguish true from spurious causal relations. Some analysts have confronted the problem; others have noted it only to put it aside; most have ignored it entirely, perhaps on the assumption that if social scientists tried to solve the unsolved problems of philosophy they would never get around to the problems of the social sciences. Yet if power is analogous to cause – or if power relations are logically a subset of causal relations – then recent analyses of causality must have relevance to the analysis of power.

In the first place, properties used to distinguish causation also serve to define power relations: covariation, temporal sequence, and asymmetry, for example. The appropriateness of these criteria has in fact been debated, not always conclusively, by various students of power (e.g., Simon [1947–56] 1957, pp. 5, 11, 12, 66; Dahl 1957, p. 204; Cartwright 1959, p. 197; Oppenheim 1961, p. 104).

Thus, the problem whether *A* can be said to cause *B* if *A* is a necessary condition for *B*, or a sufficient condition, or *both* necessary *and* sufficient, has also plagued the definition of power-terms. Some writers have explicitly stated or at least implied that relations of power mean that some action by *C* is a necessary condition for *R*'s response (Simon 1953, p. 504; March 1955, p. 435; Dahl 1957, p. 203). Oppenheim has argued, however, that such definitions permit statements that run flatly counter to common sense; he holds that it would be more appropriate to require only that *C*'s action be sufficient to produce *R*'s response (1961, p. 41). Riker has suggested in turn that 'the customary definition of power be revised . . . to reflect the necessary-and-sufficient condition theory of causality' (1964, p. 348). However, Blalock in his *Causal Inferences in Non-experimental Research* has shown that defining cause in terms of necessary and sufficient conditions leads to great practical difficulties in research. 'In real-life situations we seldom encounter instances where *B* is present if and only if *A* is also present' (1964, p. 30); moreover, specifying necessary and sufficient conditions requires the researcher 'to think always in terms of attributes and dichotomies', whereas 'there are most certainly a number of variables which are best conceived as continuously distributed, even though we may find it difficult to measure them operationally in terms of a specified unit of some kind' (p. 32). 'The use of "necessary and sufficient" terminology . . . may work well for the logician but not [for] the social scientist' (p. 34). Blalock's criticism, and indeed his whole effort to explore problems of causal inference in non-experimental research, are highly relevant to the analysis of power.

Aside from these somewhat rarefied philosophical and definitional questions, which many social scientists are prepared to abandon to metaphysicians or philosophers of science, the analogy between power and cause argues that the problem of distinguishing cause from correlation, or true from spurious causation, is bound to carry over into the analysis of power. And indeed it does. The difficulty of distinguishing true from spurious power relations has proved to be quite formidable.

The most rigorous method of distinguishing true from spurious causation is, of course, experimentation, and this would be the most rigorous method for distinguishing true from spurious power relations, provided the proper experimental conditions were present. Unfortunately, however, as in many areas of the social sciences, so too in the analysis of power, experimental methods have so far been of limited value, and for similar reasons. In non-experimental situations the optimal requirements for identifying causal relations seem to be the existence of satisfactory interval measures, a large supply of good data employing these measures, and an exhaustive analysis of alternative ways of accounting for the observations (Blalock 1964). Unfortunately, in the analysis of power, existing methods of measurement are rather inadequate, the data are often inescapably crude and limited, a variety of simple alternative explanations seem to fit the data about equally well, and in any case the complexity of the relations requires extraordinarily complex models.

*[margin annotation: CSS Here, does ho mean an analogy between power and mechanical causality?]*

The shortage of relevant models of power may disappear in time. In fact, the causal analogue suggests that the development of a great array of carefully described alternative models to compare with observations is probably a prerequisite for further development in the analysis of power. Again, the analogy between power and cause readily reveals why this would seem to be the case. In trying to determine the cause of a phenomenon it is of course impossible to know whether all the relevant factors in the real world are actually controlled during an investigation. Consequently, it is never possible to demonstrate causality.

*[margin annotation: causal inferences]*

> It is possible to make causal *inferences* concerning the adequacy of causal models, at least in the sense that we can proceed by eliminating inadequate models that make predictions that are not consistent with the data. . . . [Such] causal models involve (1) a finite set of explicitly defined variables, (2) certain assumptions about how these variables are interrelated causally, and (3) assumptions to the effect that outside variables, while operating, do not have confounding influences that disturb the causal patterning among the variables explicitly being considered. (*ibid.*, p. 62)

If power relations are a subset of causal relations, these requirements would also be applicable in the analysis of power.

In analyzing power, why have analysts so rarely attempted to describe, in rigorous language at any rate, the alternative causal models relevant to their inquiry? There seem to be several reasons. First, students of power have not always been wholly aware that distinguishing true from spurious power relations requires intellectual strategies at a rather high level of sophistication. Second, the crude quality of the observations usually available in studying power may discourage efforts to construct elegant theoretical models. Third, until recent times the whole approach to power analysis was somewhat speculative: there were a good many impressionistic works but few systematic empirical studies of power relations. Of the empirical studies now available most are investigations of power relations in American communities undertaken since 1950. These community studies have provoked a good deal of dispute over what are, in effect, alternative models of causation. So far, however, investigators have usually not described clearly the array of alternative models that might be proposed to explain their data, nor have they clearly specified the criteria they use for rejecting all the alternatives except the one they accept as their preferred explanation.

*[margin annotation: community power studies]*

Theories about power relations in various political systems are of course scattered through the writings of a number of analysts (e.g., Pareto 1916, volume 4; Mosca 1896, passim; Lasswell & Kaplan 1950, chapters 9, 10; Mills 1956; Dahl 1961; Rossi 1960; Polsby 1963; Parsons 1963*a*; 1963*b*). But a straightforward presentation of an empirical theory of power relations in political systems is a rarity. A notable exception is offered by March's formulation of six models of social choice that involve, in some sense, relationships of power.

The analogy between cause and power calls attention to one further point: any attempt to develop an empirical theory of power will run headlong into the fact that a causal chain has many links; that the links one specifies depend on what one wishes to explain; and that what one wishes to explain depends, in part, on the theory with which one begins. In causal analysis, it is usually

*the question depends on the answer !*

> ... possible to insert a very large number of additional variables between any two supposedly directly related factors. We must stop somewhere and consider the theoretical system closed. Practically, we may choose to stop at the point where the additional variables are either difficult or expensive to measure, or where they have not been associated with any operations at all. .... *A relationship that is direct in one theoretical system may be indirect in another*, or it may even be taken as spurious. (Blalock 1964, p. 18)

Some of the links that a power analyst may take as 'effects' to be explained by searching for causes are the outcomes of specific decisions; the current values, attitudes, and expectations of decision makers; their earlier or more fundamental attitudes and values; the attitudes and values of other participants – or nonparticipants – whose participation is in some way significant; the processes of selection, self-selection, recruitment, or entry by which decision makers arrive at their locations in the political system; the rules of decision making, the structures, the constitutions. No doubt a 'complete' explanation of power relations in a political system would try to account for all of these effects, and others. Yet this is an enormously ambitious task. Meanwhile, it is important to specify which effects are at the focus of an explanatory theory and which are not. A good deal of confusion, and no little controversy, are produced when different analysts focus on different links in the chain of power and causation without specifying clearly what effects they wish to explain; and a good deal of criticism of dubious relevance is produced by critics who hold that an investigator has focused on the 'wrong' links or did not provide a 'complete' explanation.

*causal factors/ links in causal chains*

## Classifying types of power

Even though the analysis of power has not produced many rigorous causal models, it has spawned a profusion of schemes for classifying types of power relations (e.g., Parsons 1963*a*; 1963*b*; Oppenheim 1961; French & Raven 1959; Cartwright 1965).

Among the characteristics most often singled out for attention are (1) legitimacy: the extent to which *R* feels normatively obliged to comply with *C*; (2) the nature of the sanctions: whether *C* uses rewards or deprivations, positive or negative sanctions; (3) the magnitude of the sanctions: extending from severe coercion to no sanctions at all; (4) the means or channels employed: whether *C* controls *R* only by means of information that changes *R*'s intentions or by actually changing *R*'s situation or his environment of rewards and deprivations. These and other characteristics can be combined to yield many different types of power relations.

As we have already indicated, no single classification system prevails, and the names for the various categories are so completely unstandardized that what is labeled power in one scheme may be called coercion or influence in another. Detached from empirical theories, these schemes are of doubtful value. In the abstract it is impossible to say why one classification system should be preferred over another.

Nonetheless, there are some subsets of power relations – types of power, as they are often called – that call attention to interesting problems of analysis and research. One of these is the distinction between *having* and *exercising* power or influence (Lasswell & Kaplan 1950, p. 71; Oppenheim 1961, chapters 2, 3). This distinction is also involved in the way anticipated reactions function as a basis for influence and power (Friedrich 1963, chapter 11).

To illustrate the problem by example, let us suppose that even in the absence of any previous communication from the president to Senator *R*, or indeed any previous action of any kind by the president, Senator *R* regularly votes *now* in a way he thinks will insure the president's favor *later*. The senator calculates that if he loses the next election, he may, as a result of the president's favorable attitude, be in line to receive a presidential appointment to a federal court. Thus, while Senator *R*'s voting behavior is oriented toward future rewards, expected or hoped for, his votes are not the result of any specific action by the president.

If one holds that *C* cannot be a cause of *R* if *C* follows *R* in time, then no act of the incumbent president *need* be a cause of Senator *R*'s favorable vote. Obviously this does not mean that Senator *R*'s actions are 'uncaused'. The immediate determinant of his vote is his expectations. If we ask what 'caused' his expectations, there are many possible answers. For example, he might have concluded that in American society if favors are extended to *C*, this makes it more likely that *C* will be indulgent later on. Or he may have acquired from political lore the understanding that the general rule applies specifically to relations of senators and presidents. Thus, the causal chain recedes into the senator's previous learning – but not necessarily to any specific *past* act of the incumbent president or any other president.

This kind of phenomenon is commonplace, important, and obviously relevant to the analysis of power. Yet some studies, critics have said, concentrate on the exercise of power and fail to account for individuals or groups in the community who, though they do not exercise power, nonetheless have power, in the sense that many people try assiduously to anticipate their reactions (Bachrach & Baratz 1962). This failure may be a result of certain paradoxical aspects of having power that can make it an exceedingly difficult phenomenon to study.

For in the limiting case of anticipated reactions, it appears, paradoxically, that it is not the president who controls the senator, but the senator who controls the president – i.e., it is the senator who, by his loyal behavior, induces the president to appoint him to a federal court. Thus, it is not $C$ who controls or even attempts to control $R$, but $R$ who attempts to control $C$ – and to the extent that $R$ anticipates $C$'s reactions correctly, $R$ does in fact control $C$. It is, then, not the king who controls the courtier but the courtier who controls the king.

Now if we examine this paradox closely we quickly discover that it arises simply because we have tried to describe the relationship between king and courtier, president and senator, $C$ and $R$ by distinguishing only one aspect, namely, the exercise of power. The courtier does indeed exercise power over the king by successfully anticipating the reactions of the monarch and thereby gaining a duchy. But it was not this that we set out to explain. For it is the king who has, holds, or possesses the capacity to confer that dukedom, and even though he does not *exercise* his power, he gains the willing compliance of the courtier.

What is it, then, that distinguishes having power from exercising power? The distinction could hinge upon the presence or absence of a manifest intention. We could define the *exercise* of power in such a way as to require $C$ to manifest an intention to act in some way in the future, his action to be contingent on $R$'s behavior. By contrast, $C$ might be said to *have* power when, though he does not manifest an intention, $R$ imputes an intention to him and shapes his behavior to meet the imputed intention. If one were to accept this distinction, then in studying the *exercise* of power, one would have to examine not only $R$'s perceptions and responses but also $C$'s intentions and actions. In studying relationships in which $C$ is thought to *have* power, even though he does not exercise it, one would in principle need only to study $R$'s perceptions, the intentions $R$ imputes to $C$, and the bearing of these on $R$'s behavior. Carried to the extreme, then this kind of analysis could lead to the discovery of as many different power structures in a political system as there are individuals who impute different intentions to other individuals, groups, or strata in the system.

The distinction between having and exercising power could also turn on the directness involved in the relation between $C$ and $R$ and on the specificity of the actions. In the most direct relationship $R$'s response would be tripped off by a signal directly from $C$. In this case, $C$ is exercising power. But some relationships are highly indirect; for example, $C$ may modify $R$'s environment in a more or less lasting way, so that $R$ continues to respond as $C$ had intended, even though $C$ makes no effort to control $R$. In these cases, one might say that although $C$ does not exercise control over $R$, he does *have* control over $R$. There are a variety of these indirect, or 'roundabout', controls (Dahl & Lindblom 1953, pp. 110 ff.).

*Measuring power*

Even more than with power terms themselves, notions of 'more' or 'less' power were in classical theory left to the realm of common sense and intuition. Efforts to develop systematic measures of power date almost wholly from the 1950s. Of those, some are stated partly in mathematical formulas, some entirely in non-mathematical language. Since the essential features can be suggested without mathematics, we shall describe these measures in ordinary language. (The reader should consult the sources cited for the precise formulations. Most of the best-known measures are presented and discussed in Riker 1964.)

In a rough way, the various criteria for measuring power can be classified into three types: game-theoretical, Newtonian, and economic.

*Game-theoretical criteria* Shapley, a mathematician, and Shubik, an econometrician, have jointly formulated a 'method for evaluating the distribution of power in a committee system' (1954). This is intended to measure the power accruing to a voter where the outcome or decision is determined exclusively by voting. In these cases the rules prescribe what proportion of votes constitutes a winning proportion (e.g., a simple majority of all committee members). Thus each member has a certain abstract probability of casting the last vote that would be needed to complete a winning coalition, in other words to occupy a pivotal position with respect to the outcome. By adding his vote at this crucial juncture, a voter may be conceived of as having made a particularly decisive contribution to the outcome; thus, gaining his vote might have considerable value to the other members of a coalition that would lose without his vote. Shapley and Shubik proposed measuring the power of a voter by the probability that he would be the pivotal voter in a winning coalition. Because their measure is entirely limited to voting situations and excludes all outcomes other than the act of voting itself, the utility of the measure is limited to cases where most of the other familiar elements of political life – various forms of persuasion, inducement, and coercion – are lacking.

*Newtonian criteria* On the analogy of the measurement of force in classical mechanics, a number of analysts propose to measure power by the amount of change in $R$ attributable to $C$. The greater the change in $R$, the greater the power of $C$; thus $C_a$ is said to exert more power than $C_b$ if $C_a$ induces more change in $R_a$ than $C_b$ induces in $R_a$ (or in some other $R$). Measures of this kind have been more frequently proposed than any other (Simon 1947–56; March 1957; Dahl 1957; 1963, chapter 5; Cartwright 1959; Oppenheim 1961, chapter 8).

'Change in $R$' is not, however, a single dimension, since many different changes in $R$ may be relevant. Some of the important dimensions of the 'change in $R$' brought about by $C$ that have been suggested for measuring the amount of $C$'s power are (1) the probability that $R$ will comply; (2) the number of persons in $R$; (3) the number of distinct items, subjects, or values in $R$; (4) the amount of change in $R$'s position, attitudes, or psychological state; (5) the speed with which $R$ changes; (6) the reduction in the size of the set of outcomes or behaviors available to $R$; and (7) the degree of $R$'s threatened or expected deprivation.

*Economic criteria* Where the game-theoretical measure focuses on the pivotal position of $C$, and Newtonian measures on changes in $R$, a third proposal would include 'costs' to both $C$ and $R$ in measuring $C$'s power. Harsanyi has argued that a complete measure of power should include (1) the opportunity costs to $C$ of attempting to influence $R$, which Harsanyi calls the *costs* of $C$'s power, and (2) the opportunity costs to $R$ of refusing to comply with $C$, which Harsanyi calls the *strength* of $C$'s power over $R$ (1962*a*, pp. 68 ff.). The measure Harsanyi proposes is not inherently limited to the kinds of cost most familiar to economists but could be extended – at least in principle – to include psychological costs of all kinds.

*Designing operational definitions*

Empirical studies discussed by Cartwright (1965), March (1965), and others, and particularly community studies, have called attention to the neglected problem of designing acceptable operational definitions.

The concepts and measures discussed in this article have not been clothed in operational language. It is not yet clear how many of them can be. Yet the researcher who seeks to observe, report, compare, and analyze power in the real world, in order to test a particular hypothesis or a broader theory, quickly discovers urgent need for operationally defined terms. Research so far has called attention to three kinds of problems. First, the gap between concept and operational definition is generally very great, so great, indeed, that it is not always possible to see what relation there is between the operations and the abstract definition. Thus a critic is likely to conclude that the studies are, no doubt, reporting *something* in the real world, but he might question whether they are reporting the phenomena we mean when we speak of *power*. Second, different operational measures do not seem to correlate with one another (March 1956), which suggests that they may tap different aspects of power relations. Third, almost every measure proposed has engendered controversy over its validity.

None of these results should be altogether surprising or even discouraging. For despite the fact that the attempt to understand political systems by analyzing power relations is ancient, the systematic empirical study of power relations is remarkably new.

# References

Agger, Robert E.; Goldrich, Daniel; and Swanson, Bert 1964 *The Rulers and the Ruled: Political Power and Impotence in American Communities*. New York: Wiley.

Aristotle *The Politics of Aristotle*. Translated and edited by Ernest Barker. New York: Oxford Univ. Press, 1962.

Bachrach, Peter; and Baratz, Morton 1962 Two Faces of Power. *American Political Science Review* 56:947–52.

Blalock, Hubert M. Jr. 1964 *Causal Inferences in Nonexperimental Research*. Chapel Hill: Univ. of North Carolina Press.

Cartwright, Dorwin (editor) 1959 *Studies in Social Power*. Research Center for Group Dynamics, Publication No. 6 Ann Arbor: Univ. of Michigan, Institute for Social Research.

Cartwright, Dorwin 1965 Influence, Leadership, Control. Pages 1–47 in James G. March (editor), *Handbook of Organizations*. Chicago: Rand McNally.

Catlin, George E.G. 1927 *The Science and Method of Politics*. New York: Knopf; London: Routledge.

Catlin, George E.G. 1930 *A Study of the Principles of Politics, Being an Essay Towards Political Rationalization*. New York: Macmillan.

Dahl, Robert A, 1957 The Concept of Power. *Behavioral Science* 2:201–15.

Dahl, Robert A. (1961) 1963 *Who Governs? Democracy and Power in an American City*. New Haven: Yale Univ. Press.

Dahl, Robert A. 1963 *Modern Political Analysis*. Englewood Cliffs, N.J.: Prentice-Hall.

Dahl, Robert A.; and Lindblom, Charles E. 1953 *Politics, Economics, and Welfare: Planning and Politico-economic Systems Resolved Into Basic Social Processes*. New York: Harper. A paperback edition was published in 1963.

French, John R.P.; and Raven, Bertram 1959 The Bases of Social Power. Pages 150–67 in Dorwin Cartwright (editor), *Studies in Social Power*. Research Center for Group Dynamics, Publication No. 6. Ann Arbor: Univ. of Michigan, Institute for Social Research.

Friedrich, Carl J. 1963 *Man and His Government: An Empirical Theory of Politics*. New York: McGraw-Hill.

Goldhamer, Herbert; and Shils, Edward 1939 Types of Power and Status. *American Journal of Sociology* 45:171–82.

Harsanyi, John C. 1962a Measurement of Social Power, Opportunity Costs, and the Theory of Two-person Bargaining Games. *Behavioral Science* 7:67–80.

Harsanyi, John C. 1962b Measurement of Social Power in *n*-Person Reciprocal Power Situations. *Behavioral Science* 7:81–91.

Jouvenel, Bertrand de (1945) 1952 *Power: The Natural History of Its Growth*. Rev. ed. London: Batchworth. First published in French.

Lasswell, Harold D. (1930) 1960 *Psychopathology and Politics*. New ed., with afterthoughts by the author. New York: Viking.

Lasswell, Harold D. 1936 *Politics: Who Gets What, When, How?* New York: McGraw-Hill.

Lasswell, Harold D.; and Kaplan, Abraham 1950 *Power and Society: A Framework for Political Inquiry*. Yale Law School Studies, Vol. 2. New Haven: Yale Univ. Press. A paperback edition was published in 1963.

Loewenstein, Karl 1957 *Political Power and the Governmental Process*. Univ. of Chicago Press.

March, James G. 1955 An Introduction to the Theory and Measurement of Influence. *American Political Science Review* 49:431–51.

March, James G. 1956 Influence Measurement in Experimental and Semiexperimental Groups. *Sociometry* 19:260–71.

March, James G. 1957 Measurement Concepts in the Theory of Influence. *Journal of Politics* 19:202–26.

March, James G. (editor) 1965 *Handbook of Organizations*. Chicago: Rand McNally.

Meinecke, Friedrich (1924) 1957 *Machiavellism: The Doctrine of Raison d'État and Its Place in Modern History*. New Haven: Yale Univ. Press. First published as *Die Idee der Staatsräson in der neueren Geschichte*.

Merriam, Charles E. 1934 *Political Power: Its Composition and Incidence*. New York: McGraw-Hill. A paperback edition was published in 1964 by Collier.

Mills, C. Wright 1956 *The Power Elite*. New York: Oxford Univ. Press.

Morgenthau, Hans J. (1948) 1967 *Politics Among Nations: The Struggle for Power and Peace*. 4th ed. New York: Knopf.

Mosca, Gaetano (1896) 1939 *The Ruling Class* (*Element di scienza politica*). New York: McGraw-Hill.

Neustadt, Richard E. 1960 *Presidential Power: The Politics of Leadership*. New York: Wiley. A paperback edition was published in 1962.

Oppenheim, Felix E. 1961 *Dimensions of Freedom: An Analysis*. New York: St. Martins; London: Macmillan.

Pareto, Vilfredo (1916) 1963 *The Mind and Society: A Treatise on General Sociology*. 4 vols. New York: Dover. First published as *Trattato di sociologia generale*. Volume 1: *Non-logical Conduct*. Volume 2: *Theory of Residues*. Volume 3: *Theory of Derivations*. Volume 4: *The General Form of Society*.

Parsons, Talcott 1963a On the Concept of Influence. *Public Opinion Quarterly* 27:37–62. A comment by J.S. Coleman appears on pages 63–82; a communication by R.A. Bauer, on pages 83–6; and a rejoinder by Talcott Parsons, on pages 87–92.

Parsons, Talcott 1963b On the Concept of Political Power. American Philosophical Society. *Proceedings* 107:232–62.

Polsby, Nelson W. 1963 *Community Power and Political Theory*. Yale Studies in Political Science, Vol. 7. New Haven: Yale Univ. Press.

Riker, William H. 1959 A Test of the Adequacy of the Power Index. *Behavioral Science* 4:120–31.

Riker, William H. 1964 Some Ambiguities in the Notion of Power. *American Political Science Review* 58:341–9.

Rogow, Arnold A.; and Lasswell, Harold D. 1963 *Power, Corruption and Rectitude*. Englewood Cliffs, N.J.: Prentice-Hall.

Rossi, Peter H. 1960 Power and Community Structure. *Midwest Journal of Political Science* 4:390–401.

Shapley, L.S.; and Shubik, Martin 1954 A Method for Evaluating the Distribution of Power in a Committee System. *American Political Science Review* 48:787–92.

Simon, Herbert A. (1947–1956) 1957 *Models of Man: Social and Rational; Mathematical Essays on Rational Human Behavior in a Social Setting*. New York: Wiley.

Simon, Herbert A. 1953 Notes on the Observation and Measurement of Political Power. *Journal of Politics* 15:500–16.

Weber, Max (1922) 1957 *The Theory of Social and Economic Organization*. Edited by Talcott Parsons. Glencoe, Ill.: Free Press. First published as Part 1 of *Wirtschaft und Gesellschaft*.

# 2  Bachrach and Baratz

## Introduction

While Bachrach and Baratz's analysis is a critique of Dahl, they fundamentally accept many aspects of Dahl's perspective. In particular they agree that it is fallacious to equate power with power resources or a reputation for power, that scope and intensity of power have to be taken into account and, most importantly, that power has to be analysed at a behavioural level. Power involves agents making things happen that would not otherwise have happened. Their critique of Dahl is that he fails to take account of institutional bias. Not only does A exercise power over B in overt decision-making (as in Dahl) but A may equally well exercise power over B by limiting the scope of the political process to issues which are relatively innocuous to A. The most obvious instance of this is the process of agenda setting whereby an issue of importance to B is deliberately left off the agenda by A. Not only is power exercised, as within the pluralist framework, in the arena of decision-making, but it is also exercised by preventing issues from reaching that arena. However, in line with Dahl's behaviourist focus, they also insist that such biases are reducible to agency. Nondecision-making, as they call this form of power, is a decision not to make a decision.

The importance of institutional neutrality is central to the workings of a truly democratic and liberal system. In a contemporary context, the central thrust of the New Social Movements is to put matters on to the agenda which have not been there previously. The women's movement has argued that family relations are not a private matter and, as a consequence, belong on the agenda and, similarly, the Green Movement has argued that emissions and the unintended consequences of production are not the private affair of producers. This is a theme which Beck analyses at great length in *Risk Society* (Beck 1992).

Recognition of the significance of institutional bias has also been central to liberal political thought. Since Rawls' *Theory of Justice* (1971) social contract theory has been dominant within liberalism. Central to this is the idea that behind political practice there exists a set of institutional norms which all members of society subscribe to irrespective of their particular political aims. However, such a hypothesis is only plausible if it is possible to find norms which

26

are neutral between competing interests. Devising such a set of neutral institutions is central to Rawls' original position and later idea of overlapping consensus (Rawls 1993). It is also found in Habermas' claim that discourse presupposes certain norms, which he described using the concept of an 'ideal speech situation'.

The idea that the social contract may be biased is central to the type of critique of the classical liberals made by McPherson in *The Theory of Possessive Individualism* (1964) – he argues that Hobbes' and Locke's social contract is neutral only between property holders. More recently the central thrust of much criticism of Rawls has demonstrated that the original position is neutral only between liberals – it is biased against non-liberals. In *Political Liberalism* Rawls has engaged with this critique by accepting that his version of the social contract does not include everyone but, significantly, that it includes everyone who is a democrat.

After the publication of 'The Two Faces of Power' Bachrach and Baratz went on to develop their own vocabulary of power, distinguishing between power and power related concepts, such as authority influence and coercion (Bachrach and Baratz 1963). While this vocabulary stimulated some debate at the time and many of the issues raised by it were taken up by Wrong (1979), most of these distinctions have not become part of the contemporary vocabulary of power. However, the second face of power is central to social and political thought, even if many theorists do not refer to Bachrach and Baratz or use their terminology. Today Dahl recognizes the importance of avoiding institutional bias and, following the contractarian liberal tradition, in *Democracy and Its Critics*, he argues that the 'general will' consists of a set of neutral institutional practices.

During the 1960s and 1970s the most significant pieces of work to operationalize the concept of the second face of power were Bachrach and Baratz's own *Power and Poverty* (in which they showed how issues of importance to poor blacks were off the agenda) and Matthew Crenson's *The Un-Politics of Air Pollution* (in which he showed that large companies could exercise power by making certain that pollution was never on the agenda). Most recently Flyvbjerg's (1998) analysis of the siting of a bus station in Aarhus, Denmark, is an ethnographically interesting analysis of the effectiveness of nondecision-making. Flyvbjerg does not refer to Bachrach and Baratz, choosing instead a form of Foucauldian analysis, but the study contains many instances of two-dimensional power – even if they are not labelled as such.

As a general word of advice to anyone undertaking power research, it is important to be clear about our level of analysis. Two-dimensional power covers many aspects of political life but, in most recent power analysis, has generally been ignored. Excluding things from the agenda, creating selective precedents, defining matters as a private affair, excluding others by endless red tape, creating committees that never reach decisions, not publishing material of general public interest, files getting lost, handing over decisions to 'experts' who are known to favour a particular outcome, exclusion by the misuse of qualifications, not having enough time, choosing a bad time for others, defining issues as inappropriate, are all instances of the second face of power. Foucauldian analysis, with which this type of phenomenon is sometimes confused, operates at a much deeper level concerning the construction of meaning. Much of what goes on in back rooms and unofficially at the level of local, national and international politics are instances of two-dimensional power. Of course, it has to be recognized that many biases are not of this form, which is where Lukes, Foucault and others come into the picture.

### Further reading

The obvious starting points are Bachrach and Baratz (1970) and Crenson (1971). For some of the debate on the concept of two-dimensional power see Frey (1971), Wolfinger (1971a and b), Debnam (1975a and b), Bachrach and Baratz (1975) and Crenson (1978).

"Mobilization of bias" - see (32)

# 'TWO FACES OF POWER'[1]
## Peter Bachrach and Morton S. Baratz
(1962)

The concept of power remains elusive despite the recent and prolific out-pourings of case studies on community power. Its elusiveness is dramatically demonstrated by the regularity of disagreement as to the locus of community power between the sociologists and the political scientists. Sociologically oriented researchers have consistently found that power is highly centralized, while scholars trained in political science have just as regularly concluded that in 'their' communities power is widely diffused.[2] Presumably, this explains why the latter group styles itself 'pluralist', its counterpart 'elitist'.

There seems no room for doubt that the sharply divergent findings of the two groups are the product, not of sheer coincidence, but of fundamental differences in both their underlying assumptions and research methodology. The political scientists have contended that these differences in findings can be explained by the faulty approach and presuppositions of the sociologists.

Reprinted by kind permission of the American Political Science Association and Peter Bachrach from the *American Political Science Review*, vol. 56. Copyright © 1962.

We contend in this paper that the pluralists themselves have not grasped the whole truth of the matter; that while their criticisms of the elitists are sound, they, like the elitists, utilize an approach and assumptions which predetermine their conclusions. Our argument is cast within the frame of our central thesis: that there are two faces of power, neither of which the sociologists see and only one of which the political scientists see.

## I

Against the elitist approach to power several criticisms may be, and have been levelled.[3] One has to do with its basic premise that in every human institution there is an ordered system of power, a 'power structure' which is an integral part and the mirror image of the organization's stratification. This postulate the pluralists emphatically – and, to our mind, correctly – reject, on the ground that

> nothing categorical can be assumed about power in any community. . . . If anything, there seems to be an unspoken notion among pluralist researchers that at bottom *nobody* dominates in a town, so that their first question is not likely to be, 'Who runs this community'?, but rather, 'Does anyone at all run this community'? The first query is somewhat like, 'Have you stopped beating your wife?', in that virtually any response short of total unwillingness to answer will supply the researchers with a 'power elite' along the lines presupposed by the stratification theory.[4]

Equally objectionable to the pluralists – and to us – is the sociologists' hypothesis that the power structure tends to be stable over time.

> Pluralists hold that power may be tied to issues, and issues can be fleeting or persistent, provoking coalitions among interested groups and citizens, ranging in their duration from momentary to semi-permanent. . . . To presume that the set of coalitions which exists in the community at any given time is a timelessly stable aspect of social structure is to introduce systematic inaccuracies into one's description of social reality.[5]

A third criticism of the elitist model is that it wrongly equates reputed with actual power:

> If a man's major life work is banking, the pluralist presumes he will spend his time at the bank, and not in manipulating community decisions. This presumption holds until the banker's activities and participations indicate otherwise. . . . If we presume that the banker is 'really' engaged in running the community, there is practically no way of disconfirming this notion, even if it is totally erroneous. On the other hand, it is easy to spot the banker who really *does* run community affairs when we presume he does not, because his activities will make this fact apparent.[6]

This is not an exhaustive bill of particulars; there are flaws other than these in the sociological model and methodology[7] – including some which the pluralists themselves have not noticed. But to go into this would not materially serve our current purposes. Suffice it simply to observe that whatever the merits of their own approach to power, the pluralists have effectively exposed the main weaknesses of the elitist model.

As the foregoing quotations make clear, the pluralists concentrate their attention, not upon the sources of power, but its exercise. Power to them means 'participation in decision-making'[8] and can be analyzed only after 'careful examination of a series of concrete decisions'.[9] As a result, the pluralist researcher is uninterested in the reputedly powerful. His concerns instead are to (a) select for study a number of 'key' as opposed to 'routine' political decisions, (b) identify the people who took an active part in the decision-making process, (c) obtain a full account of their actual behavior while the policy conflict was being resolved, and (d) determine and analyze the specific outcome of the conflict.

The advantages of this approach, relative to the elitist alternative, need no further exposition. The same may not be said, however, about its defects – two of which seem to us to be of fundamental importance. One is that the model takes no account of the fact that power may be, and often is, exercised by confining the scope of decision-making to relatively 'safe' issues. The other is that the model provides no *objective* criteria for distinguishing between 'important' and 'unimportant' issues arising in the political arena.

## II

There is no gainsaying that an analysis grounded entirely upon what is specific and visible to the outside observer is more 'scientific' than one based upon pure speculation. To put it another way,

> If we can get our social life stated in terms of activity, and of nothing else, we have not indeed succeeded in measuring it, but we have at least reached a foundation upon which a coherent system of measurements can be built up. . . . We shall cease to be blocked by the intervention of unmeasurable elements, which claim to be themselves the real causes of all that is happening, and which by their spook-like arbitrariness make impossible any progress toward dependable knowledge.[10]

The question is, however, how can one be certain in any given situation that the 'unmeasurable elements' are inconsequential, are not of decisive importance? Cast in slightly different terms, can a sound concept of power be predicated on the assumption that power is totally embodied and fully reflected in 'concrete decisions' or in activity bearing directly upon their making?

We think not. Of course power is exercised when A participates in the making of decisions that affect B. But power is also exercised when A devotes his energies to creating or reinforcing social and political values and institutional practices that limit the scope of the political process to public consideration of only those issues which are comparatively innocuous to A. To the extent that A succeeds in doing this, B is prevented, for all practical purposes, from bringing to the fore any issues that might in their resolution be seriously detrimental to A's set of preferences.[11]

Situations of this kind are common. Consider, for example, the case – surely not unfamiliar to this audience – of the discontented faculty member in an academic institution headed by a tradition-bound executive. Aggrieved about a long-standing policy around which a strong vested interest has developed, the professor resolves in the privacy of his office to launch an attack upon the policy at the next faculty meeting. But, when the moment of truth is at hand, he sits frozen in silence. Why? Among the many possible reasons, one or more of these could have been of crucial importance: (a) the professor was fearful that his intended action would be interpreted as an expression of his disloyalty to the institution; or (b) he decided that, given the beliefs and attitudes of his colleagues on the faculty, he would almost certainly constitute on this issue a minority of one; or (c) he concluded that, given the nature of the law-making process in the institution, his proposed remedies would be pigeonholed permanently. But whatever the case, the central point to be made is the same: to the extent that a person or group – consciously or unconsciously – creates or reinforces barriers to the public airing of policy conflicts, that person or group has power. Or, as Professor Schattschneider has so admirably put it:

> All forms of political organization have a bias in favor of the exploitation of some kinds of conflict and the suppression of others because *organization is the mobilization of bias*. Some issues are organized into politics while others are organized out.[12]

Is such bias not relevant to the study of power? Should not the student be continuously alert to its possible existence in the human institution that he studies, and be ever prepared to examine the forces which brought it into being and sustain it? Can he safely ignore the possibility, for instance, that an individual or group in a community participates more vigorously in supporting the *nondecision-making* process than in participating in actual decisions within the process? Stated differently, can the researcher overlook the chance that some person or association could limit decision-making to relatively non-controversial matters, by influencing community values and political procedures and rituals, notwithstanding that there are in the community serious but latent power conflicts?[13] To do so is, in our judgment, to overlook the less apparent, but nonetheless extremely important, face of power.

## III

In his critique of the 'ruling-elite model', Professor Dahl argues that 'the hypothesis of the existence of a ruling elite can be strictly tested only if . . . [t] here is a fair sample of cases involving key political decisions in which the preferences of the hypothetical ruling elite run counter to those of any other likely group that might be suggested'.[14] With this assertion we have two complaints. One we have already discussed, viz., in erroneously assuming that power is solely reflected in concrete decisions. Dahl thereby excludes the possibility that in the community in question there is a group capable of preventing contests from arising on issues of importance to it. Beyond that, however, by ignoring the less apparent face of power Dahl and those who accept his pluralist approach are unable adequately to differentiate between a 'key' and a 'routine' political decision.

Nelson Polsby, for example, proposes that 'by pre-selecting as issues for study those which are generally agreed to be significant, pluralist researchers can test stratification theory'.[15] He is silent, however, on how the researcher is to determine *what* issues are 'generally agreed to be significant', and on how the researcher is to appraise the reliability of the agreement. In fact, Polsby is guilty here of the same fault he himself has found with elitist methodology: by presupposing that in any community there are significant issues in the political arena, he takes for granted the very question which is in doubt. He accepts as issues what are reputed to be issues. As a result, his findings are fore-ordained. For even if there is no 'truly' significant issue in the community under study, there is every likelihood that Polsby (or any like-minded researcher) will find one or some and, after careful study, reach the appropriate pluralistic conclusions.[16]

Dahl's definition of 'key political issues' in his essay on the ruling-elite model is open to the same criticism. He states that it is 'a necessary although possibly not a sufficient condition that the [key] issue should involve actual disagreement in preferences among two or more groups'.[17] In our view, this is an inadequate characterization of a 'key political issue', simply because groups can have disagreements in preferences on unimportant as well as on important issues. Elite preferences which border on the indifferent are certainly not significant in determining whether a monolithic or polylithic distribution of power prevails in a given community. Using Dahl's definition of 'key political issues', the researcher would have little difficulty in finding such in practically any community; and it would not be surprising then if he ultimately concluded that power in the community was widely diffused.

The distinction between important and unimportant issues, we believe, cannot be made intelligently in the absence of an analysis of the 'mobilization of bias' in the community; of the dominant values and the political myths, rituals, and institutions which tend to favor the vested interests of one or more groups, relative to others. Armed with this knowledge, one could conclude that any challenge to the predominant values or to the established 'rules of the game' would constitute an 'important' issue; all else, unimportant. To be sure, judgments of this kind cannot be entirely objective. But to avoid making them in a study of power is both to neglect a highly significant aspect of power and thereby to undermine the only sound basis for discriminating between 'key' and 'routine' decisions. In effect, we contend, the pluralists have made each of these mistakes; that is to say, they have done just that for which Kaufman and Jones so severely taxed Floyd Hunter: they have begun 'their structure at the mezzanine without showing us a lobby or foundation',[18] *i.e.*, they have begun by studying the issues rather than the values and biases that are built into the political system and that, for the student of power, give real meaning to those issues which do enter the political arena.

## IV

There is no better fulcrum for our critique of the pluralist model than Dahl's recent study of power in New Haven.[19]

At the outset it may be observed that Dahl does not attempt in this work to define his concept, 'key political decision'. In asking whether the 'Notables' of New Haven are 'influential overtly or covertly in the making of government decisions', he simply states that he will examine 'three different 'issue-areas' in which important public decisions are made: nominations by the two political parties, urban redevelopment, and public education'. These choices are justified on the grounds that 'nominations determine which persons will hold public office. The New Haven redevelopment program measured by its cost – present and potential – is the largest in the country. Public education, aside from its intrinsic importance, is the costliest item in the city's budget'. Therefore, Dahl concludes. 'It is reasonable to expect . . . that the relative influence over public officials wielded by the . . . Notables would be revealed by an examination of their participation in these three areas of activity.'[20]

The difficulty with this latter statement is that it is evident from Dahl's own account that the Notables are in fact uninterested in two of the three 'key' decisions he has chosen. In regard to the public school issue, for example, Dahl points out that many of the Notables live in the suburbs and that those who do live in New Haven choose in the main to send their children to private schools. 'As a consequence', he writes, 'their interest in the public schools is ordinarily rather slight.'[21] Nominations by the two political parties as an important 'issue-area', is somewhat analogous to the public schools, in that the apparent lack of interest among the Notables in this issue is partially accounted for by their suburban residence – because of which they are disqualified from holding public office in New Haven. Indeed, Dahl himself concedes that with respect to both these issues the Notables are largely indifferent: 'Business leaders might ignore the public schools or the political parties without any sharp awareness that their indifference would hurt their pocketbooks . . .' He goes on, however, to say that

the prospect of profound changes [as a result of the urban-redevelopment program] in ownership, physical layout, and usage of property in the downtown area and the effects of these changes on the commercial and industrial prosperity of New Haven were all related in an obvious way to the daily concerns of businessmen.[22]

Thus, if one believes – as Professor Dahl did when he wrote his critique of the ruling-elite model – that an issue, to be considered as important, 'should involve actual disagreement in preferences among two or more groups',[23] then clearly he has now for all practical purposes written off public education and party nominations as key 'issue-areas'. But this point aside, it appears somewhat dubious at best that 'the relative influence over public officials wielded by the Social Notables' can be revealed by an examination of their nonparticipation in areas in which they were not interested.

Furthermore, we would not rule out the possibility that even on those issues to which they appear indifferent, the Notables may have a significant degree of *indirect* influence. We would suggest, for example, that although they send their children to private schools, the Notables do recognize that public school expenditures have a direct bearing upon their own tax liabilities. This being so, and given their strong representation on the New Haven Board of Finance,[24] the expectation must be that it is in their direct interest to play an active role in fiscal policy-making, in the establishment of the educational budget in particular. But as to this, Dahl is silent: he inquires not at all into either the decisions made by the Board of Finance with respect to education nor into their impact upon the public schools.[25] Let it be understood clearly that in making these points we are not attempting to refute Dahl's contention that the Notables lack power in New Haven. What we *are* saying, however, is that this conclusion is not adequately supported by his analysis of the 'issue-areas' of public education and party nominations.

The same may not be said of redevelopment. This issue is by any reasonable standard important for purposes of determining whether New Haven is ruled by 'the hidden hand of an economic elite'.[26] For the Economic Notables have taken an active interest in the program and, beyond that, the socio-economic implications of it are not necessarily in harmony with the basic interests and values of businesses and businessmen.

In an effort to assure that the redevelopment program would be acceptable to what he dubbed 'the biggest muscles' in New Haven, Mayor Lee created the Citizens Action Commission (CAC) and appointed to it primarily representatives of the economic elite. It was given the function of overseeing the work of the mayor and other officials involved in redevelopment, and, as well, the responsibility for organizing and encouraging citizens' participation in the program through an extensive committee system.

In order to weigh the relative influence of the mayor, other key officials, and the members of the CAC, Dahl reconstructs 'all the *important* decisions on redevelopment and renewal between 1950–58 . . . [to] determine which individuals most often initiated the proposals that were finally adopted or most often successfully vetoed the proposals of the others'.[27] The results of this test indicate that the mayor and his development administrator were by far the most influential, and that the 'muscles' on the Commission, excepting in a few trivial instances, 'never directly initiated, opposed, vetoed, or altered any proposal brought before them'. . . .[28]

This finding is in our view, unreliable, not so much because Dahl was compelled to make a subjective selection of what constituted *important* decisions within what he felt to be an *important* 'issue-area', as because the finding was based upon an excessively narrow test of influence. To measure relative influence solely in terms of the ability to initiate and veto proposals is to ignore the possible exercise of influence or power in limiting the scope of initiation. How, that is to say, can a judgment be made as to the relative influence of Mayor Lee and the CAC without knowing (through prior study of the political and social views of all concerned) the proposals that Lee did *not* make because he anticipated that they would provoke strenuous opposition and, perhaps, sanctions on the part of the CAC?[29]

In sum, since he does not recognize *both* faces of power. Dahl is in no position to evaluate the relative influence or power of the initiator and decision-maker, on the one hand, and of those persons, on the other, who may have been indirectly instrumental in preventing potentially dangerous issues from being raised.[30] As a result, he unduly emphasizes the importance of initiating, deciding, and vetoing, and in the process casts the pluralist conclusions of his study into serious doubt.

## V

We have contended in this paper that a fresh approach to the study of power is called for, an approach based upon a recognition of the two faces of power. Under this approach the researcher would begin – not, as does the sociologist who asks, 'Who rules?' nor as does the pluralist who asks, 'Does anyone have power?' – but by investigating the particular 'mobilization of bias' in the institution under scrutiny. Then, having analyzed the dominant values, the myths and the established political procedures and rules of the game, he would make a careful inquiry into which persons or groups, if any, gain from the existing bias and which, if any, are handicapped by it. Next, he would investigate the dynamics of *nondecision-making*; that is, he would examine the extent to which and the manner in which the *status quo* oriented persons and groups influence those community values and those political institutions (as, *e.g.*, the unanimity 'rule' of New York City's Board of Estimate[31]) which tend to limit the scope of actual decision-making to 'safe' issues. Finally, using his knowledge of the restrictive face of power as a foundation for analysis and as a standard for distinguishing between 'key' and 'routine' political decisions, the researcher would, after the manner of the pluralists, analyze participation in decision-making of concrete issues.

We reject in advance as unimpressive the possible criticism that this approach to the study of power is likely to prove fruitless because it goes beyond an investigation of what is objectively measurable. In reacting against the subjective aspects of the sociological model of power, the pluralists have, we believe, made the mistake of discarding 'unmeasurable elements' as unreal. It is ironical that, by so doing, they have exposed themselves to the same fundamental criticism they have so forcefully levelled against the elitists: their approach to and assumptions about power predetermine their findings and conclusions.

## Notes

1 This paper is an outgrowth of a seminar in Problems of Power in Contemporary Society, conducted jointly by the authors for graduate students and undergraduate majors in political science and economics.

2 Compare, for example, the sociological studies of Floyd Hunter, *Community Power Structure* (Chapel Hill, 1953); Roland Pellegrini and Charles H. Coater, 'Absentee-Owned Corporations and Community Power Structure', *American Journal of Sociology*, Vol. 61 (March 1956), pp. 413–19; and Robert O. Schulze, 'Economic Dominants and Community Power Structure', *American Sociological Review*, Vol. 23 (February 1958), pp. 3–9; with political science studies of Wallace S. Sayre and Herbert Kaufman, *Governing New York City* (New York, 1960); Robert A. Dahl, *Who Governs?* (New Haven, 1961); and Norton E. Long and George Belknap, 'A Research Program on Leadership and Decision-Making in Metropolitan Areas' (New York, Governmental Affairs Institute, 1956). See also Nelson W. Polsby, 'How to Study Community Power: The Pluralist Alternative', *Journal of Politics*, Vol. 22 (August, 1960), pp. 474–84.

3 See especially N.W. Polsby, *op. cit.*, p. 475f.

4 *Ibid.*, p. 476.

5 *Ibid.*, pp. 478–9.

6 *Ibid.*, pp. 480–1.

7 See especially Robert A. Dahl, 'A Critique of this Ruling-Elite Model', this REVIEW, Vol. 52 (June 1958), pp. 463–9; and Lawrence J.R. Herson, 'In the Footsteps of Community Power', this REVIEW, Vol. 55 (December 1961), pp. 817–31.

8 This definition originated with Harold D. Lasswell and Abraham Kaplan, *Power and Society* (New Haven, 1950), p. 75.

9 Robert A. Dahl. 'A Critique of the Ruling-Elite Model', *loc. cit.*, p. 466.

10 Arthur Bentley, *The Process of Government* (Chicago 1908), p. 202, quoted in Polsby, *op. cit.*, p. 481n.

11 As is perhaps self-evident, there are similarities in both faces of power. In each, A participates in decisions and thereby adversely affects B. But there is an important difference between the two: in the one case, A openly participates; in the other, he participates only in the sense that he works to sustain those values and rules of procedure that help him keep certain issues out of the public domain. True enough, participation of the second kind may at times be overt; that is the case, for instance, in cloture fights in the Congress. But the point is that it need not be. In fact, when the maneuver is most successfully executed, it neither involves nor can be identified with decisions arrived at on specific issues.

12 E.E. Schattschneider, *The Semi-Sovereign People* (New York, 1960), p. 71.

13 Dahl *partially* concedes this point when he observes ('A Critique of the Ruling-Elite Model', pp. 468–9) that 'one could argue that even in a society like ours a ruling elite might be so influential over ideas, attitudes, and opinions that a kind of false consensus will exist – not the phony consensus of a terroristic totalitarian dictatorship but the manipulated and superficially self-imposed adherence to the norms and goals of the elite by broad sections of a community. . . . This objection points to the need to be circumspect in interpreting the evidence'. But that he largely misses our point is clear from the succeeding sentence: 'Yet here, too, it seems to me that the hypothesis cannot be satisfactorily confirmed without something equivalent to the test

I have proposed', and that is 'by an examination of a series of concrete cases where key decisions are made....'

14 *Op. cit.*, p. 466.

15 *Op. cit.*, p. 478.

16 As he points out, the expectations of the pluralist researchers 'have seldom been disappointed'. (*Ibid.*, p. 477).

17 *Op. cit.*, p. 467.

18 Herbert Kaufman and Victor Jones, 'The Mystery of Power', *Public Administration Review*, Vol. 14 (Summer 1954), p. 207.

19 Robert A. Dahl, *Who Governs?* (New Haven, 1961).

20 *Ibid.*, p. 64.

21 *Ibid.*, p. 70.

22 *Ibid.*, p. 71.

23 *Op. cit.*, p. 467.

24 *Who Governs?*, p. 82. Dahl points out that 'the main policy thrust of the Economic Notables is to oppose tax increases; this leads them to oppose expenditures for anything more than minimal traditional city services. In this effort their two most effective weapons ordinarily are the mayor and the Board of Finance. The policies of the Notables are most easily achieved under a strong mayor if his policies coincide with theirs or under a weak mayor if they have the support of the Board of Finance.... New Haven mayors have continued to find it expedient to create confidence in their financial policies among businessmen by appointing them to the Board.' (pp. 82–2)

25 Dahl does discuss in general terms (pp. 79–84) changes in the level of tax rates and assessments in past years, but not actual decisions of the Board of Finance or their effects on the public school system.

26 *Ibid.*, p. 124.

27 *Ibid.* 'A rough test of a person's overt or covert influence', Dahl states in the first section of the book, 'is the frequency with which he successfully initiates an important policy over the opposition of others, or vetoes policies initiated by others, or initiates a policy where no opposition appears.' (*Ibid.*, p. 66)

28 *Ibid.*, p. 131.

29 Dahl is, of course, aware of the 'law of anticipated reactions'. In the case of the mayor's relationship with the CAC, Dahl notes that Lee was 'particularly skillful in estimating what the CAC could be expected to support or reject'. (p. 137). However, Dahl was not interested in analyzing or appraising to what extent the CAC limited Lee's freedom of action. Because of his restricted concept of power, Dahl did not consider that the CAC might in this respect have exercised power. That the CAC did not initiate or veto actual proposals by the mayor was to Dahl evidence enough that the CAC was virtually powerless; it might as plausibly be evidence that the CAC was (in itself or in what it represented) so powerful that Lee ventured nothing it would find worth quarrelling with.

30 The fact that the initiator of decisions also refrains – because he anticipates adverse reactions – from initiating other proposals does not obviously lessen the power of the agent who limited his initiative powers. Dahl missed this point: 'It is', he writes, 'all the more improbable, then, that a secret cabal of Notables dominates the public life of New Haven through means so clandestine that not one of the fifty prominent citizens interviewed in the course of this study – citizens who had participated extensively in various decisions – hinted at the existence of such a cabal ...' (p. 185).

In conceiving of elite domination exclusively in the form of a conscious cabal exercising the power of decision-making and vetoing, he overlooks a more subtle form of domination; one in which those who actually dominate are not conscious of it themselves, simply because their position of dominance has never seriously been challenged.

31 Sayre and Kaufman, *op. cit.*, p. 640. For perceptive study of the 'mobilization of bias' in a rural American community, see Arthur Vidich and Joseph Bensman, *Small Town in Mass Society* (Princeton, 1958).

Three-dimensional power:

# 3 Lukes

structured/culturally determined
behaviour

false consciousness

## Introduction

In *Power: A Radical View* (Lukes 1974) Dahl's and Bachrach and Baratz's theorizations of power become characterized as 'dimensions of power': Dahl's model became the first dimension of power and Bachrach and Baratz's the second. To these, Lukes adds his own third dimension of power, which has two aspects. The first constitutes a critique of the behavioural focus of Bachrach and Baratz's view. According to Lukes, biases are not necessarily reducible to individuals' actions or deliberate non-actions but are inherited from the past in the form of structured and culturally patterned behaviour of groups. The second element concerns 'false consciousness', or ideology, whereby the less powerful are not aware of their 'real interests'. In order to provide conceptual space for these two aspects, Lukes redefines power in terms of interests – '. . . A exercises power over B when A affects B in a manner contrary to B's interests.'

The first aspect of three-dimensional power (the non-agent-specific nature of bias) raises the issue of the structural constitution of relations of domination. While Lukes is entirely correct to point out that power relations are shaped by structurally constituted social relations, to call this power raises the difficult issue of distinguishing power from structural constraint. Lukes grapples with this problem towards the end of *Power* (1974) (that section is not included in the extract below) and develops his analysis further in the first article contained in *Essays in Social Theory* (1977).

Lukes framed this analysis against the backdrop of a debate within Marxism between Poulantzas and Miliband. Lukes interpreted the former as an exemplar of a structuralist Althusserian position, while the latter is presented as a methodological individualist. Within this paradigm, power and structural constraint are theorized as opposite ends of a continuous spectrum. At one end of the spectrum social relations are contingent (social life as described by Miliband), whereas at the other they are determined (Poulantzas). At the contingent end there is power (A could have acted differently) and, at the determined end, there is structure (A had no possibility of acting differently).

While this is conceptually neat, it raises three fundamental issues: 1) if power implies 'could have done otherwise' agency, it becomes difficult to see a way of distinguishing it from two-dimensional power, consequently, the third-dimension loses it radical edge; 2) while it may be empirically correct to argue that social life is both contingent and determined and, as a consequence, that Poulantzas and Miliband both describe important aspects of social life, this does not make their respective positions theoretically commensurable and/or compatible – especially since both theorists claim their perspectives to be in opposition to each other; 3) following my argument (in the general Introduction) concerning how specific debates are couched within 'local' usage, Lukes' proposed distinction between power and structure is based upon moral criteria (involving the language game of moral philosophy and normative political theory) whereas the original observation (that relations of domination entail structure, hence power) is a morally neutral empirical observation made within the language of empirical (non-normative) social and political theory. This creates a level of incoherence whereby, on the one hand, Lukes argues that power need not be agent specific yet, on the other, he defines power in terms of agency.

To turn to the second aspect of three-dimensional power, the concept of false consciousness concerns the relationship between power and knowledge and, consequently, includes the premise that power distorts knowledge. Power instrumentally warps and obscures the truth in a direction which benefits the interests of dominant groups. In contrast to Foucault, this in turn presupposes knowledge which is free from power and, hence, objective. Such a position is derived from Marxist explanations of the non-revolutionary nature of the proletariat and the theoretical opposition between science and ideology. Science is objective whereas ideology is distorted knowledge which sustains relations of domination by making the working classes internalize values and aspirations which are contrary to their long-term interests. While the concept of false consciousness is Marxist in its roots, it has applicability in wider areas than those of class – for instance: in a theoretically similar vein, feminists have argued that patriarchal relations of domination are sustained by the internalization of beliefs and expectations concerning gender differences (see Davis in this volume).

While it is undoubtedly the case that relations of domination are sustained by the social knowledge which individuals use to order interaction and shape their preferences, the concept of *false* consciousness and *real* interests is highly problematic in two ways. The first is the implicit premise that the diagnostician of this pathology him- or herself possesses true consciousness in the form of privileged access to a transcendent realm of real interests. To many Westerners some of the traditions and religious practices of other societies appear obviously 'false', furthermore, these practices legitimize hierarchies and power relations. Yet, the perception of these beliefs as 'false' and contrary to 'real' interests would appear to entail an ethnocentric privileging of the status of Western ideas as 'truth' and 'real'.

A further complication is that the concept of false consciousness lends itself to conspiracy theory. The idea that large sections of the population may believe something which is false, but in the interests of a dominant class or group, tends to have connotations of improbable and insubstantiable theories of 'mind-control' and 'brainwashing'.

Some of these problems may be overcome by insisting upon identifiable agency and interests which transcend culture and social context. Deliberately contrived propaganda and misinformation which obscure dangers to health would seem to qualify (for instance, extolling the virtues of a medicine while, simultaneously, suppressing information upon known hazardous side effects). There is clearly identifiable agency (those extolling) and transcendent interests (good health). However, while this theoretical solution does not lead to elitist claims or conspiracy theories, it also has the effect of limiting the concept of three-dimensional power to such an extent that its critical edge and wider explanatory powers are lost. While dominated groups are, sometimes, manipulated by obvious propaganda, generalized relations of domination (those pertaining to class, gender, race, ethnicity and culture) are sustained in this manner only to a small degree.

While the difficulties inherent in the more radical aspects of three-dimensional power have to be taken account of, Lukes is correct to argue that it is a mistake to overlook the relationship which exists between structure, social knowledge and power. Neither should we deny the truism that social structures and consciousness sustain relations of domination. We must strive harder, rather than abandon, the task of understanding the relationship between power and consciousness.

I would suggest that, with regard to structure, an important move in the right direction is the development of an accurate single (not combined) theory of power and structure. With respect to consciousness, theorists should abandon any evaluative notions of 'true' and 'false' and simply focus on the relationship between social knowledge and relations of domination. In general it is also vital to be clear concerning which type of language game is involved: is it empirically descriptive or normatively evaluative?

## Further reading

Gaventa's *Power and Powerlessness* (1980) is the most sustained and sophisticated attempt to apply Lukes' ideas to empirical material. In the introduction and first chapter he discusses some of the difficulties of operationalizing the theory, while the rest of the book is a sensitive account of relations of domination within mining communities. Hayward's *De-Facing Power* (2000) is both a critique of the Lukes model and, also, an interesting recent study of power relations in a school. The first chapter of Haugaard (1997a, also 1992) is largely an account of the three-dimensional debate. Clegg (1989) contains a critique and exposition of some of the problems associated with the behaviourist focus of the debate from Dahl to Lukes. As already noted, Lukes (1977, chapter 1) analyses the

relationship between power and structural constraint. The Lukes (1976) debate with
Bradshaw (1976) has received some attention in the academic literature. On the issue of
interests see: Benton (1981), McLachlan (1981), Knights and Willmott (1982), Hindess
(1982). On the analytic debate on the relationship between power, intention, influence
and related issues see: Connolly (1983), Nagel (1975), Wrong (1995) and White (1971).
Hyland (1995) contains an interesting analysis of the relationship between autonomy,
three-dimensional power and democracy. Digeser (1992) has argued that there is a
'fourth face' of power and Hayward (2000) is an insightful empirical critique.

# From *POWER: A RADICAL VIEW*
## Steven Lukes

### 4 The three-dimensional view

There is no doubt that the two-dimensional view of power represents a major
advance over the one-dimensional view: it incorporates into the analysis of
power relations the question of the control over the agenda of politics and
of the ways in which potential issues are kept out of the political process.
None the less, it is, in my view, inadequate on three counts.

In the first place, its critique of behaviourism is too qualified, or, to put it
another way, it is still too committed to behaviourism – that is, to the study
of overt, 'actual behaviour', of which 'concrete decisions' in situations of
conflict are seen as paradigmatic. In trying to assimilate all cases of exclusion
of potential issues from the political agenda to the paradigm of a decision,
it gives a misleading picture of the ways in which individuals and, above
all, groups and institutions succeed in excluding potential issues from the
political process. Decisions are choices consciously and intentionally made
by individuals between alternatives, whereas the bias of the system can be
mobilised, recreated and reinforced in ways that are neither consciously
chosen nor the intended result of particular individuals' choices. As Bachrach
and Baratz themselves maintain, the domination of defenders of the status
quo may be so secure and pervasive that they are unaware of any potential
challengers to their position and thus of any alternatives to the existing political process, whose bias they work to maintain. As 'students of power and its
consequences', they write, 'our main concern is not whether the defenders of
the status quo use their power consciously, but rather if and how they exercise it and what effects it has on the political process and other actors within
the system' ([4] p. 50).

Moreover, the bias of the system is not sustained simply by a series of individually chosen acts, but also, most importantly, by the socially structured and culturally patterned behaviour of groups, and practices of institutions, which may indeed be manifested by individuals' inaction. Bachrach and Baratz follow the pluralists in adopting too methodologically individualist a view of power. In this both parties follow in the steps of Max Weber, for whom power was the probability of *individuals realising their wills* despite the resistance of others, whereas the power to control the agenda of politics and exclude potential issues cannot be adequately analysed unless it is seen as a function of collective forces and social arrangements.[1] There are, in fact, two separable cases here. First, there is the phenomenon of collective action, where the policy or action of a collectivity (whether a group, e.g. a class, or an institution, e.g. a political party or an industrial corporation) is manifest, but not attributable to particular individuals' decisions or behaviour. Second, there is the phenomenon of 'systemic' or organisational effects, where the mobilisation of bias results, as Schattschneider put it, from the form of organisation. Of course, such collectivities and organisations are made up of individuals – but the power they exercise cannot be simply conceptualised in terms of individuals' decisions or behaviour. As Marx succinctly put it, 'Men make their own history but they do not make it just as they please; they do not make it under circumstances chosen by themselves, but under circumstances directly encountered, given and transmitted from the past.'[2]

The second count on which the two-dimensional view of power is inadequate is in its association of power with actual, observable conflict. In this respect also the pluralists' critics follow their adversaries too closely[3] (and both in turn again follow Weber, who, as we have seen, stressed the realisation of one's will, *despite the resistance of others*). This insistence on actual conflict as essential to power will not do, for at least two reasons.

The first is that, on Bachrach and Baratz's own analysis, two of the types of power may not involve such conflict: namely, manipulation and authority – which they conceive as 'agreement based upon reason' ([4] p. 20), though elsewhere they speak of it as involving a 'possible conflict of values' (p. 37).

The second reason why the insistence on actual and observable conflict will not do is simply that it is highly unsatisfactory to suppose that power is only exercised in situations of such conflict. To put the matter sharply, *A* may exercise power over *B* by getting him to do what he does not want to do, but he also exercises power over him by influencing, shaping or determining his very wants. Indeed, is it not the supreme exercise of power to get another or others to have the desires you want them to have – that is, to secure their compliance by controlling their thoughts and desires? One does not have to go to the lengths of talking about *Brave New World*, or the world of B.F. Skinner, to see this: thought control takes many less total and more mundane forms, through the control of information, through the mass media and through the processes of socialisation. Indeed, ironically, there are some excellent descriptions of this phenomenon in *Who Governs?* Consider the picture of the rule of the 'patricians' in the early nineteenth century: 'The elite seems to have possessed that most indispensable of all characteristics in a dominant group – the sense, shared not only by themselves but by the populace, that their claim to govern was legitimate' ([8] p. 17). And Dahl also sees this phenomenon at work under modern 'pluralist' conditions: leaders, he says, 'do not merely *respond* to the preferences of constituents; leaders also *shape* preferences' (p. 164), and, again, 'almost the entire adult population has been subjected to *some* degree of indoctrination through the schools' (p. 317), etc. The trouble seems to be that both Bachrach and Baratz and the pluralists suppose that because power, as they conceptualise it, only shows up in cases of actual conflict, it follows that actual conflict is necessary to power. But this is to ignore the crucial point that the most effective and insidious use of power is to prevent such conflict from arising in the first place.

The third count on which the two-dimensional view of power is inadequate is closely linked to the second: namely, its insistence that nondecision-making power only exists where there are grievances which are denied entry into the political process in the form of issues. If the observer can uncover no grievances, then he must assume there is a 'genuine' consensus on the prevailing allocation of values. To put this another way, it is here assumed that if men feel no grievances, then they have no interests that are harmed by the use of power. But this is also highly unsatisfactory. In the first place, what, in any case, is a grievance – an articulated demand, based on political knowledge, an undirected complaint arising out of everyday experience, a vague feeling of unease or sense of deprivation? (See [12].) Second, and more important, is it not the supreme and most insidious exercise of power to prevent people, to whatever degree, from having grievances by shaping their perceptions, cognitions and preferences in such a way that they accept their role in the existing order of things, either because they can see or imagine no alternative to it, or because they see it as natural and unchangeable, or because they value it as divinely ordained and beneficial? To assume that the absence of grievance equals genuine consensus is simply to rule out the possibility of false or manipulated consensus by definitional fiat.

In summary, the three-dimensional view of power involves a *thorough-going critique* of the *behavioural focus*[4] of the first two views as too individualistic and allows for consideration of the many ways in which *potential issues* are kept out of politics, whether through the operation of social forces and institutional practices or through individuals' decisions. This, moreover, can occur in the absence of actual, observable conflict, which may have been successfully averted – though there remains here an implicit reference to potential conflict. This potential, however, may never in fact be actualised.

What one may have here is a *latent conflict*, which consists in a contradiction between the interests of those exercising power and the *real interests* of those they exclude.[5] These latter may not express or even be conscious of their interests, but, as I shall argue, the identification of those interests ultimately always rests on empirically supportable and refutable hypotheses.

The distinctive features of the three views of power presented above are summarised below.

*One-dimensional view of power*

Focus on (a) behaviour
        (b) decision-making
        (c) (key) issues
        (d) observable (overt) conflict
        (e) (subjective) interests, seen as policy preferences revealed by political participation

*Two-dimensional view of power*

(Qualified) critique of behavioural focus
Focus on (a) decision-making and nondecision-making
        (b) issues and potential issues
        (c) observable (overt or covert) conflict
        (d) (subjective) interests, seen as policy preferences or grievances

*Three-dimensional view of power*

Critique of behavioural focus
Focus on (a) decision-making and control over political agenda (not necessarily through decisions)
        (b) issues and potential issues
        (c) observable (overt or covert) and latent conflict
        (d) subjective and real interests

## 5 The underlying concept of power

One feature which these three views of power share is their evaluative character: each arises out of and operates within a particular moral and political perspective. Indeed, I would maintain that power is one of those concepts which is ineradicably value-dependent. By this I mean that both its very definition and any given use of it, once defined, are inextricably tied to a given set of (probably unacknowledged) value-assumptions which predetermine the range of its empirical application – and I shall maintain below that some such uses permit that range to extend further and deeper than others. Moreover, the concept of power is, in consequence, what has been called an 'essentially contested concept' – one of those concepts which 'inevitably involve endless disputes about their proper uses on the part of their users' ([10] p. 169). Indeed, to engage in such disputes is itself to engage in politics.

The absolutely basic common core to, or primitive notion lying behind, all talk of power is the notion that *A* in some way affects *B*. But, in applying that primitive (causal) notion to the analysis of social life, something further is needed – namely, the notion that *A* does so in a non-trivial or significant manner (see [19]). Clearly, we all affect each other in countless ways all the time: the concept of power, and the related concepts of coercion, influence, authority, etc., pick out ranges of such affecting as being significant in specific ways. A way of conceiving power (or a way of defining the concept of power) that will be useful in the analysis of social relationships must imply an answer to the question: 'what counts as a significant manner?', 'what makes *A*'s affecting *B* significant?' Now, the *concept* of power, thus defined, when interpreted and put to work, yields one or more *views* of power – that is, ways of identifying cases of power in the real world. The three views we have been considering can be seen as alternative interpretations and applications of one and the same underlying concept of power, according to which *A* exercises power over *B* when *A* affects *B* in a manner contrary to *B*'s interests.[6] There are, however, alternative (no less contestable) ways of conceptualising power, involving alternative criteria of significance. Let us look at two of them.

Consider, first, the concept of power elaborated by Talcott Parsons [14, 15, 16, 17]. Parsons seeks to 'treat power as a *specific* mechanism operating to bring about changes in the action of other units, individual or collective, in the processes of social interaction' ([16], in [17] p. 299). What is it, in his view, that is specific about this mechanism, which distinguishes it as 'power'? In other words, what criteria of significance does Parsons use to identify a particular range of affecting as 'power'? The answer is, in a nutshell, the use of authoritative decisions to further collective goals. He defines power thus:

> Power then is generalized capacity to secure the performance of binding obligations by units in a system of collective organization when the obligations are legitimized with reference to their bearing on collective goals and where in case of recalcitrance there is a presumption of enforcement by negative situational sanctions – whatever the actual agency of that enforcement (p. 308).

The 'power of *A* over *B* is, in its legitimized form, the "right" of *A*, as a decision-making unit involved in collective process, to make decisions which take precedence over those of *B*, in the interest of the effectiveness of the collective operation as a whole' (p. 318).

Parsons's conceptualisation of power ties it to authority, consensus and the pursuit of collective goals, and dissociates it from conflicts of interest and, in particular, from coercion and force. Thus power depends on 'the institutionalization of authority' (p. 331) and is 'conceived as a generalized medium of mobilizing commitments or obligation for effective collective action' (p. 331). By contrast, 'the threat of coercive measures, or of compulsion, without legitimation or justification, should not properly be called the use of power at all. . . .' (p. 331). Thus Parsons criticised Wright Mills for interpreting power 'exclusively as a facility for getting what one group, the holders of power, wants by preventing another group, the "outs" from getting what it wants', rather than seeing it as 'a facility for the performance of function in and on behalf of the society as a system' ([14] p. 139).

Consider, secondly, the concept of power as defined by Hannah Arendt. *'Power'*, she writes,

> corresponds to the human ability not just to act but to act in concert. Power is never the property of an individual; it belongs to a group and remains in existence only so long as the group keeps together. When we say of somebody that he is 'in power' we actually refer to his being empowered by a certain number of people to act in their name. The moment the group, from which the power originated to begin with (*potestas in populo*, without a people or group there is no power), disappears, 'his power' also vanishes. ([1] p. 44)

It is

> the people's support that lends power to the institutions of a country, and this support is but the continuation of the consent that brought the laws into existence to begin with. Under conditions of representative government the people are supposed to rule those who govern them. All political institutions are manifestations and materializations of power; they petrify and decay as soon as the living power of the people ceases to uphold them. This is what Madison meant when he said 'all governments rest on opinion', a word no less true for the various forms of monarchy than for democracies. (p. 41)

Arendt's way of conceiving power ties it to a tradition and a vocabulary which she traces back to Athens and Rome, according to which the republic is based on the rule of law, which rests on 'the power of the people' (p. 40). In this perspective power is dissociated from 'the command–obedience relationship' (p.40) and 'the business of dominion' (p. 44). Power is consensual: it 'needs no justification, being inherent in the very existence of political communities; what it does need is legitimacy. . . . Power springs up whenever people get together and act in concert, but it derives its legitimacy from the initial getting together rather than from any action that then may follow' (p. 52). *Violence*, by contrast, is instrumental, a means to an end, but 'never will be legitimate' (p. 52). Power, 'far from being the means to an end, is actually the very condition enabling a group of people to think and act in terms of the means–end category' (p. 51).

The *point* of these rather similar definitions of power by Parsons and Arendt is to lend persuasive support to the general theoretical frameworks of their authors. In Parsons's case the linking of power to authoritative decisions and collective goals serves to reinforce his theory of social integration as based on value consensus by concealing from view the whole range of problems that have concerned so-called 'coercion' theorists, precisely under the rubric of 'power'. By definitional fiat, phenomena of coercion, exploitation, manipulation and so on cease to be phenomena of power – and in consequence disappear from the theoretical landscape. Anthony Giddens has put this point very well:

> Two obvious facts, that authoritative decisions very often do serve sectional interests and that the most radical conflicts in society stem from struggles for power, are defined out of consideration – at least as phenomena connected with 'power'. The conceptualisation of power which Parsons offers allows him to shift the entire weight of his analysis away from power as expressing a relation *between* individuals or groups, toward seeing power as a 'system property'. That collective 'goals', or even the values which lie behind them, may be the outcome of a 'negotiated order' built on conflicts between parties holding differential power is ignored, since for Parsons 'power' assumes the prior existence of collective goals. ([11] p. 265)

In the case of Arendt, similarly, the conceptualisation of power plays a persuasive role, in defence of her conception of 'the *res publica*, the public thing' to which people consent and 'behave nonviolently and argue rationally', and in opposition to the reduction of 'public affairs to the business of dominion' and to the conceptual linkage of power with force and violence. To 'speak of non-violent power', she writes, 'is actually redundant' ([1] p. 56). These distinctions enable Arendt to make statements such as the following: 'tyranny, as Montesquieu discovered, is therefore the most violent and least powerful of forms of government' (p. 41); 'Where power has disintegrated, revolutions are possible but not necessary' (p. 49); 'Even the most despotic domination we know of, the rule of master over slaves, who always outnumbered him, did not rest on superior means of coercion as such, but on a superior organization of power – that is, on the organized solidarity of the masters' (p. 50); 'Violence can always destroy power; out of the barrel of a gun grows the most effective command, resulting in the most instant and perfect obedience. What can never grow out of it is power' (p. 53); 'Power and violence are opposites; where the one rules absolutely, the other is absent. Violence appears where power is in jeopardy, but left to its own course it ends in power's disappearance' (p. 56).

These conceptualisations of power are rationally defensible. It is, however, the contention of this book that they are of less value than that advanced here for two reasons.

In the first place, they are revisionary persuasive redefinitions of power which are out of line with the central meanings of 'power' as traditionally understood and with the concerns that have always centrally preoccupied students of power. They focus on the locution 'power to', ignoring 'power over'. Thus power indicates a 'capacity', a 'facility', an 'ability', not a relationship. Accordingly, the conflictual aspect of power – the fact that it is exercised *over* people – disappears altogether from view.[7] And along with it there disappears the central interest of studying power relations in the first place – an interest in the (attempted or successful) securing of people's compliance by overcoming or averting their opposition.

In the second place, the point of these definitions is, as we have seen, to reinforce certain theoretical positions; but everything that can be said by their means can be said with greater clarity by means of the conceptual scheme here proposed, without thereby concealing from view the (central) aspects of power which they define out of existence. Thus, for instance, Parsons objects to seeing power as a 'zero-sum' phenomenon and appeals to the analogy of credit creation in the economy, arguing that the use of power, as when the ruled have justified confidence in their rulers, may achieve objectives which all desire and from which all benefit. It has been argued in defence of this view that 'in any type of group, the existence of defined "leadership" positions does "generate" power which may be used to achieve aims desired by the majority of the members of the group' ([11] p. 263). Similarly, Arendt wants to say that members of a group acting in concert are exercising power. According to the conceptual scheme here advanced, all such cases of cooperative activity, where individuals or groups significantly affect one another in the absence of a conflict of interests between them, will be identifiable, as cases of 'influence' but not of 'power'. All that Parsons and Arendt wish to say about consensual behaviour remains sayable, but so also does all that they wish to remove from the language of power.

It may be useful if at this point I set out a conceptual map (Fig. 1) of power and its cognates (all modes of 'significant affecting') – a map which broadly follows Bachrach and Baratz's typology, referred to above. Needless to say, this map is itself essentially contestable – and, in particular, although it is meant to analyse and situate the concept of power which underlies the one-, two- and three-dimensional views of power, I do not claim that it would necessarily be acceptable to all the proponents of those respective views. One reason for that, of course, is that it is developed from the perspective of the three-dimensional view, which incorporates and therefore goes further than the other two.

It will be seen that in this scheme power may or may not be a form of influence – depending on whether sanctions are involved; while influence and authority may or may not be a form of power – depending on whether a conflict of interests is involved. Consensual authority, with no conflict of interests, is not, therefore, a form of power.

The question of whether rational persuasion is a form of power and influence cannot be adequately treated here. For what it is worth, my inclination is to say both yes and no. Yes, because it is a form of significant affecting: *A* gets (causes) *B* to do or think what he would not otherwise do or think. No, because *B* autonomously accepts *A*'s reasons, so that one is inclined to say that it is not *A* but *A*'s reasons, or *B*'s acceptance of them, that is responsible

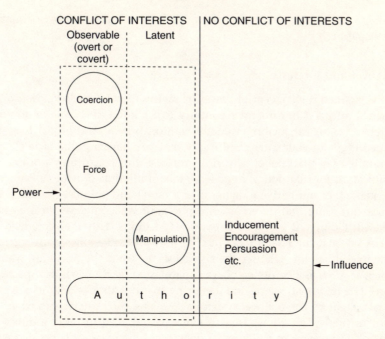

Figure 1

for *B*'s change of course. I suspect that we are here in the presence of a fundamental (Kantian) antinomy between causality, on the one hand, and autonomy and reason, on the other. I see no way of resolving this antinomy: there are simply contradictory conceptual pressures at work.

It may further be asked whether power can be exercised by *A* over *B* in *B*'s real interests. That is, suppose there is a conflict now between the preferences of *A* and *B*, but that *A*'s preferences are in *B*'s real interests. To this there are two possible responses: (1) that *A* might exercise 'short-term power' over *B* (with an observable conflict of subjective interests), but that if and when *B* recognises his real interests, the power relation ends: it is self-annihilating; or (2) that all or most forms of attempted or successful control by *A* over *B*, when *B* objects or resists, constitute a violation of *B*'s autonomy; that *B* has a real interest in his own autonomy; so that such an exercise of power cannot be in *B*'s real interests. Clearly the first of these responses is open to misuse by seeming to provide a paternalist licence for tyranny; while the second furnishes an anarchist defence against it, collapsing all or most cases of influence into power. Though attracted by the second, I am inclined to adopt the first, the dangers of which may be obviated by insisting on the empirical basis for identifying real interests. The identification of these is not up to *A*, *but to B*, exercising choice under conditions of relative autonomy and, in particular, independently of $A$'s power – e.g. through democratic participation.[8]

## 6 Power and interests

I have defined the concept of power by saying that $A$ exercises power over $B$ when $A$ affects $B$ in a manner contrary to $B$'s interests. Now the notion of 'interests' is an irreducibly evaluative notion (see [5] and [6]): if I say that something is in your interests, I imply that you have a prima facie claim to it, and if I say that 'policy $x$ is in $A$'s interest' this constitutes a prima facie justification for that policy. In general, talk of interests provides a licence for the making of normative judgments of a moral and political character. So it is not surprising that different conceptions of what interests *are* are associated with different moral and political positions. Extremely crudely, one might say that the liberal takes men as they are and applies want-regarding principles to them, relating their interests to what they actually want or prefer, to their policy preferences as manifested by their political participation.[9] The reformist, seeing and deploring that not all men's wants are given equal weight by the political system, also relates their interests to what they want or prefer, but allows that this may be revealed in more indirect and sub-political ways – in the form of deflected, submerged or concealed wants and preferences. The radical, however, maintains that men's wants may themselves be a product of a system which works against their interests, and, in such cases, relates the latter to what they would want and prefer, were they able to make the choice.[10] Each of these three picks out a certain range of the entire class of actual and potential wants as the relevant object of his moral appraisal. In brief, my suggestion is that the one-dimensional view of power presupposes a liberal conception of interests, the two-dimensional view a reformist conception, and the three-dimensional view a radical conception. (And I would maintain that any view of power rests on some normatively specific conception of interests.)[11]

## 7 The three views compared

I now turn to consider the relative strengths and weaknesses of the three views of power I have outlined.

The virtues of the decision-making or one-dimensional view are obvious and have often been stressed: by means of it, to cite Merelman again, the pluralists 'studied actual behavior, stressed operational definitions, and turned up evidence' ([13] p. 451). However, the trouble is that, by doing this, by studying the making of important decisions within the community, they were simply taking over and reproducing the bias of the system they were studying. By analysing the decisions on urban redevelopment, public education and political nominations, Dahl tells us a good deal about the *diversity* of decision-making power in New Haven. He shows that these issue areas are independent of one another, and that, by and large, different individuals exercise power in different areas and therefore no set of individuals and thus no single elite has decision-making power ranging across different issue areas. He further argues that the decision-making process is responsive to the preferences of citizens because the elected politicians and officials engaged in it anticipate the results of future elections. It would, he writes, 'be unwise to underestimate the extent to which voters may exert *indirect* influence on the decisions of leaders by means of elections ([8] p. 101): no issue of importance to the former is likely to be ignored for long by the latter. Thus Dahl pictures pluralist politics as both diverse and open: he writes, '[T]he independence, penetrability, and heterogeneity of the various segments of the political stratum all but guarantee that any dissatisfied group will find spokesmen in the political stratum' (p. 93). But the diversity and openness Dahl sees may be highly misleading if power is being exercised within the system to limit decision-making to acceptable issues. Individuals and elites may act separately in making acceptable decisions, but they may act in concert – or even fail to act at all – in such a way as to keep unacceptable issues out of politics, thereby preventing the system from becoming any more diverse than it is. 'A polity', it has been suggested, 'that is pluralistic in its decision-making can be unified in its non-decisionmaking' ([7] p. 179). The decision-making method prevents this possibility from being considered. Dahl concludes that the system is penetrable by any dissatisfied group, but he does so only by studying cases of successful penetration, and never examines failed attempts at such penetration. Moreover, the thesis that indirect influence gives the electorate control over leaders can be turned on its head. Indirect influence can equally operate to prevent politicians, officials or others from raising issues or proposals known to be unacceptable to some group or institution in the community. It can serve the interests of an elite, not only that of the electorate. In brief, the one-dimensional view of power cannot reveal the less visible ways in which a pluralist system may be biased in favour of certain groups and against others.

The two-dimensional view goes some way to revealing this – which is a considerable advance in itself – but it confines itself to studying situations where the mobilisation of bias can be attributed to individuals' decisions that have the effect of preventing currently observable grievances (overt or covert) from becoming issues within the political process. This, I think, largely accounts for the very thin and inadequate character of Bachrach and Baratz's study of poverty, race and politics in Baltimore. All that study really amounts to is an account of various decisions by the mayor and various business leaders to deflect the inchoate demands of Baltimore's blacks from becoming politically threatening issues – by such devices as making certain appointments, establishing task forces to defuse the poverty issue, by supporting certain kinds of welfare measures, etc. – together with an account of how the blacks gained political access through overt struggle involving riots. The analysis remains superficial precisely because it confines itself to studying individual decisions made to avert potentially threatening demands from becoming politically dangerous. A deeper analysis would also concern itself with all the complex and subtle ways in which the *inactivity* of leaders and the sheer weight of institutions – political, industrial and educational – served for so long to keep the blacks out of Baltimore politics; and indeed for a long period kept them from even trying to get into it.

The three-dimensional view offers the possibility of such an analysis. It offers, in other words, the prospect of a serious sociological and not merely personalised explanation of how political systems prevent demands from becoming political issues or even from being made. Now the classical objection to doing this has often been stated by pluralists: how can one study, let alone explain, what does not happen? Polsby writes:

> . . . it has been suggested that non-events make more significant policy than do policy-making events. This is the kind of statement that has a certain plausibility and attractiveness but that presents truly insuperable obstacles to research. We can sound the depth of the abyss very quickly by agreeing that non-events are much more important than events, and inquiring precisely *which* non-events are to be regarded as most significant in the community. Surely not *all* of them. For every event (no matter how defined) that occurs there must be an infinity of alternatives. Then which non-events are to be regarded as significant? One satisfactory answer might be: those outcomes desired by a significant number of actors in the community but not achieved. Insofar as these goals are in some way explicitly pursued by people in the community, the method of study used in New Haven has a reasonable chance of capturing them. A wholly unsatisfactory answer would be: certain non-events stipulated by outside observers without reference to the desires or activities of community residents. The answer is unsatisfactory because it is obviously inappropriate for outsiders to pick among all the possible outcomes that did not take place a set which they regard as important but which community citizens do not. This approach is likely to prejudice the outcomes of research. . . . ([18] pp. 96–7)

Similarly, Wolfinger argues that the 'infinite variety of possible nondecisions . . . reveals the idea's adaptability to various ideological perspectives' ([20] p. 1078). Moreover, suppose we advance 'a theory of political interests and rational behavior' specifying how people would behave in certain situations if left to themselves, and use it to support the claim that their failure so to behave is due to the exercise of power. In this case, Wolfinger argues, we have no means of deciding between two possibilities: either that there was an exercise of power, or that the theory was wrong (p. 1078).

The first point to be made against these apparently powerful arguments is that they move from a methodological difficulty to a substantive assertion. It does not follow that, just because it is difficult or even impossible to show that power has been exercised in a given situation, we can conclude that it has not. But, more importantly, I do not believe that it is impossible to identify an exercise of power of this type.

What is an exercise of power? What is it to exercise power? On close inspection it turns out that the locution 'exercise of power' and 'exercising power' is problematic in at least two ways.

In the first place, it carries, in everyday usage, a doubly unfortunate connotation: it is sometimes assumed to be both individualistic and intentional, that is, it seems to carry the suggestion that the exercise of power is a matter of individuals consciously acting to affect others. Some appear to feel discomfort in speaking either of groups, institutions, or collectivities 'exercising' power, or of individuals or collectivities doing so unconsciously. This is an interesting case of individualistic and intentional assumptions being built into our language – but that in itself provides no reason for adopting such assumptions. In what follows I propose to abandon these assumptions and to speak of the exercise of power whether by individuals or by groups, institutions, etc., and whether consciously or not. A negative justification for this revisionary usage is that there is no other available word that meets the bill (thus 'exerting' power is little different from 'exercising' it); I shall offer a positive justification below.

The second way in which the phrase 'exercising power' is problematic is that it conceals an interesting and important ambiguity. I referred above to Dahl's definition of the exercise of power in terms of $A$ getting $B$ to do something he would not otherwise do. However, this is, as it stands, too simple.

Suppose that $A$ can *normally* affect $B$. This is to suppose that, against the background of (what is assumed to be) a normally ongoing situation, if $A$ does $x$, he gets $B$ to do what he would not otherwise do. Here $A$'s action, $x$, is *sufficient* to get $B$ to do what he would not otherwise do. Suppose, however, that exactly the same is true of $A_1$. He can also normally affect $B$: his action, $y$, is also sufficient to get $B$ to do what he would not otherwise do, in just the same way. Now, suppose that $A$ and $A_1$ both act in relation to $B$ simultaneously and $B$ changes his action accordingly. Here, it is clear, $B$'s action or change of course is overdetermined: both $A$ and $A_1$ have affected $B$ by 'exercising power', but the result is the same as that which would have occurred had either affected him singly. In this case it is a pointless question to ask which of them produced the change of course, that is, which of them made a difference to the result: they both did. They both 'exercised power', in a sense – that is, a power *sufficient* to produce the result, yet one cannot say that *either* of them made a difference to the result. Let us call this sense of 'exercising power' the *operative* sense.

Contrast this case with the case where $A$ *does* make a difference to the result: that is, against the background of a normally ongoing situation, $A$, by doing $x$, actually gets $B$ to do what $B$ would not otherwise do. Here $x$ is an intervening cause which distorts the normal course of events – by contrast with the first, overdetermined case, where there are, *ex hypothesi*, two intervening sufficient conditions, so that neither can be said to have 'made a difference', just because of the presence of the other: there the normal course of events is itself distorted by the presence of the other intervening sufficient condition. In this case, by contrast, *A*'s intervention can be said to make a difference to the result. Let us call this sense of 'exercising power' the *effective* sense.

(It is worth adding a further distinction, which turns on *what* difference *A* makes to the result. *A* wishes *B* to do some particular thing, but, in exercising effective power over him, he may succeed in changing *B*'s course in a wide variety of ways. Only in the case where *B*'s change of course corresponds to *A*'s wishes, that is, where *A* secures *B*'s compliance, can we speak properly of a *successful* exercise of power: here 'affecting' becomes 'control'. It is, incidentally, this case of the successful exercise of power, or the securing of compliance, on which Bachrach and Baratz exclusively concentrate. The successful exercise of power can be seen as a sub-species of the effective exercise of power – though one could maintain that, where the operative exercise of power issues in compliance, this also is an [indeterminate] form of its successful exercise.)

We can now turn to the analysis of what exactly is involved in identifying an exercise of power. An attribution of the exercise of power involves, among other things, the double claim that *A* acts (or fails to act) in a certain way and that *B* does what he would not otherwise do (I use the term 'do' here in a very wide sense, to include 'think', 'want', 'feel', etc.). In the case of an effective exercise of power, *A* gets *B* to do what he would not otherwise do; in the case of an operative exercise of power, *A*, together with another or other sufficient conditions, gets *B* to do what he would not otherwise do. Hence, in general, any attribution of the exercise of power (including, of course, those by Dahl and his colleagues) always implies a relevant counterfactual, to the effect that (but for *A*, or but for *A* together with any other sufficient conditions) *B* would otherwise have done, let us say, *b*. This is one reason why so many thinkers (mistakenly) insist on actual, observable conflict as essential to power (though there are doubtless other theoretical and, indeed, ideological reasons). For such conflict provides the relevant counterfactual, so to speak, ready-made. If *A* and *B* are in conflict with one another, *A* wanting *a* and *B* wanting *b*, then if *A* prevails over *B*, we can assume that *B* would otherwise have done *b*. Where there is no observable conflict between *A* and *B*, then we must provide other grounds for asserting the relevant counterfactual. That is, we must provide other, indirect, grounds for asserting that if *A* had not acted (or failed to act) in a certain way – and, in the case of operative power, if other sufficient conditions had not been operative – then *B* would have thought and acted differently from the way he does actually think and act. In brief, we need to justify our expectation that *B* would have thought or acted differently; and we also need to specify the means or mechanism by which *A* has prevented, or else acted (or abstained from acting) in a manner sufficient to prevent, *B* from doing so.

I can see no reason to suppose that either of these claims cannot in principle be supported – though I do not claim it is easy.

## Notes

1 See the present author's *Individualism* (Oxford: Blackwell, 1973) ch. 17. Contrast Dahrendorf's decision to 'follow . . . the useful and well-considered definitions of Max Weber', according to which 'the important difference between power and authority consists in the fact that whereas power is essentially tied to the personality of individuals, authority is always associated with social positions or roles' ([9] p. 166).

2 Karl Marx and Friedrich Engels, 'The Eighteenth Brumaire of Louis Bonaparte', in Marx and Engels, *Selected Works* (Moscow: Foreign Languages Publishing House, 1962) vol. 1, p. 247.

3 This association is made most clearly in *Power and Poverty* ([4] esp. pp. 49–50) in reaction to the pressure of pluralist criticisms of the (potentially three-dimensional) implications of the article on nondecisions [3]. See Merelman [13] and the Communications to the Editor of the *American Political Science Review*, 62 (1968) by Bachrach and Baratz (pp. 1268–9) and Merelman (p. 1269).

4 I use the term 'behavioural' in the narrow sense indicated above, to refer to the study of overt and actual behaviour – and specifically concrete decisions. Of course, in the widest sense, the three-dimensional view of power is 'behavioural' in that it is committed to the view that behaviour (action and inaction, conscious and unconscious, actual and potential) provides evidence (direct and indirect) for an attribution of the exercise of power.

5 This conflict is latent in the sense that it is assumed that there *would be* a conflict of wants or preferences between those exercising power and those subject to it, were the latter to become aware of their interests. (My account of latent conflict and real interests is to be distinguished from Dahrendorf's account of 'objective' and 'latent' interests as 'antagonistic interests conditioned by, even inherent in, social positions', in imperatively co-ordinated associations, which are 'independent of [the individual's] conscious orientations' ([9] pp. 174, 178). Dahrendorf assumes as sociologically given what I claim to be empirically ascertainable.)

6 This distinction between 'concept' and 'view' is closely parallel to that drawn by John Rawls between 'concept' and 'conception'. It seems, writes Rawls, 'natural to think of the concept of justice as distinct from the various conceptions of justice and as being specified by the role which these different sets of principles, these different conceptions, have in common. Those who hold different conceptions of justice can, then, still agree that institutions are just when no arbitrary distinctions are made between persons in the assigning of basic rights and duties and when the rules determine a proper balance between competing claims to the advantages of social life. Men can agree to this description of just institutions since the notions of an arbitrary distinction and of a proper balance, which are included in the concept of justice, are left open for each to interpret according to the principles of justice that he accepts. These principles single out which similarities and differences among persons are relevant in determining rights and duties and they specify which division of advantages is appropriate' ( John Rawls, *A Theory of Justice*, Oxford: Clarendon Press, 1972, pp. 5–6). Analogously, those holding the three different views of power I have set out offer differing interpretations of what are to count as interests and how they may be adversely affected. I further agree with Rawls's suggestions that the various conceptions of justice (like views of power) are 'the outgrowth of different notions of society against the background of opposing views of the natural necessities and opportunities of human life. Fully to understand a conception of justice we must make explicit the conception of social co-operation from which it derives' (pp. 910). I disagree, however, with Rawls's apparent belief that there is ultimately one rational conception or set of principles of justice to be discovered. 'Justice' is no less essentially contested than 'power'.

7 Thus for Parsons 'the power of A over B' becomes a 'right' of precedence in decision-making!

8 On this last point, see the past and future writings of Peter Bachrach.

9 See Brian Barry, *Political Argument* (London: Routledge & Kegan Paul, 1965) and the present author's discussion of it in 'Varieties of Political Philosophy', *Political Studies*, 15 (1967), pp. 55–9.

10 Cf. Connolly's 'first approximation' to a definition of real interests: 'Policy *x* is more in *A*'s interest than policy *y*, if *A* were he to experience the *results* of both *x* and *y*, would *choose x* as the result he would rather have for himself' ([6] p. 472). I too connect real interests with (relative)

autonomy and choice. What is, of course, required at this point is a sustained discussion of the nature of, and conditions for, autonomy (and its relation to social determination). The reader will find the beginnings of such a discussion in the author's *Individualism*, chs. 8, 18 and 20.

11 See the present author's paper 'Relativism: Cognitive and Moral', *Supplementary Proceedings of the Aristotelian Society* (June 1974).

# References

[1] Hannah Arendt, *On Violence* (London: Allen Lane, The Penguin Press, 1970). A characteristically stimulating essay, advancing an interestingly idiosyncratic concept of power.

[2] Peter Bachrach and Morton S. Baratz, 'The Two Faces of Power', *American Political Science Review*, 56 (1962) pp. 947–52. A brilliant and by now classical contribution to the literature.

[3] ——, 'Decisions and Nondecisions: An Analytical Framework', *American Political Science Review*, 57 (1963) pp. 641–51. A crucial further development of the above.

[4] ——, *Power and Poverty. Theory and Practice* (New York: Oxford University Press, 1970). The first, theoretical part incorporates and develops the two foregoing items (toning down the potentially three-dimensional implications of the second); the second part is an empirical study of the politics of poverty and race relations in Baltimore.

[5] Isaac D. Balbus, 'The Concept of Interest in Pluralist and Marxian Analysis', *Politics and Society*, 1 (1971) pp. 151–77. Relates the subjective definition of 'interest' used by pluralists to classical liberalism and argues for the explanatory and normative superiority of Marxian class analysis.

[6] William E. Connolly, 'On "Interests" in Politics', *Politics and Society*, 2 (1972) pp. 459–77. A valuable discussion of alternative efforts to elucidate the descriptive criteria of 'interests', including a thought-provoking account of 'real interests'.

[7] Matthew A. Crenson, *The Un-Politics of Air Pollution: A Study of Non-Decisionmaking in the Cities* (Baltimore and London: The Johns Hopkins Press, 1971). A very intelligent and ingenious empirical application of the two-dimensional view of power, together with certain elements of the three-dimensional view.

[8] ——, *Who Governs? Democracy and Power in an American City* (New Haven and London: Yale University Press, 1961). The classical 'pluralist' study. A finer, subtler work than its critics and defenders might suggest, partly because it contains the evidential basis for criticising its conclusions.

[9] Ralf Dahrendorf, *Class and Class Conflict in Industrial Society* (London: Routledge & Kegan Paul, 1959). Offers a 'coercion theory of social structure' and focuses on authority relations in imperatively co-ordinated associations where there are antagonistic socially structured 'objective' interests.

[10] W.B. Gallie, 'Essentially Contested Concepts', *Proceedings of the Aristotelian Society*, 56 (1955–6) pp. 167–98. Expounds the idea of there being concepts whose application is inherently a matter of dispute.

[11] Anthony Giddens, ' "Power" in the Recent Writings of Talcott Parsons', *Sociology*, 2 (1968) pp. 257–72. An incisive critique of Parsons [14, 15, 16] for simply setting aside or ignoring the main points at issue between integration and coercion theory.

[12] Lewis Lipsitz, 'On Political Belief: The Grievances of the Poor', in *Power and Community: Dissenting Essays in Political Science*, ed. Philip Green and Sanford Levinson (New York: Random House, Vintage Books, 1970). A subtle discussion of 'political silence', focusing on unarticulated and latent grievances.

[13] Richard M. Merelman, 'On the Neo-Elitist Critique of Community Power', *American Political Science Review*, 62 (1968) pp. 451–60. A lively attack on the idea of nondecision-making and 'the false consensus argument' and a defence of a decisional methodology and pluralist premises.

[14] Talcott Parsons, 'The Distribution of Power in American Society', *World Politics*, 10 (Oct 1957) pp. 123–43. A review article of C. Wright Mills's, *The Power Elite* (New York: Oxford University Press, 1956), in which Parsons first elaborated his consensual concept of power and criticised the 'zero sum' concept as 'misleading and one-sided".

[15] ——, 'On the Concept of Influence', *Public Opinion Quarterly*, 27 (1963) pp. 37–62.

[16] ——, 'On the Concept of Political Power', *Proceedings of the American Philosophical Society*, 107 (1963) pp. 232–62. The two fullest elaborations of Parsons's later view of power.

[17] ——, *Sociological Theory and Modern Society* (New York: The Free Press; London: Collier-Macmillan, 1967). Reproduces Parsons [15, 16] as well as other relevant essays.

[18] Nelson W. Polsby, *Community Power and Political Theory* (New Haven and London: Yale University Press, 1963). An examination of the community power literature which attacks 'stratification writers' and defends a decisional methodology, testable theory and pluralist conclusions.

[19] D.M. White, 'The Problems of Power', *British Journal of Political Science*, 2 (1972) pp. 479–90. A useful, clarifying discussion which argues against the possibility of a universally satisfactory account of the meaning of 'power' and analyses it as a form of significant affecting.

[20] Raymond E. Wolfinger, 'Nondecisions and the Study of Local Politics', *American Political Science Review*, 65 (1971) pp. 1063–80. A rather diffuse defence of decisionism and pluralism and a further attack on the study of nondecision-making, concluding with scepticism about the possibility of investigating 'power structures' at all.

# 4 Poulantzas

## Introduction

As presented in the previous section, Lukes interpreted the work of Poulantzas as determinant to the point of precluding power and agency. Arguably it is the case that Poulantzas backed himself into a determinist corner in his debate with Miliband. However, the task of making sense of the nature of the relationship between structure and contingency is central to Poulantzas' wider theoretical project. In some respects, Poulantzas' work is paradigmatic of the conceptual problems entailed by, on the one hand, holding a meta-theory of history while, on the other, not wishing to reduce agents to dupes of social forces. The solution to this problem is to create a careful balance between attributing causality to anonymous social forces and winding up with a conspiracy theory within which the meta-narrative is masterminded by a powerful elite.

Poulantzas' meta-theory is Marxist and, consequently, entails the premise that, in the progress of history, the base determines the superstructure. The base is the economy while the superstructure includes the state, education, religion and any non-economic authority structures. However, if it is a premise that capitalism determines the nature of politics, it becomes a difficult, but pressing, intellectual challenge to account for the existence of the great variety of political institutions which characterize actual capitalist economies. Why has the capitalist base not always produced identical political superstructures?

Within this, the biggest conceptual problem is how to make sense of the fact that there appears to be a strong empirical association between capitalism and democratic politics. On the surface, it appears counter-intuitive that the egalitarian principles of democracy are functional to capitalism. This is particularly the case when so many democratic governments are left-wing. The easy, but theoretically unacceptable, solution to this conundrum is to argue that politics do not really matter; that the people and their elected representatives can do what they like but, behind their backs, the economy drives on and makes nothing of their actions (structural determinism without meaningful agency). The other equally (but differently) flawed alternative suggests that behind the polity there exists a capitalist elite who manage to manipulate elected representatives of all political persuasions (agent-centred conspiracy theory).

In order to avoid either of these unsophisticated, 'vulgar' Marxist, theorizations, Poulantzas developed a highly complex theory of power, agency and conflict. While the resultant perspective is complex in all its detail and terminology, it is possible to provide an overview of some of its broader contours.

At the theoretical core of Poulantzas' model lies a functional analysis of a feedback of unintended effects from the superstructure to the base. Poulantzas conceives of society as divided into social practice and structure in such a manner that structure refers to the social space within which social practice takes place. These practices are not simply the effect of structure but, rather, are constituted by meaningful choices and strategies within a structured context. Practice entails power and is constituted by struggle between classes of conflicting interests. This power conflict is the effect of contradictions within capitalism as a mode of production. However, the mode of production does not determine the outcome of specific strategic struggles: the working class may gain meaningful power over the bourgeoisie by gaining control of the instruments of state.

Within this, power is theorized in terms of the capacity of a social class to realize its specific objective interests. The possibility of meaningful control of the superstructure is open to those who are exploited by capital. Political systems can be used for the purpose of furthering all specific interests, including those of the proletariat, in their struggle against the interests of capital. Consequently, in its unity, the essence of the superstructure is constituted through class struggle and power in opposition. It is precisely because this struggle is meaningful, and that power is effective, that the democratic state is considered legitimate. If it were the case that the proletariat could never gain control of the state and, consequently, that the state always represented the interests of capital, then superstructure would be considered illegitimate. Authority would then be purely coercive, and society would be characterized by a revolutionary potential which would, obviously, be dysfunctional to the interests of capital.

Not only does the success of the power of the proletariat provide legitimacy to the state and, hence, to existing relations of domination, but this power also provides economic consequences which are functional to capital. As argued by Marx, the unintended consequences of capitalist competition are frequently contrary to the interests of capital. Left to their own devices, in order to maximize profit, capitalists will pay workers as little as possible while forcing them to work as long as possible. Yet, in the long run, such behaviour is dysfunctional to capital because it creates a dissatisfied workforce and, more significantly, a workforce which has neither the resources nor the leisure time to consume the products of capital. For the archetypal capitalist, the ideal world would be one where 'their' workers are poorly paid but those of others are sufficiently well paid to constitute effective consumers. The next best thing to that is a situation where every worker (their own and those of others) is sufficiently well paid to have time and resources to consume. The least desirable option of all is the aforementioned state of affairs where all workers are too poor to consume. By creating better working conditions and minimum wages, social-democratic governments ensure that capitalists obtain their second preference choice. In a theoretically similar fashion, other dysfunctional and unintended consequences of capitalism, all of which contribute to making capitalists their own 'gravediggers', are averted by the effective political power of the working classes.

The reason that the power of the working class never results in the actual dissolution of capitalist relations of production is because the state is ultimately paid for by the economy. There is a process of 'determinacy in the last instance' whereby no leftist government will undermine the economy which furnishes them with the resources to implement socialist policies. The moment that the welfare state is pushed so far that the economy shows signs of collapse, the government will pull back and pursue policies to protect the economy. Ironically, socialist governments are in a better position than their conservative counterparts to pursue these policies because these actions have a lower legitimacy cost for the former than for the latter. This is the case because 'socialist' policies which protect the economy tend to be perceived of as merely short-term measures to ensure prosperity whereas, in contrast, the same policies carried out by conservative parties are interpreted as policies which are in the interests of capital. Arguably, the rolling back of the welfare state by the P.S.O.E. in Spain under González in the later years and, similar policies by the Labour Party in Britain under Blair would constitute examples of this phenomenon.

In commenting upon this model it has to be observed that the above summary of aspects of Poulantzas' theory of power has been denuded of many of the complexities and contradictions which characterize his writings. There are many occasions when Poulantzas is substantially more determinist than above and, as a consequence, uses an impoverished concept of power and agency. Even if these instances are ignored (as above), his theory should be viewed only as a model which provides an important insight into aspects of power and domination rather than a theory of power and social order as a whole. This is, of course, a statement from my own theoretical view point where I would argue that we should not look for a single theory of power but, rather, construct meso-level theories which we use as conceptual tools for specific tasks.

## Further reading

The foremost interpreter of Poulantzas in English is Bob Jessop, and Jessop (1985) is his most comprehensive interpretation of Poulantzas' position. Aside from Jessop, read more of *State, Power, Socialism* (1978); *Political Power and Social Classes* (Poulantzas 1973) is also a key text for understanding his perspective on power.

For the Poulantzas/Miliband debate see Miliband (1970) and Poulantzas (1969). Ward (1987) is an interesting commentary upon Poulantzas, Jessop, Lukes and Giddens on the subject of power and structure.

# From *STATE, POWER, SOCIALISM*
## Nicos Poulantzas

[pp. 11–14]

### On the theory of the state

*I*

Who today can escape the question of the State and power? Who indeed does not talk about it? The current political situation, not only in France but in the whole of Europe, is certainly one reason for its topicality. But talk is not enough: we have to understand, know and explain. And for that, we must not hesitate to go straight to the root of the problems. We also have to grasp means adequate to the end, without giving in to the temptation of using a fashionable language of analogy and metaphor. No doubt my initial observations will seem rather arid. But unlike Alphonse Allias, I do not unfortunately have the time to pass on more quickly to the very exciting later chapters.

Whether overtly or not, all twentieth-century political theory has basically posed the same question: what is the relationship between the State, power and social classes? I repeat *twentieth-century* theory, because such was not always the case, at least not in this form. Marxism first had to make some headway. But since Max Weber, all political theory has constituted either a dialogue with Marxism or an attack upon it. At any event, who today would dream of denying the relationship between power and the dominant classes? Now, while the countless, varieties of such theory pose the same question, the great majority also give the same basic answer: first there is the State or power (which is explicated in numerous different ways) and then the ruling classes establish with it specific relations of proximity or alliance. These relations are unravelled with varying degrees of sophistication, by reference to pressure groups acting on the State or flexible strategies spreading through the networks of power and taking shape in its structures. The account always comes down to the following: the State is constituted by an original, impenetrable kernel and by 'the rest', which the ruling classes, coming on to the scene as if by chance, are able to affect and penetrate. Such a way of conceiving the State essentially rests on a Janus image, or better still, on an updated form of the half-human, half-beast Centaur-Power that already haunted Machiavelli. In some authors it is the human side that is bound up with social classes, in others it is the animal side.

There is just one problem with this. How can it explain what everyone who is not blind can observe every day, not as a philosopher but as an ordinary citizen? For it is obvious that we are hemmed in more and more tightly by a State whose most detailed practices demonstrate its connection with particular, and extremely precise, interests.

One variant of Marxism, which is still tied to a certain political tradition, claims to provide us with an answer. The State is equivalent to political domination, so the argument goes, in that each dominant class constructs a State according to its requirements, bending it at will to suit its own interests. In that sense, every State is merely a class dictatorship.

This purely instrumental conception of the State reduces *the state apparatus to state power*, thus failing to touch the heart of the matter. It is not that the State has no 'class nature'. But the real problem is the one which concerns every political theory of the State and which was posed by the founders of Marxism themselves. Indeed, although they approached the problem from a specific angle, it may be said to have obsessed them in their work. They saw the State as a *special apparatus*, exhibiting a peculiar material framework that cannot be reduced to given relations of political domination. As regards the capitalist State, the question may be formulated as follows: why, in general, does the bourgeoisie seek to maintain its domination by having recourse precisely to the national-popular State – to the modern representative State with all its characteristic institutions? For it is far from self-evident that the bourgeoisie would have chosen this particular form if it had been able to tailor a State to its requirements. While the bourgeoisie continues to derive many benefits from such a State, it is by no means always contented with it, any more than it was in the past.

This is a burning question, since it also concerns the present-day phenomenon of statism, in which, as we know only too well, the State's activity reaches into all spheres of everyday life. Here too, the variant of Marxism to which we have referred supplies a peremptory answer: these activities emanate in their entirety from the will of the dominant class or from that of its hired politicians. It is perfectly clear, however, that a number of state functions (e.g., social security) cannot be reduced to political domination alone.

Even if we try to leave behind the image of the State as a mere product or appendage of the dominant class, we encounter essentially the same snare in the traditional answer of political theory. And theorists of another, more modern variant of Marxism, do not always avoid the trap. Invoking the dual nature of the State, they see *on the one hand* (still the great divide!) a kernel of the State that somehow exists side by side with classes and the class struggle. To be sure, the explanation they give of this kernel is not that of the other theories of power and the State: in particular, they make reference to the productive forces, to which they reduce the relations of production. This is the famous economic structure from which classes and class struggle are absent – a structure that is supposed to give rise to a truly 'special' State and to the purely technical (or, in more dignified language, the purely social) measures of the State. Then *on the other hand*, there is the State's other nature, this time related to classes and the class struggle. So, we have a second State, a super-State or a State within the State, which is grafted on to the back of the first. This one does have a class nature, operating in our case as the State of the bourgeoisie and of its political domination. The second State comes along to pervert, vitiate, contaminate or deflect the functions of the first.

I spoke just now of a particular variant of Marxism. But the phenomenon is much broader, extending to that left-technocratic ideology which is currently wreaking such havoc. This is above all the case not when it points to the productive forces, but when, in more prosaic fashion, it invokes the increasing complexity of the State's technical-economic tasks in so-called post-industrial societies.

Such a line of argument does not then differ all that much from the age-old answer of political theory, whether in its traditional form or in one better adapted to the tastes of the day. For all these theorists, there is a free-standing state power which is only afterwards utilized by the dominant classes in various ways. Quite frankly, they should talk not of the class nature, but of the class utilization of the State. The term mentioned earlier, the dual nature of the State, does not encompass the reality of these analyses: namely, the view that the State's true nature lies in the first, original State, while the second is just a question of habit. Just as political theory has for centuries conceived of the State as half-human, half-beast, so the genuine State or real power are here located not on the shady side (the side of classes) but on the other, sunny side.

There is a purpose behind these schematic representations. For if all political theory and all theories of socialism (including Marxism) revolve around this question, this is because it constitutes a real problem. While not of course the only one to arise in this field, it is nevertheless of central importance; and, as the reader will have guessed, it also involves the question of the transformation of the State in the transition to democratic socialism. Anyway, there is only one road that leads somewhere, only one answer that can break the vicious circle. In fact, we may begin by expressing this answer very simply: the State really does exhibit a peculiar material framework that can by no means be reduced to mere political domination. The state apparatus – that special and hence formidable something – is not exhausted in state power. Rather political domination is itself inscribed in the institutional materiality of the State. Although the State is not created *ex nihilo* by the ruling classes, nor is it simply taken over by them: state power (that of the bourgeoisie, in the case of the capitalist State) is written into this materiality. Thus, while all the State's actions are not reducible to political domination, their composition is nevertheless marked by it.

It will be no easy matter to demonstrate these propositions. For when the simplest questions are the real ones, they are also the most complex. In order to avoid losing ourselves in the maze, we must keep hold of the guiding thread: the basis of the material framework of power and the State has to be sought in the relations of production and social division of labour – but not in the sense which is normally understood and which has come to be accepted. By these terms I do not refer to an economic structure from which classes, the class struggle and forms of power are absent. Finally, it is because this constitutes the linchpin that I shall cling on to it in order to enter the current, much broader discussion on the State and power.

[pp. 146–8, the numbers indicate specific points which Poulantzas is making.]

## Towards a relational theory of power?

**1** The analyses I have made so far show that power itself is not a quantity or object of possession, nor a quality linked to a class essence or a class-subject (the dominant class). In fact, I already stressed these points in *Political Power and Social Classes*, especially in the chapter concerning the concept of power. To be sure, I only examined power to the extent that it covers the field of class struggle, since that was my principal object of investigation; but the important thing is what was said of power in that field. As applied to social classes, power should be understood as the capacity of one or several classes to realize their specific interests. It is a concept designating the field of their struggle – that of the *relationship of forces* and of the *relations* between one class and another; the concept of class interests thus designates the horizon of action occupied by a given class in relation to others. The capacity of one class to realize its interests is in opposition to the capacity (and interests) of other classes: *the field of power is therefore strictly relational*. The power of a particular class (the dominant class, for instance) does not refer to a substance which it holds in its hand: contrary to the old zero-sum conception, power is not a measurable quantity that the various classes share or exchange among one another. The power of a class refers above all to its objective place in economic, political and ideological relations – a place which overlies the practices of struggling classes (that is, the unequal relations of domination-subordination among classes rooted in the social division of labour), and which already consists in power relationships. The place of each class, and hence its power, is delimited (i.e. at once designated and limited) by the place of the other classes. Power is not then a quality attached to a class 'in-itself', understood as a collection of agents, but depends on, and springs from, a relational system of material places occupied by particular agents.

Power, and above all the political power that is pre-eminently ascribed to the State, also refers to the power organization of a class and to class position in a given conjuncture (amongst other things, party organization): it refers to the relations of classes constituted as social forces, and thus to a strategic field properly so-called. The political power of a class, its capacity to realize its political interests, depends not only on its class place (and determination) with regard to other classes, but also on the position and strategy it displays in relation to them – on what I have called opponent strategy.

2 Contrary to the view that Foucault and Deleuze impute to Marxism, I also stressed the fact that the State is not a thing or entity endowed with an intrinsic instrumental essence and a measurable power-quantum. It refers instead to the relations of social classes and forces. By state power can only be understood the power of certain (dominant) classes – that is to say, the place of these classes in a power-relation to other (dominated) ones – and, insofar as political power is involved here, the strategic relationship of forces among these classes and their respective positions. The State is neither the instrumental depository (object) of a power-essence held by the dominant class, nor a subject possessing a quantity of power equal to the quantity it takes from the classes which face it: the State is rather the strategic site of organization of the dominant class in its relationship to the dominated classes. It is a *site* and a *centre* of the exercise of power, but it possesses no power of its own. I stressed in my earlier work that political struggles, which concern the State and bear upon it (for popular struggles are never exhausted in the latter), are never external to the State but are inscribed in its framework; from this I drew a number of political conclusions. Now, those analyses also have considerable implications for the question of transition to socialism, and it is for this reason that I now dwell upon them.

# 5   Parsons

## Introduction

In the 1950s and 1960s Parsons' structural functional account of social order was hugely influential. His main article on power 'On the concept of political power' (1963a) was developed within this overall theoretical framework. Ironically, while the main body of Parsons' theoretical framework has fallen into disfavour and, at the time of publication, his view of power was considered virtually eccentric, this article is of continuing theoretical importance because it drew attention to aspects of social power which were ignored by conflictual theorists, such as Dahl, Bachrach and Baratz, and Lukes.

Like Dahl, Parsons entered the power debate intending to defend the democraticness of American politics – a review of Mills' *The Power Elite* preceded the article Parsons (1957). However, in contrast to Dahl, his aim was not analytical clarity but, rather, to explain how power is created by society. Mills and others took for granted that power was zero-sum, i.e. that one person's loss is another's gain. Cutting a cake is zero-sum: the more cake you get, the less I can have. However, who is to say that power is zero-sum? The zero-sum perception of power is premised upon the tacit assumption that power is simply given. However, power is not simply 'out there' but has to be created. If power is produced by society then it need not be zero-sum, consequently, it may well be the case that a gain in power by some is not necessarily at the expense of others. In short, the existence of powerful individuals, or organizations, is not of necessity invidious.

While we do not necessarily have to accept the conservative implications of this argument, the observation that power is produced or created by society cannot be ignored. As we shall see, this problematic is central to the work of Barnes, Foucault, Arendt, Haugaard, and contemporary constructivist social theory.

Parsons sought to explain the production of power in terms of an analogy between the polity and economy. Within structural-functionalism society was considered in terms similar to that of biological organisms. In order for an organism to survive it needs to be able to adapt to the environment and achieve desired goals. For the former purposes, social systems have an economy and for the latter a polity. The economy is for the production of wealth, whereas the polity is for the realization of collective goals.

In order to achieve its function the economy has within it a circulatory medium – money – which is analogically equivalent to power within the polity. The analogy is not only functional but, also, substantive. The existence of money is based upon a deep tacit consensus on the value of money, which is a paradigmatic embodiment of abstract convention – money only has value because we believe it does. Similarly, the power of those in authority is based upon self-perpetuating belief in legitimacy. Parsons does not deny that some power relations are based upon coercion, or the threat of violence, but he perceived of coercion as a poor substitute for consensual legitimate power. Consensual power is power which is created by the polity and, as systems become more complex, it becomes increasingly central to the goal attainment abilities of complex social systems.

Parsons explains the analogy between money and power in terms of an ideal type historical account of the development of the two media of circulation. In a primitive economy goods are exchanged largely based upon barter. If I grow potatoes and I wish for an axe, I have to go and find someone willing to exchange axes for potatoes. Obviously this is highly inconvenient, so money is 'invented'. This early money was a commodity in itself. Coins are equivalent to their metal content. However, as the economy becomes larger and more complex, the limited availability of precious metals becomes a fetter upon economic growth, consequently, paper money replaces metal. At first the paper money is equivalent to certain quantities of metal but, over time, the value of money becomes pure abstract conventionality. Similarly, in a primitive polity leadership and compliance are based upon direct violence and coercion. However, this source of compliance is inconvenient when constructing a chain of command. A complex system presupposes actors with authoritative power which can be based upon violence only in the last resort. Over time, as the system gains in effectiveness, its members become increasingly willing to render compliance to those in authority. Just as money slowly becomes divorced from its metallic base, so, similarly, power is divorced from coercion.

Parsons does not explain the expansion of power (its non-zero-sum nature) in terms of this historical analogy (a mistake which is often made by interpreters of Parsons) but in terms of banking, the details of which are found in the article. Suffice it to say that the consensual basis of power does not entail that it can be expanded at will but, rather, the total amount of power in a system reflects the system's effectiveness at realizing goals. Power increases as legitimacy is earned through effectiveness while, conversely, it contracts as illegitimacy pervades the system due to the misuse of authority. Just as it is not possible to increase money supply simply by printing more paper money at will, legitimate power cannot be willed into existence. When leaders arbitrarily give themselves more power, a process not dissimilar to inflation is initiated. While there is more power around, its actual effectiveness has been decreased. The usual reaction of leaders in such a situation is to increase coercion (the equivalent of going back to the gold standard) as a substitute for actual power. Hence, the empirical fact that frequent use of coercion implies lack of effectiveness rather than actual control. To take an everyday example, if the only way a parent has of gaining compliance from a child is through threats and violence, this is a sign of a lack of power rather than the converse. Similarly, political regimes which coerce their populations *en masse* generally do so because they lack the type of authoritative, legitimate power which Parsons had in mind.

This model of power is deeply problematic in a number of ways. In his desire to theorize the consensual aspect of power, Parsons entirely fails to theorize conflictual power adequately – which is a theme explored by Giddens (1968). The analogy between money and power lacks a certain plausibility because we do not really understand how money works; the model is too simplistic. Furthermore, it also fails to convince because money has a tangibility which power does not – I can put my hand in my pocket and pull out legal tender while it is difficult to point to power as a thing-like entity. However, by far the greatest problem for the contemporary reader is the fact that the theory is couched in a theoretical framework – structural functionalism – which, in its stronger forms at least, has fallen entirely out of favour.

Yet, despite these failings, Parsons draws our attention to a number of aspects of power which are significant: power does not simply exist, it has to be created; the creation of power is inextricably related to the reproduction of social order; even if power is not always legitimate, it is not equivalent to violence or coercion; power is not zero-sum; and it is not inherently contrary to people's interests. These elements are central to, what I term, the consensual view of power: a view of power also evidenced in the work of Barnes, Luhmann, Crespi and Arendt. Parsons' clear perception of the need to explain the creation is central to those working within empirical social theory in general. Even if Giddens, Clegg, Bourdieu, Haugaard and Foucault cannot be described as consensual power theorists, they all share this Parsonian insight. Possibly, they would have explained the creation of social power even if Parsons had never written on the subject, who can say? Furthermore, it has to be pointed out that while Parsons' perception of power was narrow in the extreme, it was developed as a conceptual tool which was shaped for the specific task of aiding in the developing of a particular sociological theory. As argued in the general introduction (see also the introduction to Morriss, chapter 14), it is legitimate for a theorist to construct a particular language game for a specific defined purpose provided they are aware that they are no longer writing in general but concerning 'their' concepts – which may be only a particular aspect of the same words in general usage. Admittedly, Parsons is not aware in this way. He frequently over-generalizes his power claims, but, we, the readers, can bear this in mind by making the necessary conceptual adjustments.

## Further reading

The standard critique of Parsons' theory of power is Giddens (1968), which is also reprinted, with slight changes, in Giddens (1977) and Cassell (1993). In *The Nature of Power* (1988) Barnes gives a good account and critique of Parsons (not the extract included in this volume) and Haugaard (1992) does the same. Giddens (1979) includes an influential critique of functionalism.

The most significant consensual power theorists, other than Barnes and Arendt (who are included in this volume), are Blau (1964), Luhmann (1979) and Crespi (1992). Luhmann's work is influential in contemporary social theory, especially in Germany – it is also of interest for the extent to which it follows Parsons. I have termed Crespi a consensual theorist but, in actuality, his perspective is more a dialogue with Giddens than influenced by Parsons.

# 'ON THE CONCEPT OF POLITICAL POWER'
## Talcott Parsons

Power is one of the key concepts in the great Western tradition of thought about political phenomena. It is at the same time a concept on which, in spite of its long history, there is, on analytical levels, a notable lack of agreement both about its specific definition, and about many features of the conceptual context in which it should be placed. There is, however, a core complex of its meaning, having to do with the capacity of persons or collectivities 'to get things done' effectively, in particular when their goals are obstructed by some kind of human resistance or opposition. The problem of coping with resistance then leads into the question of the role of coercive measures, including the use of physical force, and the relation of coercion to the voluntary and consensual aspects of power systems.

The aim of this paper is to attempt to clarify this complex of meanings

Reprinted by kind permission of The American Philosophical Society from *Proceedings of the American Philosophical Society*, vol. 107 (pp. 232–58 – the technical note (pp. 258–62) has been omitted). Copyright © 1963.

and relations by placing the concept of power in the context of a general conceptual scheme for the analysis of large-scale and complex social systems, that is of societies. In doing so I speak as a sociologist rather than as a political scientist, but as one who believes that the interconnections of the principal social disciplines, including not only these two, but especially their relations to economics as well, are so close that on matters of general theory of this sort they cannot safely be treated in isolation; their interrelations must be made explicit and systematic. As a sociologist, I thus treat a central concept of political theory by selecting among the elements which have figured prominently in political theory in terms of their fit with and significance for the general theoretical analysis of society as a whole.

There are three principal contexts in which it seems to me that the difficulties of the concept of power, as treated in the literature of the last generation, come to a head. The first of these concerns its conceptual diffuseness, the tendency, in the tradition of Hobbes, to treat power as simply the generalized capacity to attain ends or goals in social relations, independently of the media employed or of the status of 'authorization' to make decisions or impose obligations.[1]

The effect of this diffuseness, as I call it, is to treat 'influence' and sometimes money, as well as coercion in various aspects, as 'forms' of power, thereby making it logically impossible to treat power as a *specific* mechanism operating to bring about changes in the action of other units, individual or collective, in the processes of social interaction. The latter is the line of thought I wish to pursue.

Secondly, there is the problem of the relation between the coercive and the consensual aspects. I am not aware of any treatment in the literature which presents a satisfactory solution of this problem. A major tendency is to hold that somehow 'in the last analysis' power comes down to one or the other, i.e., to 'rest on' command of coercive sanctions, *or* on consensus and the will to voluntary cooperation. If going to one or the other polar solution seems to be unacceptable, a way out, taken for example by Friedrich, is to speak of each of these as different 'forms' of power. I shall propose a solution which maintains that both aspects are essential, but that neither of the above two ways of relating them is satisfactory, namely subordinating either one to the other or treating them as discrete 'forms'.

Finally the third problem is what, since the Theory of Games, has widely come to be called the 'zero-sum' problem. The dominant tendency in the literature, for example in Lasswell and C. Wright Mills, is to maintain explicitly or implicitly that power is a zero-sum phenomenon, which is to say that there is a fixed 'quantity' of power in any relational system and hence any gain of power on the part of $A$ must by definition occur by diminishing the power at the disposal of other units, $B, C, D. \ldots$ There are, of course, restricted contexts in which this condition holds, but I shall argue that it does not hold for total systems of a sufficient level of complexity.

## Some general assumptions

The initial assumption is that, within the conception of society as a system, there is an essential parallelism in theoretical structure between the conceptual schemes appropriate for the analysis of the economic and the political aspects of societies. There are four respects in which I wish to attempt to work out and build on this parallel, showing at the same time the crucial substantive differences between the two fields.

First 'political theory' as here interpreted, which is not simply to be identified with the meaning given the term by many political scientists, is thought of as an abstract analytical scheme in the same sense in which economic theory is abstract and analytical. It is not the conceptual interpretation of any concretely complete category of social phenomena, quite definitely not those of government, though government is the area in which the political element comes nearest to having clear primacy over others. Political theory thus conceived is a conceptual scheme which deals with a restricted set of primary variables and their interrelations, which are to be found operating in all concrete parts of social systems. These variables are, however, subject to parametric conditions which constitute the values of other variables operating in the larger system which constitutes the society.

Secondly, following on this, I assume that the empirical system to which political theory in this sense applies is an analytically defined, a 'functional' subsystem of a society, not for example a concrete type of collectivity. The conception of the economy of a society is relatively well defined.[2] I should propose the conception of the *polity* as the parallel empirical system of direct relevance to political theory as here advanced. The polity of a given society is composed of the ways in which the relevant components of the total system are organized with reference to one of its fundamental functions, namely effective collective action in the attainment of the goals of collectivities. Goal-attainment in this sense is the establishment of a satisfactory relation between a collectivity and certain objects in its environment which include both other collectivities and categories of personalities, e.g. 'citizens'. A total society must in these terms be conceived, in one of its main aspects, as a collectivity, but it is also composed of an immense variety of subcollectivities, many of which are parts not only of this society but of others.[3]

A collectivity, seen in these terms, is thus clearly not a concrete 'group' but the term refers to groups, i.e. systematically related pluralities of persons, seen in the perspective of their interests in and capacities for effective collective action. The political process then is the process by which the necessary organization is built up and operated, the goals of action are determined and the resources requisite to it are mobilized.

These two parallels to economic theory can be extended to still a third. The parallel to collective action in the political case is, for the economic, production. This conception in turn must be understood in relation to three main operative contexts. The first is adjustment to the conditions of 'demand' which are conceived to be external to the economy itself, to be located in the 'consumers' of the economic process. Secondly, resources must be mobilized, also from the environment of the economy, the famous factors of production. Thirdly, the internal economic process is conceived as creatively combinatorial; it is, by the 'combination' of factors of production in the light of the utility of outputs, a process of creating more valuable facilities to meet the needs of consuming units than would be available to them without this combinatorial process. I wish most definitely to postulate that the logic of 'value added' applies to the political sphere in the present sense.[4]

In the political case, however, the value reference is not to utility in the economic sense but to effectiveness, very precisely, I think in the sense used by C.I. Barnard.[5] For the limited purposes of political analysis as such the givenness of the goal-demands of interest groups serves as the same order of factor in relation to the political system as has the corresponding givenness of consumers' wants for purposes of economic analysis – and of course the same order of qualifications on the empirical adequacy of such postulates.

Finally, fourth, political analysis as here conceived is parallel to economic in the sense that a central place in it is occupied by a generalized medium involved in the political interaction process, which is also a 'measure' of the relevant values. I conceive power as such a generalized medium in a sense directly parallel in logical structure, though very different substantively, to money as the generalized medium of the economic process. It is essentially this conception of power as a generalized medium parallel to money which will, in the theoretical context sketched above, provide the thread for guiding the following analysis through the types of historic difficulty with reference to which the paper began.

### The outputs of political process and the factors of effectiveness

The logic of the combinatorial process which I hold to be common to economic theory and the type of political theory advanced here, involves a paradigm of inputs and outputs and their relations. Again we will hold that the logic is strictly parallel to the economic case, i.e. that there should be a set of political categories strictly parallel to those of the factors of production (inputs) on the one hand, the shares of income (outputs) on the other.

In the economic case, with the exception of land, the remaining three factors must be regarded as inputs from the other three cognate functional subsystems of the society, labor from what we call the 'pattern-maintenance' system, capital from the polity and organization, in the sense of Alfred Marshall, from the integrative system.[6] Furthermore, it becomes clear that land is not, as a factor of production, simply the physical resource, but essentially the commitment, in value terms, of any resources to economic production in the system independent of price.

In the political case, similarly the equivalent of land is the commitment of resources to effective collective action, independent of any specifiable 'pay-off' for the unit which controls them.[7] Parallel to labor is the demands or 'need' for collective action as manifested in the 'public' which in some sense is the constituency of the leadership of the collectivity in question – a conception which is relatively clear for the governmental or other electoral association, but needs clarification in other connections. Parallel to capital is the control of some part of the productivity of the economy for the goals of the collectivity, in a sufficiently developed economy through financial resources at the disposal of the collectivity, acquired by earnings, gift, or taxation. Finally, parallel to organization is the legitimation of the authority under which collective decisions are taken.

It is most important to note that none of these categories of input is conceived as a form of power. In so far as they involve media, it is the media rooted in contiguous functional systems, not power as that central to the polity – e.g. control of productivity may operate through money, and constituents' demands through what I call 'influence'. Power then is the *means* of acquiring control of the factors in effectiveness; it is not itself one of these factors, any more than in the economic case money is a factor of production; to suppose it was, was the ancient mercantilist fallacy.

Though the analytical context in which they are placed is perhaps unfamiliar in the light of traditional political analysis, I hope it is clear that the actual categories used are well established, though there remain a number of problems of exact definition. Thus control of productivity through financing of collective action is very familiar, and the concept of 'demands' in the sense of what constituents want and press for, is also very familiar.[8] The concept legitimation is used in essentially the same sense in which I think Max Weber used it in a political context.[9]

The problem of what corresponds, for the political case, to the economist's 'shares of income' is not very difficult, once the essential distinction, a very old one in economic tradition, between monetary and 'real' income is clearly taken into account. Our concern is with the 'real' outputs of the political process – the analogue of the monetary here is output of power.

There is one, to us critically important revision of the traditional economic treatment of outputs which must be made, namely the bracketing together of 'goods and services', which then would be treated as outputs to the household as, in our technical terms, a part of the 'pattern-maintenance' system. The present position is that goods, i.e., more precisely property rights in the physical objects of possession, belong in this category, but that 'services', the commitment of human role-performances to an 'employer', or contracting agent constitute an output, not to the household, but to the polity, the type case (though not the only one) being an employing organization in which the role-incumbent commits himself to performance of an occupational role, a job,[10] as a contribution to the effective functioning of the collectivity.

There is, from this consideration, a conclusion which is somewhat surprising to economists, namely that service is, in the economic sense the 'real' counterpart of interest as monetary income from the use of funds. What we suggest is that the political control of productivity makes it possible, through combinatorial gains in the political context, to produce a surplus above the monetary funds committed, by virtue of which under specified conditions a premium can be paid at the monetary level which, though a result of the combinatorial process as a whole, is most directly related to the output of available services as an economic phenomenon, i.e. as a 'fluid resource'. Seen a little differently, it becomes necessary to make a clear distinction between labor as a factor of production in the economic sense and service as an output of the economic process which is utilized in a political context, that is one of organizational or collective effectiveness.

Service, however, is not a 'factor' in effectiveness, in the sense in which labor is a factor of production, precisely because it is a category of power. It is the point at which the economic utility of the human factor is matched with its potential contribution to effective collective action. Since the consumer of services is in principle the employing collectivity, it is its effectiveness for collective goals, not its capacity to satisfy the 'wants' of individuals, which is the vantage point from which the utility of the service is derived. The output of power which matches the input of services to the polity, I interpret to be the 'opportunity for effectiveness' which employment confers on those employed or contract offers to partners. Capital in the economic sense is one form of this opportunity for effectiveness which is derived from providing, for certain types of performances, a framework of effective organization.[11]

The second, particularly important context of 'real' output of the political process is the category which, in accord with much tradition, I should like to call capacity to assume leadership responsibility. This, as a category of 'real' output also is not a form of power, but this time of influence.[12] This is an output not to the economy but to what I shall call the integrative system, which in its relevance to the present context is in the first instance the sector of the 'public' which can be looked on as the 'constituencies' of the collective processes under consideration. It is the group structure of the society looked at in terms of their structured interests in particular modes of effective collective action by particular collectivities. It is only through effective organization that genuine responsibility can be taken, hence the implementation of such interest demands responsibility for collective effectiveness.[13] Again it should be made quite clear that leadership responsibility is not here conceived as an output of power, though many political theorists (e.g. Friedrich) treat both leadership and, more broadly, influence as 'forms' of power. The power category which regulates the output of leadership influence takes this form on the one side of binding policy decisions of the collectivity, on the other of political support from the constituency, in the type case through franchise. Policy decisions we would treat as a factor in integration of the system, not as a 'consumable' output of the political process.[14]

Finally, a few words need to be said about what I have called the combinatorial process itself. It is of course assumed in economic theory that the 'structures' of the factors of production on the one hand, the 'demand system' for real outputs on the other hand, are independent of each other. 'Utility' of outputs can only be enhanced, to say nothing of maximized, by processes of transformation of the factors in the direction of providing what is wanted as distinguished from what merely is available. The decision-making aspect of this transformative process, what is to be produced, how much and how offered for consumption, is what is meant by economic production, whereas the physical processes are not economic but 'technological'; they are controlled by economic considerations, but are not themselves in an analytical sense economic.

The consequence of successful adaptation of available resources to the want or demand system is an increment in the value of the resource-stock conceived in terms of utility as a type of value. But this means recombination of the components of the resource-stock in order to adapt them to the various uses in question.

The same logic applies to the combinatorial process in the political sphere. Here the resources are not land, labor, capital, and organization, but valuation of effectiveness, control of productivity, structured demands and the patterning of legitimation. The 'wants' are not for consumption in the economic sense, but for the solution of 'interest' problems in the system, including both competitive problems in the allocative sense and conflict problems, as well as problems of enhancement of the total effectiveness of the system of collective organization. In this case also the 'structure' of the available resources may not be assumed spontaneously to match the structure of the system of interest-demands. The increment of effectiveness in demand-satisfaction through the political process is, as in the economic case, arrived at through combinatorial decision-processes. The organizational 'technology' involved is not in the analytical sense political. The demand-reference is not to discrete units of the system conceived in abstraction from the system as a whole – the 'individual' consumer of the economist – but to the problem of the share of benefits and burdens to be allocated to subsystems of various orders. The 'consumption' reference is to the interest-unit's place in the allocative system rather than to the independent merits of particular 'needs'.

## The concept of power

The above may seem a highly elaborate setting in which to place the formal introduction of the main subject of the paper, namely the concept of power. Condensed and cryptic as the exposition may have been, however, understanding of its main structure is an essential basis for the special way in which it will be proposed to combine the elements which have played a crucial part in the main intellectual traditions dealing with the problems of power.

Power is here conceived as a circulating medium, analogous to money, within what is called the political system, but notably over its boundaries into all three of the other neighboring functional subsystems of a society (as I conceive them), the economic, integrative, and pattern-maintenance systems. Specification of the properties of power can best be approached through an attempt to delineate very briefly the relevant properties of money as such a medium in the economy.

Money is, as the classical economists said, both a medium of exchange and a 'measure of value'. It is symbolic in that, though measuring and thus 'standing for' economic value or utility, it does not itself possess utility in the primary consumption sense – it has no 'value in use' but only 'in exchange', i.e. for possession of things having utility. The use of money is thus a mode of communication of offers, on the one hand to purchase, on the other to sell, things of utility, with and for money. It becomes an essential medium only when exchange is neither ascriptive, as exchange of gifts between assigned categories of kin, nor takes place on a basis of barter, one item of commodity or service directly for another.

In exchange for its lack of direct utility money gives the recipient four important degrees of freedom in his participation in the total exchange system. (1) He is free to spend his money for any item or combination of items available on the market which he can afford, (2) he is free to shop around among alternative sources of supply for desired items, (3) he can choose his own time to purchase, and (4) he is free to consider terms which, because of freedom of time and source he can accept or reject or attempt to influence in the particular case. By contrast, in the case of barter, the negotiator is bound to what his particular partner has or wants in relation to what he has and will part with at the particular time. The other side of the gain in degrees of freedom is of course the risk involved in the probabilities of the acceptance of money by others and of the stability of its value.

Primitive money is a medium which is still very close to a commodity, the commonest case being precious metal, and many still feel that the value of money is 'really' grounded in the commodity value of the metallic base. On this base, however, there is, in developed monetary systems, erected a complex structure of credit instruments, so that only a tiny fraction of actual transactions is conducted in terms of the metal – it becomes a 'reserve' available for certain contingencies, and is actually used mainly in the settlement of international balances. I shall discuss the nature of credit further in another connection later. For the moment suffice it to say that, however important in certain contingencies the availability of metallic reserves may be, no modern monetary system operates primarily with metal as the actual medium, but uses 'valueless' money. Moreover, the acceptance of this 'valueless' money rests on a certain institutionalized confidence in the monetary system. If the security of monetary commitments rested only on their convertibility into metal, then the overwhelming majority of them would be worthless, for the simple reason that the total quantity of metal is far too small to redeem more than a few.

One final point is that money is 'good', i.e. works as a medium, only within a relatively defined network of market relationships which to be sure now has become world-wide, but the maintenance of which requires special measures to maintain mutual convertibility of national currencies. Such a system is on the one hand a range of exchange-potential within which money may be spent, but on the other hand, one within which certain conditions affecting the protection and management of the unit are maintained, both by law and by responsible agencies under the law.

The first focus of the concept of an institutionalized power system is, analogously, a relational system within which certain categories of commitments and obligations, ascriptive or voluntarily assumed – e.g. by contract – are treated as binding, i.e. under normatively defined conditions their fulfillment may be insisted upon by the appropriate role-reciprocal agencies. Furthermore, in case of actual or threatened resistance to 'compliance', i.e. to fulfillment of such obligations when invoked, they will be 'enforced' by the threat or actual imposition of situational negative sanctions, in the former case having the function of deterrence, in the latter of punishment. These are events in the situation of the actor of reference which intentionally alter his situation (or threaten to) to his disadvantage, whatever in specific content these alterations may be.

Power then is generalized capacity to secure the performance of binding obligations by units in a system of collective organization when the obligations are legitimized with reference to their bearing on collective goals and where in case of recalcitrance there is a presumption of enforcement by negative situational sanctions – whatever the actual agency of that enforcement.

It will be noted that I have used the conceptions of generalization and of legitimation in defining power. Securing possession of an object of utility by bartering another object for it is not a monetary transaction. Similarly, by my definition, securing compliance with a wish, whether it be defined as an obligation of the object or not, simply by threat of superior force, is not an exercise of power. I am well aware that most political theorists would draw the line differently and classify this as power (e.g. Dahl's definition), but I wish to stick to my chosen line and explore its implications. The capacity to secure compliance must, if it is to be called power in my sense, be generalized and not solely a function of one particular sanctioning act which the user is in a position to impose,[15] and the medium used must be 'symbolic'.

Secondly, I have spoken of power as involving legitimation. This is, in the present context, the necessary consequence of conceiving power as 'symbolic', which therefore, if it is exchanged for something intrinsically valuable for collective effectiveness, namely compliance with an obligation, leaves the recipient, the performer of the obligation, with 'nothing of value'. This is to say, that he has 'nothing' but a set of expectations, namely that in other contexts and on other occasions, he can invoke certain obligations of the part of other units. Legitimation is therefore, in power systems, the factor which is parallel to confidence in mutual acceptability and stability of the monetary unit in monetary systems.

The two criteria are connected in that questioning the legitimacy of the possession and use of power leads to resort to progressively more 'secure' means of gaining compliance. These must be progressively more effective 'intrinsically', hence more tailored to the particular situations of the objects and less general. Furthermore in so far as they are intrinsically effective, legitimacy becomes a progressively less important factor of their effectiveness – at the end of this series lies resort, first to various types of coercion, eventually to the use of force as the most intrinsically effective of all means of coercion.[16]

I should like now to attempt to place both money and power in the context of a more general paradigm, which is an analytical classification of ways in which, in the processes of social interaction, the actions of one unit in a system can, intentionally, be oriented to bringing about a change in what the actions of one or more other units would otherwise have been – thus all fitting into the context of Dahl's conception of power. It is convenient to state this in terms of the convention of speaking of the acting unit of reference – individual or collective – as *ego*, and the object on which he attempts to 'operate' as *alter*. We may then classify the alternatives open to ego in terms of two dichotomous variables. On the one hand ego may attempt to gain his end from alter either by using some form of control over the situation in which alter is placed, actually or contingently to change it so as to increase the probability of alter acting in the way he wishes, or, alternatively, without attempting to change alter's situation, ego may attempt to change alter's intentions, i.e. he may manipulate symbols which are meaningful to alter in such a way that he tries to make alter 'see' that what ego wants is a 'good thing' for him (alter) to do.

The second variable then concerns the type of sanctions ego may employ in attempting to guarantee the attainment of his end from alter. The dichotomy here is between positive and negative sanctions. Thus through the situational channel a positive sanction is a change in alter's situation presumptively considered by alter as to his advantage, which is used as a means by ego of having an effect on alter's actions. A negative sanction then is an alteration in alter's situation to the latter's disadvantage. In the case of the intentional channel, the positive sanction is the expression of symbolic 'reasons' why compliance with ego's wishes is 'a good thing' independently of any further action on ego's part, from alter's point of view, i.e. would be felt by him to be 'personally advantageous', whereas the negative sanction is presenting reasons why noncompliance with ego's wishes should be felt by alter to be harmful to interests in which he had a significant personal investment and should therefore be avoided. I should like to call the four types of 'strategy' open to ego respectively (1) for the situational channel, positive sanction case, 'inducement'; (2) situational channel negative sanction, 'coercion'; (3) intentional channel, positive sanction 'persuasion', and (4) intentional channel negative sanction 'activation of commitments' as shown in the following table:

| Sanction type | | | | Channel | |
|---|---|---|---|---|---|
| | Intentional | | | Situational | |
| Positive | | | 3 | 1 | |
| | Persuasion | | | Inducement | |
| Negative | Activation of Commitments | | 4 | 2 | Coercion |

A further complication now needs to be introduced. We think of a sanction as an intentional act on ego's part, expected by him to change his relation to alter from what it would otherwise have been. As a means of bringing about a change in alter's action, it can operate most obviously where the actual imposition of the sanction is made contingent on a future decision by alter. Thus a process of inducement will operate in two stages, first contingent offer on ego's part that, if alter will 'comply' with his wishes, ego will 'reward' him by the contingently promised situational change. If then alter in fact does comply, ego will perform the sanctioning act. In the case of coercion the first stage is a contingent threat that, unless alter decides to comply, ego will impose the negative sanction. If, however, alter complies, then nothing further happens, but, if he decides on noncompliance, then ego must carry out his threat, or be in a position of 'not meaning it'. In the cases of the intentional channel ego's first-stage act is either to predict the occurrence, or to announce his own intention of doing something which affects alter's sentiments or interests. The element of contingency enters in in that ego 'argues' to alter, that if this happens, on the one hand alter should be expected to 'see' that it would be a good thing for him to do what ego wants – the positive case – or that if he fails to do it it would imply an important 'subjective cost' to alter. In the positive case, beyond 'pointing out' if alter complies, ego is obligated to deliver the positive attitudinal sanction of approval. In the negative case, the corresponding attitudinal sanction of disapproval is implemented only for noncompliance.

It is hence clear that there is a basic asymmetry between the positive and negative sides of the sanction aspect of the paradigm. This is that, in the cases of inducement and persuasion, alter's compliance obligates ego to 'deliver' his promised positive sanction, in the former case the promised advantages, in the latter his approval of alter's 'good sense' in recognizing that the decision wished for by ego and accepted as 'good' by alter, in fact turns out to be good from alter's point of view. In the negative cases, on the other hand, compliance on alter's part obligates ego, in the situational case, not to carry out his threat, in the intentional case by withholding disapproval to confirm to alter that his compliance did in fact spare him what to him, without ego's intervention, would have been the undesirable subjective consequences of his previous intentions, namely guilt over violations of his commitments.

Finally, alter's freedom of action in his decisions of compliance versus noncompliance is also a variable. This range has a lower limit at which the element of contingency disappears. That is, from ego's point of view, he may not say, if you do so and so, I will intervene, either by situational manipulations or by 'arguments' in such and such a way, but he may simply perform an overt act and face alter with a *fait accompli*. In the case of inducement a gift which is an object of value and with respect to the acceptance of which alter is given no option is the limiting case. With respect to coercion, compulsion, i.e. simply imposing a disadvantageous alteration on alter's situation and then leaving it to alter to decide whether to 'do something about it' is the limiting case.

The asymmetry just referred to appears here as well. As contingent it may be said that the primary meaning of negative sanctions is as means of prevention. If they are effective, no further action is required. The case of compulsion is that in which it is rendered impossible for alter to avoid the undesired action on ego's part. In the case of positive sanctions of course ego, for example in making a gift to alter, cuts himself out from benefiting from alter's performance which is presumptively advantageous to him, in the particular exchange.

Both, however, may be oriented to their effect on alter's action in future sequences of interaction. The object of compulsion may have been 'taught a lesson' and hence be less disposed to noncompliance with ego's wishes in the future, as well as prevented from performance of a particular undesired act and the recipient of a gift may feel a 'sense of obligation' to reciprocate in some form in the future.

So far this discussion has dealt with sanctioning acts in terms of their 'intrinsic' significance both to ego and to alter. An offered inducement may thus be possession of a particular object of utility, a coercive threat, that of a particular feared loss, or other noxious experience. But just as, in the initial phase of a sequence, ego transmits his contingent intentions to alter symbolically through communication, so the sanction involved may also be symbolic, e.g. in place of possession of certain intrinsically valuable goods he may offer a sum of money. What we have called the generalized media of interaction then may be used as types of sanctions which may be analyzed in terms of the above paradigm. The factors of generalization and of legitimation of institutionalization, however, as discussed above, introduce certain complications which we must now take up with reference to power. There is a sense in which power may be regarded as the generalized medium of coercion in the above terms, but this formula at the very least requires very careful interpretation – indeed it will turn out by itself to be inadequate.

I spoke above of the 'grounding' of the value of money in the commodity value of the monetary metal, and suggested that there is a corresponding relation of the 'value', i.e. the effectiveness of power, to the intrinsic effectiveness of physical force as a means of coercion and, in the limiting case, compulsion.[17]

In interpreting this formula due account must be taken of the asymmetry just discussed. The special place of gold as a monetary base rests on such properties as its durability, high value in small bulk, etc., and high probability of acceptability in exchange, i.e. as means of inducement, in a very wide variety of conditions which are not dependent on an institutionalized order. Ego's primary aim in resorting to compulsion or coercion, however, is deterrence of unwanted action on alter's part.[18] Force, therefore, is in the first instance important as the 'ultimate' deterrent. It is the means which, again independent of any institutionalized system of order, can be assumed to be 'intrinsically' the most effective in the context of deterrence, when means of effectiveness which *are* dependent on institutionalized order are insecure or fail. Therefore, the unit of an action system which commands control of physical force adequate to cope with any potential counter threats of force is more secure than any other in a Hobbesian state of nature.[19]

But just as a monetary system resting entirely on gold as the actual medium of exchange is a very primitive one which simply cannot mediate a complex system of market exchange, so a power system in which the only negative sanction is the threat of force is a very primitive one which cannot function to mediate a complex system of organizational coordination – it is far too 'blunt' an instrument. Money cannot be only an intrinsically valuable entity if it is to serve as a generalized medium of inducement, but it must, as we have said, be institutionalized as a symbol; it must be legitimized, and must inspire 'confidence' within the system – and must also within limits be deliberately managed. Similarly power cannot be only an intrinsically effective deterrent; if it is to be the generalized medium of mobilizing resources for effective collective action, and for the fulfillment of commitments made by collectivities to what we have here called their constituents; it too must be both symbolically generalized, and legitimized.

There is a direct connection between the concept of bindingness, as introduced above, and deterrence. To treat a commitment or any other form of expectation as binding is to attribute a special importance to its fulfillment. Where it is not a matter simply of maintenance of an established routine, but of undertaking new actions in changed circumstances, where the commitment is thus to undertake types of action contingent on circumstances as they develop, then the risk to be minimized is that such contingent commitments will not be carried out when the circumstances in question appear. Treating the expectation or obligation as binding is almost the same thing as saying that appropriate steps on the other side must be taken to prevent nonfulfill-ment, if possible. Willingness to impose negative sanctions is, seen in this light, simply the carrying out of the implications of treating commitments as binding, and the agent invoking them 'meaning it' or 'being prepared to insist.

On the other hand there are areas in interaction systems where there is a range of alternatives, choice among which is optional, in the light of the promised advantageousness, situational or 'intentional', of one as compared to other choices. Positive sanctions as here conceived constitute a contingent increment of relative advantageousness, situational or intentional, of the alternative ego desires alter to choose.

If, in these latter areas, a generalized, symbolic medium, is to operate in place of intrinsic advantages, there must be an element of bindingness in the institutionalization of the medium itself – e.g. the fact that the money of a society is 'legal tender' which must be accepted in the settlement of debts which have the status of contractual obligations under the law. In the case of money, I suggest that, for the typical acting unit in a market system, what specific undertakings he enters into is overwhelmingly optional in the above sense, but whether the money involved in the transactions is or is not 'good' is not for him to judge, but his acceptance of it is binding. Essentially the same is true of the contractual obligations, typically linking monetary and intrinsic utilities, which he undertakes.

I would now like to suggest that what is in a certain sense the obverse holds true of power. Its 'intrinsic' importance lies in its capacity to ensure that obligations are 'really' binding, thus if necessary can be 'enforced' by negative sanctions. But for power to function as a generalized medium in a complex system, i.e. to mobilize resources effectively for collective action, it must be 'legitimized' which in the present context means that in certain respects compliance, which is the common factor among our media, is not binding, to say nothing of being coerced, but is optional. The range within which there exists a continuous system of interlocking binding obligations is essentially that of the internal relations of an organized collectivity in our sense, and of the contractual obligations undertaken on its behalf at its boundaries.

The points at which the optional factors come to bear are, in the bound-ary relations of the collectivity, where factors of importance for collective functioning other than binding obligations are exchanged for such binding commitments on the part of the collectivity and *vice versa*, nonbinding outputs of the collectivity for binding commitments to it. These 'optional' inputs, I have suggested above, are control of productivity of the economy at one boundary, influence through the relations between leadership and the public demands at the other.[20]

This is a point at which the dissociation of the concept of polity from exclusive relation to government becomes particularly important. In a sufficiently differentiated society, the boundary-relations of the great majority of its important units of collective organization (including some boundaries of government) are boundaries where the overwhelming majority of decisions of commitment are optional in the above sense, though once made, their fulfillment is binding. This, however, is only possible effectively within the range of a sufficiently stable, institutionalized normative order so that the requisite degrees of freedom are protected, e.g. in the fields of employment and of the promotion of interest-demands and decisions about political support.

This feature of the boundary relations of a particular political unit holds even for cases of local government, in that decisions of residence, employment, or acquisition of property within a particular jurisdiction involve the optional element, since in all these respects there is a relatively free choice among local jurisdictions, even though, once having chosen, the citizen is, for example, subject to the tax policies applying within it – and of course he cannot escape being subject to any local jurisdiction, but must choose among those available.

In the case of a 'national' political organization, however, its territorial boundaries ordinarily coincide with a relative break in the normative order regulating social interaction.[21] Hence across such boundaries an ambiguity becomes involved in the exercise of power in our sense. On the one hand the invoking of binding obligations operates normally without explicit use of coercion within certain ranges where the two territorial collectivity systems have institutionalized their relations. Thus travelers in friendly foreign countries can ordinarily enjoy personal security and the amenities of the principal public accommodations, exchange of their money at 'going' rates, etc. Where, on the other hand, the more general relations between national collectivities are at issue, the power system is especially vulnerable to the kind of insecurity of expectations which tends to be met by the explicit resort to threats of coercive sanctions. Such threats in turn, operating on both sides of a reciprocal relationship, readily enter into a vicious circle of resort to more and more 'intrinsically' effective or drastic measures of coercion, at the end of which road lies physical force. In other words, the danger of war is endemic in uninstitutionalized relations between territorially organized collectivities.

There is thus an inherent relation between both the use and the control of force and the territorial basis of organization.[22] One central condition of the integration of a power system is that it should be effective within a territorial area, and a crucial condition of this effectiveness in turn is the monopoly of control of paramount force within the area. The critical point then, at which the institutional integration of power systems is most vulnerable to strain, and to degeneration into reciprocating threats of the use of force, is between territorially organized political systems. This, notoriously, is the weakest point in the normative order of human society today, as it has been almost from time immemorial.

In this connection it should be recognized that the possession, the mutual threat, and possible use of force is only in a most proximate sense the principal 'cause' of war. The essential point is that the 'bottleneck' of mutual regression to more and more primitive means of protecting or advancing collective interests is a 'channel' into which all elements of tension between the collective units in question may flow. It is a question of the many levels at which such elements of tension may on the one hand build up, on the other be controlled, not of any simple and unequivocal conception of the 'inherent' consequences of the possession and possible uses of organized force.

It should be clear that again there is a direct parallel with the economic case. A functioning market system requires integration of the monetary medium. It cannot be a system of $N$ independent monetary units and agencies controlling them. This is the basis on which the main range of extension of a relatively integrated market system tends to coincide with the 'politically organized society', as Roscoe Pound calls it, over a territorial area. International transactions require special provisions not required for domestic.

The basic 'management' of the monetary system must then be integrated with the institutionalization of political power. Just as the latter depends on an effective monopoly of institutionally organized force, so monetary stability depends on an effective monopoly of basic reserves protecting the monetary unit and, as we shall see later, on centralization of control over the credit system.

## The hierarchical aspect of power systems

A very critical question now arises, which may be stated in terms of a crucial difference between money and power. Money is a 'measure of value', as the classical economists put it, in terms of a continuous linear variable. Objects of utility valued in money are more or less valuable than each other in numerically statable terms. Similarly, as medium of exchange, amounts of money differ in the same single dimension. One acting unit in a society has more money – or assets exchangeable for money – than another, less than, or the same.

Power involves a quite different dimension which may be formulated in terms of the conception that $A$ may have power over $B$. Of course in competitive bidding the holder of superior financial assets has an advantage in that, as economists say, the 'marginal utility of money' is less to him than to his competitor with smaller assets. But his 'bid' is no more binding on the potential exchange partner than is that of the less affluent bidder, since in 'purchasing power' all dollars are 'created free and equal'. There may be auxiliary reasons why the purveyor may think it advisable to accept the bid of the more affluent bidder; these, however, are not strictly economic, but concern the interrelations between money and other media, and other bases of status in the system.

The connection between the value of effectiveness – as distinguished from utility – and bindingness, implies a conception in turn of the focussing of responsibility for decisions, and hence of authority for their implementation.[23] This implies a special form of inequality of power which in turn implies a priority system of commitments. The implications of having assumed binding commitments, on the fulfillment of which spokesmen for the collectivity are prepared to insist to the point of imposing serious negative sanctions for noncompliance, are of an order of seriousness such that matching the priority system in the commitments themselves there must be priorities in the matter of which decisions take precedence over others and, back of that, of which decision-making agencies have the right to make decisions at what levels. Throughout this discussion the crucial question concerns bindingness. The reference is to the collectivity, and hence the strategic significance of the various 'contributions' on the performance of which the effectiveness of its action depends. Effectiveness for the collectivity as a whole is dependent on hierarchical ordering of the relative strategic importance of these contributions, and hence of the conditions governing the imposition of binding obligations on the contributors.

Hence the power of *A* over *B* is, in its legitimized form, the 'right' of *A*, as a decision-making unit involved in collective process, to make decisions which take precedence over those of *B*, in the interest of the effectiveness of the collective operation as a whole.

The right to use power, or negative sanctions on a barter basis or even compulsion to assert priority of a decision over others, I shall, following Barnard, call authority. Precedence in this sense can take different forms. The most serious ambiguity here seems to derive from the assumption that authority and its attendant power may be understood as implying opposition to the wishes of 'lower-order' echelons which hence includes the prerogative of coercing or compelling compliance. Though this is implicit, it may be that the higher-order authority and power may imply the prerogative is primarily significant as 'defining the situation' for the performance of the lower-order echelons. The higher 'authority' may then make a decision which defines terms within which other units in the collectivity will be expected to act, and this expectation is treated as binding. Thus a ruling by the Commissioner of Internal Revenue may exclude certain tax exemptions which units under his jurisdiction have thought taxpayers could claim. Such a decision need not activate an overt conflict between commissioner and taxpayer, but may rather 'channel' the decisions of revenue agents and taxpayers with reference to performance of obligations.

There does not seem to be an essential theoretical difficulty involved in this 'ambiguity'. We can say that the primary function of superior authority is clearly to define the situation for the lower echelons of the collectivity. The problem of overcoming opposition in the form of dispositions to noncompliance then arises from the incomplete institutionalization of the power of the higher authority holder. Sources of this may well include overstepping of the bounds of his legitimate authority on the part of this agent. The concept of compliance should clearly not be limited to 'obedience' by subordinates, but is just as importantly applicable to observance of the normative order by the high echelons of authority and power. The concept of constitutionalism is the critical one at this level, namely that even the highest authority is bound in the strict sense of the concept bindingness used here, by the terms of the normative order under which he operates, e.g. holds office. Hence binding obligations can clearly be 'invoked' by lower-order against higher-order agencies as well as *vice versa*.

This of course implies the relatively firm institutionalization of the normative order itself. Within the framework of a highly differentiated polity it implies, in addition to constitutionalism itself, a procedural system for the granting of high political authority, even in private, to say nothing of public organizations, and a legal framework within which such authority is legitimized. This in turn includes another order of procedural institutions within which the question of the legality of actual uses of power can be tested.

## Power and authority

The institutionalization of the normative order just referred to thus comes to focus in the concept of authority. Authority is essentially the institutional code within which the use of power as medium is organized and legitimized. It stands to power essentially as property, as an institution, does to money. Property is a bundle of rights of possession, including above all that of alienation, but also at various levels of control and use. In a highly differentiated institutional system, property rights are focussed on the valuation of utility, i.e. the economic significance of the objects, e.g. for consumption or as factors of production, and this factor comes to be differentiated from authority. Thus, in European feudalism the 'landlord' had both property rights in the land, and political jurisdiction over persons acting on the same land. In modern legal systems these components are differentiated from each other so the landowner is no longer the landlord; this function is taken over mainly by local political authority.

Precisely with greater differentiation the focus of the institution becomes more generalized and, while specific objects of possession of course continue to be highly important, the most important object of property comes to be monetary assets, and specific objects are valued as assets, i.e., in terms of potentials of marketability. Today we can say that rights to money assets, the ways in which these can be legitimately acquired and disposed of, the ways in which the interests of other parties must be protected, have come to constitute the core of the institution of property.[24]

Authority, then, is the aspect of a status in a system of social organization, namely its collective aspect, by virtue of which the incumbent is put in a position legitimately to make decisions which are binding, not only on himself but on the collectivity as a whole and hence its other member-units, in the sense that so far as their implications impinge on their respective roles and statuses, they are bound to act in accordance with these implications. This includes the right to insist on such action though, because of the general division of labor, the holder of authority very often is not himself in a position to 'enforce' his decisions, but must be dependent on specialized agencies for this.

If, then, authority be conceived as the institutional counterpart of power, the main difference lies in the fact that authority is not a circulating medium. Sometimes, speaking loosely, we suggest that someone 'gives away his property'. He can give away property rights in specific possessions but not the institution of property. Similarly the incumbent of an office can relinquish authority by resigning, but this is very different from abolishing the authority of the office. Property as institution is a code defining rights in objects of possession, in the first instance physical objects, then 'symbolic' objects, including cultural objects such as 'ideas' so far as they are valuable in monetary terms, and of course including money itself, whoever possesses them. Authority, similarly, is a set of rights in status in a collectivity, precisely in the collectivity as actor, including most especially right to acquire and use power in that status.

The institutional stability, which is essential to the conception of a code, then for property inheres in the institutional structure of the market. At a higher level the institution of property includes rights, not only to use and dispose of particular objects of value, but to participate in the system of market transactions.

It is then essentially the institutionalized code defining rights of participation in the power system which I should like to think of as authority. It is this conception which gives us the basis for the essential distinction between the internal and the external aspects of power relative to a particular collectivity. The collectivity is, by our conception, the definition of the range within which a system of institutionalized rights to hold and use power can be closed. This is to say, the implications of an authoritative decision made at one point in the system can be made genuinely binding at all the other relevant points through the relevant processes of feed-back.

The hierarchical priority system of authority and power, with which this discussion started can, by this criterion, only be binding within a given particular collectivity system. In this sense then a hierarchy of authority – as distinguished from the sheer differences of power of other coercive capacities –

must be internal to a collectively organized system in this sense. This will include authority to bind the collectivity in its relations to its environment, to persons and to other collectivities. But bindingness, legitimized and enforced through the agency of this particular collectivity, cannot be extended beyond its boundaries. If it exists at all it must be by virtue of an institutionalized normative order which transcends the particular collectivity, through contractual arrangements with others, or through other types of mutually binding obligation.

## Power, influence, equalization, and solidarity

It is on this basis that it may be held that at the boundaries of the collectivity the closed system of priorities is breached by 'free' exercise, at the constituency or integrative boundary, of influence. Status in the collectivity gives authority to settle the terms on which power will be exchanged with influence over this boundary. The wielder of influence from outside, on the collectivity, is not bound in advance to any particular terms, and it is of the essence of use of power in the 'foreign relations' of the collectivity, that authority is a right, within certain limits of discretion, to spend power in exchange for influence. This in turn can, through the offer of accepting leadership responsibility in exchange for political support, replenish the expenditure of power by a corresponding input.

By this reasoning influence should be capable of altering the priority system within the collectivity. This is what I interpret policy decision as a category of the use of power as a medium to be, the process of altering priorities in such a way that the new pattern comes to be binding on the collectivity. Similarly, the franchise must be regarded as the institutionalization of a marginal, interpenetrating status, between the main collectivity and its environment of solidary groupings in the larger system. It is the institutionalization of a marginal authority, the use of which is confined to the function of selection among candidates for leadership responsibility. In the governmental case, this is the inclusion in a common collectivity system of both the operative agencies of government and the 'constituencies' on which leadership is dependent, a grant not only in a given instance of power to the latter but a status of authority with respect to the one crucial function of selection of leadership and granting them the authority of office.

In interpreting this discussion it is essential to keep in mind that a society consists, from the present point of view, not in one collectivity, but in a ramified system of collectivities. Because, however, of the basic imperatives of effective collective action already discussed, these must in addition to the pluralistic cross-cutting which goes with functional differentiation, also have the aspect of a 'Chinese box' relation. There must be somewhere a paramount focus of collective authority and with it of the control of power – though it is crucial that this need not be the top of the total system of normative control, which may for example be religious. This complex of territoriality and the monopoly of force are central to this, because the closed system of enforceable bindingness can always be breached by the intervention of force.[25]

The bindingness of normative orders other than those upheld by the paramount territorial collectivity must be defined within limits institutionalized in relation to it. So far as such collectivities are not 'agencies' of the state, in this sense, their spheres of 'jurisdiction' must be defined in terms of a normative system, a body of law, which is binding both on government and on the nongovernmental collectivity units, though in the 'last analysis' it will, within an institutionalized order either have to be enforced by government, or contrariwise, by revolutionary action against government.

Since independent control of serious, socially organized force cannot be given to 'private' collectivities, their ultimate negative sanctions tend to be expulsion from membership, though many other types of sanction may be highly important.

Considerations such as these thus do not in any way eliminate or weaken the importance of hierarchical priorities within a collective decision-system itself. The strict 'line' structure of such authority is, however, greatly modified by the interpenetration of other systems with the political, notably for our purposes the importance of technical competence. The qualifications of the importance of hierarchy apply in principle at the boundaries of the particular collective system – analytically considered – rather than internally to it. These I would interpret as defining the limits of authority. There are two main contexts in which norms of equality may be expected to modify the concrete expectations of hierarchical decision-systems, namely on the one hand, the context of influence over the right to assume power, or decision-making authority and, on the other hand, the context of access to opportunity for status as a contributing unit in the specific political system in question.

It is essential here to recall that I have treated power as a circulating medium, moving back and forth over the boundaries of the polity. The 'real' outputs of the political process, and the factors in its effectiveness – in the sense corresponding to the real outputs and factors of economic production – are not in my sense 'forms' of power but, in the most important cases, of financial control of economic resources, and of influence, in the meaning of the category of influence, defined as a generalized mechanism of persuasion. These are very essential elements in the total political process, but it is just as important to distinguish them from power as it is to distinguish financially valuable outputs and factors of production from money itself. They may, in certain circumstances, be exchangeable for power, but this is a very different thing from being forms of power.

The circulation of power between polity and integrative system I conceive to consist in binding policy decisions on the one hand, which is a primary factor in the integrative process, and political support on the other, which is a primary output of the integrative process. Support is exchanged, by a 'public' or constituency, for the assumption of leadership responsibility, through the process of persuading those in a position to give binding support that it is advisable to do so in the particular instance – through the use of influence or some less generalized means of persuasion. In the other political 'market' *vis-à-vis* the integrative system, policy decisions are given in response to interest-demands in the sense of the above discussion. This is to say that interest groups, which, it is most important to note as a concept says nothing about the moral quality of the particular interest, attempt to persuade those who hold authority in the relevant collectivity, i.e. are in a position to make binding decisions, that they should indeed commit the collectivity to the policies the influence-wielders want. In our terms this is to persuade the decision makers to use and hence 'spend' some of their power for the purpose in hand. The spending of power is to be thought of, just as the spending of money, as essentially consisting in the sacrifice of alternative decisions which are precluded by the commitments undertaken under a policy. A member of the collectivity we conceive as noted to have authority to 'spend' power through making binding decisions through which those outside acquire claims against the collectivity. Its authority, however, is inalienable; it can only be exercised, not 'spent'.

It has been suggested that policies must be hierarchically ordered in a priority system and that the power to decide among policies must have a corresponding hierarchical ordering since such decisions bind the collectivity and its constituent units. The imperative of hierarchy does not, however, apply to the other 'market' of the power system in this direction, that involving the relations between leadership and political support. Here on the contrary it is a critically important fact that in the largest-scale and most highly differentiated systems, namely the leadership systems of the most 'advanced' national societies, the power element has been systematically equalized through the device of the franchise, so that the universal adult franchise has been evolved in all the Western democracies.[26] Equality of the franchise which, since the consequences of its exercise are very strictly binding,[27] I classify as in fact a form of power, has been part of a larger complex of its institutionalization, which includes in addition the principle of universality – its extension to all responsible adult citizens in good standing and the secrecy of the ballot, which serves to differentiate this context of political action from other contexts of involvement, and protect it against pressures, not only from hierarchical superiors but, as Rokkan points out, from status-peers as well.

Of course the same basic principle of one member, one vote, is institutionalized in a vast number of voluntary associations, including many which are subassociations of wider collectivities, such as faculties in a university, or boards and committees. Thus the difference between a chairman or presiding officer, and an executive head is clearly marked with respect to formal authority, whatever it may be with respect to influence, by the principle that a chairman, like any other member, has only one vote. Many collectivities are in this sense 'truncated' associations, e.g. in cases where fiduciary boards are self-recruiting. Nevertheless the importance of this principle of equality of power through the franchise is so great empirically that the question of how it is grounded in the structure of social systems is a crucial one.

It derives, I think, from what I should call the universalistic component in patterns of normative order. It is the value-principle that discriminations among units of a system, must be grounded in intrinsically valued differences among them, which are, for both persons and collectivities, capacities to contribute to valued societal processes. Differences of power in decision-making which mobilizes commitments, both outward in relation to the environment of the collectivity and internally, to the assignment of tasks to its members, are ideally grounded in the intrinsic conditions of effectiveness. Similarly, differences on the basis of technical competence to fulfill essential roles are grounded in the strategic conditions of effective contribution.

These considerations do not, however, apply to the functions of the choice of leadership, where this choice has been freed from ascriptive bases of right, e.g. through kinship status or some imputed 'charismatic' superiority as in such a case as 'white supremacy'. There is a persistent pressure of the sufficiently highly valued functions or outcomes, and under this pressure there seems to have been a continual, though uneven, process of erosion of discriminations in this critical field of the distribution of power.

It may be suggested that the principle of universalistic normative organization which is immediately superordinate to that of political democracy in the sense of the universal equal franchise, is the principle of equality before the law; in the case of the American Constitution, the principle of equal protection of the laws. I have emphasized that a constitutional framework is essential to advanced collective organization, given of course levels of scale and complexity which preclude purely 'informal' and traditional normative regulation. The principle in effect puts the burden of proof on the side of imposing discriminations, either in access to rights or in imposition of obligations, on the side that such discriminations are to be justified only by differences in sufficiently highly valued exigencies of operation of the system.

The principle of equality both at the level of application of the law and of the political franchise, is clearly related to a conception of the status of membership. Not all living adults have equal right to influence the affairs of all collectivities everywhere in the world, nor does an American have equal rights with a citizen of a quite different society within its territory. Membership is in fact the application to the individual unit of the concept of boundary of a social system which has the property of solidarity, in Durkheim's sense. The equal franchise is a prerogative of members, and of course the criteria of membership can be very differently institutionalized under different circumstances.

There is an important sense in which the double interchange system under consideration here, which I have called the 'support' system linking the polity with the integrative aspect of the society, is precisely the system in which power is most directly controlled, both in relation to more particularized interest-elements which seek relatively particularized policies – which of course includes wanting to prevent certain potential actions – and in relation to the more general 'tone' given to the directionality of collective action by the character of the leadership elements which assume responsibility and which, in exchange, are invested, in the type case by the electoral process, with authority to carry out their responsibilities. One central feature of this control is coming to terms with the hierarchical elements inherent in power systems in the aspects just discussed. Certain value systems may of course reinforce hierarchy, but it would be my view that a universalistically oriented value system inherently tends to counteract the spread of hierarchical patterns with respect to power beyond the range felt to be functionally necessary for effectiveness.[28]

There is, however, a crucial link between the equality of the franchise and the hierarchical structure of authority within collectivities, namely the all-or-none character of the electoral process. Every voter has an equal vote in electing to an office, but in most cases only one candidate is in fact elected – the authority of office is not divided among candidates in proportion to the numbers of votes they received, but is concentrated in the successful candidate, even though the margin be very narrow, as in the U.S. presidential election of 1960. There are, of course, considerable possible variations in electoral rules, but this basic principle is as central as is that of the equality of the franchise. This principle seems to be the obverse of the hierarchy of authority.

The hierarchical character of power systems has above been sharply contrasted with the linear quantitative character of wealth and monetary assets. This has in turn been related to the fundamental difference between the exigencies of effectiveness in collective action, and the exigencies of utility in providing for the requirements of satisfying the 'wants' of units. In order to place the foregoing discussion of the relations between power and influence in a comparable theoretical context, it is necessary to formulate the value-standard which is paramount in regulating the integrative function which corresponds to utility and effectiveness in the economic and political functions respectively.

This is, with little doubt, the famous concept of solidarity as formulated by Durkheim.[29] The two essential points of reference for present purposes concern the two main aspects of membership, as outlined above, the first of which concerns claims on executive authority for policy decisions which integrate the total collective interest on the one hand, the 'partial' interest of a subgroup on the other. The second concerns integration of rights to a 'voice' in collective affairs with the exigencies of effective leadership and the corresponding responsibility.

The principle is the 'grounding' of a collective system in a consensus in the sense of the above discussion, namely an 'acceptance' on the part of its members of their belonging together, in the sense of sharing, over a certain range, common interests, interests which are defined both by type, and by considerations of time. Time becomes relevant because of the uncertainty factor in all human action, and hence the fact that neither benefits nor burdens can be precisely predicted and planned for in advance; hence an effective collectivity must be prepared to absorb unexpected burdens, and to balance this, to carry out some sort of just distribution of benefits which are unexpected and/or are not attributable to the earned agency of any particular subunit.

Solidarity may then be thought of as the implementation of common values by definition of the requisite collective systems in which they are to be actualized. Collective action as such we have defined as political function. The famous problem of order, however, cannot be solved without a common normative system. Solidarity is the principle by virtue of which the commitment to norms, which is 'based' in turn on values, is articulated with the formation of collectivities which are capable of effective collective action. Whereas, in the economic direction, the 'problem' of effective action is coping with the scarcity of available resources, including trying to facilitate their mobility, in the integrative direction it is orderly solution of competing claims, on the one hand to receive benefits – or minimize losses – deriving from memberships, on the other to influence the processes by which collective action operates. This clearly involves some institutionalization of the subordination of unit-interest to the collective in cases where the two are in conflict, actual or potential, and hence the justification of unit interests as compatible with the more extensive collective interest. A social system then possesses solidarity in proportion as its members are committed to common interests through which discrete unit interests can be integrated and the justification of conflict resolution and subordination can be defined and implemented. It defines, not the modes of implementation of these common interests through effective agency, but the standards by which such agency should be guided and the rights of various constituent elements to have a voice in the interpretation of these standards.

## Power and equality of opportunity

We may now turn to the second major boundary of the polity, at which another order of modifications of the internal hierarchy of authority comes of focus. This is the boundary *vis-à-vis* the economy where the 'political' interest is to secure control of productivity and services, and the economic interest lies in the collective control of fluid resources and in what we may call opportunity for effectiveness. I shall not attempt here to discuss the whole interchange complex, but will confine myself to the crucial problem of the way that here also the hierarchical structure of power can, under certain conditions, be modified in an egalitarian direction.

Productivity of the economy is in principle allocable among collective (in our sense political) claimants to its control as facilities, in linear quantitative terms. This linear quantification is achieved through the medium of money, either allocation of funds with liberty to expend them at will, or at least monetary evaluation of more specific facilities.

In a sufficiently developed system, services must be evaluated in monetary terms also, both from the point of view of rational budgeting and of the monetary cost of their employment. In terms of their utilization, however, services are 'packages' of performance-capacity, which are qualitatively distinct and of unequal value as contributions to collective effectiveness. Their evaluation as facilities must hence involve an estimate of strategic significance which matches the general priority scale which has been established to regulate the internal functioning of the collectivity.

Services, however, constitute a resource to be acquired from outside the collectivity, as Weber puts it through a 'formally free' contract of employment. The contracts thus made are binding on both sides, by virtue of a normative system transcending the particular collectivity, though the obligation must articulate with the internal normative order including its hierarchical aspect. But the purveyors of service are not, in advance, bound by this internal priority system and hence an exchange, which is here interpreted to operate in the first instance as between strategic significance expressed as power-potential, and the monetary value of the service, must be arrived at.

Quite clearly, when the purveyor of service has once entered into such a contract, he is bound by the aspect of its terms which articulates the service into this internal system, including the level of authority he exercises and its implications for his power position in the collectivity. If the collectivity is making in any sense a rational arrangement, this must be tailored to an estimate of the level of the value of his strategic contribution, hence his performance-capacity.

Since, however, the boundary interchange is not integral to the internal system of bindingness, the hierarchical imperatives do not apply to the opportunity aspect of this interchange on the extrapolitical side. This is to say that the same order of pressures of a higher-order universalistic normative system can operate here that we suggested operated to bring about equality in the franchise. Again the principle is that no particularistic discriminations are to be legitimized which are not grounded in essential functional exigencies of the system of reference.

In the case of the franchise there seems to be no inherent stopping place short of complete equality, qualified only by the minimum consideration of competence attached to fully responsible membership – excluding only minors, 'defectives', through retardation and mental illness, and those morally disqualified through crime. In the service case, on the other hand, given commitments to optimum performance which in the present context can be taken for granted, the limit to the equating of universalism and equality lies in the concept of competence. Hence the principle arrived at is the famous one of equality of opportunity, by which there is equalization of access to opportunity for contribution, but selection on criteria of differential competence, both quantitative and qualitative.

Whereas the equalization of the franchise is a control on differential power 'from above' in the hierarchy of control and operates mainly through the selection of leadership, equality of opportunity is (in the corresponding sense) a control from below, and operates to check particularistic tendencies which would tend to exclude sources of service which are qualified by competence to contribute, and/or to check tendencies to retain services which are inferior to those available in competition with them.

It is the combination of these two foci of universalization, the equalitarianism of upper rights to control through the franchise, and of rights to participate through service on the basis of competence, which account for the extent to which the 'cumulative advantage',[30] which might seem to be inherent in the hierarchical internal structure of power systems, often in fact fails either to materialize at all, or to be as strong as expected.

Long and complex as it is, the above discussion may be summed up as an attempted solution of the second of the three main problems with which this paper began, namely that of the relation between the coercive and the consensual aspects of the phenomenon of power. The answer is first premised on the conception of power as a specific but generalized medium of the functioning of social relationships in complex, differentiated systems of social interaction.

Power is secondly specifically associated with the bindingness of obligations to performance within a range of circumstances which may arise in a varying and changing situation. The obligations concerned are hence in some important degree generalized so that particularities under them are contingent on circumstances. The bindingness of obligations implies that they stand on a level of seriousness such that the invoking agent, ego, may be put in the position of asserting that, since he 'means it' that alter must comply, he is prepared to insist on compliance. Partly then as a symbolic expression of this seriousness of 'meaning it' and partly as an instrument of deterrence of noncompliance,[31] this insistence is associated with command of negative situational sanctions the application of which is frequently contingent on noncompliance, and in certain cases deterrence is achieved by compulsion. We would not speak of power where situational negative sanctions or compulsion are in no circumstances attached to noncompliance in cases where a legitimate agent insists on compliance.

Thirdly, however, power is here conceived as a generalized medium of mobilizing commitments or obligation for effective collective action. As such it ordinarily does not itself possess intrinsic effectiveness, but symbolizes effectiveness and hence the bindingness of the relevant obligations to contribute to it. The operative validity of the meaningfulness of the symbolization is not a function of any one single variable but, we argue, of two primary ones. One of these is the willingness to insist upon compliance, or at least to deter noncompliance, a line of reasoning which leads to the understanding of willingness to resort to negative sanctions, the nature of which will vary, as a function of the seriousness of the question, on the dimension of their progressively more drastic nature, in the last analysis force.

The other variable concerns the collective reference and hence the justification[32] of invoking the obligations in question in the situation. This aspect concerns the dependence of power on the institutionalization of authority and hence the rights of collective agents to mobilize performances and define them as binding obligations. This justification inherently rests on some sort of consensus among the members of the collectivity of reference, if not more broadly, with respect to a system of norms under which authority and power are legitimized on a basis wider than this particular collectivity by the values of the system. More specifically, authority is the institutionalized code within which the 'language of power' is meaningful and, therefore, its use will be accepted in the requisite community, which is in the first instance the community of collective organization in our sense.

Seen in this light the threat of coercive measures, or of compulsion, without legitimation or justification, should not properly be called the use of power at all, but is the limiting case where power, losing its symbolic character, merges into an intrinsic instrumentality of securing compliance with wishes, rather than obligations. The monetary parallel is the use of a monetary metal as an instrument of barter where as a commodity it ceases to be an institutionalized medium of exchange at all.

In the history of thought there has been a very close connection between emphasis on the coercive element in power systems and on the hierarchical aspect of the structure of systems of authority and power. The above discussion has, I hope, helped to dissociate them by showing that this hierarchical aspect, important as it is, is only part of the structure of power systems. The view advanced is that it is an inherent aspect of the internal structure of collectivities. No collectivity, even the nation, however, stands alone as a total society since it is integrated with norms and values; subcollectivities can even less be claimed to be societies. The collectivity aspect of total social structure may in a particular case be dominant over others, but always in principle it impinges on at least two sorts of boundary-problems, namely that involved in its 'support' system and that involved in the mobilization of services as sources of contribution to its functioning.

In both these cases, we have argued, quite different principles are operative from that of the hierarchy of authority, namely the equality of franchise on the one hand, equality of opportunity on the other. In both cases I envisage an interchange of power, though not of authority, over the boundary of the polity, and in neither case can the principle governing the allocation of power through this interchange be considered to be hierarchical in the line authority sense. The empirical problems here are, as elsewhere, formidable, but I definitely argue that it is illegitimate to hold that, from serious consideration of the role of power as a generalized medium, it can be inferred that there is a general trend to hierarchization in the total empirical social systems involved.[33]

## The zero-sum problem

We are now in a position to take up the last of the three main problems with which the discussion started, namely whether power is a zero-sum phenomenon in the sense that, in a system, a gain in power by a unit $A$ is in the nature of the case the cause of a corresponding loss of power by other units, $B$, $C$, $D$. . . . The parallel with money on which we have been insisting throughout should give us clues to the answer, which clearly is, under certain circumstances yes, but by no means under all circumstances.

In the monetary case it is obvious that in budgeting the use of a fixed income, allocation to one use must be at the expense of alternative uses. The question is whether parallel limitations apply to an economy conceived as a total system. For long this seemed to many economists to be the case; this was the main burden of the old 'quantity theory of money'. The most obvious political parallel is that of the hierarchy of authority within a particular collectivity. It would seem to be obvious that, if $A$, who has occupied a position of substantial power, is demoted, and $B$ takes his place, $A$ loses power and B gains it, the total in the system remaining the same. Many political theorists like Lasswell and C. Wright Mills, generalized this to political systems as a whole.[34]

The most important and obvious point at which the zero-sum doctrine breaks down for money is that of credit-creation through commercial banking. This case is so important as a model that a brief discussion here is in order. Depositors, that is, entrust their money funds to a bank, not only for safe keeping, but as available to the bank for lending. In so doing, however, they do not relinquish any property rights in these funds. The funds are repayable by the bank in full on demand, the only normal restrictions being with respect to banking hours. The bank, however, uses part of the balances on deposit with it to make loans at interest, pursuant to which it not only makes the money available to the borrower, but in most cases assumes binding obligations not to demand repayment except on agreed terms, which in general leave the borrower undisturbed control for a stipulated period – or obligates him to specified installments of amortization. In other words, the same dollars come to do 'double duty', to be treated as possessions by the depositors, who retain their property rights, and also by the banker who preempts the rights to loan them, as if they were 'his'. In any case there is a corresponding net addition to the circulating medium, measured by the quantity of new bank deposits created by the loans outstanding.[35]

Perhaps the best way to describe what happens is to say that there has occurred a differentiation in the functions of money and hence there are two ways of using it in the place of one. The ordinary deposit is a reserve for meeting current expenses, whether 'private' or 'business', which is mainly important with respect to the time element of the degrees of freedom mentioned above. From the point of view of the depositor the bank is a convenience, giving him safekeeping, the privilege of writing checks rather than using cash, etc., at a cost which is low because the bank earns interest through its loaning operations. From the point of view of the borrower, on the other hand, the bank is a source of otherwise unavailable funds, ideally in the economist's sense, for investment, for financing operations promising future increments of economic productivity, which would not otherwise have been feasible.

The possibility of this 'miracle of loaves and fishes' of course rests on an empirical uniformity, namely that depositors do in fact, under normal circumstances, keep sufficient balances on hand – though they are not required to – so that it is safe for the bank to have substantial amounts out on loan at any given time. Underlying this basic uniformity is the fact that an individual bank will ordinarily also have access to 'reserves', e.g. assets which, though earning interest, are sufficiently liquid to be realized on short notice, and in the last analysis such resources as those of a federal reserve system. The individual bank, and with it its depositors, is thus ordinarily relatively secure.

We all know, however, that this is true only so long as the system operates smoothly. A particular bank can meet unusual demands for withdrawal of deposits, but if this unusual demand spreads to a whole banking system, the result may be a crisis, which only collective action can solve. Quite clearly the expectation that all depositors should be paid, all at once, in 'real' money, e.g. even 'cash' to say nothing of monetary metal, cannot be fulfilled. Any monetary system in which bank credit plays an important part is in the nature of the case normally 'insolvent' by that standard.

Back of these considerations, it may be said, lies an important relation between bindingness and 'confidence' which is in certain respects parallel to that between coercion and consensus in relation to power, indeed one which, through the element of bindingness, involves a direct articulation between money and power. How is this parallel to be defined and how does the articulation operate?

First the banking operation depends on mutual confidence or trust in that depositors entrust their funds to the bank, knowing, if they stop to think about it, that the bank will have a volume of loans outstanding which makes it impossible to repay all deposits at once. It is well known with what hesitation, historically, many classes have been brought to trust banks at all in this simple sense – the classical case of the French peasant's insistence on putting his savings in cash under the mattress is sufficient illustration. The other side of the coin, however, is the bank's trust that its depositors will not panic to the point of in fact demanding the complete fulfillment of their legal rights.

The banker here assumes binding obligations in two directions, the honoring of both of which depends on this trust. On the one hand he has loaned money on contract which he cannot recover on demand, on the other he is legally bound to repay deposits on demand. But by making loans on binding contractual terms he is enabled to create money, which is purchasing power in the literal sense that, as noted above, the status of the monetary unit is politically guaranteed – e.g. through its position as 'legal tender' – and hence the newly created dollars are 'as good as' any other dollars. Hence I suggest that what makes them good in this sense is the input of power in the form of the bindingness of the contractual obligation assumed by the banker – I should classify this as opportunity for effectiveness. The bank, as collectivity, thus enjoys a 'power position' by virtue of which it can give its borrowers effective control of certain types of opportunity.

It is, however, critically important that in general this grant of power is not unconditional. First it is power in its form of direct convertibility with money, and second, within that framework, the condition is that, per unit of time, there should be a surplus of money generated, the borrower can and must return more money than he received, the difference being 'interest'. Money, however, is a measure of productivity, and hence we may say that increasing the quantity of money in circulation is economically 'functional' only if it leads after a sequence of operations over a period of time to a corresponding increase in productivity – if it does not the consequence is inflationary. The process is known as investment, and the standard of a good investment is the expected increment of productivity which, measured in money terms, is profitability. The organizational question of allocation of responsibility for decisions and payments should of course not be too directly identified with the present level of analytical argument.

It may help round out this picture if the concept of investment is related to that of 'circular flow' in Schumpeter's sense.[36] The conception is that the routine functioning of economic processes is organized about the relation between producing and consuming units, we may say firms and households. So long as a series of parametric constants such as the state of demand and the coefficients of cost of production hold, this is a process in equilibrium through which money mediates the requisite decisions oriented to fixed reference points. This is precisely the case to which the zero-sum concept applies. On the one hand a fixed quantity and 'velocity of circulation' of the monetary medium is an essential condition of the stability of this equilibrium, whereas on the other hand, there is no place for banking operations which, through credit expansion, would change the parametric conditions.

These decisions are governed by the standard of solvency, in the sense that both producing and consuming units are normally expected to recoup their monetary expenditures, on the one hand for factors of production, on the other for consumers' goods, from monetary proceeds, on the producing side, sale of output, on the consuming, sale of factors of production, notably labor. Solvency then is a balance between monetary cost and receipts. Investment is also governed by the standard of solvency, but over a longer time period, long enough to carry out the operations necessary to bring about an increase of productivity matching the monetary obligations assumed.

There is here a crucial relation between the time-extension of the investment process and use of power to make loan contracts binding. Only if the extension of control of resources through loans creates obligations can the recipients of the loans in turn assume further obligations and expect others to assume them.

The essential principle here is that, in the sense of the hierarchy of control, a higher-order medium is used as a source of leverage to break into the 'circle' of the Schumpeterian flow, giving the recipients of this power effective control of a share of fluid resources in order to divert them from the established routine channels to new uses. It is difficult to see how this could work systematically if the element of bindingness were absent either from loan contracts or from the acceptance-status of the monetary medium.

One further element of the monetary complex needs to be mentioned here. In the case of investment there is the element of time, and hence the uncertainty that projected operations aiming at increase in productivity will in fact produce either this increase or financial proceeds sufficient to repay loans plus interest in accordance with contract. In the case of the particular borrower-lender relationship this can be handled on an individual contract-solvency basis with a legally determined basis of sharing profits and/or losses. For the system, however, it creates the possibility of inflation, namely that the net effect of credit-extension may not be increase in productivity but decline in the value of the monetary unit. Furthermore, once a system involves an important component of credit, the opposite disturbance, namely deflation with a rearrangement of the meaning of the whole network of financial and credit expectations and relationships, is also a possibility. This suggests that there is, in a ramified credit economy, a set of mechanisms which, independently of particular circular flow, and credit-extension and repayment transactions regulates the total volume of credit, rates of interest, and price-level relations in the economy.

## Zero-sum: the case of power

Let us now attempt to work out the parallel, and articulating, analysis for power systems. There is, I suggest, a circular flow operating between polity and economy in the interchange between factors in political effectiveness – in this case a share of control of the productivity of the economy – and an output to the economy in the form of the kind of control of resources which a there are various other forms. This circular flow loan for investment provides – though of course is controlled by the medium of power in the sense that the input of binding obligations, in particular through commitment to perform services, broadly balances the output of offer of opportunity for effective performance.

The suggestion is that it is a condition of the stability of this circulation system that the inputs and outputs of power on each side should balance. This is another way of saying that it is ideally formulated as a zero-sum system, so far as power is concerned, though because it includes the investment process, the same is not true for the involvement of monetary funds in the interchanges. The political circular flow system then is conceived as the locus of the 'routine' mobilization of performance expectations either through invoking obligations under old contractual – and in some cases, e.g. citizenship, ascriptive – relations, or through a stable rate of assumption of new contractual obligations, which is balanced by the liquidation, typically through fulfillment, of old ones. The balance applies to the system, of course, not to particular units.

Corresponding to utility as the value-pattern governing economic function I have put forward effectiveness as that governing political function. If it is important to distinguish utility, as the category of value to which increments are made by the combinatorial process of economic production, from solvency as the standard of satisfactory performance in handling money as the medium of economic process, then we need to distinguish effectiveness as the political value category, from a corresponding standard for the satisfactory handling of power. The best available term for this standard seems to be the success of collective goal-attainment. Where the polity is sufficiently differentiated so that power has become genuinely a generalized medium we can say that collective units are expected to be successful in the sense that the binding obligations they undertake in order to maintain and create opportunities for effectiveness, is balanced by the input of equally binding commitments to perform service, either within the collectivity in some status of employment, or for the collectivity on a contractual basis.

The unit of productive decision-making, however, is, in a sense corresponding to that applying to the household for the economic case, also expected to be successful in the sense that its expenditure of power through not only the output of services but their commitment to utilization by particular collectivities, is balanced by an input of opportunity which is dependent on collective organization, that is a unit in a position to undertake to provide opportunities which are binding on the unit.

In the light of this discussion it becomes clear that the business firm is in its aspect as collectivity in our technical sense, the case where the two standards of success and solvency coincide. The firm uses its power income primarily to maintain or increase its productivity and, as a measure of this, its money income. A surplus of power will therefore in general be exchanged for enhancement of its control of economic productivity. For a collectivity specialized in political function the primary criterion of success would be given in its power position, relative that is to other collectivities. Here there is the special problem of the meaning of the term power position. I interpret it here as relative to other collectivities in a competitive system, not as a position in an internal hierarchy of power. This distinction is of course particularly important for a pluralistic power system where government is a functionally specialized subsystem of the collectivity structure, not an approximation to the totality of that structure.[37] In somewhat corresponding fashion a collectivity specialized in integrative function would measure its success in terms of its 'level of influence' – for example, as a political interest-group in the usual sense, its capacity to influence public policy decisions. A consequence of this reasoning is that such an influence group would be disposed to 'give away' power, in the sense of trading it for an increment of influence. This could take the form of assuring political support, without barter-like conditions, to leadership elements which seemed to be likely to be able to exercise the kind of influence in question.

Is there then a political equivalent of the banking phenomenon, a way in which the circular flow of power comes to be broken through so as to bring about net additions to the amount of power in the system? The trend of the analytical argument indicates that there must be, and that its focus lies in the support system, that is the area of interchange between power and influence, between polity and integrative system.

First I suggest that, particularly conspicuous in the case of democratic electoral systems, political support should be conceived as a generalized grant of power which, if it leads to electoral success, puts elected leadership in a position analogous to that of the banker. The 'deposits' of power made by constituents are revocable, if not at will, at the next election – a condition analogous to regularity of banking hours. In some cases election is tied to barterlike conditions of expectation of carrying out certain specific measures favored by the strategically crucial voters and only these. But particularly in a system which is pluralistic not only with reference to the composition of political support, but also to issues, such a leadership element acquires freedom to make certain types of binding decision, binding in the nature of the case on elements of the collectivity other than those whose 'interest' is directly served. This freedom may be conceived to be confined to the circular flow level, which would be to say that the input of power through the channel of political support should be exactly balanced by the output through policy decisions, to interest groups which have specifically demanded these decisions.

These is, however, another component of the freedom of elected leadership which is crucial here. This is the freedom to use influence – for example through the 'prestige' of office as distinguished from its specified powers – to embark on new ventures in the 'equation' of power and influence. This is to use influence to create additions to the total supply of power. How can this be conceived to work?

One important point is that the relation between the media involved with respect to positive and negative sanctions is the obverse of the case of creating money through banking. There it was the use of power embodied in the binding character of loan contracts which 'made the difference'. Here it is the optional capacity to exert influence through persuasion. This process seems to operate through the function of leadership which, by way of the involvements it possesses with various aspects of the constituency structure of the collectivity, generates and structures new 'demands' in the specific sense of demands for policy decision.

Such demands then may be conceived, in the case of the deciders, to justify an increased output of power. This in turn is made possible by the generality of the mandate of political support, the fact that it is not given on a barter basis in exchange for specific policy decisions, but once the 'equation' of power and influence has been established through election, it is a mandate to do, within constitutional limits, what seems best, in the governmental case 'in the public interest'. Collective leadership may then be conceived as the bankers or 'brokers' who can mobilize the binding commitments of their constituents in such a way that the totality of commitments made by the collectivity as a whole can be enhanced. This enhancement must, however, be justified through the mobilization of influence; it must, that is, both be felt to be in accordance with valid norms and apply to situations which 'call for' handling at the level of binding collective commitments.

The critical problem of justification is, in one direction, that of consensus, of its bearing on the value-principle of solidarity as we have outlined this above. The standard therefore which corresponds to the value principle of solidarity is consensus in the sense in which that concept has been used above.

The problem then is that of a basis for breaking through the circular stability of a zero-sum power system. The crucial point is that this can only happen if the collectivity and its members are ready to assume new binding obligations over and above those previously in force. The crucial need is to justify this extension and to transform the 'sentiment' that something ought to be done into a commitment to implement the sentiment by positive action, including coercive sanctions if necessary. The crucial agency of this process seems to be leadership, precisely conceived as possessing a component analytically independent of the routine power position of office, which defines the leader as the mobilizer of justifications for policies which would not be undertaken under the circular flow assumptions.

It may be suggested that the parallel to credit creation holds with respect to time-extension as well as in other respects. The increments of effectiveness which are necessary to implement new binding policies which constitute an addition to the total burden on the collectivity cannot simply be willed into being; they require organizational changes through recombinations of the factors of effectiveness, development of new agencies, procurement of personnel, new norms, and even changes in bases of legitimation. Hence leadership cannot justifiably be held responsible for effective implementation immediately, and conversely, the sources of political support must be willing to trust their leadership in the sense of not demanding immediate – by the time of the next election – 'pay-off' of the power-value of their votes in their decisions dictated by their own interests.[38]

It is perhaps legitimate to call the responsibility assumed in this connection specifically leadership responsibility and distinguish it in these terms from administrative responsibility which focuses on the routine functions. In any case I should like to conceive this process of power-enhancement as strictly parallel to economic investment, in the further sense that the pay-off should be an increment to the level of collective success in the sense outlined above, i.e. enhanced effectiveness of collective action in valued areas which could not have been expected without risk-taking on the part of leadership in a sense parallel to entrepreneurial investment.

The operation of both governmental and nongovernmental collectivities is full of illustrations of the kind of phenomenon I have in mind, though because this type of formal analysis is somewhat unfamiliar, it is difficult to pin them down exactly. It has, for example, often been pointed out that the relation of executive responsibility to constituency-interests is very different in domestic and in foreign affairs. I suggest that the element of 'political banking' in the field of foreign affairs is particularly large and that the sanction of approval of policy decisions, where is occurs, cannot infallibly be translated into votes, certainly not in the short run. Similar considerations are very frequently involved in what may be called 'developmental' ventures, which cannot be expected to be 'backed' by currently well-structured interests in the same sense as maintenance of current functions. The case of support of research and training is a good one since the 'community of scholars' is not a very strong 'pressure group' in the sense of capacity directly to influence large blocks of votes.

It would follow from these considerations that there is, in developed polities, a relatively 'free-floating' element in the power system which is analogous to a credit-system. Such an element should then be subject to fluctuations on a dimension of inflation-deflation, and be in need of controls for the system as a whole, at a level above that of the activities of particular units.

The analogue of inflation seems to me to touch the credibility of the assertion of the bindingness of obligations assumed. Power, as a symbolic medium, is like money in that it is itself 'worthless', but is accepted in the expectation that it can later be 'cashed in', this time in the activation of binding obligations. If, however, 'power-credit' has been extended too far, without the necessary organizational basis for fulfillment of expectations having been laid, then attempting to invoke the obligations will result in less than a full level of performance, inhibited by various sorts of resistance. In a collectivity undergoing disintegration the same formal office may be 'worth less' than it otherwise would have been because of attrition of its basis of effectiveness. The same considerations hold when it is a case of overextension of new power-expectations without adequate provision for making them effective.

It goes without saying that a power-system in which this creditlike element is prominent is in a state analogous to the 'insolvency' of a monetary system which includes an important element of actual credit, namely its commitments cannot be fulfilled all at once, even if those to whom they have been made have formally valid rights to such fulfillment. Only a strict zero-sum power system could fulfill this condition of 'liquidity'. Perhaps the conservatism of political ideologies makes it even more difficult to accept the legitimacy of such a situation – it is all too easy to define it as 'dishonest' – than in the corresponding economic case.

There is, however, a fine line between solid, responsible and constructive political leadership which in fact commits the collectivity beyond its capacities for instantaneous fulfillment of all obligations, and reckless overextendedness, just as there is a fine line between responsible banking and 'wild-catting'.

Furthermore, under unusual pressures, even highly responsible leadership can be put in situations where a 'deflationary' spiral sets in, in a pattern analogous to that of a financial panic. I interpret, for instance McCarthyism as such a deflationary spiral in the political field. The focus of the commitments in which the widest extension had taken place was in the international field – the United States had very rapidly come into the position of bearing the largest share of responsibility for maintenance of world political order against an expansionist Communist movement. The 'loss of China' was in certain quarters a particularly traumatic experience, and the Korean war a highly charged symbol of the costs of the new stewardship.

A pluralistic political system like the American always has a large body of latent claims on the loyalty of its citizens to their government, not only for the 'right sentiments' but for 'sacrifices', but equally these are expected to be invoked only in genuine emergencies. The McCarthy definition of the situation was, however, that virtually anyone in a position of significant responsibility should not only recognize the 'in case' priority – not necessarily by our basic values the highest – of national loyalty, but should explicitly renounce all other loyalties which might conceivably compete with that to the nation, including those to kith and kin. This was in effect a demand to liquidate all other commitments in favor of the national, a demand which in the nature of the case could not be met without disastrous consequences in many different directions. It tended to 'deflate' the power system by undermining the essential basis of trust on which the influence of many elements bearing formal and informal leadership responsibilities, and which in turn sustained 'power-credit', necessarily rested. Perhaps the most striking case was the allegation of communist infiltration and hence widespread 'disloyalty' in the army, which was exploited to try to force the army leadership to put the commitments of all associated personnel, including e.g. research scientists, in completely 'liquid' form. Two features of the McCarthy movement particularly mark it as a deflationary spiral, first the vicious circle of spreading involvement with the casting of suspicion on wider and wider circles of otherwise presumptively loyal elements in the society and secondly the surprisingly abrupt end of the spiral once the 'bubble was pricked' and 'confidence restored', events associated particularly with the public reaction to McCarthy's performance in the televised army hearings, and to Senator Flanders' protest on the floor of the Senate.[39]

The focus of the McCarthy disturbance may be said to have been in the influence system, in the relation between integrative and pattern-maintenance functions in the society. The primary deflationary effect was on the 'credit' elements of pluralistic loyalties. This in turn would make leadership elements, not only in government but private groups, much less willing to take risks in claiming loyalties which might compete with those to government. Since, however, in the hierarchy of control the influence system is superordinate to the power system, deflation in the former is necessarily propagated to the latter. This takes in the first instance the form of a rush to withdraw political support – which it will be remembered is here treated as a form of power – from leadership elements which could in any sense be suspected of 'disloyalty'. The extreme perhaps was the slogan propagated by McCarthy and played with by more responsible Republican leaders like Thomas E. Dewey, of 'twenty years of treason' which impugned the loyalty of the Democratic Party as a whole. The effect was, by depriving opposition leadership of influence, to make it unsafe even to consider granting them power.

The breaking through of the zero-sum limitations of more elementary power systems opens the way to altogether new levels of collective effectiveness, but also, in the nature of the case, involves new levels of risk and uncertainty. I have already dealt briefly with this problem at the level of the particular collectivity and its extension of commitments. The problem of course is compounded for a system of collectivities because of the risk not only of particular failures, but of generalized inflationary and deflationary disturbances. There are, as we have noted, mechanisms of control which operate to regulate investment and similarly extension of the commitments of particular collectivities, both of which have to do with the attempt to ensure responsibility, on the one hand for solvency over the long run, on the other for success of the larger 'strategy' of extension. It is reasonable to suppose that beyond these, there must be mechanisms operating at the level of the system as a whole in both contexts.

In the monetary case it was the complex of central banking, credit management and their relations to governmental finance which has been seen to be the focus of these highest-level controls. In the case of power it is of course the first crucial point that there was to be some relatively paramount apex of control of the power and authority system, which we think of as in some sense the 'sovereign' stated.[40] This has mainly to do with the relations between what we have called justification and legitimacy, in relation to government as the highest-order tightly integrated collectivity structure – so far. This is the central focus of Weber's famous analysis of authority, but his analysis is in need of considerable extension in our sense. It seems, among other things, that he posed an unduly sharp alternative between charismatic and 'routine' cases, particularly the rational-legal version of the latter. In particular it would be my view that very substantial possibilities of regulated extension of power-commitments exist within the framework of certain types of 'legal' authority, especially where they are aspects of a political system which is pluralistic in general terms. These problems, however, cannot further be explored at the end of what is already a very long paper.

## Conclusion

This paper has been designed as a general theoretical attack on the ancient problem of the nature of political power and its place, not only in political systems, narrowly conceived, but in the structure and processes of societies generally. The main point of reference for the attack has been the conception that the discussion of the problem in the main traditions of political thought have not been couched at a sufficiently rigorously analytical level, but have tended to treat the nation, the state, or the lower-level collectively organized 'group', as the empirical object of reference, and to attempt to analyze its functioning without further basic analytical breakdown. The most conspicuous manifestation of this tendency has been the treatment of power.

The present paper takes a radically different position, cutting across the traditional lines. It takes its departure from the position of economic theory and, by inference, the asymmetry between it and the traditional political theory,[41] which has treated one as the theory of an analytically defined functional system of society – the economy – and the other as a concrete substructure, usually identified with government. Gradually the possibility has opened out both the extension of the analytical model of economic theory to the political field and the direct articulation of political with economic theory within the logical framework of the theory of the social system as a whole, so that the *polity* could be conceived as a functional subsystem of the society in all its theoretical fundamentals parallel to the economy.

This perspective necessarily concentrated attention on the place of money in the conception of the economy. More than that, it became increasingly clear that money was essentially a 'symbolic' phenomenon and hence that its analysis required a frame of reference closer to that of linguistics than of technology, i.e. it is not the intrinsic properties of gold which account for the value of money under a gold standard any more than it is the intrinsic properties of the sounds symbolized as 'book' which account for the valuation of physically fixed dissertations in linguistic form. This is the perspective from which the conception of power as a *generalized symbolic medium* operating in the processes of social interaction has been set forth.

This paper has not included a survey of the empirical evidence bearing on its ramified field of problems, but my strong conviction is not only that the line of analysis adopted is consistent with the broad lines of the available empirical evidence, but that it has already shown that it can illuminate a range of empirical problems which were not well understood in terms of the more conventional theoretical positions – e.g. the reasons for the general egalitarian pressure in the evolution of the political franchise, or the nature of McCarthyism as a process of political deflationary spiral.

It does not seem necessary here to recapitulate the main outline of the argument. I may conclude with the three main points with which I began. I submit, first, that the analytical path entered upon here makes it possible to treat power in conceptually specific and precise terms and thus gets away from the theoretical diffuseness called to attention, in terms of which it has been necessary to include such a very wide variety of problematical phenomena as 'forms' of power. Secondly, I think it can advance a valid claim to present a resolution of the old dilemma as to whether (in the older terms) power is 'essentially' a phenomenon of coercion or of consensus. It is both, precisely because it is a phenomenon which integrates a plurality of factors and outputs of political effectiveness and is not to be identified with any one of them. Finally, light has been thrown on the famous zero-sum problem, and a definite position taken that, though under certain specific assumptions the zero-sum condition holds, these are not constitutive of power systems in general, but under different conditions systematic 'extension' of power spheres without sacrifice of the power of other units is just as important a case.

These claims are put forward in full awareness that on one level there is an inherent arbitrariness in them, namely that I have defined power and a number of related concepts in my own way, which is different from many if not most of the definitions current in political theory. If theory were a matter only of the arbitrary choice of definitions and assumptions and reasoning from there, it might be permissible to leave the question at that and say simply, this is only one more personal 'point of view'. Any claim that it is more than that rests on the conception that the scientific understanding of societies is arrived at through a gradually developing organon of theoretical analysis and empirical interpretation and verification. My most important contention is that the line of analysis presented here is a further development of a main line of theoretical analysis of the social system as a whole, and of verified interpretation of the empirical evidence presented to that body of theory. This body of theory must ultimately be judged by its outcomes both in theoretical generality and consistency, over the whole range of social system theory, and by its empirical validity, again on levels which include not only conventionally 'political' references, but their empirical interrelations with all other aspects of the modern complex society looked at as a whole.

## Notes

1 Thus E.C. Banfield, *Political Influence* (New York, The Free Press of Glencoe, 1962), p. 348, speaks of control as the ability to cause another to give or withhold action, and power as the ability to establish control over another. Similarly Robert Dahl, 'The Concept of Power', *Behavioral Scientist* 2 (July, 1957), says that '*A* has power over *B* to the extent that he can get *B* to do something that *B* would not otherwise do'. C.J. Friedrich takes a similar position in his forthcoming book, the tentative title of which is 'Man and his Government'.

2 *Cf.* Talcott Parsons and Neil J. Smelser, *Economy and Society* (Illinois, The Free Press of Glencoe, 1956), chapter I, for a discussion of this conception.

3 E.g. the American medical profession is part of American society, but also it is part of a wider medical profession which transcends this particular society, to some extent as collectivity. Interpenetration in membership is thus a feature of the relations among collectivities.

4 For discussions of the conception of 'valued-added' in spheres of application broader than the economic alone, *cf.* Neil J. Smelser, *Social Change in the Industrial Revolution* (Glencoe, Illinois, The Free Press of Glencoe, 1959), chapter II, pp. 7–20, and Neil J. Smelser, *Theory of Collective Behavior* (New York, The Free Press of Glencoe, 1963), chapter II, pp. 23–47.

5 C.I. Barnard, *The Functions of the Executive* (Cambridge, Harvard University Press, 1938), chapter V, pp. 46–64.

6 On the rationale of these attributions, see *Economy and Society, op. cit.*, chapter II.

7 'Pay-off' may be a deciding factor in choice between particular contexts of use, but not as to whether the resource shall be devoted to collective effectiveness at all.

8 I have in fact adopted the term 'demands' from the usage of David Easton, 'An Approach to the Analysis of Political Systems', *World Politics* 9 (1957): 383–400.

9 *Cf.* Max Weber, *The Theory of Social and Economic Organization* (New York, Oxford University Press, 1947), p. 124. Translation by A.M. Henderson and Talcott Parsons; edited by Talcott Parsons.

10 The cases of services concretely rendered to a household will be considered as a limiting case where the roles of consumer and employer have not become differentiated from each other.

11 In the cases treated as typical for economic analysis the collective element in capital is delegated through the *bindingness* of the contracts of loan of financial resources. To us this is a special case, employment being another, of the binding obligation assumed by an organization, whether it employs or loans, by virtue of which the recipient can be more effective than would otherwise be the case. It is not possible to go further into these complex problems here, but they will, perhaps, be somewhat illuminated by the later discussion of the place of the concept of bindingness in the theory of power.

12 See my paper 'On the Concept of Influence', to be published in the *Public Opinion Quarterly* 27 (Spring, 1963).

13 Here again Barnard's usage of the concept of responsibility seems to me the appropriate one. See Barnard, *op. cit.*

14 In order not to complicate things too much, I shall not enter into problem of the interchange system involving legitimation here. See my paper 'Authority, Legitimation, and Political Process', in *Nomos* 1, reprinted as chapter V of my *Structure and Process in Modern Societies* (Glencoe, Illinois, The Free Press, 1960), chapter V, pp. 170–98.

15 There is a certain element of generality in physical force as a *negative* sanction, which gives it a special place in power systems. This will be taken up later in the discussion.

16 There are complications here deriving from the fact that power is associated with *negative* sanctions and hence that, in the face of severe resistance, their effectiveness is confined to deterrence.

17 I owe the insight into this parallel to Professor Karl W. Deutsch of Yale University (personal discussion).

18 'Sadistic' infliction of injury without instrumental significance to ego does not belong in this context.

19 I have attempted to develop this line of analysis of the significance of force somewhat more fully in 'Some Reflections of the Role of Force in Social Relations', in Harry Eckstein, ed., *The Problem of Internal War* (New Jersey, Princeton University Press, 1963).

20 Thus, if control of productivity operates through monetary funds, their possessor cannot 'force' e.g. prospective employees to accept employment.

21 This, of course, is a relative difference. Some hazards increase the moment one steps outside his own home, police protection may be better in one local community than the next, and crossing a state boundary may mean a considerable difference in legal or actual rights.

22 *Cf.* my paper 'The Principal Structures of Community', *Nomos* 2 and *Structure and Process, op. cit.*, chapter 8. See also W.L. Hurst, *Law and Social Process in the United States* (Ann Arbor, University of Michigan Law School, 1960).

23 As already noted, in this area, I think the analysis of Chester I. Barnard, in *The Function of the Executive, op. cit.*, is so outstandingly clear and cogent that it deserves the status of a classic of political theory in my specific sense. See especially chapter X.

24 Two particularly important manifestations of this monetization of property are, first the general legal understanding that executors of estates are not obligated to retain the exact physical inventory intact pending full statement, but may sell various items – their fiduciary obligation is focussed on the money value of the estate. Similarly in the law of contract increasing option has been given to compensate with money damages in lieu of the specific 'performance' originally contracted for.

25 Since this system is the territorially organized collectivity, the state with its government, these considerations underlie the critical importance of foreign relations in the sense of the relations to other territorially organized, force-controlling collectivities, since, once internal control of force is effectively institutionalized, the danger of this kind of breach comes from the outside in this specific sense of outside. The point is cogently made by Raymond Aron.

26 See, on this process, Stein Rokkan, 'Mass Suffrage, Secret Voting, and Political Participation', *European Journal of Sociology* 2 (1961): 132–52.

27 I.e., the aggregate of votes, evaluated by the electoral rules, determines the incumbency of office.

28 Of course where conditions are sufficiently simple, or where there is sufficient anxiety about the hierarchial implications of power, the egalitarian element may penetrate far into the political decision-making system itself, with, e.g. insistence that policy-decisions, both external and internal in reference, be made by majority vote of all members, or even under a unanimity rule. The respects in which such a system – which of course realistically often involves a sharply hierarchical stratification of influence – is incompatible with effectiveness in many spheres, can be said to be relatively clear, especially for *large* collectivities.

29 It is the central concept of *The Division of Labor in Society*. For my own relatively recent understanding of its significance, see 'Durkheim's Contribution to the Theory of Integration of Social Systems', in Kurt Wolff, ed., *Émile Durkheim, 1858–1917* (Ohio, Ohio State University Press, 1960), pp. 118–53.

30 *Cf.* C. Wright Mills, *The Power Elite* (New York, Oxford University Press, 1956) and my commentary in *Structure and Process in Modern Societies, op. cit.*, chapter 6.

31 *Cf.* Durkheim's famous essay, 'Deux lois de l'évolution pénale', *L'Année Sociologique* 4 (1899–1900): 65–95.

32 *Cf.* my paper 'On The Concept of Influence', *op. cit.*, for a discussion of the concept of justification and its distinction from legitimation.

33 Failure to see this seems to me to be a major source of the utopian strain in Marxist theory, expressed above all by the expectation of the 'withering away of the state'. There is perhaps a parallel to the confusion connected for many centuries with the Aristotelian doctrine of the 'sterility' of money.

34 H.D. Lasswell and A. Kaplan, *Power and Society* (New Haven, Yale University Press, 1950) and Mills, *The Power Elite, op. cit.*

35 Whether this be interpreted as net addition to the medium or as increase in the velocity of circulation of the 'slow' deposit funds, is indifferent, because its economic effects are the same.

36 Joseph Schumpeter, *The Theory of Economic Development* (Cambridge, Harvard University Press, 1955), translated by Redvers Opie.

37 If very carefully interpreted, perhaps the old term 'sovereignty' could be used to designate this standard somewhat more definitely than success.

38 Perhaps this is an unusually clear case of the relativity of the formal legal sense of the bindingness of commitments. Thus the populistic component in democratic government often ties both executive and legislative branches rather rigidly in what they can formally promise. However, there are many *de facto* obligations assumed by Government which are very nearly binding. Thus legally Congress could withdraw the totality of funds recently granted to universities for the support of scientific research and training, the formal appropriations being made year by year. Universities, however, plan very much in the expectation of maintenance of these funds and this maintenance is certainly something like a *de facto* obligation of Congress.

39 I have dealt with some aspects of the McCarthy episode in 'Social Strains in America', *Structure and Process, op. cit.*, chapter 7, pp. 226–49. The inherent impossibility of the demand for 'absolute security' in a pluralistic system is very cogently shown by Edward Shils in *The Torment of Secrecy* (New York, The Free Press of Glencoe, 1956), especially in chapter VI.

40 In saying this I am very far from maintaining that 'absolute' sovereignty is an essential condition of the minimal integration of political systems. On the contrary, first it is far from absolute internally, precisely because of the pluralistic character of most modern political systems and because of the openness of their boundaries in the integrative economic and other directions. Externally the relation of the territorial unit to norms and values transcending it is crucial, and steadily becoming more so. See my paper 'Polarization of the World and International Order' in Quincy Wright, William M. Evan and Morton Deutsch, eds., *Preventing World War III* (New York, Simon and Schuster, 1962), pp. 310–31.

41 I myself once accepted this. *Cf. The Social System* (Illinois, The Free Press of Glencoe, 1951), chapter V, pp. 161–3.

# 6  Barnes

## Introduction

Barry Barnes' theory of power is part of a greater project to reconstruct social theory in a cognitivist vein. While part of a larger whole, the theory of power presented in *The Nature of Power* is self-contained and makes a significant contribution to the power literature written from the perspective of social theory.

As outlined in the previous section, Parsons' theory of power marks an important break in power analysis by pointing out that power does not simply exist: it has to be created. Consequently, power is neither zero-sum nor equivalent to coercion but presupposes some level of consensus between participants. Barnes builds upon these insights while removing them from the theoretical framework of structural functionalism by incorporating them within a new theory of social order with contemporary theoretical relevance. While Barnes' theory of power can broadly be conceptualized as a consensual theory of power, the consensus is neither on system goals nor explicit perceptions of legitimacy but, rather, on a shared cognitive framework. Barnes' conceptualization owes much to the Kuhnian concept of paradigms, and rational choice views of agency.

For Barnes, both natural and social power denote a capacity for action. Power is not simply reducible to its exercise. He uses the example of a car to illustrate this point: a car is not simply powerful when driven at a high speed but it is equally powerful when parked. What distinguishes natural and social power is their source: physical power is derived from a knowledge and manipulation of physical objects, while social power is based upon knowledge and membership of social systems.

Hobbes first analysed the problem of social order and, consequently, forms a common reference point for theorizations of social order. The underlying problematic for Hobbes was to understand how rationally egoistic individuals could be prevented from entering into a continual state of war with each other as a consequence of competition for scarce resources. Hobbes assumed, mistakenly in Barnes' view, that the natural consequence of rational egoism is competition and hence conflict. According to Barnes, rational egoism does not lead to a propensity to conflict, but, rather, towards a certain level of cooperation. To take the ultimate example of a complex social order, even in a situation of extreme conflict, linguistic order benefits all; consequently, the result is not linguistic disorder or Babel (the linguistic equivalent of Hobbes' state of nature). Because rational egoism does not entail the absence of social order, neither is it the case that social order presupposes the type of massive internalization of norms, a virtual 'taming of wild beasts', presupposed by Parsons. Rather, as has been argued by Chomsky with respect to language acquisition, the human mind has a predisposition for order. The rational egoist who pursues power after power, does so by perceiving and manipulating the orderedness of the natural and social worlds, not by spreading anarchy.

The predisposition to perceive order is a cognitive facility which Barnes theorizes along the lines of Kuhn's description of paradigms. Kuhn argues that science does not develop in a slow incremental way (as is generally assumed) but through a series of scientific revolutions. What lends a scientific revolution its revolutionary character is, essentially, a discontinuity in norms which shape practices. A revolution is not only a 'great' discovery but, more significantly, one that leads to a change in everyday practice through a reordering of norms.

The paradigmatic ordering facility of the human mind gives individuals a capacity for action which is both derivable from the physical world (natural power) and from the social world (social power). What distinguishes the two worlds from each other is the fact that ordering of the social world constitutes a self-fulfilling prophecy (the equivalent of 'operation boot strap' in Parsons) whereas this is not the case with the natural world (ignoring Heisenberg's uncertainty principle – I believe). How exactly the social process constitutes itself as a self-fulfilling prophecy, and hence power, is the subject of the extract which follows.

As the extract is self-explanatory, suffice it to say that the reputational power theorists to whom Barnes frequently refers include Hunter, with whom Dahl entered into debate (see introduction pp. 5–6). When reading Barnes' account it is important to note the extent to which the emergent concept of power is interactive. The power which a leader has is not derived from him or her but from the perceptions of those who perceive them as powerful. Power is not a property and cannot be possessed in the way that material objects can. In this vein, notice also the extent to which Barnes' account of the fall of the Shah has similarities with Parsons' description of McCarthyism in the US.

Since Parsons was widely criticized for his inability to take account of conflictual power, Barnes is highly conscious of the need to provide conceptual space for conflict within his consensual theory. Barnes' view of leadership is one where power is conferred by the less powerful, so it might be expected that illegitimate power would be theoretically problematic. This is an issue which

Barnes deals with in the latter half of his book. As an extract from this section is not included, I will outline a few of the salient points.

Barnes' solution to the problem of theorizing conflictual power within a consensual theory is to build massive inertia into his theory of empowerment through the use of rational choice theory and Weberian views of bureaucracy. The rational choice aspects include the following. 1) Divide and rule: in a society consisting of groups A, B and C, group A exploits and manages to dominate both B and C by making alliances with one at a time while simultaneously dividing them against each other. While this may appear problematic with respect to just three parties, it is not at all implausible in a real society composed of *many* cross-cutting cleavages – Stalin was renowned for this. 2) Time: if illegitimate leadership can be made to endure a significant span of time there will be a tendency for it to strengthen as time passes by virtue of its very persistence. Routine reinforces the taken-for-granted aspect of a leader's power which can, in turn, be reinforced through pomp and ceremony. Over time, power will be made to *appear intrinsic* to the leader; consequently, relations of domination take on a 'could not be otherwise' aspect. 3) 'Fear of being first': a despot can be overthrown only if a large number of people rebel at once. However, being first is a costly option. Even in a successful revolution, those who rebel first are confronted with the full, and as yet unweakened, power of the despot. The obvious option for a rational egoist is to wait for someone else to be first. The aggregate of everyone wishing to be second is that no one does anything – the despot remains in power.

Using Weberian analysis, Barnes argues that illegitimate power is reinforced by instrumental rationality, the division of labour and the complex chains of command which constitute modern bureaucracies. In such a context, individuals frequently lead a schizophrenic existence whereby, in their private lives they evaluate the consequences of their actions while in their bureaucratic existence they concern themselves simply with performing their job to maximum efficiency. Thus, the same actors may privately condemn the actions of the very regime which they scrupulously obey at work – Bauman's (1989) portrayal of the Holocaust would confirm this analysis.

As a whole, Barnes' theory of power is essentially a Weberian ideal type. It is a distillation of certain aspects of power which will never be found in their pure form. The theory is presented as a general theory of power but it is more correctly viewed as a theory which deals with certain aspects of power. The use of Kuhnian cognitive theory offers significant insights into the nature of the consensual basis of social order and the use of rational choice explains how rationality, consent and conflict can coexist in particular situations. However, as with all ideal types, this does not constitute an explanation of many aspects of power and domination – for instance: false consciousness, class, power/ knowledge (Foucault), discipline, stigma, consensus through reification, 'obligatory passage points' (Clegg) and the many instances when conflictual power is not reducible to the type of rationality presupposed by rational choice. The last point, of course, highlights a wider issue: the theoretical impoverishment of insisting that agency can be reducible to rational choice theory. I would not deny that agents frequently behave as economically rational utility maximizers and to that extent (but only to that extent) rational choice solutions are pertinent but, as often as not, actors are religiously motivated, conformers to tradition, in the grip of charismatic leadership, driven by emotion, altruism, the search for truth or beauty, etc. This is symptomatic of a more general point, it is my conviction that most social theorists undermine their work through failure to specify the scope of their ideas and, thus, they overextend their analysis.

### Further reading

Aside from reading *The Nature of Power* in its entirety, Barnes (1986), (1995) and (2000) are useful next ports of call. Barnes (1982) gives an illuminating account of the importance of Kuhn for social science. The main secondary analysis of Barnes' theory is contained in Haugaard (1997a), chapter 2.

# From *THE NATURE OF POWER*
## Barry Barnes

[pp. 46–53]

### Self-reference and self-validation

A society is everything its members know, including everything they know about each other, and each others' knowledge of each other and so on. Such a body of knowledge will be used by its possessors to make reference to each other, and to make reference to each other as possessors of knowledge. What is known will be something that is referred to in using the knowledge itself: the use of knowledge will involve the specification of the content of the knowledge, its basis and its distribution as references. The knowledge that constitutes society is *self-referring*.

Whatever the members of a society know may be referred to by members within the framework of what they know. If a society is a distribution of knowledge then it is a self-referring distribution of knowledge. To learn such knowledge is to do two things. It is to become *informed* about whatever the knowledge is used to refer to, and it is to be *constituted* or reconstituted as a referent, an entity that may be referred to by others, or indeed oneself, using that very same knowledge. It is easy to overlook the constitutive or performative dimension of learning when a single individual is concerned, but if we think of the entire membership of a society at once this dimension becomes vividly apparent. In learning what a society knows the members as a whole thereby constitute the society itself as a distribution of knowledge, much of which knowledge will be *about* the society itself, and hence valid and 'consonant with social experience' only when it has been learned. Where knowledge is self-referring it must also be self-validating. A membership must learn it in order to become what it correctly describes.

Neither epistemologists and philosophers of science nor sociologists of knowledge have given much detailed consideration to systems of knowledge that involve self-reference. Yet if social action is indeed generated by knowledgeable human beings, acting calculatively and reflectively, this is a topic of great importance. Even in the present context it is worthwhile to pause whilst it is given some extended consideration. The fact that society and knowledge of society are not fully separable independent entities is of some importance when we seek to identify the basis of power.

Let us begin on familiar ground by considering our knowledge of everyday material objects (see figure 1 [number of figure changed, M.H.]). We know that the billiard-ball is spherical. On one side, there we are, with our knowledge, or, if preferred, our shared belief. On the other side is the billiard-ball, completely separate from us. To check whether our belief is or is not correct we move to the ball, observe it, measure it, rotate it. The shape of the ball remains unaffected by what we do to it or what we believe about it: it is there to be investigated as an external phenomenon. If the shape is indeed found to be that of a sphere, this shows that our belief is correct, that we were indeed properly informed about the nature of the billiard-ball (1.a).

This is perhaps our commonest paradigm of knowing. We have a shared belief about some separate, distinct, independently identifiable thing, and if the nature of that thing is as we believe it to be then our belief is correct. But not all our beliefs about the objects in our physical environment are like this. Suppose we believe that this rock is the summit of the mountain. Once again there we are, with our knowledge; and there, separate from us, is a thing or object that can be pointed out, the summit. But now it is no longer the nature of the object itself that makes it a proper referent of our belief: now it is the relationship of the object with things outside itself. Suppose that some vandal hammers the top from the Matterhorn and makes off with it. Should the headlines read 'Vandal steals Matterhorn summit!' or 'Vandal lowers Matterhorn summit!'? The newspapers may take their choice, but what is certain is that the Matterhorn would not subsequently be known as a mountain without a summit. The weather may indeed have scraped an

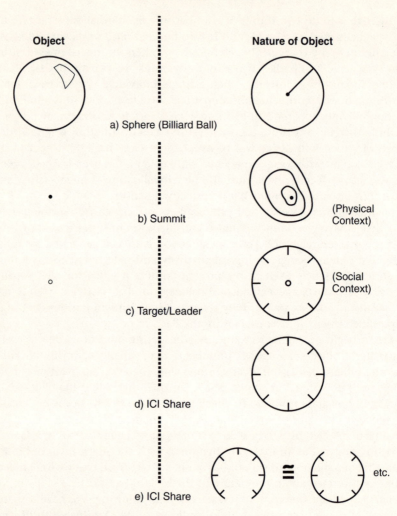

Figure 1  Objects and their natures

inch or two from the Matterhorn over the last century or so, without depriving it of its summit. A summit is that part of a mountain which exists in a
certain relationship with all its other parts. To check that something is a
summit is not the same kind of process as checking that it is a sphere: with
the latter one looks to the nature of the thing itself – one looks at or inside
the thing; whereas with the former one looks outside the thing itself, to its
relationship with its context. Our belief that what we are pointing to is a
summit is valid only if what we are pointing to relates to its context in a
specific way. Indeed we cannot even understand what summits are as we

understand what spherical objects are, by looking at them in isolation and noting their properties.

Summits are physical objects, quite separate from us, but objects which are what they are only because of circumstances outside themselves (1.b). There are other physical objects just like summits, but objects of a nature defined not by a context of physical circumstances, but by a context of human activity. The list of such objects is endless: auguries and omens, cups and reliquaries, jewellery; more mundanely, pets, pollutions, rubbish; at a yet more practical level, reagents and solvents, targets and weapons, vermin and weeds. All these are independent entities which can be pointed to and identified, picked up and examined, described and measured; yet they are only what they are because of how we act in relation to them.

With objects of this kind it is no longer a matter of us and our belief here, and the object and its nature there. It is no longer even a matter of us here, and object in context there. We now *are* the context which makes the object what it is. The target is the target because we believe it to be the target, and hence treat it as the target. Physical object though it is, the target is a target only to the extent that it is believed to be such and treated as such. In ceasing to believe that an object is a target, we dissolve away its nature as a target. In coming to believe that an object is a target, we constitute the context that makes it a target, and hence we constitute it as a target. Our believing self-validates: we validate what we believe by referring to what we believe (1.c).

Here at last is a simple stereotypical example that captures something of the nature of our knowledge of society (which is the most intensely self-referring component of the knowledge that is society). Social objects, if we may call them that, are often very much like the objects we call targets. They are identifiable as objects, as substantial bounded entities, but their nature is constituted by our beliefs about them: our beliefs constitute the context that makes them what they are. John is the leader of the gang. He is the leader because the members know him to be the leader, and act routinely on the basis of what they know. Whoever the leader is, he is the leader, in just the way that whatever is the target is the target. Both the physical and the social object are the objects that they are because of the context of belief and action that rings them about (1.c).

Most, indeed probably all terms denoting a social status or position are analogous to the terms 'target' and 'leader' in this respect. Status terms denote objects the natures of which are constituted by the surrounding context of belief and action. Beliefs about the status of individuals in society are accordingly not fully independent of that to which they refer. To come to believe something about the status of an individual is to do two things at once: it is to accept a *claim about* his status and at the same time to contribute to the *constitution of* his status.

Given that the nature of a social object is constituted by what rings it about, the actual physical manifestation of the object itself may actually be dispensed with. Only the hollow ring of belief and action is actually necessary. Consider shares in Imperial Chemical Industries (ICI), or the value of a share in ICI, or the voting power of a share. Here are three hollow rings of belief and action: neither the share, nor its value, nor its power, exist or are manifested as tangible objects. It is only our general familiarity with objects and how to treat them, and their mnemonic convenience, that induces us occasionally to set marker-objects at the centre of such hollow rings; and then it is important not to confuse the marker with what is marked, the share certificate with what is certified, the paper banknotes with the value of the share (1.d).

## The invisibility of self-reference

When a social object is designated one quickly looks out from the object to check the correctness of the designation, and, in practice, to acquire a sense of its point and significance. What one looks toward is the generally accepted designation of the object, and the generally accepted way of acting in relation to it. An object is designated validly if that is how it is designated generally, and/or if action in relation to it is action routinely associated with that designation. A social object is constituted as a social object to the extent that it is generally believed to be such an object.[1] Analogously, if a social structure is an array of social objects, then it too is constituted by being believed to exist. Social structure is the product of those who live in it; they encounter it through the actions that flow from their belief in its existence. But if this is the case, why are we not more aware of a fundamental and profound contrast between natural and social knowledge?[2]

It is very important to recognize that even where a society makes a strong and explicit divide between its conceptions of natural and social order, the discernible differences between the two kinds of order are very slight. Natural order is an ordering constructed by people and used to make sense of nature, not an ordering insisted upon by nature and imposed upon people by nature. Natural order is just as much a system of conventions as social order. Conversely, the objects classified into a social order may be just as material and tangible as those classified into a natural order: John the gang-leader is just as substantial as the spherical billiard-ball, and once designated he is identified and reidentified by his physical characteristics just like the billiard-ball – indeed, recognition of John's physical form is crucially important in the continuing routine treatment of him in terms of his social status as gang-leader.

Natural order and social order are not just similar conventional orderings. They are orderings which are taught and transmitted in just the same way. In particular, in both cases, specific objects and processes are pointed out and displayed directly as examples of terms: natural and social order are both transmitted by *ostension*. The ball is pointed out as a spherical ball; John is pointed out as the leader of the gang. Thus, learning about nature and learning about society are the same kind of process: they feel the same; they can be run together; indeed they are the same. Just the competences and procedures which allow us to learn about our physical environment and respond appropriately to it also allow us to learn about society, respond appropriately to it, and thereby keep it in existence as something we have learned about and know how to respond to. There is a marvellous economy of explanation here: people have to be assigned learning capabilities in order to account for how they cope as organisms in a physical environment, and those very same learning capabilities may be what is necessary both to account for how people cope as agents in a social environment and how they constitute that environment in the course of coping with it.

The small difference between knowledge of physical nature and knowledge of society only becomes evident when we take an interest in the grounds for accepting the knowledge, the features that make it valid. At this point, with our knowledge of nature, we often find ourselves giving closer and closer attention to the independent referents of the knowledge, whereas with our knowledge of our own society we usually find ourselves referring back to our own collective action, our own practice, as the focus of our reflection. Even at this point, the distinction between the social and the natural may be exceedingly slight and difficult to discern for the isolated individual. Durkheim says that, like material objects, social facts are external to the individual – and so they are, almost. Every individual in John's gang observes John to be the leader by noting the actions and inferring the beliefs of the other members. Every individual, when reflecting upon John's putative leadership, looks outward at a near-complete ring of confirming action, action confirming and thus constituting John's social position as leader.

That all these slightly different contexts around the social position may be brought together as perceptions of essentially 'the same' context allows an agreed social order to be created and sustained. The 'error' in individual perception involved here is so extremely small as to be for all practical purposes no error at all. The individual who accepts the 'external' social fact of John's leadership will be making no mistake, even though a tiny part of what constitutes John's leadership is not 'external' to that individual at all but internal to him, being nothing more nor less than his own belief in John's leadership. For most practical purposes the individual may neglect his own contribution to the social reality in which he believes. The gang-member may take the leader as externally given, provided the gang is not too small; the share-seller may take the share-price as externally fixed, provided his holding is not too large (1.e).

## The ubiquity of self-reference

The contribution of any given individual to the constitution of a social object may be minute, but however minute it is the nature of that object will nonetheless be *wholly and entirely* constituted by the totality of the individuals in the relevant society: its crucial characteristics, its nature as a social object, are the surrounding activities of all these individuals. However 'external' to any individual a social object may be, it is completely 'internal' to his community. The gang-leader is constituted as such by gang-members' actions. The share-price is constituted by market transactions. However many the individual pieces into which the hollow ring of belief and action around a social object is broken, it remains a ring of belief and action, nothing more. As with social objects, so it is with knowledge of society generally. Whereas knowledge of nature refers in the last analysis to entities and processes beyond itself, knowledge of society refers in the last analysis to knowledge, and hence precisely to itself. Whereas knowledge of nature may be confirmed or disconfirmed by processes involving reference to states of affairs that exist independently of the knowledge, knowledge of society must be confirmed or disconfirmed by processes involving reference to states of affairs that exist only because the knowledge is generally presumed to be true. If we step back from all these ongoing processes, and focus on knowledge of society as a core constituent of society itself as a distribution of knowledge, then society is revealed as a sublime, monumental, self-fulfilling prophesy.[3]

Knowledge of society self-refers. There are no objects beyond its existing domain of application waiting to be discovered, nor any existing social objects with features other than those they are already known to possess. Yet individuals may nonetheless rightly feel dissatisfaction with the accuracy or the extent of their knowledge of their society, and may rightly seek to correct mistakes therein or to add to it and extend its scope. For individuals may be systematically incorrect in their beliefs about each other, or ignorant of pattern and order in their own beliefs. Consider the cyclic character of fashion in clothing. A few people, opinion-leaders, at the top of the social hierarchy, may seek to dress distinctively, differently from everyone else. The rest of the society may seek to dress like those just above them in the hierarchy. If at a given time the opinion-leaders know what is generally being worn, then they will set in motion a wave of activity which will eventually invalidate that knowledge. They will dress at variance with the norm, whereupon their new mode of dress will pass down the society and become a new norm. As they correct their increasingly inadequate knowledge, so they will increasingly tend to vary their dress yet again, inaugurating new waves of change, so that the familiar cyclic pattern in fashionable dressing is established and sustained. A recurring oscillation in social practice is established, associated with a continuing small degree of inadequacy in social knowledge. Note too that once it is established the oscillation itself becomes a complex social object, available for examination and reflection. A new layer of knowledge may be built up, as it were, by scanning what exists already. And the new knowledge may inspire new practice: explicitly formulated knowledge of the cyclic tendencies in dress-routines does indeed inspire a significant range of economic activities in our society.

Knowledge of society is therefore open to correction, modification and development. People can learn more about their society just as they can learn more about their physical environment. But there is a crucial difference between the two kinds of learning. Ideally, to learn about the physical environment is to take account of more information about an independent realm, which realm remains unchanged by the learning process. We may proceed, confident that the acquisition of knowledge makes no difference to that which is known. But to learn about our own society may be to change that society, since in learning we change ourselves and we are part of our own society. An act of learning in this case may both take account of the nature of society and change the nature of society. The act alters knowledge of society and at the same time alters the referents of that knowledge. It is both an act of learning and an act of reconstitution of the phenomena being learned about. It is at once cognitive and performative. Learning involves the adjustment of belief, but society just is constituted of rings of belief and action, so that the performative role of learning is indeed immediately and straightforwardly intelligible.[4]

This is a key point to keep in mind in what follows. Society is a distribution of knowledge. Power, as will shortly be argued, is an aspect of that distribution. But the knowledge in question is self-referring, and to acquire it or forget it has not just a cognitive but also a performative significance. We shall not be able to treat power as independent of knowledge of power, or the distribution of power as independent of knowledge of that distribution. Many difficulties will have to be faced because of this.

[pp. 57–63]

**Power redescribed**

A society is a distribution of knowledge, part of which knowledge is self-referring knowledge of the nature of the society itself: the self-referring knowledge of the society includes the normative order of the society. Power, therefore, that is to say social power, must be an aspect or a characteristic of a distribution of knowledge, and indeed this is precisely how I propose to define it and conceive of it. Any specific distribution of knowledge confers a generalized capacity for action upon those individuals who carry and constitute it, and that capacity for action is their social power, the power of the society they constitute by bearing and sharing the knowledge in question. Social power is the added capacity for action that accrues to individuals through their constituting a distribution of knowledge and thereby a society.

Consider an isolated individual in a given environment. Such an individual possesses general capacities for action and can thus be said to possess power, the power to act that resides in his own body. It is not easy to specify what such power amounts to, but it is easy enough to notice losses and gains therein: loss of strength involves loss of power; gain of skill involves gain of power; and so on. Similarly, in a collection of isolated individuals in a given environment, all possess general capacities for action, and hence all possess power separately. The totality of the power possessed separately is roughly the sum of all the separate capacities for action of the different individuals, although there is little point in referring to such a total capacity for action since it is never exercised coherently.

Consider now a genuine society of individuals, who carry and constitute a distribution of knowledge and act and interact coherently on the basis of it. The total power available is considerably increased; overall capacity for action is larger and wider ranging than that of so many isolated individuals: things are now possible that were not possible before; other things may be done more quickly and with less effort. A shared distribution of knowledge confers a capacity to carry out routines and execute projects in concert, which is an added capacity for action, which is social power.

Much more power resides in a genuine society than resides in so many isolated individuals. But the additional power is never available equally to all the individuals of the society. As action becomes routinized and coherently ordered, so discretion in its direction tends to concentrate. Most individuals cease actively to exercise discretion over many of the actions of their own bodies, and a few acquire effective discretion over those actions. Those who gain discretion in the direction of the capacity for action of a society, discretion in the use of power, are those who in conventional usage are called 'powerful' individuals: in what follows I often refer to them as 'powers' or 'power-holders'. Although, in theory, an increase in the power of a society need not be accompanied by such a concentration of discretion in the use of that power, in practice the one thing is accompanied by the other. The elaboration of systems of concerted, routinized interaction tends to occur in association with a concentration of discretion in the use and direction of such systems and hence an unevenness in what is conventionally called the distribution of power.[5] Typically, some individuals constitute a set of routines and others direct it. As often as not some individuals predominate in constituting the entire social system of routines and other individuals predominate in directing its operations. The capacity for action in the society is made available to some much more than others. Routine social actions are directed predominantly at the discretion of a subset of members.

Social power *is* the capacity for action in a society, and hence is predominantly but not wholly identifiable as that which is routinely possible therein. Social power is *possessed* by those with discretion in the direction of social action, and hence predominantly by those with discretion in the use of routines. A routine may be thought of as a potential or capacity, to be set in operation or not, pointed this way or that, combined with other routines or kept apart, at the discretion of a controlling agent. Such an agent possesses social power. The possession of power is the possession of discretion: to gain power is to gain such discretion; to lose power is to lose such discretion. Such gains and losses are effectively gains and losses in the agent's capacity to act through the bodies of others. (In contrast, if an entire society is said to gain or lose power the implication is that it has gained or lost competences and capabilities, parts of its general capacity for action.)

We have here a very simple, embryonic account of power and its distribution. Later, it will have to be elaborated and modified, but it will do for the moment. Note that the account raises no new fundamental problems of the kind discussed in chapter 2 [this selection is from chapter 3; the previous selection is from chapter 2 – M.H.]. Successfully to exercise discretion in the direction of social actions is usually to exercise a known and recognized right. To accept direction in the performance of social actions is usually to take account of the existence of a right, and may involve recognition of the existence of sanctions in support of the right. The social order problems associated with the possession and use of power are the problems of the stability of calculative action under reflective awareness already considered. The problem of why a power is obeyed is no deeper than that of why a traffic-light is obeyed.

### Consequences of the redescription

How does this account compare with the common sense conceptions of power, and the sociological definitions and methods of measurement outlined in chapter 1? [Chapter 1 analyses 'common sense' views, as well as those of Dahl and Weber (among others) but especially Parsons – M.H.] It is actually very close indeed to common sense. As common sense requires, power is a potential or capacity which may or may not be used. Again as common sense requires, power is possessed, and its possessors have something real at their disposal. Where the present account goes beyond common sense is in specifying what that 'something real' actually is. Social power is the capacity for action embedded in the society, the capacity implicit in the existence of a shared distribution of knowledge, the capacity largely known to members as their own routine practices and competences. In equating the possession of power with the possession of discretion in the direction of these practices and competences the present account points to the source of the ability to get things done characteristic of powerful agents.

The present account also accords with some of the features of the most widely accepted sociological definitions of power. As it stands at the moment it treats discretion in the use of power as something attributable to an individual, and power itself as embedded in the social relationships surrounding that individual. Where the present account may represent an advance upon sociological orthodoxy is in its allowing power to be characterized independently of any particular effects it may have. Nor is this virtue bought at the price of empirical irrelevance. There are many empirical methods of identifying a capacity for action which do not need to refer to the effects of its use.

As far as the systematic identification and measurement of power via indicators is concerned, the present conception is incompatible with the 'event' approach. It asserts that power exists independently of particular acts of use and can be identified independently of its use. It is willing to assume, for example, despite the paucity of confirming events, that there is probably a person or persons with discretion to use our nuclear weapons. This discretion exists, indeed is exercised, all the time, but it will be manifested in an event only when a change in the mode or extent of use of the capacity is ordained.

There is no similar fundamental clash with the reputational approach to the measurement of power, since reputationalists accept that power is a capacity and seek to map its distribution by drawing upon members' beliefs about that distribution. There is indeed a close affinity between reputationalism and the present approach, although the two are not identical. Reputationalism takes the overall distribution of belief about power in a society as an *indicator* of the distribution of power itself. The present conception takes a distribution of knowledge in society to *define* the distribution of power itself. On the present conception a system of routines and an associated distribution of discretion in the use of those routines exist as a distribution of knowledge, simply that. To possess power an agent must be known to possess it.[6] That distribution of knowledge which makes the discretionary activities of the agent possible is not an indicator of the power he possesses but the very embodiment of that power: the capacity of the agent to generate action inheres in the relevant structure of knowledge, just as the capacity of the car engine to generate motion inheres in the structure of the engine.

On the face of it, this may seem to indicate the clear superiority of the reputational approach; for if the powerful are merely those who are believed to be powerful, then it must be impossible for an individual to be mistaken with regard to who has power, and this is counter-intuitive. It is, however, perfectly possible for individuals to be mistaken about power within the framework advocated here. Social power is identified as a distribution of *knowledge*, not of mere individual *belief*. Knowledge is accepted belief, generally held belief, belief routinely implicated in social action.[7] Recall how a society may know that red means stop at the traffic light. An individual may nonetheless believe that red means go, and only come to realize his mistake as he realizes what everyone else knows. Similarly, an agent may believe someone to be powerful and only realize his mistake as he realizes what everyone else knows.[8] Every individual in a society may be in error about some aspect of social power in this way, so that none of them truly knows where power lies overall, and yet power will lie, necessarily, by its nature, where it is known to lie.

Social power is not the simple product of individual beliefs. Reputationalists are entirely justified in taking such beliefs, even massive samples of such beliefs, as nothing more than indicators; for social power is constituted as a distribution of knowledge. Because power resides in a patterned distribution of knowledge over many people, it appears to any given individual as being external to himself. To a very good approximation that is a correct perception. But the perception is often rationalized by the claim that power is really there, independent not just of belief but of knowledge. Norms, institutions and social structures are often accorded a 'fully objective' reality in much the same way. The problem stems from an impoverished way of thinking, which allows attributes, characteristics and capacities to manifest a real and genuine existence if they reside within the individual or within external nature, but not if they reside within a number of interacting individuals. This impoverished conception allows for the subjective (that with a basis within the single individual), and for the objective (that with a basis in the natural external order), but fails to recognize that which is largely external to any individual yet wholly internal to the set of interacting individuals.[9] It fails to recognize intersubjective phenomena, and often ends up by mistreating them as analogues of fully 'external' natural phenomena.

Social power is precisely a feature of a set of interacting individuals. It is their general capacity for action, and exists as a distribution of knowledge which they carry and sustain. There is nothing obscure or opaque about such a conception; indeed it makes power visible and accessible in a way which other conceptions fail to do. It makes it clear, for example, why a society with a highly developed technology is, on the whole, more powerful than a similarly sized society which lacks one. It is curious how few sociological accounts of power are able to deal straight-forwardly with this simple contrast.

Power is embedded in society as a whole. But discretion in its use is usually distributed more selectively. Power structures or distributions of power are actually, in my view of the matter, distributions of discretion in the use of power. The possession of power is the possession of discretion in the use of that power. When one person is said to have more power than another it is a matter of the one having discretion over a greater capacity for action than the other. Nonetheless, it is cumbersome to refer always to discretion in the use of power when a reference simply to power will do, and I shall adopt the latter usage as a kind of shorthand much of the time. Indeed, I have occasionally lapsed into this idiom already, and referred to power when to be precise I should have referred to discretion in its use.

A power-holder holds power that actually resides in the capacity for action of others. He is like a driver who has at his disposal the 100 b.h.p. of his motor car. The power is in the car; it resides in the nature of the engine and so forth; but the driver has it at his disposal and may be said to possess it. Strictly analogously, the powerful agent possesses power in a sense, but the power he possesses resides in the social context and outside its possessor.

Perhaps all this will seem obvious, and the explicit discussion of it pedantic. Nonetheless, there is no harm in labouring the point. We are far too prone to think of power inhering in the individual who possesses it. Even when we explicitly recognize it as erroneous we are still liable to lapse back into this mode of thought in unguarded moments and to make mistaken inferences in consequence. Perhaps we should blame our history for the difficulty. In Europe, since feudal times or earlier we have made a fetish of hierarchy and assumed that all of value is concentrated at the 'top' of society. Power has radiated from heroic figures; they have glowed with it and illuminated everyone else. There could be no question that they might actually need anyone else. The lower orders were the dross through which the mythical knight cut swathes, *en route* to a true knightly opponent: all power was in the knight and his opponent; none in the hundreds who fell as he cut his path. Later, idealist doctrines conceived of spirit emanating from God into the higher realms of His Church and His society, animating human clay and forcing it into motion: brute matter was inert and incapable of independent action, becoming active only as spiritual power suffused into it, spiritual power mediated by God's agents and deputies at the head of society, spiritual power which radiated from above to activate and direct the clay below. Thus was initiated many centuries of controversy between a dominant idealism and materialism, and thus was defined and established the enduring ideological dimension of this controversy.[10]

Our very language and linguistic idiom are structured around this emanationist conception. Dominant figures are 'powerful', as if jugs of power have been poured down their throats. They 'possess' power, like the finery they wear and the silver in their dining-rooms. Power is 'divided' or 'distributed' amongst them like the spoils of war or the food at a banquet. Custom being what it is, one must needs employ this emanationist idiom, at least to some extent. But it remains the case that power, capacity for action, is actually right down there amongst the supposedly powerless, and that it is only discretion in use which is strongly concentrated at the higher levels of society.

The deposition of the Shah in 1979 marked the onset of revolutionary change in Iran. Many Western politicians and their advisors found it surprising. Many social scientists and political theorists found their ideas in need of revision. The Shah, after all, 'had' vast oil revenues; immense stocks of armaments and advanced weapons; formidable resources for coercion including the notorious secret police force Savak; a developed state apparatus and goodness knows what else. The clerics who engineered the Revolution 'had' very little. How then could the latter overwhelm the former? The problem, of course, is formulated wrongly. No doubt cartoonists were entitled to draw the Shah with bombs protruding from his hip-pocket and fighter-planes from his attaché case, but nobody should have thought in that way. What the Shah 'had' was a certain degree of discretion established in an overall distribution of knowledge. The fighter-planes and bombs were elsewhere. What had to be done was to shift the structure of discretion, a difficult enough task no doubt but much easier than to destroy the entire capacity for action embedded in an entire society. The Revolution shifted discretion and succeeded: this is all that successful revolutions ever have to do. We need to ensure that we have broken completely free of the residue of an emanationist view of power, and explicitly to recognize that power lies outside and beyond the power-holder is as good a way as any of doing this.[11]

## Notes

1 Some sociologists of knowledge will be inclined to say the same of physical objects of all kinds, to say, for example, that what makes an object a sphere is simply general agreement that it is a sphere. An important source of confusion needs to be eliminated here. Knowledge is indeed a matter of agreement in belief. Nonetheless, we cannot know that a ball is a sphere simply by looking to other people, who will be looking to yet other people, and so on endlessly. We must all first look to the ball and decide for ourselves as to its shape – and only then look to others to discern the agreed verdict, if there is one. We have practices for determining the shapes of things which we apply to the things themselves and which tell us (collectively) what shapes the things are. In contrast, our practices for determining the leadership statuses of persons we apply to the contexts around those persons, in fact to other persons applying similar practices. There is a difference between material objects classified by intrinsic or internal properties and social objects classified by reference to contexts, and persons in the contexts.

2 Our usual conception has natural knowledge referring clearly and directly to the external world without any element of self-reference. It will be evident already that natural knowledge cannot be represented adequately in this way, but the usual conception remains useful for purposes of contrast. Indeed, although systems of natural knowledge are not devoid of self-reference loops, that knowledge is nonetheless used to refer to independent entities.

3 R.K. Merton (1949) is seminal on self-fulfilling prophesies, but his treatment considers them only as errors which may become truths. Krishna (1971), in a curiously neglected paper, produces an account close to that offered here. See also Barnes (1983), Henshel (1978).

4 I say that an act of learning is 'performative' in that it makes something which may in turn be learned of. To make something generally involves the performance of an action or actions. Normally, we do not recognize learning, or indeed forgetting, as performances which may make or unmake states of affairs.

5 Overwhelmingly, in the sociological literature, 'power' is equated with what I call 'discretion in the use of power', and the notion of power as capacity for action is set aside in favour of the notion of power as capacity to gain compliance. This reflects the intense concern of many sociologists with relative standing in society, with themes such as 'equality', and their comparatively weaker concern with what societies can actually do.

6 That is, the agent's capacity for social action must be known under some description or other. Clearly, my, or our, concept of power need not be known in the agent's society. But what then is the 'power' which is being discussed here, in this book? Is it our conception of power, or is it that of agents in the relevant society? The answer is that 'power' in this book is our concept, a sociological concept, but defined as an aspect of their knowledge. Power in their society is not whatever they believe it to be, but what their knowledge makes it by fixing their capacity for action, and hence their power, on our definition. Any topic that is to be the subject of sociological enquiry, involving cross-cultural comparison and the systematic study of more than one social order, must be described 'externally', in the terminology of the sociologists' own society, even though it is constituted 'internally' by members of the society being studied. Power cannot be defined as whatever is taken to be power, and powerful persons as whichever agents are generally taken to be powerful, in the society being studied. If such a definition were to be adhered to consistently and uncompromisingly then power in a given society would be identified only when the written sign 'power' was encountered, or the phonetic sequence 'powr'. If, in a given society, with its own specific language and culture, 'power' just happened to be used entirely in relation to sausages, then a sociological account of power in that society would relate to sausages. Given that our interest concerns power, not sausages, what we have to do is to describe the focus of our interest using the terms and concepts of ordinary everyday English usage, using familiar examples and instances, and then to find as close an analogy as we can for that focus

in the discourse and practice of other societies. We have to start with an 'external' description or definition of something or other, and then look for aspects of practice in other societies which offer the strongest possible analogy with our description. Only in this way can sausage-like phenomena referred to with power-sounding noises reliably be avoided. In identifying power-like phenomena in other societies we are metaphorically extending use of our term 'power' away from its root or core use in the context of our own society. But once identified, these phenomena have to be described and understood more thoroughly, in richer detail: each needs to be analysed separately as it is constituted by ongoing practice in its specific context, with all its idiosyncrasies and unique features. We must identify powerful agents in alien societies by analogy with such agents as they are defined and exist in our own society: our own society must serve as the familiar system from which we extend our understanding to the unfamiliar systems of alien societies. But the phenomena we seek to understand in the alien society are constituted by alien practice, not ours, and exist as features of the alien distribution of knowledge.

7 The standard conception of knowledge as accepted or acceptable belief is being deployed here, the currently accepted usage of sociologists of knowledge. The alternative conception current in philosophy, according to which knowledge is belief justified and true in some absolute sense, is not employed in this book. Curiously, however, in the present context it probably does not make a great deal of difference which conception of knowledge is used, since the knowledge self-validates.

8 Needless to say, the mistaken belief that an agent has power in society may induce a given individual to obey that agent, and hence make the agent powerful in a certain sense. But such a mistaken belief may only be sustained if the individual believer is isolated from the society, and denied the possibility of learning of it and the supposedly powerful agent's actual role in it. It is tempting to suggest that power based on mistaken belief of this kind should not be considered to be social power, just as power based solely on larger biceps than the next person, or a longer sword, is best treated as other than social power. It must be remembered, however, that belief of this kind is 'mistaken' only in the sense of being deviant. The mistaken belief about an agent's power is much like the mistaken belief that green means stop at the traffic-light. Should such a 'mistaken' belief spread and be entertained more widely, should it become institutionalized, normal and hence true, then social power would have come into existence as an aspect of a reconstituted distribution of knowledge. Knowledge about power is more vulnerable to reconstitutions of this kind than knowledge about traffic-lights. See Barnes (1983) and also Wrong (1979, p. 9).

9 In the wider context of sociological theory this failure is evident in much of the controversy over the merits of methodological individualism.

10 This is a long and fascinating story, and an endless source of materials and problems for sociologists of knowledge. For one particularly intriguing part of the story see M.C. Jacob (1976) and J.R. Jacob (1977); for a sociological overview and further references see Shapin (1982).

11 The view that power is immanent in entities and emanates from entities is ubiquitous, and will remain so for reasons which I have yet to discuss. Innumerable further examples of such a view and its consequences could be cited. Durkheim's (1915) discussion of the power of the aboriginal totem is of great interest, as is Marx on the power of capital: 'The productive power developed by the labourer when working *in cooperation* is the *productive power of capital*. This productive power of associated labour is developed gratuitously, whenever the workmen are placed under given conditions, and it is capital that places them under such conditions. Because this power costs capital nothing, and because, on the other hand, the labourer himself does not develop it before his labour belongs to capital, it appears as a power with which capital is endowed by Nature – a productive power that is immanent in capital' (1867, p. 349).

## References

Barnes, B. (1983) 'Social Life as Bootstrapped Induction', *Sociology*, 17, 4, pp. 524–45.

Durkheim, E. (1915) *The Elementary Forms of the Religious Life*, tr. J.W. Swain, London, George Allen and Unwin.

Henshel, R.L. (1978) 'Self Altering Predictions', in Fowles, J. (ed.) *Handbook of Futures Research*, Westport, Greenwood Press.

Jacob, J.R. (1977) *Robert Boyle and the English Revolution*, New York, Franklin.

Jacob, M.C. (1976) *The Newtonians and the English Revolution, 1689–1720*, Hassocks, Harvester Press.

Krishna, D. (1971) ' "The Self-Fulfilling Prophesy" and the Nature of Society', *American Sociological Review*, 36, 4, pp. 1104–7.

Marx, K. (1867) *Capital*, English tr. 1958, London, Lawrence and Wishart.

Merton, R.K. (1949) 'The Self-Fulfilling Prophesy', in *Social Theory and Social Structure*, New York, Free Press.

Shapin, S. (1982) 'History of Science and its Sociological Reconstructions', *History of Science*, 20, pp. 157–211.

Wrong, D. (1979) *Power: Its Forms, Bases and Uses*, Oxford, Basil Blackwell.

# 7 Arendt

## Introduction

In the work of Parsons and Barnes we have encountered the mutually related ideas that power is not the same as violence, that it presupposes some level of consensus, and is something which is created through social interaction. In both instances these perceptions are empirically derived observations around which a non-normative social theory is constructed. In the work of Hannah Arendt similar observations are fused with a sophisticated civic republican normative political theory.

Arendt's political thought is dominated by her experience of politics – the rise and fall of Nazism, Stalinism, the foundation of the state of Israel, US politics from the 1940s to the 1970s, Hungary 1956 and the global student movements of the 1960s. Rather than developing a systemic vision of how politics should be constituted, Arendt's legacy consists, rather, of a number of insights with an overlapping coherence. Because her perception of the world is highly original, her use of terminology is often unique. These are elements which render it imperative, although difficult, to write a concise introduction to her thoughts on power.

At the most general level, the intellectual problem which preoccupied Arendt was how to theorize the distinction between perverted politics, anti-politics, totalitarianism, politics which prevent human flourishing, on the one hand, and a form of virtue politics which contributes to human freedom and emancipation, on the other. Power is central to the latter politics while violence and coercion characterize the former regimes. Her experience of Nazism is obviously central to this problematic.

The intellectually easy way of making sense of Nazism is to characterize it as a unique event – a momentary German descent into madness and evil. Such a solution is, of course, comforting because it means Nazism can be marginalized as 'their' problem. However, aside from being intellectually facile, a number of facts point against this. These include that: a) Marxism led to the totalitarianism of Stalinism which bears many affinities with Nazism; b) some of the atrocities committed by colonizing powers could be interpreted as precursors of the Holocaust (the British invented the concentration camp – although not the death camp); c) even a great philosopher (and personal friend), such as Martin Heidegger, could become a Nazi; and d) Eichmann, whose trial Arendt attended (Arendt 1959), was no ranting anti-Semite but, rather, an ordinary, banal, agent of modernity – a bureaucrat. Not only do these elements point away from the unique Germanness of Nazism but they also point towards the hypothesis that totalitarianism is a consequence of modernity, albeit, the darkest possible side of modernity.

In order to reconstitute political philosophy on a new footing, Arendt looked back to the Greeks for inspiration. The ancient Athenian idea that 'man' is naturally a political animal, was not an empirical observation but a moral assertion to the effect that politics was necessary in order to become fully human. Greek political thought is premised upon a teleological world-view whereby growth and change take place as a consequence of things realizing their ultimate ends, which constitute their true essence. An acorn becomes an oak because that is its ultimate end. As an empirical fact, a person (unlike an acorn) has the capacity to choose not to realize their true essence by not participating in politics. A person of 'private affairs' is not fully human, whereas citizenship entails the possibility of realizing full human development through political participation. Infamously, of course, in Athens this presupposed slavery and the nonenfranchisement of women in order to create the conditions whereby (male) citizens had the facility to use the labour of others in order to carry out their private, or economic, affairs.

One of the great errors of modern political philosophy is that essentially 'private affairs' have become central to normative concerns, while the vision of politics as end in itself has become lost. In both Marxism and Locke's variant of liberalism, labour (a means to an end) is sacred in itself. A communist society is one in which the state has withered away and the control of one's labour is equated with emancipation. In Locke's liberalism the bourgeois preoccupation with protection of private property (embodied labour) is central to the concept of social contract. Mistaking means for the end is also characteristic of utilitarian liberalism: the very basis of morality – utility – is not an end in itself but, rather, a means to an end. The net result is that the private aspects of humanity, which the ancient Greeks would have considered a means to an end, have become central to political thought while, simultaneously, the idea of human development through political participation has become entirely lost.

Private affairs are, in essence, things of the body (eating, sleeping and procreating), which constitute aspects of life that humans share with the animal world. Consequently, politics that concern themselves with these elements are an extension of nature and, as such, not 'real politics' in Arendt's sense of politics as an end in itself.

Totalitarianism is the ultimate example of this form of naturalistic antipolitics. At its core Nazism was based upon a form of biologism. The Holocaust was not simply age-old anti-Semitism writ large but was a racial theory of breeding whereby the ultimate aim of politics was a superior biological organism. Consistent with this, it was also characterized by a fatalism borrowed from the natural world. Nazism was not an arbitrary social construct but reflected the forces of nature (Darwinism) carried into politics – the Nazis were enacting the dictates of the laws of nature. As a consequence of this, the average Germans did not view themselves as responsible agents, free subjects, creating a new social order and, for this reason, they could not grasp the moral implications of their actions.

This vision of politics as an extension of nature is inextricably linked to the influence of science upon the ontology of modernity. Central to modern scientific endeavour is the insight that the universe is governed by laws which, once understood, turn common sense reality upon its head – Copernicus, Galileo and Darwin are paradigm examples. Carried into politics this constitutes a 'naturalization' of moral philosophy which is morally dangerous. Not only were Nazis obeying the laws of nature, but the 'scientific' nature of Marxism also contributed to Stalinism. Marx considered himself scientific in the manner of natural scientists. He turned philosophy upside-down by replacing reason with labour and, in so doing, discovering historical laws which had a force and inevitability which is analogical to natural laws. The terrifying result is a politics where all responsibility is lost to a scientific vision which is the embodiment of natural laws. Stalin saw himself as enacting the laws of historical materialism, hence, not as a moral agent of social change.

The horror of Nazism and Stalinism was further augmented by another error derived from this inability to distinguish politics from 'natural' activities. This was the conception of politics as another form of 'work', like architecture or carpentry (a mistaken perception which goes back to Plato). According to this vision, politics result in human creations similar to buildings or chairs. In the hands of Hitler and Stalin this vision legitimizes the moulding of a new society – totalitarianism is merely a 'job of work'. Just as trees have to be felled in order to construct chairs and build houses so, too, humans have to be changed and sacrificed toward the creation of a new artifice, the 'body politic'. This new creation is both an extension of nature in that it is the culmination of natural laws, and is also constructed using the logic which humans use in their natural activities.

If we think of political power as the energy and vitality created by virtuous politics and, if totalitarianism is an extension of nature, then the opposition between political power and violence is both empirical and normative. Violence, which acts upon the human body, is the antipolitics of nature extended into social life, whereas political power is the opposite. Violence, but not political power, flows from the barrel of a gun. If a political regime continually uses violence to gain compliance this is the manifestation of the absence of power, of 'real politics' and of moral foundations.

While liberal democratic regimes, such as the United States, do not suffer from the terrifying 'natural' logic of totalitarianism, they do not embody the political vitality of the type which Arendt was advocating. One of the key characteristics of modernity is the discovery (and normative endorsement) of 'society', the private realm, as the key to human flourishing. The modern bourgeois is essentially a private individual for whom the state is a necessary evil for the preservation of law and order – an ordered society in which commerce can flourish. This lends itself to an ethic of moral introspection. In itself, this does not lead to totalitarianism, although it contributes to an inability to resist it and a failure to engage in politics for the purposes of human development. Reflecting upon her own experience of political inactivity as a youth, Arendt argued that one of the factors that made the Jews such easy victims was that they were essentially apolitical – they were preoccupied by society. With regard to Heidegger, the philosophical mistake which allowed him to embrace Nazism was that his philosophy was entirely introspective. For Arendt, moral philosophy and ethics do not come from inside the mind but from an active engagement with other members of a political community. In this regard, Socrates is the ultimate political philosopher. He did not attempt to construct political philosophy from an introspective insight but, rather, realized himself through engaging in political activity in the form of dialogue with others. Heidegger escaped from the world while, in contrast, Socrates created moral philosophy by engagement with the ideas of others. Citizenship should be an active engagement in dialogues with others, not an escape from them. Consequently, the state should not simply be viewed as an assembled set of laws and institutions constructed to allow people to get on with their private business (as in liberalism) but should be constructed for the purpose of dialogic interaction.

Humans have a potential for freedom in politics. What makes the human world different from that of nature is the ability which humans have to make unpredictable things happen. Revolutions are paradigmatic in this regard. They are a manifestation of a human bid for freedom against any form of historical determinacy. This fact makes the idea of revolution as a consequence of historical determinism (as in Marxism) an ultimate tragedy – a moment of freedom turned into enslavement. The American revolution was another manifestation of the human capacity for freedom but this time it was partly successful because it was inspired by the desire for meaningful citizenship. The motivation was not primarily economic; consequently, it was not a mistaken quest to be subject to nature – although capitalism and consumerism have taken much of the 'political' meaning out of American citizenship. The revolutions which demonstrate the human capacity for freedom to the greatest extent are the Hungarian revolution of 1956, some of the student movements, and Gandhi's passive resistance. Particularly in the latter, the distinction between true political power, derived from political activity, and violence can be seen. Violence was the only resource left to the British if they had wished to retain possession of India. Since Arendt's death (1975), the events of 1989 and Mandela's leadership against apartheid in South Africa also demonstrate the distinction between power and violence.

On a normative level, Arendt's dialogic concept of citizenship owes much to a phenomenological and existentialist world view. Humans make sense of the world by imposing meaning upon it. This meaning is, in turn, a reflection of some perception of truth. If this truth is considered external to the self (in nature) all moral responsibility is lost. Furthermore, if reality turns out not to correspond with this vision, then the external world, at least if it consists of humans, can be shaped – people can be killed or resocialized. On the other hand, if the logical implication of the 'localness' of our interpretative horizons is taken seriously, then truth is an emergent property derived through reflecting upon the diversity of possible interpretations. Because we, as humans, have the potential for freedom we have the potential to change ourselves and, consequently, attain responsibility for being the way we are – a responsibility which is evaded in the naturalistic determinism of totalitarianism. The only way forward is not an escape into our particular interpretative horizon (philosophical introspection) but a life of active citizenship where interpretative horizons are continually reflected against each other. The source of moral philosophy is not that there exists such a thing as a single human nature but that people are essentially different. Human diversity is not simply to be tolerated but constitutes the premise from which human development is possible. The consequence is power. A power which is truly political in the strong sense that, not only is it created by society (as in Barnes and Parsons), but is derived from the unique capacity of humans to act in concert through dialogue and, as a consequence, to transform themselves by realizing their true essences.

Arendt's work on power was produced over thirty years ago. Yet, her theoretical fusion of power with a lack of foundationalism and social philosophy of the self is probably more pertinent today than when she wrote. Globalization, postmodernity, social movements and identity politics make her vision of citizenship relevant. Identity politics is about the meaning of self as a political project and the whole idea of empowerment, so fashionable among social movements, concerns power as the ability to act in concert.

**Further reading**

At the time of publication Arendt's analysis of power was not widely commented upon. The first serious analysis was Habermas' article 'Hannah Arendt's Communications Concept of Power' (Habermas 1977). In the light of the obvious similarities between ideal speech and Arendt's dialogic moral philosophy, it is interesting to note that Habermas was highly critical of Arendt's consensual view of power. More recently, Gehard Goehler has used Arendt's analysis of power to develop a contrast between transitive and intransitive power (see Goverde *et al.* 2000).

Aside from the excerpt which follows, Arendt also analyses power in *The Human Condition* (1958, pp. 200–5).

The best general introduction to Hannah Arendt's political philosophy is Canovan *Hannah Arendt: A Reinterpretation* (1992). Other useful points of departure include Bradshaw (1989), Hansen (1993) and Benhabib (1988).

# From *ON VIOLENCE*
## Hannah Arendt

*Power* corresponds to the human ability not just to act but to act in concert. Power is never the property of an individual; it belongs to a group and remains in existence only so long as the group keeps together. When we say of somebody that he is 'in power' we actually refer to his being empowered by a certain number of people to act in their name. The moment the group, from which the power originated to begin with (*potestas in populo*, without a people or group there is no power), disappears, 'his power' also vanishes. In current usage, when we speak of a 'powerful man' or a 'powerful personality', we already use the word 'power' metaphorically; what we refer to without metaphor is 'strength'.

*Strength* unequivocally designates something in the singular, an individual entity; it is the property inherent in an object or person and belongs to its character, which may prove itself in relation to other things or persons, but is essentially independent of them. The strength of even the strongest individual can always be overpowered by the many, who often will combine for no other purpose than to ruin strength precisely because of its peculiar independence. The almost instinctive hostility of the many toward the one has always, from Plato to Nietzsche, been ascribed to resentment, to the envy of the weak for the strong, but this psychological interpretation misses the point. It is in the nature of a group and its power to turn against independence, the property of individual strength.

*Force*, which we often use in daily speech as a synonym for violence, especially if violence serves as a means of coercion, should be reserved, in terminological language, for the 'forces of nature' or the 'force of circumstances' (*la force des choses*), that is, to indicate the energy released by physical or social movements.

*Authority*, relating to the most elusive of these phenomena and therefore, as a term, most frequently abused,[1] can be vested in persons – there is such a thing as personal authority, as, for instance, in the relation between parent and child, between teacher and pupil – or it can be vested in offices, as, for instance, in the Roman senate (*auctoritas in senatu*) or in the hierarchical offices of the Church (a priest can grant valid absolution even though he is drunk). Its hallmark is unquestioning recognition by those who are asked to obey; neither coercion nor persuasion is needed. (A father can lose his authority either by beating his child or by starting to argue with him, that is, either by behaving to him like a tyrant or by treating him as an equal.) To remain in authority requires respect for the person or the office. The greatest enemy of authority, therefore, is contempt, and the surest way to undermine it is laughter.[2]

*Violence*, finally, as I have said, is distinguished by its instrumental character. Phenomenologically, it is close to strength, since the implements of violence, like all other tools, are designed and used for the purpose of multiplying natural strength until, in the last stage of their development, they can substitute for it.

It is perhaps not superfluous to add that these distinctions, though by no means arbitrary, hardly ever correspond to watertight compartments in the real world, from which nevertheless they are drawn. Thus institutionalized power in organized communities often appears in the guise of authority, demanding instant, unquestioning recognition; no society could function without it. (A small, and still isolated, incident in New York shows what can happen if authentic authority in social relations has broken down to the point where it cannot work any longer even in its derivative, purely functional form. A minor mishap in the subway system – the doors on a train failed to operate – turned into a serious shutdown on the line lasting four hours and involving more than fifty thousand passengers, because when the transit authorities asked the passengers to leave the defective train, they simply refused.)[3] Moreover, nothing, as we shall see, is more common than the combination of violence and power, nothing less frequent than to find them in their pure and therefore extreme form. From this, it does not follow that authority, power, and violence are all the same.

Still it must be admitted that it is particularly tempting to think of power in terms of command and obedience, and hence to equate power with violence, in a discussion of what actually is only one of power's special cases – namely, the power of government. Since in foreign relations as well as domestic affairs violence appears as a last resort to keep the power structure intact against individual challengers – the foreign enemy, the native criminal – it looks indeed as though violence were the prerequisite of power and power nothing but a façade, the velvet glove which either conceals the iron hand or will turn out to belong to a paper tiger. On closer inspection, though, this notion loses much of its plausibility. For our purpose, the gap between theory and reality is perhaps best illustrated by the phenomenon of revolution.

Since the beginning of the century theoreticians of revolution have told us that the chances of revolution have significantly decreased in proportion to the increased destructive capacities of weapons at the unique disposition of governments.[4] The history of the last seventy years, with its extraordinary record of successful and unsuccessful revolutions, tells a different story. Were people mad who even tried against such overwhelming odds? And, leaving out instances of full success, how can even a temporary success be explained? The fact is that the gap between state-owned means of violence and what people can muster by themselves – from beer bottles to Molotov cocktails and guns – has always been so enormous that technical improvements make hardly any difference. Textbook instructions on 'how to make a revolution' in a step-by-step progression from dissent to conspiracy, from resistance to armed uprising, are all based on the mistaken notion that revolutions are 'made'. In a contest of violence against violence the superiority of the government has always been absolute; but this superiority lasts only as long as the power structure of the government is intact – that is, as long as commands are obeyed and the army or police forces are prepared to use their weapons. When this is no longer the case, the situation changes abruptly. Not only is the rebellion not put down, but the arms themselves change hands – sometimes, as in the Hungarian revolution, within a few hours. (We should know about such things after all these years of futile fighting in Vietnam, where for a long time, before getting massive Russian aid, the National Liberation Front fought us with weapons that were made in the United States.) Only after this has happened, when the disintegration of the government in power has permitted the rebels to arm themselves, can one speak of an 'armed uprising', which often does not take place at all or occurs when it is no longer necessary. Where commands are no longer obeyed, the means of violence are of no use; and the question of this obedience is not decided by the command-obedience relation but by opinion, and, of course, by the number of those who share it. Everything depends on the power behind the violence. The sudden dramatic breakdown of power that ushers in revolutions reveals in a flash how civil obedience – to laws, to rulers, to institutions – is but the outward manifestation of support and consent.

Where power has disintegrated, revolutions are possible but not necessary. We know of many instances when utterly impotent regimes were permitted to continue in existence for long periods of time – either because there was no one to test their strength and reveal their weakness or because they were lucky enough not to be engaged in war and suffer defeat. Disintegration often becomes manifest only in direct confrontation; and even then, when power is already in the street, some group of men prepared for such an eventuality is needed to pick it up and assume responsibility. We have recently witnessed how it did not take more than the relatively harmless, essentially nonviolent French students' rebellion to reveal the vulnerability of the whole political system, which rapidly disintegrated before the astonished eyes of the young rebels. Unknowingly they had tested it; they intended only to challenge the ossified university system, and down came the system of governmental power, together with that of the huge party bureaucracies – *'une sorte de désintégration de toutes les hiérarchies'*.[5] It was a textbook case of a revolutionary situation[6] that did not develop into a revolution because there was nobody, least of all the students, prepared to seize power and the responsibility that goes with it. Nobody except, of course, de Gaulle. Nothing was more characteristic of the seriousness of the situation than his appeal to the army, his journey to see Massu and the generals in Germany, a walk to Canossa, if there ever was one, in view of what had happened only a few years before. But what he sought and received was support, not obedience, and the means were not commands but concessions.[7] If commands had been enough, he would never have had to leave Paris.

No government exclusively based on the means of violence has ever existed. Even the totalitarian ruler, whose chief instrument of rule is torture, needs a power basis – the secret police and its net of informers. Only the development of robot soldiers, which, as previously mentioned, would eliminate the human factor completely and, conceivably, permit one man with a push button to destroy whomever he pleased, could change this fundamental ascendancy of power over violence. Even the most despotic domination we know of, the rule of master over slaves, who always outnumbered him, did not rest on superior means of coercion as such, but on a superior organization of power – that is, on the organized solidarity of the masters.[8] Single men without others to support them never have enough power to use violence successfully. Hence, in domestic affairs, violence functions as the last resort of power against criminals or rebels – that is, against single individuals who, as it were, refuse to be overpowered by the consensus of the majority. And as for actual warfare, we have seen in Vietnam how an enormous superiority in the means of violence can become helpless if confronted with an ill-equipped but well-organized opponent who is much more powerful. This lesson, to be sure, was there to be learned from the history of guerrilla warfare, which is at least as old as the defeat in Spain of Napoleon's still-unvanquished army.

To switch for a moment to conceptual language: Power is indeed of the essence of all government, but violence is not. Violence is by nature instrumental; like all means, it always stands in need of guidance and justification through the end it pursues. And what needs justification by something else cannot be the essence of anything. The end of war – end taken in its twofold meaning – is peace or victory; but to the question. And what is the end of peace? There is no answer. Peace is an absolute, even though in recorded history periods of warfare have nearly always outlasted periods of peace. Power is in the same category; it is, as they say, 'an end in itself'. (This, of course, is not to deny that governments pursue policies and employ their power to achieve prescribed goals. But the power structure itself precedes and outlasts all aims, so that power, far from being the means to an end, is actually the very condition enabling a group of people to think and act in terms of the means-end category.) And since government is essentially organized and institutionalized power, the current question What is the end of government? does not make much sense either. The answer will be either question-begging – to enable men to live together – or dangerously utopian – to promote happiness or to realize a classless society or some other non-political ideal, which if tried out in earnest cannot but end in some kind of tyranny.

Power needs no justification, being inherent in the very existence of political communities; what it does need is legitimacy. The common treatment of these two words as synonyms is no less misleading and confusing than the current equation of obedience and support. Power springs up whenever people get together and act in concert, but it derives its legitimacy from the initial getting together rather than from any action that then may follow. Legitimacy, when challenged, bases itself on an appeal to the past, while justification relates to an end that lies in the future. Violence can be justifiable, but it never will be legitimate. Its justification loses in plausibility the farther its intended end recedes into the future. No one questions the use of violence in self-defense, because the danger is not only clear but also present, and the end justifying the means is immediate.

Power and violence, though they are distinct phenomena, usually appear together. Wherever they are combined, power, we have found, is the primary and predominant factor. The situation, however, is entirely different when we deal with them in their pure states – as, for instance, with foreign invasion and occupation. We saw that the current equation of violence with power rests on government's being understood as domination of man over man by means of violence. If a foreign conqueror is confronted by an impotent government and by a nation unused to the exercise of political power, it is easy for him to achieve such domination. In all other cases the difficulties are great indeed, and the occupying invader will try immediately to establish Quisling governments, that is, to find a native power base to support his dominion. The head-on clash between Russian tanks and the entirely nonviolent resistance of the Czechoslovak people is a textbook case of a confrontation between violence and power in their pure states. But while domination in such an instance is difficult to achieve, it is not impossible. Violence, we must remember, does not depend on numbers or opinions, but on implements, and the implements of violence, as I mentioned before, like all other tools, increase and multiply human strength. Those who oppose violence with mere power will soon find that they are confronted not by men but by men's artifacts, whose inhumanity and destructive effectiveness increase in proportion to the distance separating the opponents. Violence can always destroy power; out of the barrel of a gun grows the most effective command, resulting in the most instant and perfect obedience. What never can grow out of it is power.

In a head-on clash between violence and power, the outcome is hardly in doubt. If Gandhi's enormously powerful and successful strategy of nonviolent resistance had met with a different enemy – Stalin's Russia, Hitler's Germany, even prewar Japan, instead of England – the outcome would not have been decolonization, but massacre and submission. However, England in India and France in Algeria had good reasons for their restraint. Rule by sheer violence comes into play where power is being lost; it is precisely the shrinking power of the Russian government, internally and externally, that became manifest in its 'solution' of the Czechoslovak problem – just as it was the shrinking power of European imperialism that became manifest in the alternative between decolonization and massacre. To substitute violence for power can bring victory, but the price is very high; for it is not only paid by the vanquished, it is also paid by the victor in terms of his own power. This is especially true when the victor happens to enjoy domestically the blessings of constitutional government. Henry Steele Commager is entirely right: 'If we subvert world order and destroy world peace we must inevitably subvert and destroy our own political institutions first.'[9] The much-feared boomerang effect of the 'government of subject races' (Lord Cromer) on the home government during the imperialist era meant that rule by violence in faraway lands would end by affecting the government of England, that the last 'subject race' would be the English themselves. The recent gas attack on the campus at Berkeley, where not just tear gas but also another gas, 'outlawed by the Geneva Convention and used by the Army to flush out guerrillas in Vietnam', was laid down while gas-masked Guardsmen stopped anybody and everybody 'from fleeing the gassed area', is an excellent example of this 'backlash' phenomenon. It has often been said that impotence breeds violence, and psychologically this is quite true, at least of persons possessing natural strength, moral or physical. Politically speaking, the point is that loss of power becomes a temptation to substitute violence for power – in 1968 during the Democratic convention in Chicago we could watch this process on television[10] – and that violence itself results in impotence. Where violence is no longer backed and restrained by power, the well-known reversal in reckoning with means and ends has taken place. The means, the means of destruction, now determine the end – with the consequence that the end will be the destruction of all power.

Nowhere is the self-defeating factor in the victory of violence over power more evident than in the use of terror to maintain domination, about whose weird successes and eventual failures we know perhaps more than any generation before us. Terror is not the same as violence; it is, rather, the form of government that comes into being when violence, having destroyed all power, does not abdicate but, on the contrary, remains in full control. It has often been noticed that the effectiveness of terror depends almost entirely on the degree of social atomization. Every kind of organized opposition must disappear before the full force of terror can be let loose. This atomization –

an outrageously pale, academic word for the horror it implies – is maintained and intensified through the ubiquity of the informer, who can be literally omnipresent because he no longer is merely a professional agent in the pay of the police but potentially every person one comes into contact with. How such a fully developed police state is established and how it works – or, rather, how nothing works where it holds sway – can now be learned in Aleksandr I. Solzhenitsyn's *The First Circle*, which will probably remain one of the masterpieces of twentieth-century literature and certainly contains the best documentation on Stalin's regime in existence.[11] The decisive difference between totalitarian domination, based on terror, and tyrannies and dictatorships, established by violence, is that the former turns not only against its enemies but against its friends and supporters as well, being afraid of all power, even the power of its friends. The climax of terror is reached when the police state begins to devour its own children, when yesterday's executioner becomes today's victim. And this is also the moment when power disappears entirely. There exist now a great many plausible explanations for the de-Stalinization of Russia – none, I believe, so compelling as the realization by the Stalinist functionaries themselves that a continuation of the regime would lead, not to an insurrection, against which terror is indeed the best safeguard, but to paralysis of the whole country.

To sum up: politically speaking, it is insufficient to say that power and violence are not the same. Power and violence are opposites; where the one rules absolutely, the other is absent. Violence appears where power is in jeopardy, but left to its own course it ends in power's disappearance. This implies that it is not correct to think of the opposite of violence as nonviolence; to speak of nonviolent power is actually redundant. Violence can destroy power; it is utterly incapable of creating it. Hegel's and Marx's great trust in the dialectial 'power of negation', by virtue of which opposites do not destroy but smoothly develop into each other because contradictions promote and do not paralyze development, rests on a much older philosophical prejudice: that evil is no more than a privative *modus* of the good, that good can come out of evil; that, in short, evil is but a temporary manifestation of a still-hidden good. Such time-honored opinions have become dangerous. They are shared by many who have never heard of Hegel or Marx, for the simple reason that they inspire hope and dispel fear – a treacherous hope used to dispel legitimate fear. By this, I do not mean to equate violence with evil; I only want to stress that violence cannot be derived from its opposite, which is power, and that in order to understand it for what it is, we shall have to examine its roots and nature.

## Notes

1 There is such a thing as authoritarian government, but it certainly has nothing in common with tyranny, dictatorship, or totalitarian rule. For a discussion of the historical background and

political significance of the term, see my 'What is Authority?' in *Between Past and Future: Exercises in Political Thought*, New York, 1968, and Part I of Karl-Heinz Lübke's valuable study, *Auctoritas bei Augustin*, Stuttgart, 1968, with extensive bibliography.

2 Sheldon Wolin and John Schaar, in 'Berkeley: The Battle of People's Park', *New York Review of Books*, June 19, 1969, are entirely right: 'The rules are being broken because University authorities, administrators and faculty alike, have lost the respect of many of the students.' They then conclude, 'When authority leaves, power enters.' This too is true, but, I am afraid, not quite in the sense they meant it. What entered first at Berkeley was student power, obviously the strongest power on every campus simply because of the students' superior numbers. It was in order to break this power that authorities resorted to violence, and it is precisely because the university is essentially an institution based on authority, and therefore in need of respect, that it finds it so difficult to deal with power in nonviolent terms. The university today calls upon the police for protection exactly as the Catholic church used to do before the separation of state and church forced it to rely on authority alone. It is perhaps more than an oddity that the severest crisis of the church as an institution should coincide with the severest crisis in the history of the university, the only secular institution still based on authority. Both may indeed be ascribed to 'the progressing explosion of the atom 'obedience' whose stability was allegedly eternal', as Heinrich Böll remarked of the crisis in the churches. See 'Es wird immer später', in *Antwort an Sacharow*, Zürich, 1969.

3 See the New York *Times*, January 4, 1969, pp. 1 and 29.

4 Thus Franz Borkenau, reflecting on the defeat of the Spanish revolution, states: 'In this tremendous contrast with previous revolutions one fact is reflected. Before these latter years, counterrevolution usually depended upon the support of reactionary powers, which were technically and intellectually inferior to the forces of revolution. This has changed with the advent of fascism. Now, every revolution is likely to meet the attack of the most modern, most efficient, most ruthless machinery yet in existence. It means that the age of revolutions free to evolve according to their own laws is over.' This was written more than thirty years ago (*The Spanish Cockpit*, London, 1937: Ann Arbor, 1963, pp. 288–9) and is now quoted with approval by Noam Chomsky (*American Power and the New Mandarins*, New York, 1969, p. 310). He believes that American and French intervention in the civil war in Vietnam proves Borkenau's prediction accurate, 'with substitution of "liberal imperialism" for "fascism"'. I think that this example is rather apt to prove the opposite.

5 Raymond Aron, *La Révolution Introuvable*, Paris, 1968, p. 41.

6 Stephen Spender, *The Year of the Young Rebels*, New York, 1969, p. 56, disagrees: 'What was so much more apparent than the revolutionary situation [was] the nonrevolutionary one.' It may be 'difficult to think of a revolution taking place when . . . everyone looks particularly good humoured', but this is what usually happens in the beginning of revolutions – during the early great ecstasy of fraternity.

7 There is some controversy on the purpose of de Gaulle's visit. The evidence of the events themselves seems to suggest that the price he had to pay for the army's support was public rehabilitation of his enemies – amnesty for General Salan, return of Bidault, return also of Colonel Lacheroy, sometimes called the 'torturer in Algeria'. Not much seems to be known about the negotiations. One is tempted to think that the recent rehabilitation of Pétain, again glorified as the 'victor of Verdun', and, more importantly, de Gaulle's incredible, blatantly lying statement immediately after his return, blaming the Communist party for what the French now call *les événements*, were part of the bargain. God knows, the only reproach the government could have addressed to the Communist party and the trade unions was that they lacked the power to prevent *les événements*.

8 In ancient Greece, such an organization of power was the polis, whose chief merit, according to Xenophon, was that it permitted the 'citizens to act as bodyguards to one another against slaves and criminals so that none of the citizens may die a violent death'. (*Hiero*, IV, 3.)

9 'Can We Limit Presidential Power?' in *The New Republic*, April 6, 1968.

10 It would be interesting to know if, and to what an extent, the alarming rate of unsolved crimes is matched not only by the well-known spectacular rise in criminal offenses but also by a definite increase in police brutality. The recently published *Uniform Crime Report for the United States*, by J. Edgar Hoover (Federal Bureau of Investigation, United States Department of Justice, 1967), gives no indication how many crimes are actually solved – as distinguished from 'cleared by arrest' – but does mention in the Summary that police solutions of serious crimes declined in

1967 by 8%. Only 21.7 (or 21.9)% of all crimes are 'cleared by arrest', and of these only 75% could be turned over to the courts, where only about 60% of the indicted were found guilty! Hence, the odds in favor of the criminal are so high that the constant rise in criminal offenses seems only natural. Whatever the causes for the spectacular decline of police efficiency, the decline of police power is evident, and with it the likelihood of brutality increases. Students and other demonstrators are like sitting ducks for police who have become used to hardly ever catching a criminal.

A comparison of the situation with that of other countries is difficult because of the different statistical methods employed. Still, it appears that, though the rise of undetected crime seems to be a fairly general problem, it has nowhere reached such alarming proportions as in America. In Paris, for instance, the rate of solved crimes declined from 62% in 1967 to 56% in 1968, in Germany from 73.4% in 1954 to 52.2% in 1967, and in Sweden 41% of crimes were solved in 1967. (See 'Deutsche Polizei', in *Der Spiegel*, April 7, 1967.)

11 Solzhenitsyn shows in concrete detail how attempts at a rational economic development were wrecked by Stalin's methods, and one hopes this book will put to rest the myth that terror and the enormous losses in human lives were the price that had to be paid for rapid industrialization of the country. Rapid progress was made after Stalin's death, and what is striking in Russia today is that the country is still backward in comparison not only with the West but also with most of the satellite countries. In Russia there seems not much illusion left on this point, if there ever was any. The younger generation, especially the veterans of the Second World War, knows very well that only a miracle saved Russia from defeat in 1941, and that this miracle was the brutal fact that the enemy turned out to be even worse than the native ruler. What then turned the scales was that police terror abated under the pressure of the national emergency; the people, left to themselves, could again gather together and generate enough power to defeat the foreign invader. When they returned from prisoner-of-war camps or from occupation duty they were promptly sent for long years to labor and concentration camps in order to break them of the habits of freedom. It is precisely this generation, which tasted freedom during the war and terror afterward, that is challenging the tyranny of the present regime.

# 8 Giddens

## Introduction

Anthony Giddens' analysis of power is inextricably bound up with his theory of structuration, which is one of the most influential perspectives in contemporary social thought. For this reason it is necessary to understand the basics of the theory of structuration in order to appreciate his theory of power.

The theory of structuration was developed in response to the dualism, or division, which exists between subject-centred and object-centred social theories. The former refers to social theories which place primary emphasis upon individuals as creators of society, whereas objectivist theories focus upon society itself and conceptualize agents as the effect of social order. Subjectivist perspectives include hermeneutics, rational choice and phenomenology, while objectivist theories include structuralism and functionalism. This division between subject and object-centred social theories is a reflection of a Cartesian world view where the problem of philosophy is an epistemological one of building a bridge between thinking subject and external reality – at it simplest, the problem for Descartes was to understand how it is we can be certain that the world 'out there' is as we see it; after all it could all be a dream. In place of this division between 'self' and the 'world', Giddens substitutes a Heideggerian perspective where the thinking subject is part of the world by constituting it in the act of 'being'. The world is as it is because we interpret that way in our 'being-in-the-world' – the act of seeing a tree as a tree is, in reality, an extension of our existence; the 'treeness' of the tree is not pregiven by the 'world-out-there' but is part of the interpretive horizon which constitutes our being. Translated into social theory terms, social structures (social object and conceptual equivalent of the 'world-out-there') exist in the moment that they are reproduced by agents while, simultaneously, social agents constitute themselves as such through structured action. This moment of the reproduction of agency and structure is structuration.

In Heidegger there are two levels of being: one which all things that 'are' have in common while the other is the 'being' of particular things. The former is constituted by being in time and space (all things exist in time and space) while the particular being of things is constituted through their meaning givenness. In the moment of structuration all structures are reproduced in time and space – Giddens prefers to write 'time-space' as the two are inseparable. The existence of structure in the moment of structuration is only a *virtual* or momentary existence in time-space. Structures do not have a permanent existence outside the act of structuration – which is distinct from structuralism where social structures are described in a manner which suggests they exist externally to social action. In the moment of structural reproduction – structuration – the individual orders or 'binds' time-space; an act which constitutes the most basic and shared aspect of all agency. At this level structuration constitutes the realization of agency through the ability of actors to order their actions in time-space. Hence, neither structure nor agency is ontologically separable, consequently, agency and structure constitute a dualism rather than a duality.

While structures exist only in the moment of structuration, in aggregate form they have a more enduring existence as social systems. As an assembled set of structures, systems have a more 'solid' time-space existence by 'bracketing' patterns of time-spaces which are continually being recreated. This is akin to a television image which is composed of dots (structures) which exist only momentarily but which as a totality constitute a picture (system). The momentary actions whereby individuals order their everyday lives, in aggregate form, constitute elements of the social system of which they are a part. The moment of going to work or buying a pound of sugar are acts of structuration (ordering of time-space) which in their small way contribute to the reproduction of the capitalist system as a whole.

While the common existence of all structures is as an ordering of time-space, this is not how they are experienced (we do not experience going to work or buying a pound of sugar primarily as 'binding' time-space) and this experiential element constitutes the particular existence of structures. Structures exist through meaning. The particularity of an ordered act, and hence its structuredness, is derived from its meaning. This meaning is singular to the act but simultaneously systemic, by virtue of the fact that meaning is relational. As was argued by de Saussure, the meaning of words is not derived by a direct relationship between the word and the thing or idea which the word denotes (the signifier does not derive its meaning from the signified), but, rather, from the systemic context of other words from which it differs. To take the example of chess as a simplified language where each piece constitutes the equivalent of a word (and each move is like speaking a word), it would be impossible to explain the meaning of a pawn, for instance, without explaining its relationship to and difference from the other pieces. A pawn gains its meaning from the game of chess as a system. Similarly, going to work is only meaningful relative to particular systemically constituted relations of production.

The meaningfulness of structured acts is both a reflection of our ontology and, simultaneously, the source of our ability to reproduce structure in the future.

Outside of the moment of reproduction social structure exists as social knowledge. What enables social actors to reproduce structure is their knowledge of social life. This knowledge is both the knowledge which they use to order their own actions and make sense of the actions of others in an interactive context. Because social life is so complex, the knowledge of structure is largely of a tacit and taken-for-granted nature. When actors speak a language fluently, interact competently or see reality in a meaning-given familiar way, the knowledge which enables them to do so is of a practical, unevaluated, taken-for-granted, character.

The individuals who reproduce structures are not unreflective agents driven by social forces – the 'dopes' of functionalism or structurally overdetermined beings of structuralism. They are purposive agents realizing projects which have been reflectively thought out and are actualized through the tacit knowledge which enables them to 'go on' in a practical and socially competent manner. Giddens refers to the latter knowledge as 'practical consciousness knowledge' while the former more consciously reflective knowledge is termed 'discursive consciousness knowledge'. At this very moment I am presenting Giddens' theory discursively while, simultaneously, using my practical consciousness of the English language in order to accomplish this act. My intention is to explain Giddens but the unintentional effect of my action is to reproduce the structures of the English language. Social structures are the unintended consequence of purposive action. Buying a pound of sugar is a discursively constructed task which is made possible by practical consciousness knowledge of structure (the value of money and nature of shops) which unintentionally contributes to the structuredness of the capitalist system.

Under the influence of theories of psychology – Freud, R.D. Laing and Erik Erikson in particular – Giddens argues that practical consciousness knowledge is central to the maintenance of ontological security. For an agent to feel secure in themselves they must be able to take the world for granted, and this presupposes that meaning is stable. If this does not happen anxiety comes flooding through from the unconscious. Because of the relationship between ontological security and stability of meaning, apparently trivial (from the perspective of discursive consciousness knowledge) disruptions of social life can be experienced as quite threatening. For instance, part of our practical consciousness knowledge includes knowledge of the appropriate distance to stand from another person when in conversation. Try next time you are conversing with someone to stand just that bit closer than normal – both you and the person with whom you conversing will find it disturbing! The fact that appropriate reproduction of the structuredness of interaction is conducive to ontological security constitutes an important aspect of structural constraint. Actors are not structurally constrained because they are dupes but because routinization, hence structuration, is conducive to ontological security. One of the first acts of socialization is when an infant gains the necessary ontological security to let his or her mother out of sight because of a taken-for-granted knowledge that she always returns. The fact that structures are constraining is a prerequisite to explaining their continuity over time. If structures could be changed at will they would cease to exist – imagine a game or language in which you could change the rules as you went along!

Following Wittgenstein, Giddens argues that practical consciousness knowledge is a knowledge of rules with constitutive and regulative characteristics which also have the type of infinite applicability associated with a mathematical formula. To take the instance given of spatial distantiation in interaction, this may be expressed constitutively ('In England it is customary to stand so far apart'), or regulatively ('You should not stand that close!') but neither is adequate to explain the infinitely fine variations on rule following appropriate to different social circumstances – formal settings, informal ones, between the sexes, in lifts, restaurants, etc. The type of analytical rule which best captures this image of a rule applicable to a variety of circumstances is a mathematical formula. A formula has the quality of rails laid to infinity – remember, you have the capacity to construct and interpret an infinite variety of sentences, none of which you have never heard or said before, in the same way that the mathematical statement of the law of gravity applies to objects you have never seen before. Nevertheless, social rules also have a regulative aspect (try standing too close to strangers in lifts and joining their conversation into the bargain!) which is of theoretical significance because it ties structures to legitimacy and domination. When a social rule is broken it is frequently considered an infraction and, as such, is subject to sanctions unlike a violation of the law of gravity, should it occur.

Not only do structures offer ontological security but they also facilitate agency. The meaning-givenness, hence structuredness, of the world-out-there makes it possible for us to accomplish acts which we could not otherwise do. This facility is the essence of the concept of power.[1] Agency is possible only because of resources which exist only as a potential facility because they are meaning given. The resources of a wealthy person or of a political leader exist only because of the meaning of money and authority. As the carrier of meaning, structure is central to the constitution of power resources. When a social agent acts, he or she draws upon certain resources to bring about certain situations which would not otherwise have occurred. When action takes place, an agent uses structures which, in the moment of being drawn upon, are recreated and, simultaneously with this act of structuration, the individual is facilitated in producing effects. In short, power is generated by structural reproduction which takes place in the moment of agency.

Not only does the existence of structure presuppose constraint but so also does agency. If structures were changed at will, collaborative interaction would be an impossibility. Furthermore, since resources presuppose meaning and meaning entails constraint, resources presuppose constraint. Consequently, social structures can be conceptualized as both enabling and constraining social action. When actors realize agency they structure their action by drawing upon tacit knowledge, they reproduce structure, and, in so doing, unintentionally reproduce resources and intentionally produce the power necessary for the realization of their specific projects. Following the constitutive and regulative aspects of rule following, structures have both a signifying and legitimizing aspect both of which facilitate agency, hence, power.

The above is a somewhat simplified but, hopefully sufficient, account of Giddens' theory of structuration to give the reader the conceptual tools necessary to make sense of the short selection from *The Constitution of Society* which follows. The theory of power is a significant one. As with the consensual power theorists, Giddens provides us with a theory of how power is created. It is not zero-sum, consequently, not always contrary to the interests of the less powerful. His theorization of practical consciousness knowledge has strong affinity with Barnes' analysis, the most significant difference being Barnes' use of Kuhn's image of paradigms and Giddens' use of Wittgenstein on rule following.[2] A more theoretically significant difference between the two is Giddens' more complex and sophisticated view of agency. However, while Giddens' theory allows us to make sense of many aspects of power it can be argued that his view of structural reproduction is too consensual. As we shall see in the analysis of Foucault, meaning is substantially more contested than Giddens' theory provides conceptual space for.

## Further reading

The quantity of material written on and by Giddens is truly immense. With respect to primary material, as a first port of call, I would recommend: *The Constitution of Society* (1984), *Contemporary Critique of Historical Materialism* (1985) and *The Giddens Reader* (1993). Secondary commentary includes: Barbalet (1987), Cohen (1989), Haugaard (1992 and 1997a), Craib (1992), Held and Thompson (1989), Layder (1985 and 1987), Callinicos (1985). Crespi (1992) is an interesting alternative to Giddens' theory of power.

## Notes

1 It has to be acknowledged that Giddens is not entirely consistent in this regard. In some instances Giddens is at pains to emphasize that '[I]t is mistaken . . . to treat power *itself* as a resource as many theorists of power do. Resources are the media through which power is exercised. . . .' (Giddens 1979 p. 91) and '. . . power is *instantiated* in action . . .' (Giddens 1979 p. 91 italics not original, see also 1984 p. 16). However, at variance with this, he also writes: 'power does not come into being only when being "exercised" . . . This is important, because we can talk of power being "*stored up*" for future occasion of use' (Giddens 1976 pp. 111–12 emphasis not original). In other words, he sometimes follows Dahl in linking power to its exercise yet elsewhere he equates it with resources – there are many more instances of this inconsistency. However, as the former usage is substantially more consistent with his theory of structuration than the latter, I have taken the liberty of presenting Giddens as if he clearly distinguished between power and power resources.

2 However, this may not be as significant a divergence as it appears. Kuhn also incorporates the idea of rule following into the concept of paradigms (see Kuhn 1970 pp. 188–9).

# From *THE CONSTITUTION OF SOCIETY*

## Anthony Giddens

[pp. 14–17]

### Agency and power

What is the nature of the logical connection between action and power? Although the ramifications of the issue are complex, the basic relation involved can easily be pointed to. To be able to 'act otherwise' means being able to intervene in the world, or to refrain from such intervention, with the effect of influencing a specific process or state of affairs. This presumes that to be an agent is to be able to deploy (chronically, in the flow of daily life) a range of causal powers, including that of influencing those deployed by others. Action depends upon the capability of the individual to 'make a difference' to a pre-existing state of affairs or course of events. An agent ceases to be such if he or she loses the capability to 'make a difference', that is, to exercise some sort of power. Many interesting cases for social analysis centre upon the margins of what can count as action – where the power of the individual is confined by a range of specifiable circumstances.[1] But it is of the first importance to recognize that circumstances of social constraint in which individuals 'have no choice' are not to be equated with the dissolution of action as such. To 'have no choice' does not mean that action has been replaced by reaction (in the way in which a person blinks when a rapid movement is made near the eyes). This might appear so obvious as not to need saying. But some very prominent schools of social theory, associated mainly with objectivism and with 'structural sociology', have not acknowledged the distinction. They have supposed that constraints operate like forces in nature, as if to 'have no choice' were equivalent to being driven irresistibly and uncomprehendingly by mechanical pressures (see pp. 211–13 [not included – M.H.]).

Expressing these observations in another way, we can say that action logically involves power in the sense of transformative capacity. In this sense, the most all-embracing meaning of 'power', power is logically prior to subjectivity, to the constitution of the reflexive monitoring of conduct. It is worth emphasizing this because conceptions of power in the social sciences tend faithfully to reflect the dualism of subject and object referred to previously. Thus 'power' is very often defined in terms of intent or the will, as the capacity to achieve desired and intended outcomes. Other writers by contrast, including both Parsons and Foucault, see power as above all a property of society or the social community.

The point is not to eliminate one of these types of conception at the expense of the other, but to express their relation as a feature of the duality of structure. In my opinion, Bachrach and Baratz are right when, in their well-known discussion of the matter, they say that there are two 'faces' of power (not three, as Lukes declares).[2] They represent these as the capability of actors to enact decisions which they favour on the one hand and the 'mobilization of bias' that is built into institutions on the other. This is not wholly satisfactory because it preserves a zero-sum conception of power. Rather than using their terminology we can express the duality of structure in power relations in the following way. Resources (focused via signification and legitimation) are structured properties of social systems, drawn upon and reproduced by knowledgeable agents in the course of interaction. Power is not intrinsically connected to the achievement of sectional interests. In this conception the use of power characterizes not specific types of conduct but all action, and power is not itself a resource. Resources are media through which power is exercised, as a routine element of the instantiation of conduct in social reproduction. We should not conceive of the structures of domination built into social institutions as in some way grinding out 'docile bodies' who behave like the automata suggested by objectivist social science. Power within social systems which enjoy some continuity over time and space presumes regularized relations of autonomy and dependence between actors or collectivities in contexts of social interaction. But all forms of dependence offer some resources whereby those who are subordinate can influence the activities of their superiors. This is what I call the *dialectic of control* in social systems.

## Structure, structuration

Let me now move to the core of structuration theory: the concepts of 'structure', 'system' and 'duality of structure'. The notion of structure (or 'social structure'), of course, is very prominent in the writings of most functionalist authors and has lent its name to the traditions of 'structuralism'. But in neither instance is this conceptualized in a fashion best suited to the demands of social theory. Functionalist authors and their critics have given much more attention to the idea of 'function' than to that of 'structure', and consequently the latter has tended to be used as a received notion. But there can be no doubt about how 'structure' is usually understood by functionalists and, indeed, by the vast majority of social analysts – as some kind of 'patterning' of social relations or social phenomena. This is often naively conceived of in terms of visual imagery, akin to the skeleton or morphology of an organism or to the girders of a building. Such conceptions are closely connected to the dualism of subject and social object: 'structure' here appears as 'external' to human action, as a source of constraint on the free initiative of the independently constituted subject. As conceptualized in structuralist and post-structuralist thought, on the other hand, the notion of structure is more interesting. Here it is characteristically thought of not as a patterning of presences but as an intersection of presence and absence; underlying codes have to be inferred from surface manifestations.

These two ideas of structure might seem at first sight to have nothing to do with one another, but in fact each relates to important aspects of the structuring of social relations, aspects which, in the theory of structuration, are grasped by recognizing a differentiation between the concepts of 'structure' and 'system'. In analysing social relations we have to acknowledge both a syntagmatic dimension, the patterning of social relations in time-space involving the reproduction of situated practices, and a paradigmatic dimension, involving a virtual order of 'modes of structuring' recursively implicated in such reproduction. In structuralist traditions there is usually ambiguity over whether structures refer to a matrix of admissible transformations within a set or to rules of transformation governing the matrix. I treat structure, in its most elemental meaning at least, as referring to such rules (and resources). It is misleading, however, to speak of 'rules of transformation' because all rules are inherently transformational. Structure thus refers, in social analysis, to the structuring properties allowing the 'binding' of time-space in social systems, the properties which make it possible for discernibly similar social practices to exist across varying spans of time and space and which lend them 'systemic' form. To say that structure is a 'virtual order' of transformative relations means that social systems, as reproduced social practices, do not have 'structures' but rather exhibit 'structural properties' and that structure exists, as time-space presence, only in its instantiations in such practices and as memory traces orienting the conduct of knowledgeable human agents. This does not prevent us from conceiving of structural properties as hierarchically organized in terms of the time-space extension of the practices they recursively organize. The most deeply embedded structural properties, implicated in the reproduction of societal totalities, I call *structural principles*. Those practices which have the greatest time-space extension within such totalities can be referred to as *institutions*.

[pp. 28–34]

## Forms of institution

The division of rules into modes of signifying or meaning constitution and normative sanctions, together with the concept of resources – fundamental to the conceptualization of power – carries various implications which need to be spelled out.[3] What I call the 'modalities' of structuration serve to clarify the main dimensions of the duality of structure in interaction, relating the knowledgeable capacities of agents to structural features. Actors draw upon the modalities of structuration in the reproduction of systems of interaction,

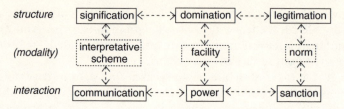

Figure 1

by the same token reconstituting their structural properties. The communication of meaning in interaction, it should be stressed, is separable only analytically from the operation of normative sanctions. This is obvious, for example, in so far as language use is itself sanctioned by the very nature of its 'public' character.[4] The very identification of acts or of aspects of interaction – their accurate description, as grounded hermeneutically in the capability of an observer to 'go on' in a form of life – implies the interlacing of meaning, normative elements and power. This is most evident in the not infrequent contexts of social life where what social phenomena 'are', how they are aptly described, is contested. Awareness of such contestation, of divergent and overlapping characterizations of activity, is an essential part of 'knowing a form of life', although this is not made clear in the writings of authors such as Winch, who treat forms of life as both unified and consensual.[5]

The dimensions of the duality of structure are portrayed in Figure 1.[6] Human actors are not only able to monitor their activities and those of others in the regularity of day-to-day conduct; they are also able to 'monitor that monitoring' in discursive consciousness. 'Interpretative schemes' are the modes of typification incorporated within actors' stocks of knowledge, applied reflexively in the sustaining of communication. The stocks of knowledge which actors draw upon in the production and reproduction of interaction are the same as those whereby they are able to make accounts, offer reasons, etc.[7] The communication of meaning, as with all aspects of the contextuality of action, does not have to be seen merely as happening 'in' time-space. Agents routinely incorporate temporal and spatial features of encounters in processes of meaning constitution. Communication, as a general element of interaction, is a more inclusive concept than communicative intent (i.e. what an actor 'means' to say or do). There are once more two forms of reductionism to be avoided here. Some philosophers have tried to derive overall theories of meaning or communication from communicative intent; others, by contrast, have supposed that communicative intent is at best marginal to the constitution of the meaningful qualities of interaction, 'meaning' being governed by the structural ordering of sign systems.

In the theory of structuration, however, these are regarded as of equivalent interest and importance, aspects of a duality rather than a mutually exclusive dualism.

The idea of 'accountability' in everyday English gives cogent expression to the intersection of interpretative schemes and norms. To be 'accountable' for one's activities is both to explicate the reasons for them and to supply the normative grounds whereby they may be 'justified'. Normative components of interaction always centre upon relations between the rights and obligations 'expected' of those participating in a range of interaction contexts. Formal codes of conduct, as, for example, those enshrined in law (in contemporary societies at least), usually express some sort of claimed symmetry between rights and obligations, the one being the justification of the other. But no such symmetry necessarily exists in practice, a phenomenon which it is important to emphasize, since both the 'normative functionalism' of Parsons and the 'structuralist Marxism' of Althusser exaggerates the degree to which normative obligations are 'internalized' by the members of societies.[8] Neither standpoint incorporates a theory of action which recognizes human beings as knowledgeable agents, reflexively monitoring the flow of interaction with one another. When social systems are conceived of primarily from the point of view of the 'social object', the emphasis comes to be placed upon the pervasive influence of a normatively co-ordinated legitimate order as an overall determinant or 'programmer' of social conduct. Such a perspective masks the fact that the normative elements of social systems are contingent claims which have to be sustained and 'made to count' through the effective mobilization of sanctions in the contexts of actual encounters. Normative sanctions express structural asymmetries of domination, and the relations of those 'nominally subject to them may be of various sorts other than expressions of the commitments those norms supposedly engender.

Concentration upon the analysis of the structural properties of social systems, it should be stressed, is a valid procedure only if it is recognized as placing an *epoché* upon – holding in suspension – reflexively monitored social conduct. Under such an *epoché* we may distinguish three structural dimensions of social systems: signification, domination and legitimation. The connotations of the analysis of these structural properties are indicated in the table below. The theory of coding presumed in the study of structures of signification must look to the extraordinary advances in semiotics which have been pioneered in recent decades. At the same time we have to guard against the association of semiotics with structuralism and with the shortcomings of the latter in respect of the analysis of human agency. Signs 'exist' only as the medium and outcome of communicative processes in interaction. Structuralist conceptions of language, in common with similar discussions of legitimation, tend to take signs as the given properties of speaking and writing rather than examining their recursive grounding in the communication of meaning.

| Structure(s) | Theoretical Domain | Institutional Order |
|---|---|---|
| Signification | Theory of coding | Symbolic orders/modes of discourse |
| Domination | Theory of resource authorization | Political institutions |
|  | Theory of resource allocation | Economic institutions |
| Legitimation | Theory of normative regulation | Legal institutions |

Structures of signification always have to be grasped in connection with domination and legitimation. Once more this bears upon the pervasive influence of power in social life. There are certain positions which have to be carefully skirted here. Thus some relevant issues have been brought to the fore by Habermas's critique of Gadamer and ensuing debates.[9] Among other things, Habermas criticized Gadamer's conception of linguistically saturated 'traditions' for failing to demonstrate that frames of meaning incorporate differentials of power. The criticism is valid enough, but Habermas sought to develop the point in the direction of showing the significance of 'systematically distorted' forms of communication. He has not been able on this basis, however, satisfactorily to integrate the concept of power with an institutional theory. 'Domination' is not the same as 'systematically distorted' structures of signification because domination – as I conceive of it – is the very condition of existence of codes of signification.[10] 'Domination' and 'power' cannot be thought of only in terms of asymmetries of distribution but have to be recognized as inherent in social association (or, I would say, in human action as such). Thus – and here we must also reckon with the implications of the writings of Foucault – power is not an inherently noxious phenomenon, not just the capacity to 'say no'; nor can domination be 'transcended' in some kind of putative society of the future, as has been the characteristic aspiration of at least some strands of socialist thought.

What are the connotations of the claim that the semantic has priority over the semiotic rather than vice versa? They can be spelled out, I think, through a comparison of structuralist and post-structuralist conceptions of meaning on the one hand, and that which can be derived from the later Wittgenstein on the other.[11] The foundation of a theory of meaning in 'difference' in which, following Saussure, there are no 'positive values' leads almost inevitably to a view accentuating the primacy of the semiotic. The field of signs, the grids of meaning, are created by the ordered nature of differences which comprise codes. The 'retreat into the code' – whence it is difficult or impossible to re-emerge into the world of activity and event – is a characteristic tactic adopted by structuralist and post-structuralist authors. Such a retreat, however, is not necessary at all if we understand the relational character of the codes that generate meaning to be located in the ordering of social practices, in the very capacity to 'go on' in the multiplicity of contexts of social activity. This is a discovery which Wittgenstein himself surely made, albeit against a very different philosophical backdrop, when he abandoned some of the main parameters of his early writings. Whereas his earlier analysis of language and meaning terminates in paradox – a sort of Indian rope trick, pulling up the ladder after it has been climbed – his later view hugs the ground of routine social practices. Even the most complicated semiotic relations have a grounding in the semantic properties generated by the rule-governed properties of daily activities.

In the terminology indicated in the table above the 'signs' implied in 'signification' should not be equated with 'symbols'. Many writers treat the two terms as equivalent, but I regard symbols, interpolated within symbolic orders, as one main dimension of the 'clustering' of institutions.[12] Symbols coagulate the 'surpluses of meaning' implied in the polyvalent character of signs; they conjoin those intersections of codes which are especially rich in diverse forms of meaning association, operating along the axes of metaphor and metonymy. Symbolic orders and associated modes of discourse are a major institutional locus of ideology. However, in the theory of structuration ideology is not a particular 'type' of symbolic order or form of discourse. One cannot separate off 'ideological discourse' from 'science', for example. Ideology' refers only to those asymmetries of domination which connect signification to the legitimation of sectional interests.[13]

We can see from the case of ideology that structures of signification are separable only analytically either from domination and from legitimation. Domination depends upon the mobilization of two distinguishable types of resource. Allocative resources refer to capabilities – or, more accurately, to forms of transformative capacity – generating command over objects, goods or material phenomena. Authoritative resources refer to types of transformative capacity generating command over persons or actors. Some forms of allocative resources (such as raw materials, land, etc.) might seem to have a 'real existence' in a way which I have claimed that structural properties as a whole do not. In the sense of having a time-space 'presence', in a certain way such is obviously the case. But their 'materiality' does not affect the fact that such phenomena become resources, in the manner in which I apply that term here, only when incorporated within processes of structuration. The transformational character of resources is logically equivalent to, as well as inherently bound up with the instantiation of, that of codes and normative sanctions.

The classification of institutional orders offered above depends upon resisting what has sometimes been called 'substantivist' concepts of 'economic', 'political' and other institutions. We can conceive of the relationships involved as follows:

| | |
|---|---|
| S-D-L | Symbolic orders/modes of discourse |
| D (auth)-S-L | Political institutions |
| D (alloc)-S-L | Economic institutions |
| L-D-S | Legal institutions |

where S = signification, D = domination, L = legitimation

'Substantivist' conceptions presume concrete institutional differentiation of these various orders. That is to say, it is held, for example, that 'politics' exists only in societies having distinct forms of state apparatus and so on. But the work of anthropologists demonstrates effectively enough that there are 'political' phenomena – to do with the ordering of authority relations – in all societies. The same applies to the other institutional orders. We have to be particularly careful in conceptualizing the 'economic', even having made the point that this does not presuppose the existence of a clearly differentiated 'economy'. There has been a strong tendency in some of the literature of economics to 'read back' into traditional cultures concepts that have meaning only in the context of market economies. The 'economic' cannot properly be defined, in a generic way at least, as concerning struggles for scarce resources.[14] This is somewhat like defining power solely by reference to sectional struggles. It is not scarcity of resources as such, far less struggles or sectional divisions centred upon distribution, that is the main feature of the 'economic'. Rather, the sphere of the 'economic' is given by the inherently constitutive role of allocative resources in the structuration of societal totalities. Other cautionary notes should be added here. If it is held that all societies are haunted by the possibility of material scarcity, it is only a short step to the supposition that conflicts over scarce resources make up the fundamental motor of social change, as is presumed in at least some versions of historical materialism and in many non-Marxist theories also. But this presumption is both logically wanting, usually depending upon a specious form of functional reasoning, and empirically false.[15]

[pp. 256–62]

## Change and power

Anyone who reflects upon the phrase 'human beings make history', particularly within the broader scope of Marx's writings, is inevitably led to consider questions of conflict and power. For, in Marx's view, the making of history is done not just in relation to the natural world but also through the struggles which some human beings wage against others in circumstances of domination. A deconstruction of historical materialism means discarding some of the main parameters in terms of which Marx organized his work. But in the case of power and its relation to conflict – somewhat paradoxically – it is an effort of reconstruction that is needed. Let me look at why that should be.

A relatively superficial, although by no means unimportant, objection to Marx's various observations on conflict and domination might be that they greatly exaggerate the significance of class struggle and class relations in history. Whatever 'history' is, it is certainly not primarily 'the history of class struggles', and domination is not founded in some generalized sense upon class domination, even in the 'last instance'. A more fundamental problem, however, is the concept of power presumed, although rarely given direct expression, in Marx's writings. For Marx associates power (and the state, as its embodiment) with schism, with a division of interest between classes. Power is thus linked to conflict and is represented as characteristic only of class societies. While Marx was able to develop a formidable analysis and indictment of domination in class-divided and capitalist societies, socialism appears as a society in which domination is transcended. In this respect Marxism and socialism more generally, as Durkheim discerned,[16] share a good deal in common with their nineteenth-century opponent, utilitarian liberalism. Each participates in a 'flight from power', and each ties power inherently to conflict. Since in Marx power is grounded in class conflict, it poses no specific threat in the anticipated society of the future: class division will be overcome as part and parcel of the initiation of that society. For liberals, however, who deny the possibility of achieving such a revolutionary reorganization of society, the threat of power is omnipresent. Power signals the existence of conflict and the potentiality of oppression; thus the state should be organized in such a way as to minimize its scope, taming it through parcelling it out in a democratic fashion.[17]

A reconstructed theory of power would begin from the premise that such views are untenable. Power is not necessarily linked with conflict in the sense of either division of interest or active struggle, and power is not inherently oppressive. The barrage of critical attacks which Parsons's analysis of power provoked[18] should not allow us to ignore the basic correctives which he helped to introduce into the literature. Power is the capacity to achieve outcomes; whether or not these are connected to purely sectional interests is not germane to its definition. Power is not, as such, an obstacle to freedom or emancipation but is their very medium – although it would be foolish, of course, to ignore its constraining properties. The existence of power presumes structures of domination whereby power that 'flows smoothly' in processes of social reproduction (and is, as it were, 'unseen') operates. The development of force or its threat is thus not the type case of the use of power. Blood and fury, the heat of battle, direct confrontation of rival camps – these are not necessarily the historical conjunctures in which the most far-reaching effects of power are either felt or established.

These things having been said, however, it is necessary to separate structuration theory from both of the variant pathways trodden by Parsons and by Foucault. In associating power with so-called 'collective goals', Parsons sacrifices part of the insight that the concept of power has no intrinsic relation to that of interest. If power has no logical connection with the realization of sectional interests, neither does it have any with the realization of collective interests or 'goals'. More substantively, Parsons's concentration upon normative consensus as the foundation of the integration of societies leads him seriously to underestimate the significance of contestation of norms; and of the manifold circumstances in which force and violence, and the fear of them, are directly involved in the sanctioning of action.[19] Foucault's rehabilitation of the concept of power, on the other hand, is achieved only at the cost of succumbing to a Nietzschean strain in which power is seemingly prior to truth. In Foucault, as in Parsons, although for different reasons, power is not related to a satisfactory account of agency and knowledgeability as involved in the 'making of history'.

In order to develop these various observations further, I want to discuss several aspects of power within the conceptual framework of the theory of structuration. A primary concern must be the issue of how power is generated. We have to take very seriously indeed Parsons's contention that power is not a static quantity but expandable in relation to divergent forms of system property, although I shall not adopt the ideas he worked out in pursuing the implications of this view.

The notion of time-space distanciation, I propose, connects in a very direct way with the theory of power. In exploring this connection we can elaborate some of the main outlines of domination as an expandable property of social systems. Power, I have described in the opening chapter, is generated in and through the reproduction of structures of domination. The resources which constitute structures of domination are of two sorts – allocative and authoritative. Any co-ordination of social systems across time and space necessarily involves a definite combination of these two types of resources, which can be classified as below:

| *Allocative Resources* | *Authoritative Resources* |
|---|---|
| 1 Material features of the environment (raw materials, material power sources) | 1 Organization of social time-space (temporal-spatial constitution of paths and regions) |
| 2 Means of material production/ reproduction (instruments of production, technology) | 2 Production/reproduction of the body (organization and relation of human beings in mutual association) |
| 3 Produced goods (artifacts created by the interaction of 1 and 2) | 3 Organization of life chances (constitution of chances of self-development and self-expression) |

These are not fixed resources; they form the media of the expandable character of power in different types of society. Evolutionary theories have always tended to give priority to those in the left-hand column, the various sorts of material resources employed in 'adaptation' to the environment. But, as my preceding discussion has indicated, authoritative resources are every bit as 'infrastructural' as allocative resources are. I do not at all want to deny the influence of the surrounding natural habitat upon patterns of social life, the impact that major sorts of technological invention may have or the relevance of the material power resources that may be available and harnessed to human use. But it has long been conventional to emphasize these, and I think it very important to demonstrate the parallel significance of authoritative resources. For, like Marxism, we are still prisoners of the Victorian era in so far as we look first of all to the transformation of the material world as the generic motive force of human history.

It is clear that the garnering of allocative resources is closely involved with time-space distanciation, the continuity of societies across time and space and thus the generation of power. Hunters and gatherers have little means of storing food and other material requisites and utilize the given storehouse of nature in providing for their needs the year around. They are in a very immediate fashion dependent upon the bounty of nature – a fact which, however, does not necessarily imply impoverishment. Moreover, ritual, ceremonial and religious activities ordinarily loom much larger than do the relatively limited material requirements of daily life. In agrarian communities at least some kind of productive technology is employed, and the storehouse which the natural world provides is augmented in various ways that facilitate the 'stretching' of social relations across time-space. That is to say, different seasonal crops are grown, products are stored where this is technically possible, fields are allowed to lie fallow to protect the productive capacity of the society in the long term and so on. In class-divided societies there may be a further development of agrarian *per capita* productivity, although this is certainly by no means always the case as compared with that of smaller peasant communities. Irrigation schemes and other technical innovations usually do not so much increase average productivity as regularize and co-ordinate production. In larger agrarian states storage of food and other perishable goods becomes of the first importance. In modern capitalism purchase and sale of manufactured foods is as fundamental to social existence as the exchange of the whole gamut of other commodities: it is not an exaggeration to say that the expansion of capitalism to form a new world economy would not have been possible without the development of a range of techniques for the preservation and storage of perishable goods, particularly food.[20] But then capitalism also generates, and is dependent upon, rates of technical innovation, coupled with a massive utilization of natural resources, which are on an altogether different plane from anything which went before.

Described in such a manner, human history would sound (and has very often been made to sound) like a sequence of enlargements of the 'forces of production'. The augmenting of material resources *is* fundamental to the expansion of power, but allocative resources cannot be developed without the transmutation of authoritative resources, and the latter are undoubtedly at least as important in providing 'levers' of social change as the former. The organization of social time-space refers to the forms of regionalization within (and across) societies in terms of which the time-space paths of daily life are constituted. Hunting-and-gathering communities, and the relatively few instances of larger nomadic cultures, are the only societies whose overall time-space organization implies regular movement of the whole group through time-space. 'Only' is misplaced here. For hunting-and-gathering societies have been the most typical form of human social organization upon this earth until very recent times. Spatial fixity – the pinning down of locales to definite 'built environments', especially in the form of cities – marks a new departure in human history.

The second category of authoritative resources, the production/reproduction of the body, should not be assimilated to category 2 in the classification of allocative resources. Of course, the means of material repro-duction are necessary to the reproduction of the human organism; for most of human history material limits of various sorts have kept down the overall growth of population. But the *co-ordination* of numbers of people together in a society and their reproduction over time is an authorita-tive resource of a fundamental sort. Power does not, of course, depend solely upon the size of a population brought together within an administrative order. But size of system organization does make a very significant con-tribution to the generation of power. The various constraining and enabling characteristics of the body that I discussed in chapter 3 [not included – M.H.] are relevant here – indeed, they are the basis upon which administrative resources in this sense are to be analysed. However, we have to add to these the category of life chances, a phenomenon again by no means sheerly dependent upon the material productivity of a society. The nature and scale of power generated by authoritative resources depends not only on the arrangement of bodies, regionalized on time-space paths, but also on the life chances open to agents. 'Life chances' means, in the first instance, the chances of sheer survival for human beings in different forms and regions of society. But it also connotes the whole range of aptitudes and capabilities which Weber had in mind when he introduced the term. Take just one example: mass literacy. A literate population can be mobilized, and can mobilize itself, across time-space in ways quite distinct from those pertaining within largely oral cultures.

I have already referred to the importance of storage of allocative resources as a medium of the expansion of domination, a theme familiar in the litera-ture of evolutionary theory. Much less familiar, but of essential importance to the engendering of power, is the storage of authoritative resources. 'Storage' is a medium of 'binding' time-space involving, on the level of action, the knowledgeable management of a projected future and recall of an elapsed past. In oral cultures human memory is virtually the sole repository of information storage. However, as we have seen, memory (or recall) is to be understood not only in relation to the psychological qualities of individual agents but also as inhering in the recursiveness of institutional reproduction. Storage here already presumes modes of time-space control, as well as a phenomenal experience of 'lived time', and the 'container' that stores authoritative resources is the community itself.

The storage of authoritative and allocative resources may be understood as involving the retention and control of information or knowledge whereby social relations are perpetuated across time-space. Storage presumes *media* of information representation, modes of information *retrieval* or recall and, as with all power resources, modes of its dissemination. Notches on wood, written lists, books, files, films, tapes – all these are media of information storage of widely varying capacity and detail. All depend for their retrieval upon the recall capacities of the human memory but also upon skills of interpretation that may be possessed by only a minority within any given population. The dissemination of stored information is, of course, influenced by the technology available for its production. The existence of mechanized printing, for instance, conditions what forms of information are available and who can make use of it. Moreover, the character of the information medium – as McLuhan, that now forgotten prophet, consistently stressed – directly influences the nature of the social relations which it helps to organize.[21]

It is the containers which store allocative and authoritative resources that generate the major types of structural principle in the constitution of societies indicated in the previous chapter. Information storage, I wish to claim, is a fundamental phenomenon permitting time-space distanciation and a thread that ties together the various sorts of allocative and authoritative resources in reproduced structures of domination. The city, which only ever develops in conjunction with the elaboration of new forms of information storage, above all writing, is the container or 'crucible of power' upon which the formation of class-divided societies depends. Although I have quoted it before elsewhere,[22] I cannot resist mentioning again here Mumford's observation, which summarizes this point in an exemplary way:

> the first beginning of urban life, the first time the city proper becomes visible, was marked by a sudden increase in power in every department and by a magnification of the role of power itself in the affairs of men. A variety of institutions had hitherto existed separately, bringing their numbers together in a common meeting place, at seasonable intervals: the hunters' camp, the sacred monument or shrine, the palaeolithic ritual cave, the neolithic agricultural village – all of these coalesced in a bigger meeting place, the city. . . . The original form of

this container lasted for some six thousand years; only a few centuries ago did it begin to break up.[23]

It began to break up, one should say, under the impact of modern capitalism, which developed in societal contexts that helped to form, and were shaped by, a new type of power container: the nation-state. The disappearance of city walls is a process convergent with the consolidation of a highly elaborated type of administrative order operating within tightly defined territorial boundaries of its own.

## Abbreviations

CCHM: *A Contemporary Critique of Historical Materialism:* Vol. I (London: Macmillan / Berkeley: University of California Press, 1981).
CPST: *Central Problems in Social Theory* (London: Macmillan / Berkeley: University of California Press, 1979).
NRSM: *New Rules of Sociological Method* (London: Hutchinson / New York: Basic Books, 1976).
SSPT: *Studies in Social and Political Theory* (London Hutchinson / New York: Basic Books, 1977).

## Notes

1 For a further development of this point, see 'Power, the dialectic of control and class structuration', in Anthony Giddens and Gavin Mackenzie, *Social Class and The Division of Labour* (Cambridge: Cambridge University Press, 1982).
2 Peter Bachrach and Morton S. Baratz, 'The two faces of power', *American Political Science Review*, vol. 56, 1962; *Power and Poverty* (New York: Oxford University Press, 1970); Steven Lukes, *Power, a Radical View* (London: Macmillan, 1974). For further discussion of these points, cf. *CPST*, pp. 88–94.
3 *CPST*, chapter 2.
4 Cf. Paul Ziff, *Semantic Analysis* (Ithaca: Cornell University Press, 1960).
5 Cf. Hanna F. Pitkin, *Wittgenstein and Justice* (Berkeley: University of California Press, 1972), pp. 241–64.
6 For this style of representing these relations I am indebted to Derek Gregory; see his *Regional Transformation and Industrial Revolution* (London: Macmillan, 1982), p. 17.
7 Peter Marsh *et al.*, *The Rules of Disorder* (London: Routledge, 1978), p. 15 and *passim*.
8 *NRSM*, pp. 108–10.
9 Jürgen Habermas, *Zur Logik der Sozialwissenschaften* (Tübingen: Siebeck & Mohr, 1967); 'On systematically distorted communication', *Inquiry*, vol. 13, 1970.
10 Cf. my 'Habermas's critique of hermeneutics', in *SSPT*.
11 See *CPST*, pp. 33–8.
12 Paul Ricoeur, 'Existence and hermeneutics', in *The Conflict of Interpretations* (Evanston: Northwestern University Press, 1974).
13 For an elaboration of this position, see *CPST*, chapter 5. Symbolic orders and modes of discourse constitute the 'cultural' aspects of social systems. But, as with 'society' and 'history', I call upon the term 'culture' to fulfil a double duty. Thus I shall speak of 'cultures' in a general way, as a term interchangeable with 'societies', although in some contexts these terms have to be accorded more precision.
14 Cf. Karl Polanyi *et al.*, *Trade and Market in the Early Empires* (New York: Free Press, 1957), pp. 243–70 and *passim*.
15 My reasons for making these claims are given at some length in *CCHM*, especially in the introduction and in chapter 3.
16 Emile Durkheim, *Socialism* (New York: Collier-Macmillan, 1962).
17 Cf. Bertrand Badie and Pierre Birnbaum, *Sociologie de l'Etat* (Paris: Grasset, 1979), pp. 189ff.

18 Including my own commentary in ' "Power" in the writings of Talcott Parsons', in *SSPT*.

19 Cf. also Niklas Luhmann, *Trust and Power* (Chichester: Wiley, 1979), p. 127, who asserts that 'the close association of the powerful with the dangerous is really only adequate for archaic societies and archaic ways of thinking. . . .' This seems extraordinarily sanguine in a nuclear age.

20 Cf. Boris Frankel, *Beyond the State* (London: Macmillan, 1983). This is one of the few books to emphasize the significance of mass food production and preservation for the development of capitalism.

21 Marshall McLuhan, *The Gutenberg Galaxy* (London: Routledge, 1962).

22 *CCHM*, p. 96.

23 Lewis Mumford, 'University city', in Carl H. Kraeling and Robert M. Adams, *City Invisible* (Chicago: University of Chicago Press, 1960), p. 7.

# 9 Mann

## Introduction

The extract which follows comes from the introduction to volume 1 of Michael Mann's monumental study of the sources of power 'from the beginning to the present'. So far two volumes have been published (Mann 1986 and 1993) but volumes 3 and 4 are forthcoming. The beginning is not, of course, the beginning of human biological existence upon earth but the moment at which humans began to create permanent power sources within relatively complex civilized societies – about 3000 BC. As Mann acknowledges, the idea of writing a history of this scope has a slightly old-fashioned ring about it and fits within the tradition of the founders of sociology (Marx, Durkheim and Weber).

Mann's objective is to write sociological history which falls neither into the potential sociological trap of historical determinism, nor tends towards a naive empiricism whereby history is viewed as a set of relatively contingent, but empirically self-evident, events to be recorded – a view which is tacitly held by many professional historians. As a sociologist, he views history as a *selection* of events which are *not self-evidently* important but become so, relative to *a particular* ordering interpretative framework (a scientific theory or framework). In the case of *The Sources of Social Power* this interpretative framework entails a particular view of the relationship between social agents and power sources.

In similar fashion to Giddens, Mann's objective is to accommodate human freedom, and contingency of historical record, with constraint and determinacy. At any particular juncture the choices of social agents are both enabled and constrained by the particular power sources available at a moment in time. In contrast to Marxism, history is not driven by one power source, the economy, nor is it the case that agents are the effects of power sources. Rather, historical agents are active beings situated within complex overlapping networks of power which are continually negotiated in novel ways and, in the process, transformed. In essence, Mann writes a history of these transformations and this determines the geographical location of his narrative. He is not writing the history of a single space but, rather, of wherever happens to be the cutting edge of power sources. Consequently, the analysis opens with a focus primarily upon the complex irrigational civilizations of Mesopotamia, Egypt, China and Central and South America and culminates in North Western Europe and the United States.

Mann argues that agents are social but not societal. In making this assertion he wants to get away from the perception of history as the history of a single subject, a system, or even systems. Rather, he writes a history of agents who find themselves enmeshed in different interconnecting networks and organizations of power sources. Like Giddens, Mann considers the equation of society with systems (most typically found in Parsons) to be the product of a modern sensibility whereby the world is divided into distinct sovereign states. In Mann's framework, the state is not all-embracing, in the sense defined by systemic boundaries, but, rather, one among many social phenomena within a complex network of power sources that link agents to each other. Because the state exists through the negotiation of networks of power, the state cannot be defined in terms of a particular power source such as, for instance, the monopoly of physical force (Weber's definition). Within Mann's framework military force is but one among four sources of power which states exploit. The other three are economic, political and ideological power and, as will be seen, the nature of these power sources is clearly analysed in the extract which follows.

Since the state cannot be defined in terms of any single power source, Mann refers to it as 'functionally promiscuous'. Functional promiscuity applies not only to the state but to other institutions as well. For instance, we may think of the Roman Catholic church as solely exploiting ideological power sources but we do not have to go back very far in time to find use being made of economic, authoritative and military power sources – albeit to a lesser extent.

Aside from an explicitness of theoretical premises, another characteristic which typically distinguishes historical sociology from conventional history is a manifest orientation towards using the past in order to understand the present. The objective of historical sociology is to construct histories of the present (to borrow a phrase from Foucault). This task is accomplished by presenting us with past social orders, which are clearly different from the present and, in so doing, allowing us to perceive contemporary taken-for-granted aspects of social life as unique and surprising.

We do not have to go back further than the medieval period, to see that Weber's definition of the state makes sense only relative to specific, historically unique, states. This also applies to the currently common definition of the state as having a monopoly of military power *and* taxation. Prior to the sixteenth century, no state had either a monopoly of military power or taxation. The inability of states to monopolize military power was partly a consequence of the fact that, prior to the modern period, armies could sustain themselves on continuous march only for about three days – after that time they would have to make camp and replenish their food resources. Consequently, a monopoly of violence was difficult to maintain beyond a radius of ninety miles (an army marched about thirty miles a day). This limitation upon military power was not purely technological but also authoritative and, in that sense, political. The ability of modern armies to sustain themselves for much longer is, in part, a consequence of the invention of complex and sophisticated models of command and discipline. The circumscribed nature of pre-modern military power had, in turn, a direct impact upon taxation. Collection of taxes could not be routinized as a standard monopoly function of the state due to the difficulty of penalizing defaulters living at any distance. As a consequence, tax was negotiated on an ad hoc exchange basis, frequently being bartered for political power in the form of exchange of tax for feudal privilege – a practice which continually weakened the state.

Echoing the work of Michels and Mosca, Mann argues that the sources of social power become effective resources only when they are organized. In mobilizing resources, actors reorganize social life. What determines dominance in any specific system is the ability of people to 'organizationally outflank' each other – in the transition from feudalism to capitalism the bourgeoisie organizationally outflanked the aristocracy. In writing a history of the cutting edge of power, Mann is, in essence, tracing a history of organizational outflanking by one group over another. It is for these reasons that Mann's history shifts geographically to north-western Europe and the US: these spaces have organizationally outflanked the rest of the world.

Organizational networks of power sources are not qualitatively uniform in nature. Rather, they are either intensive or extensive and, either authoritative or diffuse. In principle, the Holy Roman Emperor claimed authoritative power over all of Europe but, in practice, had effective, intensive, authoritative power only over whatever heartland in which he chose to base himself. However, claims of extensive authoritative power were not entirely spurious – complex negotiation could yield tribute from faraway parts.

On an ideological level, Christianity constituted a shared set of norms which were highly extensive. These norms were a prerequisite for the development of economic exchange across Europe. It is part of Mann's hypothesis that much of the groundwork for capitalism was laid in the medieval period through the development of a complex, diffuse, but extensive, system of trade. In essence, Mann proposes that it was not so much puritanism which was the essential ideological catalyst for capitalism (as argued by Weber in *The Protestant Ethic*) but, rather, Christianity as a whole which contributed to the creation of an extensively shared set of norms which enabled the growth of early capitalism. Again, in order to emphasize the institutional promiscuity of power sources (and consequent lack of determinacy of any single source), Mann argues that this common set of norms was only one among the many necessary (though not singly sufficient) conditions for modern capitalism. Another was, for instance, the invention of deep ploughing in North Western Europe – again an example of organizational outflanking.

Organizational outflanking takes place in many ways and, in many instances, can be the consequence of fortuitous events. However, once outflanking occurs, history is propelled in a new direction. Borrowing and amending Weberian terminology, Mann writes of moments of tracklaying (switchmen – in Weber) where power sources are sent in new directions across the social and historical landscape. In the extract included here, the rise of the European pike phalanx constitutes an instance of the reorganization of power sources, through organizational outflanking, which took place because of relatively contingent circumstances.

### Further reading

The entirety of *The Sources of Social Power* (1986) provides a clear understanding of this model of power. Volume 2 Mann (1993) and Mann (1984) are of particular interest to those wishing to understand the formation of the modern state. Anderson (1974), Elias (2000), Giddens (1985), Hall (1994), Poggi (1978), Tilly (1990) and Spruyt (1994) offer important rival accounts of the relationship between power sources and the formation of the modern state. Poggi (2000) is a recent, and important, contribution which also develops this Weberian and organizational tradition of political sociology.

# From *THE SOURCES OF SOCIAL POWER*, VOL. 1
## Michael Mann

### Organizations of power

If the problem [of understanding the nature of the organization of power sources – M.H.] is so difficult, what is the solution? In this section I give two empirical examples of relative predominance by a particular power source. These point to a solution in terms of power *organization*. The first example is of military power. It is often easy to see the emergence of a new military power because the fortunes of war can have such a sudden and clear-cut issue. One such was the rise of the European pike phalanx.

*Example 1: the rise of the European pike phalanx*

Important social changes were precipitated by military events just after A.D. 1300 in Europe. In a series of battles the old feudal levy, whose core was semi-independent groups of armored mounted knights surrounded by their retainers, was defeated by armies (mainly Swiss and Flemish) that placed greater reliance on dense masses of infantry pikemen (see Verbruggen 1977). This sudden shift in the fortunes of war led to important changes in social power. It hastened the demise of Powers that did not adjust to the lessons of war – for example, the great duchy of Burgundy. But in the long run it strengthened the power of centralized states. They could more easily provide resources to maintain the mixed infantry-cavalry-artillery armies that proved the answer to the pike phalanx. This hastened the demise of classic feudalism in general because it strengthened the central state and weakened the autonomous lord.

Let us consider this first in the light of 'factors'. Considered narrowly, it seems a simple causal pattern – changes in the technology of military power relations lead to changes in political and economic power relations. With this model we have an apparent case of military determinism. But this takes no account of the many other factors contributing to the military victory. Most crucial was probably the form of morale possessed by the victors – confidence in the pikeman to the right and to the left and at one's back. In turn, this probably derived from the relatively egalitarian, communal life of Flemish burghers, Swiss burghers, and yeoman farmers. We could continue elaborating until we had a multifactor explanation; or perhaps we could argue that the decisive point was the mode of economic production of the two groups. The stage is set for the kind of argument between economic, military, ideological, and other factors that looms in virtually every area of historical and sociological research. It is a ritual without hope and an end. For military power, like all the power sources, is itself promiscuous. It requires morale and economic surpluses – that is, ideological and economic supports – as well as drawing upon more narrowly military traditions and development. *All* are necessary factors to the exercise of military power, so how can we rank their importance?

But let us try to look at the military innovations in a different, *organizational* light. Of course, they had economic, ideological, and other preconditions. But they also had an intrinsically military, emergent, interstitial power of reorganization – a capacity through particular battlefield superiority to restructure general social networks distinct from those provided by existing dominant institutions. Let us call the latter 'feudalism', – comprising a mode of production (extraction of surplus from a dependent peasantry, interrelation of peasant plots of land and lords' manors, delivery of surplus as commodities to the towns, etc.); political institutions (the hierarchy of courts from the vassal to lord to monarch); military institutions (the feudal levy); and a

European-wide ideology, Christianity. 'Feudalism' is a loose way of describing the dominant way in which the myriad factors of social life, and, at the core, the four sources of social power, were organized and institutionalized across medieval western Europe. But other areas of social life were less central to, and less controlled by, feudalism. Social life is always more complex than its dominant institutions because, as I have emphasized, the dynamic of society comes from the myriad social networks that humans set up to pursue their goals. Among social networks that were not at the core of feudalism were towns and free peasant communities. Their further development was relatively interstitial to feudalism. And in a crucial respect two of them, in Flanders and Switzerland, found that their social organization contributed a particularly effective form of 'concentrated coercion' (as I shall define military organization later) to the battlefield. This was unsuspected by anyone, even themselves. It is sometimes argued that the first victory was accidental. At the battle of Courtrai the Flemish burghers were penned against the river by the French knights. They were unable to engage in their usual tactic against charging knights – flight! Not desirous of being slaughtered, they dug their pikes into the ground, gritted their teeth, and unhorsed the first knightly rank. It is a good example of interstitial surprise – for everyone concerned.

But it is *not* an example of 'military' versus 'economic' factors. Instead it is an example of a competition between two ways of life, one dominant and feudal, the other hitherto less important and burgher or free peasant, which took a decisive turn on the battlefield. One way of life generated the feudal levy, the other the pike phalanx. Both forms required the myriad 'factors' and the functions of all four major power sources necessary for social existence. Hitherto one dominant organizational configuration, the feudal, had predominated and partially incorporated the other into its networks. Now, however, the interstitial development of aspects of Flemish and Swiss life found a rival military organization capable of unhorsing this predominance. Military power *reorganized* existing social life, through the effectiveness of a particular form of 'concentrated coercion' on the battlefield.

Indeed the reorganization continued. The pike phalanx sold itself (literally) to rich states whose power over feudal, and town, and independent peasant networks was enhanced (as it was also over religion). An area of social life – undoubtedly a part of European feudalism, but not at its core and so only weakly institutionalized – unexpectedly and interstitially developed a highly concentrated and coercive military organization that first threatened, but then induced a restructuring of, the core. The emergence of an autonomous military organization was in this case short-lived. Both its origins and its destiny were promiscuous – not accidentally so, but in its very nature. Military power enabled a reorganizing spurt, a regrouping both of the myriad networks of society and of its dominant power configurations.

*Example 2: the emergence of civilizational cultures and religions*

In many times and places, ideologies have spread over a more extensive social space than that covered by states, armies, or modes of economic production. For example, the six best-known pristine civilizations – Mesopotamia, Egypt, the Indus Valley, Yellow River China, Mesoamerica, and Andean America – (with the possible exception of Egypt) arose as a series of small states situated within a larger cultural/civilizational unit, sharing common monumental and artistic styles, forms of symbolic representation, and religious pantheons. In later history, federations of states within a broader cultural unit are also found in many cases (e.g., classical Greece or medieval Europe). The world-salvation religions spread over much of the globe more extensively than any other power organization. Since then, secular ideologies like liberalism and socialism have also spread extensively across the boundaries of other power networks.

So religions and other ideologies are extremely important historical phenomena. Scholars drawing our attention to this argue in factorial terms: It shows, they claim, the autonomy of 'ideal' factors from 'material' ones (e.g., Coe 1982, and Keatinge 1982 in relation to ancient American civilizations; and Bendix 1978, in relation to the spread of liberalism across the early modern world). Again the materialist counterblast comes: These ideologies are not 'free floating' but the product of real social circumstances. True, the ideology does not 'float above' social life. Unless ideology stems from divine intervention in social life, then it must explain and reflect real-life experience. But – and in this lies its autonomy – it explains and reflects aspects of social life that existing dominant power institutions (modes of economic production, states, armed forces, and other ideologies) do not explain and organize effectively. An ideology will emerge as a powerful, autonomous movement when it can put together in a single explanation and organization a number of aspects of existence that have hitherto been marginal, interstitial to the dominant institutions of power. This is always a potential development in societies because there are many interstitial aspects of experience and many sources of contact between human beings other than those that form the core networks of dominant institutions.

Let me take up the example of the cultural unity of pristine civilizations (elaborated in Chapters 3 and 4). We observe a common pantheon of gods, festivals, calendars, styles of writing, decoration, and monumental building. We see the broader 'material' roles religious institutions performed – predominantly the economic role of storing and redistributing produce and regulating trade, and the political/military role of devising rules of war and diplomacy. And we examine the content of the ideology: the concern with genealogy and the origins of society, with life-cycle transitions, with influencing the fertility of nature and controlling human reproduction, with justifying yet regulating violence, with establishing sources of legitimate authority beyond one's own kin group, village, or state. Thus a religiously centered culture provided to people who lived in similar conditions over a broad region with a sense of collective normative identity and an ability to cooperate that was not intense in its powers of mobilization but that was more extensive and diffuse than state, army, or mode of production provided. A religiously centered culture offered a particular way of organizing social relations. It fused in a coherent organizational form a number of social needs, hitherto interstitial to the dominant institutions of the small familial/village/state societies of the region. Then the power organization of temples, priests, scribes, and so forth, acted back and reorganized those institutions, in particular establishing forms of long-distance economic and political regulation.

Was this the result of its ideological content? Not if we mean by this its ideological answers. After all, the answers that ideologies give to the 'meaning of life' questions are not all that varied. Nor are they particularly impressive, both in the sense that they can never be tested and found true, and in the sense that the contradictions they are supposed to resolve (e.g., the question of theodicy: Why do apparent order and meaning coexist with chaos and evil?) still remain after the answer has been given. Why then do a few ideological movements conquer their region, even much of the world, whereas most do not? The explanation for the difference may reside less in the answers ideologies provide than in the way they set about answering. Ideological movements argue that human problems can be overcome with the aid of *transcendent, sacred authority*, authority that cuts through and across the 'secular' reach of economic, military, and political power institutions. Ideological power converts into a distinctive form of social organization, pursuing a diversity of ends, 'secular' and 'material' (e.g., the legitimation of particular forms of authority) as well as those conventionally considered as religious or ideal (e.g., the search for meaning). If ideological movements are distinct as *organizations*, we can then analyze the situations in which their form seems to answer human needs. There should be determinate conditions of the capacity of transcendent social authority, reaching through, 'above', and beyond the reach of established power authorities to solve human problems. It is one of the conclusions of my historical analysis to argue that this is so.

Therefore, the power sources are not composed internally of a number of stable 'factors' all showing the same coloration. When an independent source of power emerges, it is promiscuous in relation to 'factors', gathering them from all crannies of social life, giving them only a distinctive organizational configuration. We can now turn to the four sources and the distinctive organizational means they imply.

## The four sources and organizations of power

*Ideological power* derives from three interrelated arguments in the sociological tradition. First, we cannot understand (and so act upon) the world merely by direct sense perception. We require concepts and categories of *meaning* imposed upon sense perceptions. The social organization of ultimate knowledge and meaning is necessary to social life, as Weber argued. Thus collective and distributive power can be wielded by those who monopolize a claim to meaning. Second, *norms*, shared understandings of how people should act morally in their relations with each other, are necessary for sustained social cooperation. Durkheim demonstrated that shared normative understandings are required for stable, efficient social cooperation, and that ideological movements like religions are often the bearers of these. An ideological movement that increases the mutual trust and collective morale of a group may enhance their collective powers and be rewarded with more zealous adherence. To monopolize norms is thus a route to power. The third source of ideological power is *aesthetic/ritual practices*. These are not reducible to rational science. As Bloch (1974) has expressed it, in dealing with the power of religious myth, 'You cannot argue with a song.' A distinctive power is conveyed through song, dance, visual art forms, and rituals. As all but the most fervent materialists recognize, where meaning, norms, and aesthetic and ritual practices are monopolized by a distinctive group, it may possess considerable extensive and intensive power. It can exploit its functionality and build distributive on top of collective power. In later chapters I analyze the conditions under which an ideological movement can attain such power, as well as its overall extent. Religious movements provide the most obvious examples of ideological power, but more secular examples in this volume are the cultures of early Mesopotamia and classical Greece. Predominantly secular ideologies are characteristic of our own era – for example, Marxism.

In some formulations the terms 'ideology' and 'ideological power' contain two additional elements, that the knowledge purveyed is false and/or that it is a mere mask for material domination. I imply neither. Knowledge purveyed by an ideological power movement necessarily 'surpasses experience' (as Parsons puts it). It cannot be totally tested by experience, and therein lies its distinctive power to persuade and dominate. But it need not be false; if it is, it is less likely to spread. People are not manipulated fools. And though ideologies always do contain legitimations of private interests and material domination, they are unlikely to attain a hold over people if they are merely this. Powerful ideologies are at least highly plausible in the conditions of the time, and they are genuinely adhered to.

These are the functions of ideological power, but to what distinct organizational contours do they give rise?

*Ideological organization* comes in two main types. In the first, more autonomous form it is sociospatially *transcendent*. It transcends the existing institutions of ideological, economic, military, and political power and generates a 'sacred' form of authority (in Durkheim's sense), set apart from and above more secular authority structures. It develops a powerful autonomous role when emergent properties of social life create the possibility of greater cooperation or exploitation that transcend the organizational reach of secular authorities. Technically, therefore, ideological organizations may be unusually dependent on what I called *diffused* power techniques, and therefore boosted by the extension of such 'universal infrastructures' as literacy, coinage, and markets.

As Durkheim argued, religion arises out of the usefulness of normative integration (and of meaning and aesthetics and ritual), and it is 'sacred', set apart from secular power relations. But it does not merely integrate and reflect an already established 'society'; indeed it may actually create a society-like network, a religious or cultural community, out of emergent, interstitial social needs and relations. Such is the model I apply in Chapters 3 and 4 to the first extensive civilizations, and in Chapters 10 and 11 to the world-salvation religions. Ideological power offers a distinctive sociospatial method of dealing with emergent social problems.

The second configuration is ideology as immanent *morale*, as intensifying the cohesion, the confidence, and, therefore, the power of an already-established social group. Immanent ideology is less dramatically autonomous in its impact, for it largely strengthens whatever is there. Nevertheless, ideologies of class or nation (the main examples) with their distinctive infrastructures, usually extensive and diffuse, contributed importantly to the exercise of power from the times of the ancient Assyrian and Persian empires onward.

*Economic power* derives from the satisfaction of subsistence needs through the social organization of the extraction, transformation, distribution, and consumption of the objects of nature. A grouping formed around these tasks is called a *class* – which in this work, therefore, is purely an *economic* concept. Economic production, distribution, exchange, and consumption relations normally combine a high level of intensive and extensive power, and have been a large part of social development. Thus classes form a large part of overall social-stratification relations. Those able to monopolize control over production, distribution, exchange, and consumption, that is, a dominant class, can obtain general collective and distributive power in societies. Again I shall analyze the conditions under which such power arises.

I will not enter here into the many debates concerning the role of classes in history. I prefer the context of actual historical problems, beginning in Chapter 7 with class struggle in ancient Greece (the first historical era for which we have good evidence). There I distinguish four phases in the development of class relations and class struggle – *latent*, *extensive*, *symmetrical*, and *political* class structures. I use these in succeeding chapters. My conclusions are stated in the last chapter. We will see that classes, though important, are not 'the motor of history' as Marx, for one, believed.

On one important issue the two main traditions of theory differ. Marxists stress control over labor as the source of economic power, and so they concentrate on 'modes of *production*'. Neo-Weberians (and others, like the substantivist school of Karl Polanyi) stress the organization of economic *exchange*. We cannot elevate one above the other on a priori theoretical grounds; historical evidence must decide the issue. To assert, as many Marxists do, that production relations must be decisive because 'production comes first' (i.e., it precedes distribution, exchange, and consumption) is to miss the point of 'emergence'. Once a form of exchange emerges, it is a social fact, potentially powerful. Traders can react to opportunity at their end of the economic chain and then act back upon the organization of production that originally spawned them. A trading empire like the Phoenician is an example of a trading group whose actions decisively altered the lives of the producing groups whose needs originally created their power (e.g., developing the alphabet – see Chapter 7). Relations between production and exchange are complex and often attenuated: Whereas production is high on intensive power, mobilizing intense local social cooperation to exploit nature, exchange may occur extremely extensively. At its fringes, exchange may encounter influences and opportunities that are far removed from the production relations that originally generated selling activities. Economic power is generally diffuse, not controllable from a center. This means that class structure may not be unitary, a single hierarchy of economic power. Production and exchange relations may, if attenuated, fragment class structure.

Thus classes are groups with differential power over the social organization of the extraction, transformation, distribution, and consumption of the objects of nature. I repeat that I use the term *class* to denote a purely economic power grouping, and the term *social stratification* to denote any type of distribution of power. The term *ruling class* will denote an economic class that has successfully monopolized other power sources to dominate a state-centered society at large. I leave open for historical analysis questions concerning the inter-relations of classes to other stratification groupings.

*Economic organization* comprises circuits of production, distribution, exchange, and consumption. Its main sociospatial peculiarity is that although those circuits are extensive, they also involve the intensive practical, everyday labor – what Marx called the praxis – of the mass of the population. Economic organization thus offers a distinctively stable, sociospatial blend of extensive and intensive power, and of diffused and authoritative power. Therefore, I shall call economic organization *circuits of praxis*. This perhaps rather pompous term is intended to build upon two of Marx's insights. First, at one 'end' of a reasonably developed mode of production are a mass of workers laboring and expressing themselves through the conquest of nature. Second, at the other 'end' of the mode are complex, extensive circuits of exchange into which millions may be locked by impersonal, seemingly 'natural', forces. The contrast is extreme in the case of capitalism, but nonetheless present in all types of economic-power organization. Groups defined in relation to the circuits of praxis are classes. The degree to which they are 'extensive', 'symmetrical', and 'political' across the whole circuit of praxis of a mode of production will determine the organizing power of class and class struggle. And this will turn on the tightness of linkage between intensive local production and extensive circuits of exchange.

*Military power* was partly defined earlier. It derives from the necessity of organized physical defense and its usefulness for aggression. It has both intensive and extensive aspects, for it concerns questions of life and death, as well as the organization of defense and offense in large geographical and social spaces. Those who monopolize it, as military elites, can obtain collective and distributive power. Such power has been neglected of late in social theory, and I return to nineteenth- and early-twentieth-century writers like Spencer, Gumplowicz, and Oppenheimer (although they usually exaggerated its capacities).

*Military organization* is essentially *concentrated-coercive*. It mobilizes violence, the most concentrated, if bluntest, instrument of human power. This is obvious in wartime. Concentration of force forms the keystone of most classic discussions of military tactics. But as we shall see in various historical chapters (especially 5–9), it may endure beyond the battlefield and the campaign. Militaristic forms of social control attempted in peacetime are also highly concentrated. For example, directly coerced labor, whether slave or corvée, often built city fortifications, monumental buildings, or main communication roads or channels. Coerced labor appears also in mines, on plantations, and on other large estates, and in the households of the powerful. But it is less suited to normal dispersed agriculture, to industry where discretion and skill are required, or to the dispersed activities of commerce and trade. The costs of effectively enforcing direct coercion in these areas have been beyond the resources of any known historical regime. Militarism has thus proved useful where concentrated, intensive, authoritative power has yielded disproportionate results.

Second, military power also has a more extensive reach, of a negative, terroristic form. As Lattimore pointed out, throughout most of history military striking range was greater than the range of either state control or economic-production relations. But this is minimal control. The logistics are daunting. In Chapter 5, I calculate that throughout ancient history the maximum unsupported march practicable for an army was about 90 kilometers – scant basis for intensive military control over large areas. Faced with a powerful military force located, let us say, 300 kilometers away, locals might be concerned to comply externally with its dictates – supply annual tribute, recognize the suzerainty of its leader, send young men and women to be 'educated' at its court – but everyday behavior could be otherwise unconstrained.

Thus military power is sociospatially dual: a concentrated core in which positive, coerced controls can be exercised, surrounded by an extensive penumbra in which terrorized populations will not normally step beyond certain niceties of compliance but whose behavior cannot be positively controlled.

*Political power* (also partly defined earlier) derives from the usefulness of centralized, institutionalized, territorialized regulation of many aspects of social relations. I am not defining it in purely 'functional' terms, in terms of judicial regulation backed by coercion. Such functions can be possessed by any power organization – ideological, economic, military, as well as states. I restrict it to regulations and coercion centrally administered and territorially bounded – that is, to *state* power. By concentrating on the state, we can analyze its distinctive contribution to social life. As here defined, political power heightens boundaries, whereas the other power sources may transcend them. Second, military, economic, and ideological power can be involved in *any* social relationships, wherever located. Any A or group of As can exercise these forms of power against any B or group of Bs. By contrast, political relations concern one particular area, the 'center'. Political power is located in that center and exercised outward. Political power is necessarily centralized and territorial, and in these respects differs from the other power sources (see Mann 1984, for fuller discussions; a formal definition of the state is also given in my next chapter). Those who control the state, the state elite, can obtain both collective and distributive power and trap others within their distinctive 'organization chart'.

*Political organization* is also sociospatially dual, though in a different sense. Here we must distinguish domestic from 'international' organization. Domestically, the state is *territorially centralized* and territorially-bounded. States can thus attain greater autonomous power when social life generates emergent possibilities for enhanced cooperation and exploitation of a centralized form over a confined territorial area (elaborated in Mann 1984). It depends predominantly upon techniques of authoritative power, because centralized, though not as much so as military organization. When discussing the actual powers of state elites, we will find it useful to distinguish formal 'despotic' powers from real 'infrastructural' powers. This is explained in Chapter 5 in the section titled 'The Comparative Study of Ancient Empires'.

But states' territorial boundaries – in a world never yet dominated by a single state – also give rise to an area of regulated interstate relations. *Geopolitical diplomacy* is a second important form of political-power organization. Two geopolitical types – the hegemonic empire dominating marcher and neighboring clients, and varying forms of multistate civilization – will play a considerable role in this volume. Clearly, geopolitical organization is very different in form from the other power organizations mentioned so far. It is indeed normally ignored by sociological theory. But it is an essential part of social life and it is not reducible to the 'internal' power configurations of its component states. For example, the successive hegemonic and despotic pretensions of the German emperor Henry IV, Philip II of Spain, and Bonaparte of France were only in a superficial sense humbled by the strength of the states and others who opposed them – they were really humbled by the deep-rooted, multistate diplomatic civilization of Europe. Geopolitical power organization is thus an essential part of overall social stratification.

To summarize so far: Human beings pursuing many goals set up many networks of social interaction. The boundaries and capacities of these networks do not coincide. Some networks have greater capacity for organizing intensive and extensive, authoritative and diffused, social cooperation than others. The greatest are the networks of ideological, economic, military, and political power – the four sources of social power. Each then implies distinctive forms of sociospatial organization by which humans can attain a very broad, but not exhaustive, package of their myriad goals. The importance of these four lies in their combination of intensive and extensive power. But this is translated into historical determinacy through the various organizational means that impose their general shape onto a large part of general social life. The main shapes I identified were *transcendent* or *immanent* (from ideological power), *circuits of praxis* (economic), *concentrated-coercive* (military), and *centralized-territorial* and *geopolitical diplomatic* (political) organization. Such configurations become what I called 'promiscuous', drawing in and structuring elements from many areas of social life. In example 2 above, the transcendent organization of the culture of early civilizations drew in aspects of economic redistribution, of rules of warfare, and of political and geopolitical regulation. Thus we are dealing not with the external relations between different sources, dimensions, or levels of social power but rather with (1) the sources as ideal types that (2) attain intermittent existence as distinct organizations within the division of labor and that (3) may exert more general, promiscuous shaping of social life. In (3) one or more of these organizational means will emerge interstitially as the primary reorganizing force in either the short term, as in the military example, or the long term, as in the ideological example. This is the IEMP model of organized power.

Max Weber once used a metaphor drawn from the railways of his time when trying to explain the importance of ideology – he was discussing the power of salvation religions. He wrote that such ideas were like 'switchmen' (i.e., 'pointsmen' in British railways) determining down which of several tracks social development would proceed. Perhaps the metaphor should be amended. The sources of social power are 'tracklaying vehicles' – for the tracks do not exist before the direction is chosen – laying different gauges of track across the social and historical terrain. *The 'moments' of tracklaying, and of converting to a new gauge, are the closest that we can approach the issue of primacy.* In these moments we find an autonomy of social concentration, organization, and direction that is lacking in more institutionalized times.

That is the key to the importance of the power sources. They give collective organization and unity to the infinite variety of social existence. They provide such significant patterning as there is in large-scale social structure (which may or may not be very great) because they are capable of generating collective action. They are 'the generalized means' through which human beings make their own history.

## References

Bendix, R. 1978. *Kings or People*. Berkeley: University of California Press.

Bloch, M. 1974. Symbols, song, dance and features of articulation. In *Archives Européenes de Sociologie*, 15.

Coe, M.D. 1982. Religion and the rise of Mesoamerican states. In *The Transition to Statehood in the New World*, ed. G.D. Jones and R.R. Kautz. Cambridge: Cambridge University Press.

Keatinge, R. 1982. The nature and role of religious diffusion in the early stages of state formation. In *The Transition to Statehood in the New World*, ed. G.D. Jones and R.R. Kautz. Cambridge: Cambridge University Press.

Lattimore, O. 1962. *Studies in Frontier History*. London: Oxford University Press.

Mann, M. 1984. The Autonomous Power of the State. In *Archives Européennes de Sociologie*, 25.

Verbruggen, J.F. 1977. *The Art of Warfare in Western Europe During the Middle Ages*. Amsterdam: North-Holland.

# 10   Foucault

## Introduction

Foucault's concept of power is linked to a project of social critique which is accomplished by writing what he termed 'histories of the present'. While Foucault always resisted the label 'postmodern', this form of critique displays many characteristics of discontinuity with the Enlightenment perception of the relationship between power, knowledge and truth. As is exemplified by the three-dimensional power debate, the modern/Enlightenment perception of the relationship between power and knowledge is a negative one whereby power distorts truth – the third dimension of power. In the work of Foucault, the relationship between power and knowledge is not oppositional but, rather, mutually constitutive. As he puts it in the extract which follows: 'Perhaps we should abandon the belief that power makes mad and that, by the same token, the renunciation of power is one of the conditions of knowledge.'

The modern perception of an opposition between truth and power derives from a desire for an undistorted relationship between the subject and world-out-there. This is exemplified by Descartes for whom the problem of philosophy is an epistemological one of building a bridge between the I and the world. In postmodern social thought, this division of the self from the world out there presupposed by Cartesian epistemology is displaced by a perception of the self as constituting the world ontologically. Our being in the world is inseparable from our perception of it. At this moment I recreate the 'chairness' of the chair upon which I am sitting in a manner which is inseparable from my being or ontology – the chairness of the object is not 'out-there'. However, my being-in-the-world is not a self-creational process but a product of the specific historicity of the world into which I happen to have been born; consequently, a reflection of a particular set of social relations. Because truth is inextricably tied to particular existences and social relations, the Enlightenment quest for truth as perceptions which are true everywhere is considered an illusion. In the modern view of truth, scientific procedure is a method whereby the distorting effects of context are filtered out. In moral philosophy, Habermas' ideal speech situation and Rawls' original position are conceptual devices which mirror the intentions of this scientific quest for undistorted knowledge. Scientific procedure is a view of the world from nowhere while moral philosophy is a judgement from nowhere.

The history of knowledge is a story of struggle for certain truths and judgements as views from nowhere. The outcome is constitutive of particular social relations and modes of being which become dominant at certain historical conjunctures. While the quest for truth is perceived as an escape from distorting social relations, the outcome is, in fact, a consequence of a power conflict whereby certain realities are privileged and others disqualified.

A history of the present is an analysis of the power relations which have constituted our interpretative horizon and consequent being. Social critique is not, as in modern social critique (exemplified by critical theory), the attempt to privilege yet another interpretative horizon as the truth. Rather, it is an attempt to undermine relations of domination by showing how the crutches of legitimacy of modern truth and impartial judgement are simply a reflection of social relations saturated with power.

Foucault's work falls into three distinct phases: the archaeology, the genealogy and the 'care of the self'. The archaeology includes, among others, *Madness and Civilization* (1971) and *The Order of Things* (1970); the genealogy *Discipline and Punish* (1979) *Power/Knowledge* (1980) and *History of Sexuality, Volume 1* (1981); and 'the care of the self' the other two volumes of *History of Sexuality* (1986 and 1990). In the archaeology, his theory of power is implicit, while the genealogical works are explicitly concerned with power. In the 'care of the self', power again becomes implicit. In other words, in the archaeology Foucault is primarily concerned with the tacit knowledge which constitutes the conditions of possibility without the mechanics of how they are fought for or resisted. In the genealogy, this archaeological description of systems of thought is supplemented with an account of how they are constituted by, and in turn, constitute, relations of power. If our being-in-the-world is inseparable from our interpretation of it, then any system of thought presupposes subjection both of certain knowledges and, inseparably from it, certain modes of being. This creates an inevitable struggle between knowledges, not simply as roads to truth, but as modes of existence. In the 'care of the self' the possibilities of the constitution of self, as resistance to dominant knowledges, becomes a project of emancipation. However, unlike modern epistemologically guided emancipation, the 'care of the self' does not presuppose escape into a realm of undistorted truth but, rather, an experimentation with subversive knowledges as new ways of being.

In writing a history of the present, Foucault wished to understand how it is that we have come to understand (and be in) the world the way we do (are). This entails exploring the tacit and taken-for-granted which enables us to order things in the way we do. In Giddens' vocabulary, it involves exploring our practical consciousness knowledge (habitus in Bourdieu). Typically, Foucault's histories open with a surprising statement which is intended to startle the reader out of the complacent taken-for-grantedness of their way of making sense of the world. For instance, *The Order of Things* opens with a list of animals quoted from what is purported to be an ancient Chinese encyclopaedia which included, among other things: '(a) belonging to the emperor, (b) embalmed, (c) tame, (d) suckling pigs, (e) sirens, (f) fabulous, (g) stray dogs, (h) included in the present classification, (i) frenzied, . . .' (Foucault 1970, p. xv). To us this may appear chaos or a dystopia where nothing makes sense. It is well-nigh impossible to believe that a mind could view this as an ordered list. Yet, it is Foucault's belief that this list could have made sense relative to a particular tacit knowledge, or what he termed *episteme*, which is now absent from the world. The fact that it is theoretically possible to order the world in this way, is intended to sensitize us to the idea that 'our' interpretative horizon, and 'our' consequent being-in-the-world, could be entirely different than it is.

Foucault was essentially a meaning holist whereby meaning constitutes itself relationally through difference within an ordered totality. Imagine the pieces in a game of chess as symbols or words. Each piece has its specific meaning. Then picture yourself trying to explain to someone who knows nothing about chess what a single piece – the queen, for instance – means. What is manifest in the thought experiment is that understanding what queen means is incomprehensible without an understanding of the game as a whole. Thomas Kuhn once used an example to explain a similar point: imagine a father taking his two-year-old daughter for a walk in a city park. They come to a pond, the child sees a duck and says 'bird'. The father informs her, more specifically, that it is a duck. Shortly afterwards they come to a flock of geese and the child says 'duck'. The father explains that it is a goose something like this: 'Geese are like ducks, except they are larger and they . . .' Later they come to swans and the child identifies them as geese whereupon her father explains the difference between geese and swans. Again the meaning of the duck, goose and swan is not constituted singly. It is created not by the relationship between the signifier (word) and the signified (bird swimming about) but through relational difference between the signifiers. What is also obvious is that in the act of learning these words the child is learning not simply something external to the self but, significantly, is actually being transformed through her newly acquired ability to make sense of the world – next time she comes to the park it will appear different to her. Learning the meaning of the world is inextricably tied to ontological transformation, consequently systems of meaning entail specific ways of being. Hence, writing a history of the present is inextricably tied to understanding how it is that we are what we are.

Since systems of meaning are relationally constituted, the type of histories Foucault wrote are marked by discontinuities. Epistemes are shared systems of knowledge which are relationally self-constituting layers of historical thought. There is not continuous development across time (as in conventional historiography) but, rather, self-contained systems of thought which, as in an archaeological site, are situated horizontally relative to each other.

Foucault argued that modern European history is characterized by three separate systems of thought, as follows: the Renaissance from about 1450 to 1650, the classical period from 1650 to 1800 and the modern period from 1800 to the present. Within each of these periods it was possible to say different things which made sense locally. For instance, in the Renaissance period there were debates which, to our ears, sound as absurd as the Chinese encyclopaedia. In that period we can witness the debate between those who argued that plants mirrored animals except that they were upside-down (the roots corresponding to the mouth) whereas others argued that they were right-side up (the flower corresponding to the face). In the classical period this type of pursuit of the resemblance between things became a source of error. Instead the classical system of meaning sustained the creation of elaborate systems of classifications. Interestingly, man [sic],[1] the compiler of these tables, was missing from the system of classification.

For Foucault, a key element in the transition to the modern period was the introduction of man as an object of knowledge. In many respects, Kant is paradigmatic in this regard. When Kant tried to answer the epistemological question 'how do we know the world?' his answer was that we know it by imposing categories of thought upon it. Consequently, seeing is not only a faculty of the sense but, for instance, entails classifying objects in terms of time and space. If I look out my window I can see slender cypress trees in the foreground and rolling hills behind. This perception presupposes not only sense data (light-rays hitting the surface of my eye) but, additionally, my mind ordering these things in space – and the view makes sense only because it is so ordered.

In modernity, knowledge is not reducible to an order which exists prior to our interpretation of it. The classical quest for classification presupposes the idea that order exists in the world irrespective of our ordering it, hence, man is absent. This prior existent order was a reflection of the perfect order of the mind of God. However, with the 'death of God', this is replaced with the Kantian insight that man, by the act of ordering the world, according to *a priori* categories, finds the truth. By limiting the world through ordering it according to the categories of the human mind, 'man' imposes his own finity upon the world and, in an ultimate irony of fate, through this act of limitation, 'man' becomes the source of truth. At the end of *The Order of Things* Foucault predicts the death of 'man' and, in many respects, his archaeological method is intended as a nail in that coffin. If it is the case that the being in the world of the person is contingently determined by systems of thought then 'man', the classifier of the universe, is not the source of truth but, rather, a reflection of a local system of thought. Kant saw man as the source of truth because the categories were *a priori* and, consequently, a-historical.

In contrast to Kant and the moderns, in Foucault we find 'historical *a prioris*' which are not *a priori* to all experience, but simply prior to any given experience and constitute the 'conditions of possibility' of a given epoch – they are the interpretative grid that shape the perceptions of an era. These *a prioris* presuppose particular ontologies which are variable relative to social relations: hence, they cannot be the source of any absolute invariable truth.

Associated with the modern shift to 'man' as a source of knowledge, the human sciences were born. Truth is to be found in humans as living beings. While, in general, there is no escape from knowledge saturated by power, each historical period involves particular relations between power and knowledge. Once the person becomes a source of knowledge then particular ways of being are no longer a source of indifference. The discovery of man becomes inextricably tied to a model of judgemental normality. Certain behavioural patterns are classified as mad or delinquent by human sciences proclaiming truth. Social deviants are created as objects to be studied, judged on their abnormality and ultimately resocialized. As objects, individuals become subjectified, subjects of knowledge, in a one-way judgemental monologue which is legitimated by having truth on its side and being confronted merely by pure irrationality as its only opposition.

While the classical and Renaissance periods entailed struggles over knowledge contested on the grounds of claims to truth, because man was absent, the outcome of these struggles did not mean man's subjectification to a particular normalizing judgement. In his genealogical works, *Discipline and Punish* and *History of Sexuality*, Foucault charts the conflicts over which interpretative horizons have a claim to truth and how the victory of the modern one entails the creation of new power relations. The prisoner who resists, the homosexual who will not admit deviance, are not simply individuals resisting a particular set of social relations which disempower materially. No, they are people who by their particular being-in-the-world are resisting truth and power. In the genealogical works power is more explicitly central than in the archaeology and the term 'discourse' replaces 'episteme' as the technical term for the tacit knowledge which informs particular ways of making sense of the world.

In *Discipline and Punish* (see below) and *Power/Knowledge* (Foucault 1980, p. 90) Foucault uses the image of a reversal of Clausewitz's view that war is politics by other means to the idea that politics is war by other means. The opposite of war is peace although peace does not represent the absence of war but, rather, the reinscription of the rules of war through the use of power to privilege certain knowledges as truth. What interests Foucault is not the surest path to truth, which is the modern Enlightenment project, but rather, how truth is used to pacify others by privileging certain ways of interpreting the world, particular discourses, and disqualifying others. Power is a form of pacification which works by codifying and taming war though the imposition of particular knowledge as truth.

Social life is characterized by two levels of conflict. There exist 'local' struggles which take place within a regime of power and truth production as well as the deeper struggles which take place over the regime of truth production. In an ongoing game, for instance, there is conflict between players which is controlled and managed according to impartial rules of the game, i.e. shallow conflict. In contrast, in real life, the rules of procedure are continually contested and the appeal to truth is merely a particular type of strategy. In order to obtain release from prison, the modern subject has to admit to the truth of the system of knowledge which classifies them. *Discipline and Punish* describes how prisoners are placed in a Panopticon consisting of prison cells which, through ingenious design, are subject to continual visibility. Because prisoners are aware of being subjected to continual normalizing judgement, they start to subject themselves to the judgement of others by adopting that viewpoint. In *The History of Sexuality Volume 1*, the sexual deviants look into themselves and help the expert to classify them. By admitting to the truth of 'what they really are' the subject constitutes the truth of the regime which classifies them. In contrast, the resisting subject is the (irrational) 'other' who, 'perversely', constitutes themselves through recourse to subjected knowledge with which there cannot be dialogue if the modern monologue of power/knowledge is to sustain itself.

Typical of Foucault's method, *Discipline and Punish* opens with a scene which is intended to shock the reader. It is a description of the sentence given to Damines in 1757: it astounds the reader, but the real horror is about to come. The reality of being hanged, drawn and quartered is far worse than the instructions. This is followed by a description of the dull monotony of a prison regime from a mere eighty years later. What has changed? The obvious and banal answer, which is usually given, is that people have become more civilized. However, according to Foucault, the explanation lies in the fact that we are confronted by a discontinuity of interpretative horizon. The horrific execution is representative of power as repression and violence. This is the 'sovereign' model whereby the King demonstrates his surplus of power by making war on the subject and pulverizing their physical body – a war between the body-politic and the actual body of the recalcitrant subject. Here power works from the top down, with the king at the apex of the pyramid. In contrast, in the prison regime we see power as knowledge with its point of application as the human subject. The creation and transformation of the soul is the logical application of power within a system of thought in which 'man' has been discovered.

The ultimate physical embodiment of this new regime of power is Bentham's Panopticon. While the body is necessary to confine the prisoner (there is no way of confining the soul without it) the objective is no longer the body in itself. The object is to transform this being (ontology) of the human subject by making it an object of knowledge. The fact that the body is no longer the object of punishment is exemplified in the contrast between modern capital punishment and previous modes. Within the technological limits of the eighteenth century the guillotine was an attempt to kill the soul without hurting the body – it is a relatively instant death. Lethal injection combined with painkillers is a contemporary refinement of this technique.

The Panopticon is a power machine that produces truth about the subject as an object of knowledge. It is a one-way monologue which defines the subject through the physical construction of an environment in which prisoners cannot tell whether they are observed. This both renders the prisoners mute and induces them into objectifying themselves in terms of the dominant discourse or system of thought. In effect, alternative realities are filtered out and the resocialized prisoners come to see themselves as others see them.

In an ironic twist, the implementation of the Panopticon in the form of the prison frequently failed to resocialize but this failure reinforced the dominant discourse by producing delinquents who legitimate the system of knowledge which sustains the prison regime. Delinquents and other 'species' of malsocialized individuals are objects of knowledge and truth and, just as the classification of plants is necessary for botany, so too the delinquent is necessary for criminology and the other scientific disciplines of 'man'.

The actualization of the Panopticon principle is not confined solely to prisons but also to many other institutions, especially the school and the open-plan workplace. Here again visibility, knowledge, classification and exact division are used as instruments of power. In schools, and educational institutions in general, this is combined with examinations and certificates which are validated by the state.

## Further reading

Among Foucault's general theoretical writings on power, pp. 78–165 of *Power/Knowledge* (1980) and the 'Afterword', entitled 'The Subject and Power' in Dreyfus and Rabinow (1982 pp. 208–26 – also reproduced in Faubion 2000 pp. 326–48) are especially recommended. Like *Discipline and Punish,* Foucault's *History of Sexuality Volume 1* is a clearly integrated combination of the theoretical and empirical analysis of power. There are also many interviews with Foucault containing his analysis on power. Probably the most relevant among these is Foucault (1988). Usefully, there has recently been published an edited volume, *Foucault and Power* (Foucault 2000 – ed. Faubion), which contains most of Foucault's essays and interviews on power. Rabinow (1984) also includes a number of Foucault's writings on power.

The secondary literature on Foucault's work is extensive. Recommended starting points are Sheridan (1980), Haugaard (1997a – especially pp. 41–98), Clegg (1989), Smart (1983), Shumway (1989), McNay (1994), and Dreyfus and Rabinow (1982). Flyvbjerg (1997) has undertaken an ethnographic study of the siting of a bus station in Aarhus, Denmark, which draws upon Foucault's analysis.

### Note

1 Please note that the use of 'man' to signify both man and woman is derived from Foucault and has become conventional usage in the analysis of Foucault. I have followed in the use of this gender-biased terminology purely for the purpose of exposition of his ideas – I do not endorse it and would not otherwise use it.

# From *DISCIPLINE AND PUNISH*
## Michel Foucault

[pp. 16–19]

The reduction in penal severity in the last 200 years is a phenomenon with which legal historians are well acquainted. But, for a long time, it has been regarded in an overall way as a quantitative phenomenon: less cruelty, less pain, more kindness, more respect, more 'humanity'. In fact, these changes are accompanied by a displacement in the very object of the punitive operation. Is there a diminution of intensity? Perhaps. There is certainly a change of objective.

If the penality in its most severe forms no longer addresses itself to the body, on what does it lay hold? The answer of the theoreticians – those who, about 1760, opened up a new period that is not yet at an end – is simple, almost obvious. It seems to be contained in the question itself: since it is no longer the body, it must be the soul. The expiation that once rained down upon the body must be replaced by a punishment that acts in depth on the heart, the thoughts, the will, the inclinations. Mably formulated the principle once and for all: 'Punishment, if I may so put it, should strike the soul rather than the body' (Mably, 326).

It was an important moment. The old partners of the spectacle of punishment, the body and the blood, gave way. A new character came on the scene, masked. It was the end of a certain kind of tragedy, comedy began, with shadow play, faceless voices, impalpable entities. The apparatus of punitive justice must now bite into this bodiless reality.

Is this any more than a mere theoretical assertion, contradicted by penal practice? Such a conclusion would be over-hasty. It is true that, today, to punish is not simply a matter of converting a soul; but Mably's principle has not remained a pious wish. Its effects can be felt throughout modern penality.

Reprinted by kind permission of Georges Borchardt, Inc. and Penguin Books from *Discipline and Punish: The Birth of the Prison*, trans. Alan Sheridan (New York: Pantheon 1977 and Harmondsworth: Penguin 1979) (pp. 16–19, 25–31; 200–4 and 249–55). Originally published in French as *Surveiller et Punir; Naissance de la Prison*. Copyright © 1975 by Les Éditions Gallimard; translation Copyright © 1977.

To begin with, there is a substitution of objects. By this I do not mean that one has suddenly set about punishing other crimes. No doubt the definition of offences, the hierarchy of their seriousness, the margins of indulgence, what was tolerated in fact and what was legally permitted – all this has considerably changed over the last 200 years; many crimes have ceased to be so because they were bound up with a certain exercise of religious authority or a particular type of economic activity; blasphemy has lost its status as a crime; smuggling and domestic larceny some of their seriousness. But these displacements are perhaps not the most important fact: the division between the permitted and the forbidden has preserved a certain constancy from one century to another. On the other hand, 'crime', the object with which penal practice is concerned, has profoundly altered: the quality, the nature, in a sense the substance of which the punishable element is made, rather than its formal definition. Undercover of the relative stability of the law, a mass of subtle and rapid changes has occurred. Certainly the 'crimes' and 'offences' on which judgement is passed are juridical objects defined by the code, but judgement is also passed on the passions, instincts, anomalies, infirmities, maladjustments, effects of environment or heredity; acts of aggression are punished, so also, through them, is aggressivity; rape, but at the same time perversions; murders, but also drives and desires. But, it will be objected, judgement is not actually being passed on them; if they are referred to at all it is to explain the actions in question, and to determine to what extent the subject's will was involved in the crime. This is no answer. For it *is* these shadows lurking behind the case itself that are judged and punished. They are judged indirectly as 'attenuating circumstances' that introduce into the verdict not only 'circumstantial' evidence, but something quite different, which is not juridically codifiable: the knowledge of the criminal, one's estimation of him, what is known about the relations between him, his past and his crime, and what might be expected of him in the future. They are also judged by the interplay of all those notions that have circulated between medicine and jurisprudence since the nineteenth century (the 'monsters' of Georget's times, Chaumié's 'psychical anomalies', the 'perverts' and 'maladjusted' of our own experts) and which, behind the pretext of explaining an action, are ways of defining an individual. They are punished by means of a punishment that has the function of making the offender 'not only desirous, but also capable, of living within the law and of providing for his own needs'; they are punished by the internal economy of a penalty which, while intended to punish the crime, may be altered (shortened or, in certain cases, extended) according to changes in the prisoner's behaviour; and they are punished by the 'security measures' that accompany the penalty (prohibition of entering certain areas, probation, obligatory medical treatment), and which are intended not to punish the offence, but to supervise the individual, to neutralize his dangerous state of mind, to alter his criminal tendencies, and to continue even when this change has been achieved. The criminal's soul is not referred to in the trial merely to explain his crime and as a factor in the juridical apportioning of responsibility; if it is brought before the court, with such pomp and circumstance, such concern to understand and such 'scientific' application, it is because it too, as well as the crime itself, is to be judged and to share in the punishment. Throughout the penal ritual, from the preliminary investigation to the sentence and the final effects of the penalty, a domain has been penetrated by objects that not only duplicate, but also dissociate the juridically defined and coded objects. Psychiatric expertise, but also in a more general way criminal anthropology and the repetitive discourse of criminology, find one of their precise functions here: by solemnly inscribing offences in the field of objects susceptible of scientific knowledge, they provide the mechanisms of legal punishment with a justifiable hold not only on offences, but on individuals; not only on what they do, but also on what they are, will be, may be. The additional factor of the offender's soul, which the legal system has laid hold of, is only apparently explanatory and limitative, and is in fact expansionist. During the 150 or 200 years that Europe has been setting up its new penal systems, the judges have gradually, by means of a process that goes back very far indeed, taken to judging something other than crimes, namely, the 'soul' of the criminal.

And, by that very fact, they have begun to do something other than pass judgement. Or, to be more precise, within the very judicial modality of judgement, other types of assessment have slipped in, profoundly altering its rules of elaboration. Ever since the Middle Ages slowly and painfully built up the great procedure of investigation, to judge was to establish the truth of a crime, it was to determine its author and to apply a legal punishment. Knowledge of the offence, knowledge of the offender, knowledge of the law: these three conditions made it possible to ground a judgement in truth. But now a quite different question of truth is inscribed in the course of the penal judgement. The question is no longer simply: 'Has the act been established and is it punishable?' But also: 'What *is* this act, what *is* this act of violence or this murder? To what level or to what field of reality does it belong? Is it a phantasy, a psychotic reaction, a delusional episode, a perverse action?' It is no longer simply: 'Who committed it?' But: 'How can we assign the causal process that produced it? Where did it originate in the author himself? Instinct, unconscious, environment, heredity?' It is no longer simply: 'What law punishes this offence?' But: 'What would be the most appropriate measures to take? How do we see the future development of the offender? What would be the best way of rehabilitating him?' A whole set of assessing, diagnostic, prognostic, normative judgements concerning the criminal have become lodged in the framework of penal judgement. Another truth has penetrated the truth that was required by the legal machinery; a truth which, entangled with the first, has turned the assertion of guilt into a strange scientifico-juridical complex.

[pp. 25–31]

Historians long ago began to write the history of the body. They have studied the body in the field of historical demography or pathology; they have considered it as the seat of needs and appetites, as the locus of physiological processes and metabolisms, as a target for the attacks of germs or viruses; they have shown to what extent historical processes were involved in what might seem to be the purely biological base of existence; and what place should be given in the history of society to biological 'events' such as the circulation of bacilli, or the extension of the life-span (cf. Le Roy-Ladurie). But the body is also directly involved in a political field; power relations have an immediate hold upon it; they invest it, mark it, train it, torture it, force it to carry out tasks, to perform ceremonies, to emit signs. This political investment of the body is bound up, in accordance with complex reciprocal relations, with its economic use; it is largely as a force of production that the body is invested with relations of power and domination; but, on the other hand, its constitution as labour power is possible only if it is caught up in a system of subjection (in which need is also a political instrument meticulously prepared, calculated and used); the body becomes a useful force only if it is both a productive body and a subjected body. This subjection is not only obtained by the instruments of violence or ideology; it can also be direct, physical, pitting force against force, bearing on material elements, and yet without involving violence; it may be calculated, organized, technically thought out; it may be subtle, make use neither of weapons nor of terror and yet remain of a physical order. That is to say, there may be a 'knowledge' of the body that is not exactly the science of its functioning, and a mastery of its forces that is more than the ability to conquer them: this knowledge and this mastery constitute what might be called the political technology of the body. Of course, this technology is diffuse, rarely formulated in continuous, systematic discourse; it is often made up of bits and pieces; it implements a disparate set of tools or methods. In spite of the coherence of its results, it is generally no more than a multiform instrumentation. Moreover, it cannot be localized in a particular type of institution or state apparatus. For they have recourse to it; they use, select or impose certain of its methods. But, in its mechanisms and its effects, it is situated at a quite different level. What the apparatuses and institutions operate is, in a sense, a micro-physics of power, whose field of validity is situated in a sense between these great functionings and the bodies themselves with their materiality and their forces.

Now, the study of this micro-physics presupposes that the power exercised on the body is conceived not as a property, but as a strategy, that its effects of domination are attributed not to 'appropriation', but to dispositions, manoeuvres, tactics, techniques, functionings; that one should decipher in it a network of relations, constantly in tension, in activity, rather than a privilege that one might possess; that one should take as its model a perpetual battle rather than a contract regulating a transaction or the conquest of a territory. In short this power is exercised rather than possessed; it is not the 'privilege', acquired or preserved, of the dominant class, but the overall effect of its strategic positions – an effect that is manifested and sometimes extended by the position of those who are dominated. Furthermore, this power is not exercised simply as an obligation or a prohibition on those who 'do not have it'; it invests them, is transmitted by them and through them; it exerts pressure upon them, just as they themselves, in their struggle against it, resist the grip it has on them. This means that these relations go right down into the depths of society, that they are not localized in the relations between the state and its citizens or on the frontier between classes and that they do not merely reproduce, at the level of individuals, bodies, gestures and behaviour, the general form of the law or government; that, although there is continuity (they are indeed articulated on this form through a whole series of complex mechanisms), there is neither analogy nor homology, but a specificity of mechanism and modality. Lastly, they are not univocal; they define innumerable points of confrontation, focuses of instability, each of which has its own risks of conflict, of struggles, and of an at least temporary inversion of the power relations. The overthrow of these 'micro-powers' does not, then, obey the law of all or nothing; it is not acquired once and for all by a new control of the apparatuses nor by a new functioning or a destruction of the institutions; on the other hand, none of its localized episodes may be inscribed in history except by the effects that it induces on the entire network in which it is caught up.

Perhaps, too, we should abandon a whole tradition that allows us to imagine that knowledge can exist only where the power relations are suspended and that knowledge can develop only outside its injunctions, its demands and its interests. Perhaps we should abandon the belief that power makes mad and that, by the same token, the renunciation of power is one of the conditions of knowledge. We should admit rather that power produces knowledge (and not simply by encouraging it because it serves power or by applying it because it is useful); that power and knowledge directly imply one another; that there is no power relation without the correlative constitution of a field of knowledge, nor any knowledge that does not presuppose and constitute at the same time power relations. These 'power-knowledge relations' are to be analysed, therefore, not on the basis of a subject of knowledge who is or is not free in relation to the power system, but, on the contrary, the subject who knows, the objects to be known and the modalities of knowledge must be regarded as so many effects of these fundamental implications of power-knowledge and their historical transformations. In short, it is not the activity of the subject of knowledge that produces a corpus of knowledge, useful or resistant to power, but power-knowledge, the processes and struggles that traverse it and of which it is made up, that determines the forms and possible domains of knowledge.

To analyse the political investment of the body and the micro-physics of power presupposes, therefore, that one abandons – where power is concerned – the violence-ideology opposition, the metaphor of property, the model of the contract or of conquest; that – where knowledge is concerned – one abandons the opposition between what is 'interested' and what is 'disinterested', the model of knowledge and the primacy of the subject. Borrowing a word from Petty and his contemporaries, but giving it a different meaning from the one current in the seventeenth century, one might imagine a political 'anatomy'. This would not be the study of a state in terms of a 'body' (with its elements, its resources and its forces), nor would it be the study of the body and its surroundings in terms of a small state. One would be concerned with the 'body politic', as a set of material elements and techniques that serve as weapons, relays, communication routes and supports for the power and knowledge relations that invest human bodies and subjugate them by turning them into objects of knowledge.

It is a question of situating the techniques of punishment – whether they seize the body in the ritual of public torture and execution or whether they are addressed to the soul – in the history of this body politic; of considering penal practices less as a consequence of legal theories than as a chapter of political anatomy.

Kantorowitz gives a remarkable analysis of 'The King's Body': a double body according to the juridical theology of the Middle Ages, since it involves not only the transitory element that is born and dies, but another that remains unchanged by time and is maintained as the physical yet intangible support of the kingdom; around this duality, which was originally close to the Christological model, are organized an iconography, a political theory of monarchy, legal mechanisms that distinguish between as well as link the person of the king and the demands of the Crown, and a whole ritual that reaches its height in the coronation, the funeral and the ceremonies of submission. At the opposite pole one might imagine placing the body of the condemned man; he, too, has his legal status; he gives rise to his own ceremonial and he calls forth a whole theoretical discourse, not in order to ground the 'surplus power' possessed by the person of the sovereign, but in order to code the 'lack of power' with which those subjected to punishment are marked. In the darkest region of the political field the condemned man represents the symmetrical, inverted figure of the king. We should analyse what might be called, in homage to Kantorowitz, 'the least body of the condemned man'.

If the surplus power possessed by the king gives rise to the duplication of his body, has not the surplus power exercised on the subjected body of the condemned man given rise to another type of duplication? That of a 'non-corporal', a 'soul', as Mably called it. The history of this 'micro-physics' of the punitive power would then be a genealogy or an element in a genealogy of the modern 'soul'. Rather than seeing this soul as the reactivated remnants of an ideology, one would see it as the present correlative of a certain technology of power over the body. It would be wrong to say that the soul is an illusion, or an ideological effect. On the contrary, it exists, it has a reality, it is produced permanently around, on, within the body by the functioning of a power that is exercised on those punished – and, in a more general way, on those one supervises, trains and corrects, over madmen, children at home and at school, the colonized, over those who are stuck at a machine and supervised for the rest of their lives. This is the historical reality of this soul, which, unlike the soul represented by Christian theology, is not born in sin and subject to punishment, but is born rather out of methods of punishment, supervision and constraint. This real, non-corporal soul is not a substance; it is the element in which are articulated the effects of a certain type of power and the reference of a certain type of knowledge, the machinery by which the power relations give rise to a possible corpus of knowledge, and knowledge extends and reinforces the effects of this power. On this reality-reference, various concepts have been constructed and domains of analysis carved out: psyche, subjectivity, personality, consciousness, etc.; on it have been built scientific techniques and discourses, and the moral claims of humanism. But let there be no misunderstanding: it is not that a real man, the object of knowledge, philosophical reflection or technical intervention, has been substituted for the soul, the illusion of the theologians. The man described for us, whom we are invited to free, is already in himself the effect of a subjection much more profound than himself. A 'soul' inhabits him and brings him to existence, which is itself a factor in the mastery that power exercises over the body. The soul is the effect and instrument of a political anatomy; the soul is the prison of the body.

That punishment in general and the prison in particular belong to a political technology of the body is a lesson that I have learnt not so much from history as from the present. In recent years, prison revolts have occurred throughout the world. There was certainly something paradoxical about their aims, their slogans and the way they took place. They were revolts against an entire state of physical misery that is over a century old: against cold, suffocation and overcrowding, against decrepit walls, hunger, physical maltreatment. But they were also revolts against model prisons, tranquillizers, isolation, the medical or educational services. Were they revolts whose aims were merely material? Or contradictory revolts: against the obsolete, but also against comfort; against the warders, but also against the psychiatrists? In fact, all these movements – and the innumerable discourses that the prison has given rise to since the early nineteenth century – have been about the body and material things. What has sustained these discourses, these memories and invectives are indeed those minute material details. One may, if one is so disposed, see them as no more than blind demands or suspect the existence behind them of alien strategies. In fact, they were revolts, at the level of the body, against the very body of the prison. What was at issue was not whether the prison environment was too harsh or too aseptic, too primitive or too efficient, but its very materiality as an instrument and vector of power; it is this whole technology of power over the body that the technology of the 'soul' – that of the educationalists, psychologists and psychiatrists – fails either to conceal or to compensate, for the simple reason that it is one of its tools. I would like to write the history of this prison, with all the political investments of the body that it gathers together in its closed architecture. Why? Simply because I am interested in the past? No, if one means by that writing a history of the past in terms of the present. Yes, if one means writing the history of the present.[1]

[pp. 200–4, A description of Bentham's Panopticon]

Bentham's *Panopticon* is the architectural figure of this composition. We know the principle on which it was based: at the periphery, an annular building; at the centre, a tower; this tower is pierced with wide windows that open onto the inner side of the ring; the peripheric building is divided into cells, each of which extends the whole width of the building; they have two windows, one on the inside, corresponding to the windows of the tower; the other, on the outside, allows the light to cross the cell from one end to the other. All that is needed, then, is to place a supervisor in a central tower and to shut up in each cell a madman, a patient, a condemned man, a worker or a schoolboy. By the effect of backlighting, one can observe from the tower, standing out precisely against the light, the small captive shadows in the cells of the periphery. They are like so many cages, so many small theatres, in which each actor is alone, perfectly individualized and constantly visible. The panoptic mechanism arranges spatial unities that make it possible to see constantly and to recognize immediately. In short, it reverses the principle of the dungeon; or rather of its three functions – to enclose, to deprive of light and to hide – it preserves only the first and eliminates the other two. Full lighting and the eye of a supervisor capture better than darkness, which ultimately protected. Visibility is a trap.

To begin with, this made it possible – as a negative effect – to avoid those compact, swarming, howling masses that were to be found in places of confinement, those painted by Goya or described by Howard. Each individual, in his place, is securely confined to a cell from which he is seen from the front by the supervisor; but the side walls prevent him from coming into contact with his companions. He is seen, but he does not see; he is the object of information, never a subject in communication. The arrangement of his room, opposite the central tower, imposes on him an axial visibility; but the divisions of the ring, those separated cells, imply a lateral invisibility. And this invisibility is a guarantee of order. If the inmates are convicts, there is no danger of a plot, an attempt at collective escape, the planning of new crimes for the future, bad reciprocal influences; if they are patients, there is no danger of contagion; if they are madmen there is no risk of their committing violence upon one another; if they are schoolchildren, there is no copying, no noise, no chatter, no waste of time; if they are workers, there are no disorders, no theft, no coalitions, none of those distractions that slow down the rate of work, make it less perfect or cause accidents. The crowd, a compact mass, a locus of multiple exchanges, individualities merging together, a collective effect, is abolished and replaced by a collection of separated individualities. From the point of view of the guardian, it is replaced by a multiplicity that can be numbered and supervised; from the point of view of the inmates, by a sequestered and observed solitude (Bentham, 60–4).

Hence the major effect of the Panopticon: to induce in the inmate a state of conscious and permanent visibility that assures the automatic functioning of power. So to arrange things that the surveillance is permanent in its effects, even if it is discontinuous in its action; that the perfection of power should tend to render its actual exercise unnecessary; that this architectural apparatus should be a machine for creating and sustaining a power relation independent of the person who exercises it; in short, that the inmates should be caught up in a power situation of which they are themselves the bearers. To achieve this, it is at once too much and too little that the prisoner should be constantly observed by an inspector: too little, for what matters is that he knows himself to be observed; too much, because he has no need in fact of being so. In view of this, Bentham laid down the principle that power should be visible and unverifiable. Visible: the inmate will constantly have before his eyes the tall outline of the central tower from which he is spied upon. Unverifiable: the inmate must never know whether he is being looked at at any one moment; but he must be sure that he may always be so. In order to make the presence or absence of the inspector unverifiable, so that the prisoners, in their cells, cannot even see a shadow, Bentham envisaged not only venetian blinds on the windows of the central observation hall, but, on the inside, partitions that intersected the hall at right angles and, in order to pass from one quarter to the other, not doors but zig-zag openings; for the slightest noise, a gleam of light, a brightness in a half-opened door would betray the presence of the guardian.[2] The Panopticon is a machine for dissociating the see/being seen dyad: in the peripheric ring, one is totally seen, without ever seeing; in the central tower, one sees everything without ever being seen.[3]

It is an important mechanism, for it automatizes and disindividualizes power. Power has its principle not so much in a person as in a certain concerted distribution of bodies, surfaces, lights, gazes; in an arrangement whose internal mechanisms produce the relation in which individuals are caught up. The ceremonies, the rituals, the marks by which the sovereign's surplus power was manifested are useless. There is a machinery that assures dissymmetry, disequilibrium, difference. Consequently, it does not matter who exercises power. Any individual, taken almost at random, can operate the machine: in the absence of the director, his family, his friends, his visitors, even his servants (Bentham, 45). Similarly, it does not matter what motive animates him: the curiosity of the indiscreet, the malice of a child, the thirst for knowledge of a philosopher who wishes to visit this museum of human nature, or the perversity of those who take pleasure in spying and punishing. The more numerous those anonymous and temporary observers are, the greater the risk for the inmate of being surprised and the greater his anxious awareness of being observed. The Panopticon is a marvellous machine which, whatever use one may wish to put it to, produces homogeneous effects of power.

A real subjection is born mechanically from a fictitious relation. So it is not necessary to use force to constrain the convict to good behaviour, the madman to calm, the worker to work, the schoolboy to application, the patient to the observation of the regulations. Bentham was surprised that panoptic institutions could be so light: there were no more bars, no more chains, no more heavy locks; all that was needed was that the separations should be clear and the openings well arranged. The heaviness of the old 'houses of security', with their fortress-like architecture, could be replaced by the simple, economic geometry of a 'house of certainty'. The efficiency of power, its constraining force have, in a sense, passed over to the other side – to the side of its surface of application. He who is subjected to a field of visibility, and who knows it, assumes responsibility for the constraints of power; he makes them play spontaneously upon himself; he inscribes in himself the power relation in which he simultaneously plays both roles; he becomes the principle of his own subjection. By this very fact, the external power may throw off its physical weight; it tends to the non-corporal; and, the more it approaches this limit, the more constant, profound and permanent are its effects: it is a perpetual victory that avoids any physical confrontation and which is always decided in advance.

Bentham does not say whether he was inspired, in his project, by Le Vaux's menagerie at Versailles: the first menagerie in which the different elements are not, as they traditionally were, distributed in a park (Loisel, 104–7). At the centre was an octagonal pavilion which, on the first floor, consisted of only a single room, the king's *salon*; on every side large windows looked out onto seven cages (the eighth side was reserved for the entrance), containing different species of animals. By Bentham's time, this menagerie had disappeared. But one finds in the programme of the Panopticon a similar concern with individualizing observation, with characterization and classification, with the analytical arrangement of space. The Panopticon is a royal menagerie; the animal is replaced by man, individual distribution by specific grouping and the king by the machinery of a furtive power. With this exception, the Panopticon also does the work of a naturalist. It makes it possible to draw up differences: among patients, to observe the symptoms of each individual, without the proximity of beds, the circulation of miasmas, the effects of contagion confusing the clinical tables; among schoolchildren, it makes it possible to observe performances (without there being any imitation or copying), to map aptitudes, to assess characters, to draw up rigorous classifications and, in relation to normal development, to distinguish laziness and stubbornness' from 'incurable imbecility'; among workers, it makes it possible to note the aptitudes of each worker, compare the time he takes to perform a task, and if they are paid by the day, to calculate their wages (Bentham, 60–4).

So much for the question of observation. But the Panopticon was also a laboratory; it could be used as a machine to carry out experiments, to alter behaviour, to train or correct individuals. To experiment with medicines and monitor their effects. To try out different punishments on prisoners, according to their crimes and character, and to seek the most effective ones. To teach different techniques simultaneously to the workers, to decide which is the best. To try out pedagogical experiments – and in particular to take up once again the well-debated problem of secluded education, by using orphans. One would see what would happen when, in their sixteenth or eighteenth year, they were presented with other boys or girls, one could verify whether, as Helvetius thought, anyone could learn anything; one would follow 'the genealogy of every observable idea'; one could bring up different children according to different systems of thought, making certain children believe that two and two do not make four or that the moon is a cheese, then put them together when they are twenty or twenty-five years old; one would then have discussions that would be worth a great deal more than the sermons or lectures on which so much money is spent; one would have at least an opportunity of making discoveries in the domain of metaphysics. The Panopticon is a privileged place for experiments on men, and for analysing with complete certainty the transformations that may be obtained from them. The Panopticon may even provide an apparatus for supervising its own mechanisms. In this central tower, the director may spy on all the employees that he has under his orders: nurses, doctors, foremen, teachers, warders; he will be able to judge them continuously, alter their behaviour, impose upon them the methods he thinks best; and it will even be possible to observe the director himself. An inspector arriving unexpectedly at the centre of the Panopticon will be able to judge at a glance, without anything being concealed from him, how the entire establishment is functioning. And, in any case, enclosed as he is in the middle of this architectural mechanism, is not the director's own fate entirely bound up with it? The incompetent physician who has allowed contagion to spread, the incompetent prison governor or workshop manager will be the first victims of an epidemic or a revolt. ' "By every tie I could devise", said the master of the Panopticon, "my own fate had been bound up by me with theirs" ' (Bentham, 177). The Panopticon functions as a kind of laboratory of power. Thanks to its mechanisms of observation, it gains in efficiency and in the ability to penetrate into men's behaviour; knowledge follows the advances of power, discovering new objects of knowledge over all the surfaces on which power is exercised.

[pp. 249–55]

The prison, the place where the penalty is carried out, is also the place of observation of punished individuals. This takes two forms: surveillance, of course, but also knowledge of each inmate, of his behaviour, his deeper states of mind, his gradual improvement; the prisons must be conceived as places for the formation of clinical knowledge about the convicts; 'the penitentiary system cannot be an *a priori* conception; it is an induction of the social state. There are moral diseases, as well as breakdowns in health, where the treatment depends on the site and direction of the illness' (Faucher, 6). This involves two essential mechanisms. It must be possible to hold the prisoner under permanent observation; every report that can be made about him must be recorded and computed. The theme of the Panopticon – at once surveillance and observation, security and knowledge, individualization and totalization, isolation and transparency – found in the prison its privileged locus of realization. Although the panoptic procedures, as concrete forms of the exercise of power, have become extremely widespread, at least in their less concentrated forms, it was really only in the penitentiary institutions that Bentham's utopia could be fully expressed in a material form. In the 1830s, the Panopticon became the architectural programme of most prison projects. It was the most direct way of expressing 'the intelligence of discipline in stone' (Lucas, I, 69); of making architecture transparent to the administration of power;[4] of making it possible to substitute for force or other violent constraints the gentle efficiency of total surveillance; of ordering space according to the recent humanization of the codes and the new penitentiary theory: 'The authorities, on the one hand, and the architect, on the other, must know, therefore, whether the prisons are to be based on the principle of milder penalties or on a system of reforming convicts, in accordance with legislation which, by getting to the root cause of the people's vices, becomes a principle that will regenerate the virtues that they must practice' (Baltard, 4–5).

In short, its task was to constitute a prison-machine[5] with a cell of visibility in which the inmate will find himself caught as 'in the glass house of the Greek philosopher' (Harou-Romain, 8) and a central point from which a permanent gaze may control prisoners and staff. Around these two requirements, several variations were possible: the Benthamite Panopticon in its strict form, the semicircle, the cross-plan, the star shape. In the midst of all these discussions, the Minister of the Interior in 1841 sums up the fundamental principles: 'The central inspection hall is the pivot of the system. Without a central point of inspection, surveillance ceases to be guaranteed, continuous and general; for it is impossible to have complete trust in the activity, zeal and intelligence of the warder who immediately supervises the cells . . . The architect must therefore bring all his attention to bear on this object; it is a question both of discipline and economy. The more accurate and easy the surveillance, the less need will there be to seek in the strength of the building guarantees against attempted escape and communication between the inmates. But surveillance will be perfect if from a central hall the director or head-warder sees, without moving and without being seen, not only the entrances of all the cells and even the inside of most of them when the unglazed door is open, but also the warders guarding the prisoners on every floor . . . With the formula of circular or semi-circular prisons, it would be possible to see from a single centre all the prisoners in their cells and the warders in the inspection galleries' (Ducatel, 9).

But the penitential Panopticon was also a system of individualizing and permanent documentation. The same year in which variants of the Benthamite schema were recommended for the building of prisons, the system of 'moral accounting' was made compulsory: an individual report of a uniform kind in every prison, on which the governor or head-warder, the chaplain and the instructor had to fill in their observations on each inmate: 'It is in a way the *vade mecum* of prison administration, making it possible to assess each case, each circumstance and, consequently, to know what treatment to apply to each prisoner individually' (Ducpétiaux, 56–7). Many other, much more complete, systems of recording were planned or tried out (cf., for example, Gregory, 199ff; Grellet-Wammy, 23–5 and 199–203). The overall aim was to make the prison a place for the constitution of a body of knowledge that would regulate the exercise of penitentiary practice. The prison has not only to know the decision of the judges and to apply it in terms of the established regulations: it has to extract unceasingly from the inmate a body of knowledge that will make it possible to transform the penal measure into a penitentiary operation; which will make of the penalty required by the offence a modification of the inmate that will be of use to society. The autonomy of the carceral régime and the knowledge that it creates make it possible to increase the utility of the penalty, which the code had made the very principle of its punitive philosophy: 'The governor must not lose sight of a single inmate, because in whatever part of the prison the inmate is to be found, whether he is entering or leaving, or whether he is staying there, the governor must also justify the motives for his staying in a particular classification or for his movement from one to another. He is a veritable accountant. Each inmate is for him, in the sphere of individual education, a capital invested with penitentiary interest' (Lucas, II, 449–50). As a highly efficient technology, penitentiary practice produces a return on the capital invested in the penal system and in the building of heavy prisons.

Similarly, the offender becomes an individual to know. This demand for knowledge was not, in the first instance, inserted into the legislation itself, in order to provide substance for the sentence and to determine the true degree of guilt. It is as a convict, as a point of application for punitive mechanisms, that the offender is constituted himself as the object of possible knowledge.

But this implies that the penitentiary apparatus, with the whole technological programme that accompanies it, brings about a curious substitution: from the hands of justice, it certainly receives a convicted person; but what it must apply itself to is not, of course, the offence, nor even exactly the offender, but a rather different object, one defined by variables which at the outset at least were not taken into account in the sentence, for they were relevant only for a corrective technology. This other character, whom the penitentiary apparatus substitutes for the convicted offender, is the *delinquent*.

The delinquent is to be distinguished from the offender by the fact that it is not so much his act as his life that is relevant in characterizing him. The penitentiary operation, if it is to be a genuine re-education, must become the sum total existence of the delinquent, making of the prison a sort of artificial and coercive theatre in which his life will be examined from top to bottom. The legal punishment bears upon an act, the punitive technique on a life; it falls to this punitive technique, therefore, to reconstitute all the sordid detail of a life in the form of knowledge, to fill in the gaps of that knowledge and to act upon it by a practice of compulsion. It is a biographical knowledge and a technique for correcting individual lives. The observation of the delinquent 'should go back not only to the circumstances, but also to the causes of his crime; they must be sought in the story of his life, from the triple point of view of psychology, social position and upbringing, in order to discover the dangerous proclivities of the first, the harmful predispositions of the second and the bad antecedents of the third. This biographical investigation is an essential part of the preliminary investigation for the classification of penalties before it becomes a condition for the classification of moralities in the penitentiary system. It must accompany the convict from the court to the prison, where the governor's task is not only to receive it, but also to complete, supervise and rectify its various factors during the period of detention' (Lucas, II, 440–2). Behind the offender, to whom the investigation of the facts may attribute responsibility for an offence, stands the delinquent whose slow formation is shown in a biographical investigation. The introduction of the 'biographical' is important in the history of penality. Because it establishes the 'criminal' as existing before the crime and even outside it. And, for this reason, a psychological causality, duplicating the juridical attribution of responsibility, confuses its effects. At this point one enters the 'criminological' labyrinth from which we have certainly not yet emerged: any determining cause, because it reduces responsibility, marks the author of the offence with a criminality all the more formidable and demands penitentiary measures that are all the more strict. As the biography of the criminal duplicates in penal practice the analysis of circumstances used in gauging the crime, so one sees penal discourse and psychiatric discourse crossing each other's frontiers and there, at their point of junction, is formed the notion of the 'dangerous' individual, which makes it possible to draw up a network of causality in terms of an entire biography and to present a verdict of punishment-correction.[6]

The delinquent is also to be distinguished from the offender in that he is not only the author of his acts (the author responsible in terms of certain criteria of free, conscious will), but is linked to his offence by a whole bundle of complex threads (instincts, drives, tendencies, character). The penitentiary technique bears not on the relation between author and crime, but on the criminal's affinity with his crime. The delinquent, the strange manifestation of an overall phenomenon of criminality, is to be found in quasi-natural classes, each endowed with its own characteristics and requiring a specific treatment, what Marquet-Wasselot called in 1841 the 'ethnography of the prisons'; 'The convicts are . . . another people within the same people; with its own habits, instincts, morals' (Marquet-Wasselot, 9). We are still very close here to the 'picturesque' descriptions of the world of the malefactors – an old tradition that goes back a long way and gained new vigour in the early nineteenth century, at a time when the perception of another form of life was being articulated upon that of another class and another human species. A zoology of social sub-species and an ethnology of the civilizations of malefactors, with their own rites and language, was beginning to emerge in a parody form. But an attempt was also being made to constitute a new objectivity in which the criminal belongs to a typology that is both natural and deviant. Delinquency, a pathological gap in the human species, may be analysed as morbid syndromes or as great teratological forms. With Ferrus's classification, we probably have one of the first conversions of the old 'ethnography' of crime into a systematic typology of delinquents. The analysis is slender, certainly, but it reveals quite clearly the principle that delinquency must be specified in terms not so much of the law as of the norm. There are three types of convict; there are those who are endowed 'with intellectual resources above the average of intelligence that we have established', but who have been perverted either by the 'tendencies of their organization' and a 'native predisposition', or by 'pernicious logic', an 'iniquitous morality', a 'dangerous attitude to social duties'. Those that belong to this category require isolation day and night, solitary exercise, and, when one is forced to bring them into contact with the others, they should wear 'a light mask made of metal netting, of the kind used for stone-cutting or fencing'. The second category is made up of 'vicious, stupid or passive convicts, who have been led into evil by indifference to either shame or honour, through cowardice, that is to say, laziness, and because of a lack of resistance to bad incitements'; the régime suitable to them is not so much that of punishment as of education, and if possible of mutual education: isolation at night, work in common during the day, conversations permitted provided they are conducted aloud, reading in common, followed by mutual questioning, for which rewards may be given. Lastly, there are the 'inept or incapable convicts', who are 'rendered incapable, by an incomplete organization, of any occupation requiring considered effort and consistent will, and who are therefore incapable of competing in work with intelligent workers and who, having neither enough education to know their social duties, nor enough intelligence to understand this fact or to struggle against their personal instincts, are led to evil by their very incapacity. For these, solitude would merely encourage their inertia; they must therefore live in common, but in such a way as to form small groups, constantly stimulated by collective operations, and subjected to rigid surveillance' (Ferrus, 182ff and 278ff). Thus a 'positive' knowledge of the delinquents and their species, very different from the juridical definition of offences and their circumstances, is gradually established; but this knowledge is also distinct from the medical knowledge that makes it possible to introduce the insanity of the individual and, consequently, to efface the criminal character of the act. Ferrus states the principle quite clearly: 'Considered as a whole, criminals are nothing less than madmen; it would be unjust to the latter to confuse them with consciously perverted men'. The task of this new knowledge is to define the act 'scientifically' *qua* offence and above all the individual *qua* delinquent. Criminology is thus made possible.

The correlative of penal justice may well be the offender, but the correlative of the penitentiary apparatus is someone other; this is the delinquent, a biographical unity, a kernel of danger, representing a type of anomaly. And, although it is true that to a detention that deprives of liberty, as defined by law, the prison added the additional element of the penitentiary, this penitentiary element introduced in turn a third character who slipped between the individual condemned by the law and the individual who carries out this law. At the point that marks the disappearance of the branded, dismembered, burnt, annihilated body of the tortured criminal, there appeared the body of the prisoner, duplicated by the individuality of the 'delinquent', by the little soul of the criminal, which the very apparatus of punishment fabricated as a point of application of the power to punish and as the object of what is still called today penitentiary science. It is said that the prison fabricated delinquents; it is true that it brings back, almost inevitably, before the courts those who have been sent there. But it also fabricates them in the sense that it has introduced into the operation of the law and the offence, the judge and the offender, the condemned man and the executioner, the non-corporal reality of the delinquency that links them together and, for a century and a half, has caught them in the same trap.

## Notes

1 I shall study the birth of the prison only in the French penal system. Differences in historical developments and institutions would make a detailed comparative examination too burdensome and any attempt to describe the phenomenon as a whole too schematic.

2 In the *Postscript to the Panopticon*, Bentham adds dark inspection galleries painted in black around the inspector's lodge, each making it possible to observe two storeys of cells.

3 In the first version of the *Panopticon*, Bentham had also imagined an acoustic surveillance, operated by means of pipes leading from cells to the central tower. In the *Postcript* he abandoned the
idea, perhaps because he could not introduce into it the principle of disymmetry and prevent
the prisoners from hearing the inspector as well as the inspector hearing them. Julius tried to
develop a system of disymmetrical listening (Julius, 18).

4 'If one treats of the administrative question by abstracting the question of buildings, one runs
the risk of drawing up principles that are based on no reality; whereas, with a sufficient knowledge of administrative needs, an architect may accept a particular system of imprisonment that
theory may have dismissed as Utopian' (Blouet, 1).

5 'The English reveal their genius for mechanics in everything they do . . . and they want their
buildings to function as a machine subject to the action of a singular motor' (Baltard, 18).

6 One should study how the practice of biography became widespread at about the same time as
the constitution of the individual delinquent in the punitive mechanisms: the biography or auto-
biography of prisoners in Appert; the drawing up of biographical files on the psychiatric model;
the use of biography in the defence of accused persons. On the last point one might compare
the great justificatory memoirs of the late eighteenth century written for the three men condemned to the wheel, or for Jean Salmon – and the defences of criminals in the period of Louis
Philippe. Chaix d'Est-Ange pleaded for La Roncière: 'If long before the crime, long before the
charge is laid, you can scrutinize the defendant's life, penetrate into his heart, find its most hidden
corners, lay bare all his thoughts, his entire soul . . .' (*Discours et plaidoyers*, II, 166).

## References

Baltard L., *Architectonographie des prison*, 1829.
Bentham, J., *Works*, ed. Bowring, IV, 1843.
Blouet, Apel, *Projet de prisons cellulaires*, 1843.
*Discours et plaidoyers* [not included in the bibliography – M.H.].
Ducatel, *Instruction pour la construction des maisons d'arrêt*, 1841.
Ducpétiaux E., *De la réforme pénitentiaire*, III, 1837.
Faucher, L., *De la réforme des prisons*, 1838.
Ferrus, G., *Des prisonniers*, 1850.
Grégory, G. de, *Projet de Code penal universel*, 1832.
Grellet-Wammy, *Manuel des prisons*, II, 1832.
Harou-Roman, N.P., *Project de pénitencier*, 1840.
Julius, N.H., *Leçons sur les prisons*, I, 1831 (Fr. Trans.).
Kantorowitz, E., *The King's Two Bodies*, 1959.
Le Roy-Ladurier, E., *Contrepoint*, 1973.
—— 'L'historie immobile', *Annales*, May–June 1974.
Loisel, G., *Historic des ménageries*, II, 1912.
Lucas, C., *De la réforme des prisons*, 1836.
Malby, G. de, *De la Législation, Oeuvres complètes*, IX, 1789.
Marquet-Wasselot, J.J., *L'Ethnographie des prisons*, 1841.

# 11   Davis

## Introduction

In many respects, Kathy Davis' article is a reflection upon the themes of power, feminism, gender and the nature of social research. It first appeared in *The Gender of Power* (a collection of articles on feminist power research) and represents Davis thinking back over her experience researching and writing the monograph *Power Under the Microscope* (1988) – an account of power relations between male doctors and female patients.

If one were to select one theme which underlies the central dynamic of power relations between men and women, it has to be gender. However, the existence of this central thread does not make researching the topic of women and power straightforward because the theorization of gender cuts into the core of some of the biggest debates in contemporary social thought.

At the most general (and most innocuous) level gender gains its meaning in opposition to sex. Gender is the social construction of 'male' and 'female' while sex is the biological given. We 'do' gender but we are born sexed. However, understanding this easily stated opposition entails theorizing one of the fundamental problems of social thought: the construction of identity through the transformation of the human biological organism into a socialized person. There are two broad aspects to this problem: the nature versus nurture debate and, secondly, the problem of how to theorize the constructedness of social life.

Perceptions of the relationship between nature and nurture, the biological and the social, are scalar. At one end of the scale the person is theorized as an essentially biological being whose social appearances have only deceptive depth. In this type of sociobiologism, exemplified by Desmond Morris, the complexities of social life are merely a façade behind which lies the 'naked ape'. The male ape hunts, the female nurtures and social organization is purely epiphenomenal – places of work are merely elaborate hunting grounds etc.

At the opposite end of the scale from sociobiologism is the sociological perception of gender as constructed through social processes. In fact, at the extremities of this position lies the idea that not only gender but, in some postmodern feminism (for instance Wittig 1981), sex itself is not biological but socially constructed – the body is a social product.

The thorough-going biologistic position is, with few exceptions, hostile to feminism. Put crudely, though not inaccurately, it is a theoretical position which leads to reification of male relations of domination. As argued in our analyses of Foucault and Bourdieu, if certain power relations are perceived as socially constructed then it is implicitly the case that they need not be as they are. In order to stabilize social relations against this form of social deconstruction, an effective strategy is to claim that power relations are not cultural but, rather, reflect a reality outside of the 'merely social' and, consequently, 'merely conventional'. If male–female relations are beyond convention, any normative debate is bypassed (it is irrelevant if domination is unjust) because any attempt at change is irrational, or even perverse, since it runs counter to the immutable reality of the physical world. This denial of gender and the reduction of difference to biological sex precludes the theorization of social power (although there is conceptual space for natural or physical power). It is, in essence, an exercise of the very social power which is denied and is integral to the construction of gender.

Simone de Beauvoir's well-known observation, from *The Second Sex*, that 'one is not born a woman, but rather becomes one' is a paradigmatic assertion which is easily stated but difficult to theorize. There are a number of approaches which may be followed in order theoretically to unpack it.

Marxist approaches have been used by some feminist scholars (see Connell 1987) but this approach has the disadvantage of economic reductionism and the consequent necessity to subordinate gender to class. In order to remain faithful to the premises of Marxist discourse, gender division has to be theorized as a reflection of relations of production and consequent class antagonisms. Implicit in this is a reduction of gender/power to the status of epiphenomenal relative to the 'real' foundations of power: the ability of a specific class to realize its objective interests in the continual struggle over exploitation (see chapter 4, Poulantzas). Class becomes the mediating link between power and gender and, as a consequence, the significance of gender is trivialized – not a promising prospect for the feminist researcher. Given that feminist gender theory is a critique of patriarchal essentialism, there is also something unsatisfactory about replacing one essentialism with another.

Another common mode of analysis is sex-role theory. In general, role theory has deep foundations in sociological thought. When Durkheim first confronted the problem of social order he argued that many aspects of the orderedness of social life were reducible to social norms deriving from the specificity of social roles. When, for instance, an individual physically enters a university they automatically conform to certain norms pertaining to the construction of what it is to be either a 'lecturer' or 'student'. While one would tend not to think of lecturer or student as normative concepts, once one reflects upon 'inappropriate behaviour' (lecturer) or 'uncool behaviour' (student) it is manifestly obvious that these social roles are highly normatively regulated. This applies equally to sex-roles such as husband or wife. To use Durkheim's felicitous phrase, these norms are 'social facts' which confront social agents as an external reality which has to be negotiated. Viewed from the perspective of the sociologist, the aggregate of these social facts adds up to a complex orderedness which constitutes society as an object which exists in its own right.

The perception of the centrality of social roles in the constitution of social life is developed by Parsons in his functional systems theory. In Parsons' treatment, these roles were interpreted in terms of the 'needs' of the social system. This interpretation has the unfortunate theoretical consequence that agents conforming to their respective roles become 'cultural dopes' or, as I prefer, 'dupes' – 'oversocialized' beings who are merely the effects of the social system which they reproduce. While theoretically flawed, role theory has obvious applicability for the analysis of construction of gender. Essentially, the construction of female gender becomes reducible to a combination of stereotypical female roles (nurse, carers etc.) and 'female modes' of performing roles which are not specifically gendered (female politician etc.).

Even when structural functionalist theoretical premises are not explicit, sex-role analysis has all the flaws of the Parsonsian world view. Essentially roles are taken as given – created in advance by either whatever or whoever. Unfortunately for social theory this type of analysis has an immediate appeal because it corresponds with the stereotypes which dominate much of 'common sense' thought. However, these stereotypes explain very little because they are viciously circular to the point of being tautological – people conform to stereotypes as a result of stereotypes. The descriptive nature of this analysis presupposes taking as given, what the power theorist wishes to understand: the dynamics of power in the construction of sex-roles.

In her work, Davis set out to avoid a merely descriptive analysis of gender by explicitly examining the construction of gender through the dynamics of power. In accomplishing this task, Davis takes a theoretically and methodologically novel approach. Critics of Giddens' theory of structuration have frequently argued that, while the theory of structuration is obviously theoretically sophisticated and, to a large extent, succeeds in the task of balancing agency and structure, or subject-centredness against object-centredness, the approach appears difficult to apply empirically. Giddens' standard response has been to cite Willis' *Learning to Labour* as a paradigmatic piece of empirical research using structuration theory – which is not all that convincing given that Willis' work predates the theory of structuration. However, Davis' analysis is a better example of how structuration theory can be applied empirically. For her mode of collecting empirical data, Davis looks to ethnomethodology and conversation analysis. This is also a significant methodological move because both these approaches are frequently criticized for the fact that they fail to provide conceptual space for power.

Both ethnomethodology and conversation analysis derive from phenomenology and symbolic interactionism. Based upon these traditions ethnomethodologists and conversation analysts view identity as constructed through a series of mediations with the symbolic universe and, as a consequence, both approaches share an acute sensitivity to the complexity of the symbolically mediated aspects of social life. It is central to ethnomethodology that even the most fleeting and trivial interactions presuppose complex interactive symbolic mediation. In his 'breaching experiments' Garfinkel demonstrated that even minor breaches in the construction of interaction would lead to failure in communication (Garfinkel 1984). Promisingly for gender theory, Garfinkel and colleagues undertook a detailed ethnomethodological study of an individual, known as Agnes, who was born biologically male but who insisted that she was female. Through her behaviour, which Garfinkel described as '120% female', Agnes demonstrated the constructedness of gender (Garfinkel 1984). Because Agnes could not take femaleness for granted she was more conscious than most women of the performativity of gender and, as a consequence, made an excellent source for the analysis of how femaleness is 'accomplished'. Interestingly, while this was a constructivist analysis of gender, power was curiously absent. This could in part be explained by Agnes' idealized image of femaleness although, in all probability, it was a consequence of the phenomenological theoretical underpinnings of ethnomethodology. While conversation analysis is sensitive to power relations with regard to turn taking (men find it much easier to hold the floor than women and are less frequently interrupted), conversation analysis does not have a power perspective built into it either.

Kathy Davis made up for this lack of power perspective in conversation analysis and ethnomethodology by the introduction of Giddens' theory of structuration as a theoretical base. In the theory of structuration, power is not seen as negative, as saying no or top down but, rather, power is constituted through the structuring of relations of domination. Because structuration is 'done', it is substantially more compatible with ethnomethodology and conversation analysis than with Foucauldian theory where power tends to exist 'out there' (Davis' interpretation) in some mysterious and reified form – a reification which is reinforced by the supposed death of the subject. The moment of structuration is a moment in which multi-faceted meaning is reproduced. The meanings reproduced include the context and, as ethnomethodologists would argue, context is far from trivial. To take a Davis-type example (Davis 1988), when a female patient describes her symptoms and hesitantly suggests a particular course of medical intervention and, in response, the doctor is excessively polite, while simultaneously taking control of diagnosis and cure, both actors are reproducing the meaning of gender and the doctor–patient relationship. The tentative hesitation of the female patient is part of what it means to be a woman, a patient and a doctor engaged in interaction and, furthermore, the polite reply is equally a structuring of these three elements. In this context, a slight pause or hesitation are significant acts of structuration which reproduce specific meanings which are saturated with power. The hesitation of the woman is not power which is exercised over her but, rather, her actively structuring specific power differentials which are intrinsic to the meaning-givenness and power relations of the female patient and male doctor. In this sense, power is positive by constituting reality. Gender and patient would lose their meaning if the power differential, revealed in a moment's hesitation, were subtracted from the moment of structuration.

As I have argued in (1997a) and (2001) (and is also implicit in my introduction to Foucault pp. 181–7), Foucault's death of the subject and characterization of power as a mysterious force is not actually intrinsic to his position as practised in writing his 'histories of the present'. In the genealogy Foucault describes actors both creating and resisting power in a manner which implies that the subject is 'alive and well'. However, until this is theoretically generally accepted, Foucault's observations concerning the positive constitutive aspects of power will not be combined with structuration theory despite a shared perception of power as constituting.

**Further reading**

After 'Critical Sociology and Gender Relations', I would recommend the other articles contained in *The Gender of Power* and Davis' study *Power Under the Microscope* (1988). Radtke and Stam (eds) (1994) is another useful collection of articles on power and gender. Connell *Power and Gender* (1987) is a sophisticated critique of several feminist perspectives for their failure to take account of power and also offers an original theorization of power and gender which is reminiscent of aspects of structuration theory and Bourdieu. Judith Butler's *Gender Trouble* (1990) is a good starting point for those wishing to explore a Foucauldian analysis of gender and power.

# 'CRITICAL SOCIOLOGY AND GENDER RELATIONS'
## Kathy Davis

Within feminist scholarship, gender has occupied a privileged position as the central concept, undisputedly part and parcel of any study in the field. Based on their critique of traditional disciplines, feminists have formulated

Reprinted by kind permission of Sage Publications Ltd. from *The Gender of Power* by Kathy Davis, Monique Leijenaar and Jantine Oldersma (pp. 65–86). Copyright © 1991, Sage.

theoretical frameworks for analyzing social life using gender as focus and ana-lytic tool, 'through which the division of social experience along gender lines tends to give men and women different conceptions of themselves, their activities and beliefs, and the world around them' (Harding 1986: 31).

Gender has been investigated in terms of the individual (how men and women behave, their beliefs and attitudes, gender identity), in terms of social structure (gendered divisions in the social activities or labor of men and women) and in terms of symbolic orders (gender symbolism, how we think about 'masculinity' and 'feminity'). At each of these levels, gender has not simply been regarded as a matter of difference between individuals or social organizations or human thought, but rather as a power asymmetry. In other words, whereas gender differences may – in and of themselves – be of some academic interest, for feminists the primary concern has been with how this difference constructs asymmetrical power relations between men and women – relations involving domination and subordination. Thus, it is at the moment that the issue of gender embraces the issue of power that it becomes of particular interest and relevance to feminists.

The issue of power has not fared nearly as well as gender within feminist scholarship, however. Originally, power was viewed as something that only men 'had'. Since we were going to devote ourselves to the position of women, we found ourselves focusing on oppression as the female experience *par excellence*. In our dealings with one another, power was an even less accept-able item. In fact, it was something of a dirty word, conjuring up images of competitive, career-oriented females, stepping over the backs of their less fortunate sisters or hob-nobbing with men for a piece of the pie. It obviously had no place in the egalitarian women's communities we envisioned for ourselves.

Times have changed. We soon discovered that even women's groups were not free of power; that women were different; and – to make matters worse – some of us were more powerful than others of us. Within feminist scholar-ship, power has since become a legitimate topic of study. Gender relations now tend to be automatically viewed as relations of power. Feminist scholars are increasingly concerning themselves with how these relations come to be constructed, maintained and, of course, undermined in the various areas of social life.

Having established that power and gender are inevitably connected and that this relation is of primary concern to feminists, including the scholars among us, the next question becomes: how can the relationship between gender and power best be theorized? There are basically two possibilities. In the first case, gender is taken as the central concept and an attempt is made to develop a specifically feminist theory on power and gender. This assumes that social experience, including relations of power between the sexes, can best be understood in terms of gender. It also assumes that power has indeed a gender, i.e. that there are specific forms of power operating in gender relations. And, finally, it assumes that a specifically feminist perspective on power is required.

In the second case, power is taken as the central concept and an attempt is made to elaborate traditional or critical theories on power within the social sciences to include relations between the sexes. This assumes that social experience, including gender relations, can best be understood in terms of power. It also assumes that power does not have a gender (although the two go hand-in-hand in practice). And, finally, it assumes that a feminist critique of existing theories of power is required in order to make them applicable to understanding how power works in gender relations.

In the context of a study on power and gender in medical encounters, I was faced with this choice as well (Davis 1988a, b). My research concerned how women's complaints were being defined, diagnosed and treated in consultations with male general practitioners and how asymmetrical relations of power are being produced, reproduced and undermined in the process. It was, in short, a microanalysis of power in a specific institutionalized gender relationship.

It could have been tackled using either gender or power as theoretical focus. On the one hand, a theory of gender might have been employed in order to account for asymmetries between male physicians and female patients in medical interaction. On the other hand, a theory of power could have been selected from those available within the social sciences in order to analyze gender relations in the context of general practice consultations. In both cases, however, the theoretical framework would have had some missing pieces. Theories of gender do not deal with power explicitly; theories of power tend to be silent when it comes to the subject of gender. Thus, either way gaps would need to be filled in and adaptations made to meet the particular requirements of my own inquiry. Faced with this difficult choice, I ultimately opted for the latter route and turned to current (critical) social theory on power, in particular Giddens' (1976, 1979, 1984) theory of structuration, for help in delineating the workings of power in encounters between women and their doctors.

In this chapter, an attempt will be made to discuss some of the advantages and disadvantages of Giddens' theory for coming to terms with some of the problems which can emerge in the analysis of power and gender at the level of face-to-face interaction. After locating the theory of structuration within current debates about power in the social sciences and setting out some of its central features, an attempt will be made to demonstrate its merits for my own inquiry. Although I shall be showing why Giddens' theory of power proved a felicitous choice for my own study of power and gender in medical encounters, my conclusion will not be that I have, therefore, discovered the solution to the problems currently faced by feminist theory on gender and power. On the contrary, I shall be arguing that the entire question of choice – which theory is most adequate for investigating power relations between the sexes – is itself in need of revision. In conclusion, I shall be making some suggestions for a direction that feminist theorizing on power and gender might more profitably take.

## Problems in theorizing power

Feminists are not the first (social) scientists to encounter difficulties in theorizing power. In fact, since the inception of sociology as a science, power has been rather standard fare for debate. Despite massive theorizing concerning the 'nature of the beast', however, there appears to be little agreement as to how it should be defined. As Lukes (1982), himself a leading theorist on power, notes: when it comes to power, one is left with the unavoidable impression that 'anything goes'.[1]

Whereas the last word has yet to be said on the subject of power, several attempts have been made to sort out some of the dilemmas involved in theorizing about it. According to Lukes (1979), there are primarily three bones of contention or 'contests', which regularly emerge in discussions about power.

### Agency v. structural determinism

Should power be linked to human agency or is it a form of structural determinism? This question concerns the extent to which a person has some freedom of choice ('could have done otherwise'), even in asymmetrical power relations or whether individual activity can best be described as determined by socially structured systems of domination.

### The nature of power

Whereas everyone seems to agree that power involves A exercising some control over B's activities, the exact nature of that control is open to debate. Does power have to involve an overt or observable manifestation or can it be covert or even latent? To what extent does it have to be 'against B's interests' and, indeed, can we reasonably talk about 'interests' at all? Is power essentially a straight-forward exercise of control or is it more likely to be elusive, ambiguous, complex and subtle?

### Consensus v. coercion

Theories on power have tended to focus on power as consensus or power as coercion, but not both. To what extent should power be viewed as an essential and desirable component of highly organized societies? Or should power be regarded primarily in terms of domination and authority? Which approach has the most to offer for understanding contemporary society?

If these are the kinds of issue which inevitably arise in discussions about power, then it makes sense to look for theories which attempt to resolve them or, at least, take them a step in the right direction. I shall now take a look at one such theory: Giddens' theory of structuration and, in particular, his notions of power.

## Giddens' conception of power

Giddens attempts to resolve some of the controversies involved in the debates about power by providing a critique of the classics (Weber, Durkheim, Marx) as well as the more recent contributions to social theory (Goffman, Habermas, Althusser, Foucault). In an attempt to uncover some of their inherent theoretical weaknesses, he also tries to salvage their respective merits. This admittedly eclectic approach led to the development of his own theory of structuration, a 'grand theory' which – as he modestly notes – is applicable to 'all the concrete processes of social life' (Giddens 1984: xviii).

Within this 'grand theory', power occupies a central role. It is not something which can be 'tacked on' to other more basic concepts as, for example, to functionalism, where power is secondary to 'norms' and 'values' or in Marxist theory where 'class interest' is central and power an appendage which will disappear miraculously along with class divisions. In his view, social theories which disregard the centrality of power in social life will inevitably prove to be inadequate.

Taking the position that power is central to the study of social life does not, however, mean that it automatically becomes more central than other concepts. He rejects the tendency of Foucault and company who, under the influence of a 'Nietzschean radicalization of power', give power primacy over everything else. Power appears as some kind of 'mysterious phenomenon, that hovers everywhere and underlies everything' (Giddens 1984: 226). The result is a reductionism every bit as faulty as functionalist and Marxist reductionisms were.

In his framework, Giddens treats power as one of several primary concepts, each essential for the analysis of social life. They are all clustered around relations involving action and structure and cannot be explicated without reference to this relationship. In this relationship, which Giddens calls 'duality of structure', social structure and human action do not stand in opposition, but rather presuppose one another: 'Structure [is] the medium and outcome of the conduct it recursively organizes; the structural properties of social systems do not exist outside of action but are chronically implicated in its production and reproduction' (Giddens 1984: 374).

Taking the 'duality of structure' as starting point, Giddens is able to conceptualize power in a way which is dynamic, processual and, at the same time, highly complex. It goes beyond the scope of this chapter to deal with Giddens' theory of structuration, including his notions on power, in any comprehensive way.[2] Instead, I shall limit myself to those dimensions of his concept of power which make it especially relevant to the study of power at the level of face-to-face interaction; that is, how actors draw upon rules and resources in order to influence the course of a conversation and, in the process, construct (asymmetrical) relations of power.

Giddens' conception of power has the following five dimensions:

1 *Power is integral to social interaction*  Power is implicated at all levels of social life, from the level of 'global cultures and ideologies' all the way down to the 'most mundane levels of everyday interactions' (Giddens 1976: 113). The analysis of power is not limited to social institutions or political collectivities, but can also take a face-to-face encounter as its starting point. Any instance of social interaction involves three elements: its constitution as meaningful; its constitution as a moral or normative order; and its constitution as the operation of relations of power. These elements are 'subtly, but tightly' interwoven, making it impossible to deal with one without taking the other into account (Giddens 1979: 104–13). Power involves the skills and resources which members bring to and mobilize in the production of interaction, thereby directing or influencing its course. It is implicated in the production of meaning in the sense that actors have capabilities for making certain 'accounts count'. It is also involved in ensuring compliance to moral claims. Members exercise power by enacting or resisting sanctions. Analyzing power entails showing how it is involved in both the production of meaning as well as the constitution and maintenance of normative orders concerning how the situation and the respective social position of the participants are to be defined.

2 *Power is intrinsic to human agency*  There can be no study of power which does not take agency into account. In its most general sense, power is agency. It is the 'can' which mediates the desired or intended outcomes of social actors and the actual realization of these outcomes in their daily social practices. It is also the 'could have done otherwise' which is implicated in every situation, even the most restrictive and oppressive (Giddens 1976: 11). By linking power to agency, the possibility is rejected that social actors are ever completely governed by social forces. Even when they display outward compliance with the oppressive contingencies of their situations, the conclusion is not warranted that they have been 'driven irresistibly and uncomprehendingly by mechanical pressures' beyond their control (Giddens 1984: 15). Compliance is often the result of a decidedly rational assessment of the situation and the viable alternatives; it does not automatically entail agreement.

Whereas Giddens rejects the notion that individuals can ever be completely powerless, he does not go to the other extreme and argue that society is made under circumstances of their own choosing. Social action is always bounded by 'unacknowledged conditions' and 'unintended consequences' (Giddens 1984: 9–14); that is, by conditions lying outside the actors' self-understanding. The analysis of power entails uncovering the subtle mix of what actors do (and refrain from doing), what they *achieve* (and fail to achieve) and what they might have done (but did not do).

3 *Power is relational, involving relations of dependence and autonomy*  Giddens locates power in a relationship between actors, whereby it can be 'harnessed to actors' attempts to get others to comply with their wants' (Giddens 1976: 93). To this end, resources and skills are mobilized by actors to accomplish their respective goals or influence the course of events in a desired direction. Unfortunately, members do not have equal access to resources for effecting the outcome of the interaction. Resources are asymmetrically distributed in accordance with structures of domination.

Despite this asymmetry, however, power relations are always reciprocal, involving some degree of autonomy and dependence in both directions. Power is never a simple matter of 'haves' and 'have nots'. Such a conception can only lead to an overestimation of the power of the powerful, closing our eyes to both the chinks in the armor of the powerful as well as the myriad ways that the less powerful have to exercise control over their lives, even in situations where stable, institutionalized power relations are in operation. Investigating power will therefore also involve uncovering the 'dialectic of control': 'how the less powerful manage resources in such a way as to exert control over the more powerful in established power relationships' (Giddens 1984: 374).

4 *Power is enabling as well as constraining*  In many of the contexts of every-day life, power does go hand-in-hand with structured forms of domination. Actors do not simply intervene in the course of events, but they also try to exercise control over one another. This is accomplished by means of sanctions which are structurally available. By means of sanctioning processes, some actors can restrict the activities of other actors or get them to do things that they might not normally have done under other circumstances. Whereas this sanctioning can be accomplished by means of threat, force or violence, this is the exception. More common or mundane sanctions entail disapproval, criticism or simply an absence of response (Giddens 1984: 175).

Sanctions are not only restrictive, however. They can be enabling as well, inducing actors to engage in specific activities. In fact, sanctions are the very means by which social interaction comes to be constituted as orderly and 'normal'. This means that power cannot be equated with forms of domination despite their 'inherent social association'; nor is power an 'inherently noxious phenomenon'. A person always retains the 'capacity to say no' (Giddens 1984: 32). Power is also involved in the very constitution of social life, making it productive, enabling and even positive.

Any analysis of power, then, will entail sorting out both dimensions and showing how power is connected to constraint and enablement in specific instances of social interaction.

5 *Power is processual* Power is exercised as a process, part and parcel of the perpetual flux of situated practices of social actors. Structured relations of power involving domination and subordination are produced and reproduced through these practices. Just as members routinely and continually construct the 'normal appearances' of their everyday lives, they will simultaneously, and in similar ways, be constructing power relations. Power will be exercised as members reflexively monitor their interaction and employ skills and resources in flexible, on-the-spot and, above all, habitual ways in order to gain control over the encounter. This conception of power does not focus on the outcome or product of power or who has 'more' of it, but rather on the 'hows' of power. In other words, the focus is on how actors routinely construct, maintain, but also change and transform their relations of power.

In conclusion, Giddens' conception of power is suited to a micro-analysis of power. It does not treat power as straight-forward, top-down or repressive. Far from being a matter of openly authoritarian forms of control, power can also be enabling or productive. It has a Janus-face. Power is regarded as mundane, processual and multidimensional, whereby relations of power involving domination and subordination are constructed in the course of interaction by means of the same reflexive procedures employed by actors to structure or sustain any situation.

Having briefly described Giddens' conception of power, particularly as it can be applied to the analysis of face-to-face interaction, I shall return to the question posed at the beginning of this chapter. What does Giddens' view of power have to offer specifically for an inquiry like mine into how power works in medical interaction and, more generally, for feminist theorizing on the relationship between gender and power?

## Conceptualizing power in interaction between the sexes

At the outset of my inquiry into medical consultations between female patients and male GPs, I expected to find the kinds of phenomena so abundantly and convincingly described in feminist literature on women and health care: physicians undermining women's control and authority over their reproduction (Arms 1975; Culpepper 1978; Ehrenreich and English 1979; Oakley 1979; Fisher 1986; Martin 1987), making moralistic statements about women's roles as wives and mothers or about their sexuality (Scully and Bart 1973; Lorber 1976; Fidell 1980; Scully 1980; Standing 1980; Fisher and Groce 1985), not taking their complaints seriously (Homans 1985;

MacPherson 1988), finding psychological disorder in even the most harmless complaint (Lenanne and Lenanne 1973; Davis 1986), prescribing tranquilizers at the drop of a hat (Cooperstock 1978) and so on.

Much to my surprise (and, admittedly, chagrin),[3] I was forced to conclude, having listened to numerous taped consultations, that the GPs were behaving in an undisputedly friendly and benevolent fashion. They displayed an unflaggingly sympathetic interest in their patients' problems, even the most trivial ones. They had obviously received social skills training and were familiar with the more holistic approaches to medicine. Whereas they did prescribe tranquilizers for their female patients, it was only with great hesitancy and reluctance. In fact, it was almost as though I had wandered into a conversation between two friends rather than an institutional encounter. It did not look anything like a power struggle.

Just as I had expected the doctors of my study to display the behavior of the powerful, authoritatively wielding the sceptre of control throughout the consultations, I was prepared to discover the patients scarcely able to hold their own, hapless and helpless in the face of the combined forces of institutional authority and male domination. Whereas it was undoubtedly true that the patients did not, when all was said and done, come out on top in the interactional power struggles, I could not help but notice that they were not going down without a fight. It was abundantly clear that, just as male doctors could be nice and friendly while exercising control, patients were often surprisingly recalcitrant and rebellious. In fact, the patients routinely exercised power in all sorts of subtle, sneaky and even somewhat unorthodox ways. Although the consultations were conducted in a cooperative and – as previously mentioned – friendly fashion, patients could engage in activities that served to undermine the physician's authority over their problems as well as what was to be done about them. These power practices were not dramatic, but rather microscopic attempts to shift the power imbalance in favor of the patient.

Even my initial confrontation with my data convinced me that power was not going to be an easy thing to come to terms with. This conviction was fuelled, however, by my experience with feminist literature on interaction between the sexes. Whereas power had become an undeniable topic within these studies, it was often conceptualized in a way which was problematic. Originally, studies on interaction were not about power and gender at all.[4]

Social interaction tended to be viewed as an essentially orderly and harmonious enterprise – a cooperative coproduction involving the activities of all participants (Garfinkel 1967). These participants, otherwise referred to as 'members' had, in principle at least, access to the same kinds of interactional resources for engaging in social interaction. In other words, they were peers in the interaction game. Apparently, they did not have a gender. Feminist scholars have since taken issue with this stance. They specifically examined interaction between men and women in a variety of social contexts: private conversations between couples and mixed groups (Henley 1977; Fishman 1978), the public arena of television talkshows and meetings (Trömel-Plötz 1984), and institutional settings like medical consultations, the courtroom and the classroom (Fisher and Todd 1983, 1986). What they discovered, quite simply, was that where gender was a part of the interaction, power was soon to follow. An explicit attempt was made to uncover how the asymmetrical power relations between men and women were being constructed within and through their talk.

In most cases, this was accomplished by studying the sequential organization of the conversations and showing how women and men do not have equal access to the interactional resources for ordering that talk. The findings are of no great surprise. It would seem that men have a tendency to hog the conversational floor. They get their topics initiated and talked about more often, interrupt with equanimity and are notably reticent about performing the 'interactional shit-work' (Fishman 1978) which is necessary for any conversation, if it is to proceed in a pleasant and well-oiled fashion. Just as unsurprisingly, women seem to have considerable difficulty getting the floor. Once they do, their topics tend to get broken off midstream or are taken over by others. They are subject to constant interruption and are rarely the recipients of 'interactional shit-work', but rather the ones who do it. It is my contention that these studies have primarily two things to tell us about gender and power in face-to-face interaction. First, conversational power is something that men have and women do not. Secondly, power relations between the sexes in conversational contexts have as their most distinguishing feature control, restraint and repression. In other words, the model of power and gender relations being employed in feminist studies on interaction is a top-down, repressive one.

At this point, the reader, particularly if she is a feminist, might be inclined to ask: 'So what's wrong with that'? In fact, this model of power and gender relations does bear considerable resemblance to our interactional experiences as women. Or, as Trömel-Plötz (1984) rather pessimistically notes, this is women's 'conversational lot in life'. Moreover, it is a model which has stood us in good stead as we have attempted to uncover the inequities faced by women in the various contexts of their everyday lives.

While I do not believe that this model is entirely wrong, it clearly had some rather serious drawbacks as a conceptual framework for understanding the workings of power in my own research. How was I to come to terms with my friendly doctors and resistant patients? Moreover, it is a model which is of limited usefulness in understanding gender and power more generally. The main problem is that it draws implicitly upon what I shall refer to as feminist 'common-sense' notions on gender relations.[5] Despite the merits of these notions, they are not infallible and, in fact, are in need of some elaboration. It is to this issue that I shall now direct my attention.

## Feminist common sense on power

Feminist 'common sense', both traditionally and in the present, tends to treat power within gender relations as basically top-down and repressive. Women are regarded as the inevitable victims of male supremacy, helpless and hapless at the hands of the evil-intentioned, omnipotent male. Power, by the same token, is automatically linked to relations involving domination and author-itarian forms of control or coercion, making it difficult to see it as anything but negative and repressive. This view of power has methodological and political implications for investigating interaction between men and women.

I shall begin with the notion that power between the sexes can best be viewed as top-down. One of the main contributions of conversation analysis and, more generally, ethnomethodology and the 'interpretative sociologies' was to break radically with mainstream Parsonian sociology and its treatment of the individual as 'cultural dope', blindly driven by social forces beyond her control. A valiant attempt was made to retrieve the social actor as basically competent and knowledgeable. Studies in the field were, in fact, devoted to displaying just how – often surprisingly – capable members were at finding their way about in social life. Social interaction was always and everywhere viewed as a human accomplishment, actively and knowledgeably negotiated by the participants themselves.

This stance of uncovering how ordinary people 'do social life' and giving them at least a little credit for knowing what was going on is one of the initial attractions of conversation analysis as research orientation. It is a stance, however, which seems to disappear as soon as the participants turn out to have a gender. In that case, it is suddenly the man who does the interacting, negotiating the encounter all by himself, while the woman sits passively and helplessly on the sidelines, at best the respondent to his activities. Unwit-tingly, perhaps, it would seem that as soon as gender enters the interactional scene, women are transformed into that 'cultural dope' we used to be so inter-ested in avoiding. This is more than a methodological inconsistency, however. It has political implications as well.

It goes almost without saying that feminist scholars have always been espe-cially interested in how women fare in the various contexts of their daily lives. Whereas the original concern was with domination or 'systems of male control and coercion', there has been a growing emphasis in recent years on how women themselves 'participate in setting up, maintaining, and altering the system of gender relations' (Gerson and Peiss 1985: 322). The idea is not to deny the fact that structured asymmetries exist in the resources available to men and women for exercising control over what happens in any encounter, nor to blame women for their own oppression. It is, however, important to delineate how relations of power are being negotiated; that is, the process by which relations involving domination and subordination are produced, reproduced and transformed. This requires, among other things, being particularly alert to how women exercise control, even when their resources are limited, or when they do not, when all is said and done, come out on top. It also involves directing our attention at the often microscopic and sometimes even trivial ways in which women routinely undermine asymmetrical power relations or display some degree of penetration of what is going on, despite being unable or unwilling at that particular moment to do anything to alter the course of events.

It is this concern with the 'boundaries' – how women and men delineate their relations at any given time or place – that is essential for coming to terms with processes of change. Uncovering how they 'make and reshape their social worlds' (Gerson and Peiss 1985: 321) enables us, ultimately, to explain how and why these boundaries change or, more to the point, might be changed at some future date. In short, an adequate feminist analysis of gender relations requires replacing a top-down model of power with a model which treats power relations as something to be negotiated by parties who both have access to some resources, albeit unequal ones.

The second notion inherent in feminist common sense concerning power in gender relations is that power is inevitably linked to domination and subordination. The implication of this linkage is that power is basically a nasty business, employed by men for the sole purpose of keeping women down, silencing them or otherwise preventing them from acting, thinking or feeling as they would choose to do, when left to their own devices. There are several difficulties with such a conception of power.

First, if we want to investigate power we will be forced to look for it in situations which involve overt and authoritarian forms of control by men over women. This eliminates those instances of interaction between the sexes which are friendly, pleasant or intimate. Since much of the interaction between men and women could be characterized in precisely this way, including my own research, a model of power is clearly required which will enable us to investigate it anywhere. In other words, we need a model of power relations which can also deal with power as it is exercised in friendly or intimate encounters.

Secondly, if power relations are strictly of the coercive or repressive kind, it is difficult to account for why women continue to go along with them. The only possible explanation becomes that they are, indeed, powerless to do anything about them or, more probably, the misguided victims of what used to be dubbed 'false consciousness'. This, once again, relegates women squarely to the position of 'cultural dope', that passive and unenlightened victim of circumstances beyond her control.

Thirdly, if power is equated with domination and subordination, it is difficult to see how we as feminists could ever develop forms of social action and interaction which are something different from that. What would our feminist alternative be? We can criticize, but we are unable to come up with anything better. In other words, we are forced into a kind of political nihilism.

An adequate feminist model of power will need to take into account that power is not only linked to domination, but can also be a potentially positive or enabling force.[6] In conclusion, whereas 'feminist common sense' is an essential prerequisite for examining power in gender relations, it is neither complex nor dynamic enough to come to terms with many of the everyday encounters between the sexes.

## Theorizing power and gender

In order to come to terms with how power works to construct asymmetrical gender relations at the level of face-to-face interaction, a conception of power is needed which enables us to link agency to structured relations involving domination and subordination. We need to be able to reinstate women to the position of agency without falling into the concomitant stance of blaming them for social inequities. And, we have to come to terms with the Janus-face of power, uncovering the subtle and multifaceted complexities of its workings in many everyday encounters between the sexes. As we have seen, Giddens' theory of structuration deals with precisely these issues, making it a useful starting point for coming to terms with power in interaction between the sexes. Before closing this chapter with an unqualified endorsement of his theory, however, a few words of caution are in order.

Giddens, like most social theorists of power, does not address the subject of gender, gender relations or power relations between the sexes.[7] In fact, both his theory of structuration as well as his conception of power are completely devoid of any connection with concrete contexts or the situated practices of social actors. His theory is general and highly abstract, making it, at best, a heuristic framework for the enterprising investigator brave enough to try to use it.

Power is, of course, always and everywhere contextual. It entails a relationship between specific actors or groups, drawing upon specific rules and resources, organized in specifically structured ways. Power cannot be analyzed without reference to sex, class, region, historical period or whatever. As Thompson notes:

> what is at issue is the fact that the restrictions on opportunities operate differentially, affecting unevenly various groups of individuals whose categorization depends on certain assumptions about social structure; and it is this differential operation or effect which cannot be grasped by the analysis of rules alone. (Thompson 1984:159)

This means that Giddens' notions of power, as well as his theory of structuration as a whole, are urgently in need of both empirical and theoretical grounding. When this is done – as I have attempted in my own research on medical encounters (Davis 1988a, b) – the result is a grounded theory of gender relations as power relations in a specific social context. Using both structural and individual approaches to power, it becomes possible to show how power works without losing women as subjects. Their contributions in producing, sustaining, but also undermining and transforming relations involving domination and subordination can be uncovered without having to blame them for structured inequities. We can see power as something which is complex and subtle enough to account for much of the routine inter-action between the sexes where straightforward forms of repression are not the order of the day.

In conclusion, an attempt has been made to show how it is possible to use a theory of power, taken from the (critical) sociological tradition, and apply it to the analysis of gender relations in a specific context. Whereas it enabled me to tackle certain theoretical problems which I had encountered within feminist scholarship in my own particular field of inquiry, it did so in abstract. The business of supplying the empirical grounding – showing how power worked in face-to-face interaction between women and men in medical set-tings – was left entirely to me. My choice for a suitable theoretical framework for analyzing gender and power was made on the basis of theoretical and empirical problems which arose in the course of my inquiry.

It is my contention that this is exactly how it should be. The question of which theoretical approach is best for the study of gender and power is itself a faulty one. It presupposes that there is a theory (or that one could be developed) which could, in principle, be used to account for gender and power at all levels of social life. It is this pretension which is in need of revi-sion. The question is not whether we need a specific theory to explain how power is gendered. Neither is the issue whether or not we should re-enter the sociological mainstream in search of that one glorious theory which can be revised to meet our feminist ends. The relationship between gender and power is a complicated one; that much is clear. We need theories to help us to analyze asymmetrical relations involving power and gender in all areas and at all levels of social life. Considering the dazzling variety and complexity of social life, it seems highly improbable that any one theory – regardless of whether its starting point is gender or power – can ever hope to explain it all.

Instead of putting our efforts into the zealous pursuit of the 'perfect theory', I would suggest that we should move in the other direction. We need theories which are, above all, anchored in our experiences – as women, as feminists, but also as scholars grappling with specific questions about power and gender, applied to specific settings and analyzed with specific research methods. Taking these experiences as starting point, we must develop theories which will help us come to terms with the concrete social practices of the women and men in the contexts we are investigating. Moreover, they must be based on a sophisticated and reflective feminist critique of how asymmetrical gender relations are being constructed, maintained and under-mined in those specific contexts. It is my contention that one theoretical perspective on gender and power – a kind of feminist 'grand theory' – is not what we need. We need feminist theory on gender and power which is grounded.

## Notes

1 For example, power is something which is possessed; it can only be exercised; it is a matter of authority. Power belongs to the individual; it belongs only to collectivities; power doesn't belong to anyone, but is a feature of social relations. Power usually involves conflict, but it doesn't have to. Power presupposes resistance; power is primarily involved in compliance (to norms); power is both. Power is tied to repression and domination; power is productive and enabling. Power is bad, good, demonic or routine (Lukes 1982).
2 For a more complete discussion of how the theory of structuration can be applied to the study of power and gender, particularly in institutional settings, the reader is referred to Davis (1988b).
3 It was a project carried out explicitly under the banner of women's studies.
4 While there is also a variety of linguistic approaches to the study of language and interaction, my focus here will be on the sociological tradition of conversation analysis and ethnomethodology. Studies within this tradition have been concerned with how ordinary people engage in social practices using talk as a medium. For a good discussion of this approach, see Garfinkel (1967), Sacks et al. (1974) and, more recently, Atkinson and Heritage (1983).
5 The Schutzian notion of 'common sense' refers to mundane understandings of social life or what people need to know in order to make sense of what they or others are doing in the course of their everyday lives. Obviously, for feminists, part of this 'common sense' will concern our (and other women's) experience with oppression and exploitation in social life. This experience as well as our beliefs about it form the basis of what I am calling feminist 'common sense' here. See also Stanley and Wise (1983).
6 This point has been made by Hartsock (1983) who argues that female theorists on power have always emphasized the positive aspects of power: 'power to' rather than 'power over'. A feminist perspective on power would need to include this along with an analysis of how relations involving domination and subordination are produced and reproduced between the sexes.
7 With the exception of the occasional gratuitous reference to the 'importance' of feminism as contemporary social movement or the 'desirability' of avoiding sexist pronoun usage in scientific texts (Giddens in Munters et al. 1985) – a bit scanty for someone who claims to have produced a 'grand theory' for explicating 'all the concrete processes of social life'.

## References

Arms, S. (1975) *Immaculate Deception*. New York: Bantam Books.

Atkinson, J.M. and Heritage, J. (eds.) (1983) *Structures of Social Action: Studies in Conversation Analysis*. Cambridge: Cambridge University Press.

Cooperstock, R. (1978) 'Sex Differences in Psychotropic Drug Use', *Social Science and Medicine*, 12B: 179–86.

Culpepper, E. (1978) 'Exploring Menstrual Attitudes', in: M.S. Hennifin (ed.), *Women Looking at Biology Looking at Women*. Cambridge, MA: Schenckman.

Davis, Kathy (1986) The Process of Problem (Re)formulation in Psychotherapy', *Sociology of Health and Illness*, 8 (1): 44–74.

Davis, K. (1988a) 'Paternalism under the Microscope', in: A.D. Todd and S. Fisher (eds.), *Gender and Discourse: the Power of Talk*. Norwood: Ablex Publishing Company, pp. 19–54.

Davis, K. (1988b) *Power under the Microscope: Toward a Grounded Theory of Gender Relations in Medical Encounters*. Dordrecht: Foris Publications.

Ehrenreich, B. and English, D. (1979) *For Her Own Good*. London: Pluto Press.

Fidell, L.S. (1980) 'Sex Role Stereotypes and the American Physician', *Psychology of Women Quarterly*, 4 (3): 313–30.

Fisher, S. (1986) *In the Patient's Best Interest: Women and the Politics of Medical Decisions*. New Brunswick, NJ: Rutgers University Press.

Fisher, S. and Groce, S.B. (1985) 'Doctor-Patient Negotiation of Cultural Assumptions', *Sociology of Health and Illness*, 7 (3): 342–74.

Fisher, S. and Todd, A.D. (eds.) (1983) *The Social Organization of Doctor–Patient Communication*. Washington, DC: Center For Applied Linguistics.

Fisher, S. and Todd, A.D. (eds.) (1986) *Discourse and Institutional Authority: Medicine, Education and Law*. Norwood: Ablex Publishing Company.

Fishman, P.M. (1978) 'Interaction: the Work Women Do', *Social Problems*, 26: 397–406.

Garfinkel, H. (1967) *Studies in Ethnomethodology*. Englewood Cliffs, NJ: Prentice-Hall.

Gerson, J.M. and Peiss, K. (1985) 'Boundaries, Negotiation, Consciousness: Reconceptualizing Gender Relations', *Social Problems*, 32 (4): 317–31.

Giddens, A. (1976) *New Rules of Sociological Method*. London: Hutchinson.

Giddens, A. (1979) *Central Problems in Social Theory*. London: Macmillan Press.

Giddens, A. (1984) *The Constitution of Society*. Cambridge: Polity Press.

Harding, S. (1986) *The Science Question in Feminism*. Ithaca and London: Cornell University Press.

Hartsock, N. (1983) *Money, Sex and Power: Toward a Feminist Historical Materialism*. New York: Longman.

Henley, N.M. (1977) *Body Politics: Power, Sex and Nonverbal Communication*. Englewood Cliffs, NJ: Prentice Hall.

Homans, H. (ed.) (1985) *The Sexual Politics of Reproduction*. Aldershot: Gower.

Lenanne, K.J. and Lenanne, J. (1973) 'Alleged Psychogenic Disorders in Women – a Possible Manifestation of Sexual Prejudice', *New England Journal of Medicine*, 288 (6): 288–92.

Lorber, J. (1976) 'Women and Medical Sociology: Invisible Professionals and Ubiquitous Patients', in: M. Millman and R. Moss Kanter (eds.), *In Another Voice: Feminist Perspectives on Social Life and Social Science*. New York: Octagon Books.

Lukes, S. (1979) 'On the Relativity of Power', in: S.C. Brown (ed.), *Philosophical Disputes in the Social Sciences*. Sussex: Harvester Press, Ltd. pp. 261–74.

Lukes, S. (1982) 'Panoptikon: Macht und Herrschaft bei Weber, Marx, Foucault', *Kursbuch*, 70: 135–48.

MacPherson, A. (ed.) (1988) *Women's Problems in General Practice*. Oxford: Oxford University Press.

Martin, E. (1987) *The Woman in the Body: a Cultural Analysis of Reproduction*. Boston: Beacon Press.

Munters, Q.J., Meijer, E., Mommaas, H., Poel, H. v.d., Rosendal, R. and Spaargaren, G. (1985) *Anthony Giddens: een kennismaking met de structuratietheorie*. Wageningen: Landbouwhogeschool Wageningen.

Oakley, A. (1979) 'A Case of Maternity: Paradigms of Women as Maternity Cases', *Signs*, 4 (4): 607–31.

Sacks, H., Schegloff, E.A. and Jefferson, G. (1974) 'A Simple Systematics for the Organization of Turn-taking in Conversation', *Language*, 50: 696–735.

Scully, D. (1980) *Men Who Control Women's Health*. Boston: Houghton Mifflin.

Scully, D. and Bart, P. (1973) 'A Funny Thing Happened on the Way to the Orifice: Women in Gynecological Textbooks', *American Journal of Sociology*, 78: 1045–50.

Standing, H. (1980) 'Sickness is a Woman's Business? Reflections on the Attribution of Illness', in: Brighton Women and Science Group (eds.), *Alice through the Microscope*. London: Virago.

Stanley, L. and Wise, S. (1983) *Breaking Out: Feminist Consciousness and Feminist Research*. London: Routledge & Kegan Paul.

Thompson, J.B. (1984) *Studies in the Theory of Ideology*. Cambridge: Polity Press.

Trömel-Plötz, S. (1984) *Gewalt durch Sprache*. Frankfurt am Main: Fischer Taschenbuch Verlag.

# 12   Bourdieu

## Introduction

As stated by Bourdieu in the beginning of the text which follows, a central aspect of his objective is to construct a sociology or anthropology which is neither objectivist nor subjectivist. While this aim is identical to Giddens' it is noteworthy that there has been little significant dialogue between the two. There are also striking affinities between Bourdieu's theory of power and Foucault's.

As with the theory of structuration, for Bourdieu the key to overcoming the dualism of social thought is the theorization of social practice. Under the influence of Heidegger, this is theorized as the flowing together of past and future through the process of 'becoming'. Practical social action is what links history to the future. The past, or historicity, is found in an actor's knowledge of the social world. This knowledge is not primarily discursive but forms part of what Bourdieu terms (following Elias) their 'habitus'. The concept of habitus is equivalent to Giddens' concept of practical consciousness knowledge and bears a resemblance to Foucault's concept of *épistémes*. Habitus is a tacit knowledge of how to 'go on' as a competent social agent. It is a form of disposition derived from life experience. In this sense, habitus is both an internalization of reality and, in the moment of practice, an externalization of self as constituted through past experience. Through the use of habitus in social practice, history, as past experience, becomes projected into the future. When actors interpret their past they impose a particular order upon it which, in turn, determines their ordering the future. Hence the ability to reproduce the orderedness of social life as a whole, is a reflection of the orderedness which actors perceive to exist in the past.

Because habitus is tacit knowledge, it does not reflect the type of highly discursive instrumental rationality presupposed by rational choice theory or other such models. Yet, Bourdieu views much of social interaction as strategic. It is a strategy which is informed by a habitus consciousness of meaning and value which reflects relations of domination and, as such, power.

In the work of Poulantzas we saw that power is theorized as the ability of a class to realize its objective interests. In Bourdieu, power is similarly class-related but the concept of class is both wider and more fragmented than the traditional Marxist one and, furthermore, interests are not considered 'objective' (or systemically determined). Bourdieu combines Marx and Weber to construct a view of class which is both economically constituted and linked to status. The latter is a manifestation of domination expressed through the subtleties of meaning which characterize lifestyles. One particular expression of habitus is bodily posture, or 'hexis', whereby the body conveys meaning. Among the Kabylia, female gender is constructed according to ideals of modesty and restraint which results in a bodily posture oriented towards the ground. This is in contrast to men who stand straight, facing the sky. Haute cuisine, classical music and Oxford English are all expressions of habitus which convey surplus meaning beyond the act of eating, listening to music and communication. They convey to others that a specific individual belongs to a dominant class.

Because habitus represents past experience, status has a tendency to be both self-reproducing and self-reinforcing. It is self-reproducing in the moment that the dominated class use their past experience to shape future expectations. In this case, habitus, as embodied history, repeats itself as an endless, self-fulfilling prophecy. Individuals find themselves in a particular place in society; as a result they undergo certain experiences, they then internalize a habitus concerning the order of things, and, consequently, structure their future behaviour in a manner which reproduces their social position. Instances of this include the expectation by working-class children that education is 'not really for them'. They order their actions relative to this predisposition and the more they do so, the more accurate they find their habitus to be – they underachieve within the educational system.

The alternative to the self-fulfilling prophecy is to try to move up the social ladder. This has the unintended consequence of reinforcing relations of domination. What constitutes status is valued because people desire it. Consequently, the act of raising expectations towards social mobility is, ironically, to validate the system of hierarchy. Furthermore, the attempt at advancement usually culminates in failure because the newly acquired habitus, the new manners and meanings, do not form part of the actor's deeply internalized habitus, the habitus of childhood, which is what renders actions easy and natural to perform. The recently acquired condition of the habitus of social advancement is betrayed in the actions of such individuals. Their actions are characterized as 'affected', 'unnatural' or 'pedantic' in contrast to the 'natural ease' and 'effortless elegance' of those who carry out the very same actions with reference to a habitus which is truly 'theirs'. In the social hierarchy the petit-bourgeoisie are the most likely to find themselves in this position. They are caught between the habitus of those above and below them and, ultimately, may feel at home with neither. To borrow a phrase from Bauman, they have become universal strangers.

If we look to consensual theories of power (Parsons and Barnes, especially) one of the central problems is to understand how power is created in a quantity which surpasses what can be explained in terms of access either to coercion or scarce material resources. Social systems produce substantially more power than is explicable in terms of violence or economic capital. In Parsons, consensus derives from system goals while, in Barnes, convergence of paradigms provides the key. While the answers provided are different, both underline the idea of tacit consensus which forms part of the key to understanding the creation of power. It is relatively easy to make sense of power as coercion or economic capital, but what is much more difficult (although more interesting) is to comprehend how relations of domination are sustained by the tacit consensus of the dominated. How do we understand this surplus of power?

Given that individuals are knowledgeable agents, one answer to this question is in terms of the theorization of the knowledge which actors use in order to structure their actions: tacit social knowledge becomes the locus of the consensus. Once this conceptual move is made, we have a problematic which links Barnes (though not Parsons, who lost sight of the extent of the knowledge of social actors) to Lukes, Giddens, Davis and Foucault. In one way or another, these authors and Bourdieu all share the view that non-coercive and non-economic power bases can be explained in terms of social knowledge. In Barnes, the social knowledge is Kuhnian, in Lukes false consciousness, in Foucault systems of thought, in Giddens practical consciousness knowledge of structuration, in Davis knowledge of how 'to do' gender, and in Bourdieu it is habitus. What distinguishes these positions is the theorization of how these variants on tacit knowledge accomplish this task.

Social order is ordered by virtue of its meaning-givenness. Meaning is relationally constituted and, as attested by the existence of societies with different symbolic systems, could be otherwise than it is. Foucault's histories of the present are a form of social criticism which is practised by making this arbitrariness manifest. In a manner which is similar to Foucault, for Bourdieu power also works by obscuring arbitrariness. This process of, what I would call, reification of meaning is central to the idea of 'symbolic capital'. This form of capital is, in essence, world constructing through the capacity to make certain interpretations of the world count. Bourdieu views this ability to privilege meanings as a form of 'symbolic violence'. While Foucault focuses upon the use of truth to stabilize meaning, Bourdieu analyses how this process is brought about by the state, educational institutions and appeals to nature.

The word 'culture' has two meanings: one is anthropological (an analytical usage) while the other is linked to status and has normative connotations. In the anthropological usage, culture refers to systems of meaning and consequent habits and customs while culture as status is the 'local culture' of a particular elite group. In order for elite culture to be more than simply another arbitrary local way of life, its conventionality has to be disguised. Since cultures vary so enormously, it is diffi-cult for anyone aware of this diversity to imagine how this task can be accom-plished. However, the ease and consequent apparent naturalness of those to whom this culture is a 'natural' habitus (i.e. they are socialized into it from early childhood) is part of the key to this process of social alchemy. The observed naturalness of those of a certain social class can easily be transmogrified into an empirical claim of actual 'naturalness'. Nature is beyond convention and, as a consequence, if a particular habitus is 'natural' it is no longer a matter of 'mere' convention. In short, the difference between those who are 'born into' 'culture' and those who have to 'learn' it becomes evidence which suggests an essentialist difference between them. It is for this reason that the analysis of Davis finds that patriarchy and sociobiologism go together. If something is natural it is not mere convention and, consequently, could not be otherwise than it is. The fact that those who 'learn' it go through the motions but it is not natural to them is evidence of the fact that elite culture is not simply just another local culture (anthropological sense). Rather, the 'ease' of use of this culture by the elite reflects a (claimed) 'naturalness' and, hence, innate predisposition. Furthermore, given that it is only 'natural' to those who are already elite, this constitutes proof of their innate superiority and legitimizes existing relations of domination. As one of the great aesthetes of the culinary art observed with regard to taste: ' ". . . *taste* is a natural gift of recognizing and loving perfection . . . There is such a thing as bad taste . . . and persons of *refinement* know this *instinctively*. For those who do not, *rules* are needed" ' (Bourdieu 1984, p. 68).

Once a culture becomes reified as natural, it constitutes a scarce commodity which confers distinction, hence status, upon those who possess it (they are not simply adhering to local custom). Hence, culture becomes capital which confers power in the same manner as economic capital. Cultural capital presupposes a process of misrecognition of the arbitrariness of a local culture and the consequent legitimization as a sign of distinction, hence, status. In this sense it is intrinsically tied to symbolic capital.

A similar process occurs in education through symbolic violence in education. Educational institutions reflect the habitus of the bourgeoisie and, as a consequence, those to whom this order of things is taken for granted. In this instance, it is not nature which disguises the perception of cultural arbitrarines but academic knowledge which is validated by the state (educational qualifications) and (as in Foucault) by a claimed link to truth. The latter is reinforced within academia through a continual struggle between academics. Much of this takes place through the use of linguistic capital whereby complex linguistic expression and obfuscation are used to create a distance between scholarly knowledge and mere 'common sense'.

The struggle for power takes place in many arenas and Bourdieu refers to these as fields. Each field is governed by a local way of doing things which make particular strategies worth pursuing.

To return to the problem of objectivism and subjectivism, the actions of individuals are tied to those of structured systems by virtue of strategies and possibilities within given fields. Actors gain knowledge of the field, which becomes part of their habitus while, simultaneously, it is a reflection of the conditions of possibility within the field. The latter conditions constitute constellations of structural relations of different groups – classes – in the conflict over power. In this sense, power is both interpersonal and systemic. Because individuals exercise it over each other, power is negative but, equally, since strategy entails habitus, order and culture it is simultaneously positively constitutive. In contrast to the theory of structuration, structural reproduction is carried on through conflict but, simultaneously (as in the theory of structuration) there is consensus on shared social knowledge. However, this consensus is not derived from a desire for ontological security but, in its place, a process of reification whereby conventionality is obscured.

This theorization of the struggle over power bears a resemblance to Foucault's description of the manner in which systems of thought change through local conflicts. In Foucault, we see individuals fighting for local knowledge by claiming that they are not simply another arbitrary way of life, but constitute the truth. This is similar to Clegg's obligatory passage points which are derived from the work of Laclau and Mouffe. However, Bourdieu's position is not postmodern but links back to the older tradition of ideology and 'false consciousness' because it is a process whereby the dominated misrecognize reality. In contrast to Foucault, but as in Lukes, there would appear to exist a potential for knowledge which is undistorted by power.

## Further reading

As with Giddens and Foucault, there is an immense body of literature by and on Bourdieu. His writings on power include (1984), (1986) and (1991b) and the most accessible of his general writings is Bourdieu, Pierre and Loic J.D. Wacquant (1992). With regard to secondary material, the following are particularly useful: Fowler (1997), Harker, Mahar and Wilkes (1990) Calhoun, LiPuma and Postone (1993), Swartz (1997) Jenkins (1992), and Robbins (1991, 1999 and 2000).

# 'SOCIAL SPACE AND SYMBOLIC POWER'*
## Pierre Bourdieu

I would like, within the limits of a lecture, to try and present the theoretical principles which are at the base of the research whose results are presented

Reprinted by kind permission of the American Sociological Association and Pierre Bourdieu from *Sociological Theory*, vol. 7 (pp. 14–15). Copyright © 1989.

* This is the text of a lecture delivered at the University of California, San Diego, in March of 1986, translated from the French by Loic J.D. Wacquant. A French version appeared in Pierre Bourdieu, *Choses dites* (Paris, Editions de Minuit, 1987, pp. 147–66).

in my book *Distinction* (Bourdieu 1984a), and draw out those of its theoretical implications that are most likely to elude its readers, particularly here in the United States, due to the differences between our respective cultural and scholarly traditions.

If I had to characterize my work in two words, that is, as is the fashion these days, to label it, I would speak of *constructivist structuralism* or of *structuralist constructivism*, taking the word structuralism in a sense very different from the one it has acquired in the Saussurean or Lévi-Straussian tradition. By structuralism or structuralist, I mean that there exist, within the social world itself and not only within symbolic systems (language, myths, etc.), objective structures independent of the consciousness and will of agents, which are capable of guiding and constraining their practices or their representations. By constructivism, I mean that there is a twofold social genesis, on the one hand of the schemes of perception, thought, and action which are constitutive of what I call habitus, and on the other hand of social structures, and particularly of what I call fields and of groups, notably those we ordinarily call social classes.

I think that it is particularly necessary to set the record straight here: indeed, the hazards of translation are such that, for instance, my book *Reproduction in Education, Society and Culture* (Bourdieu and Passeron 1977) is well known, which will lead certain commentators – and some of them have not hesitated to do so – to classify me squarely among the structuralists, while works that come from a much earlier period (so old, in fact, that they even precede the emergence of the typically 'constructivist' writings on the same topics) and which would probably make them perceive me as a 'constructivist' have characteristically been ignored. Thus, in a book entitled *Pedagogic Relationship and Communication* (Bourdieu et al. 1965), we showed how the social relation of understanding in the classroom is constructed in and through misunderstanding, or in spite of misunderstanding; how teachers and students agree, by a sort of tacit transaction tacitly guided by the concern to minimize costs and risks, to agree on a minimal definition of the situation of communication. Likewise, in another study entitled 'The Categories of Professorial Judgment' (Bourdieu and de Saint Martin 1975), we tried to analyze the genesis and functioning of the categories of perception and appreciation through which professors construct an image of their students, of their performance and of their value, and (re)produce, through practices of cooptation guided by the same categories, the very group of their colleagues and the faculty. I now close this digression and return to my argument.

# I

Speaking in the most general terms, social science, be it anthropology, sociology or history, oscillates between two seemingly incompatible points of view, two apparently irreconcilable perspectives: objectivism and subjectivism or, if you prefer, between physicalism and psychologism (which can take on various colorings, phenomenological, semiological, etc.). On the one hand, it can 'treat social facts as things', according to the old Durkheimian precept, and thus leave out everything that they owe to the fact that they are objects of knowledge, of cognition – or misrecognition – within social existence. On the other hand, it can reduce the social world to the representations that agents have of it, the task of social science consisting then in producing an 'account of the accounts' produced by social subjects.

Rarely are these two positions expressed and above all realized in scientific practice in such a radical and contrasted manner. We know that Durkheim is no doubt, together with Marx, the one who expressed the *objectivist* position in the most consistent manner. 'We believe this idea to be fruitful, he wrote (Durkheim 1970, p. 250), that social life must be explained, not by the conception of those who participate in it, but by deep causes which lie outside of consciousness'. However, being a good Kantian, Durkheim was not unaware of the fact that this reality can only be grasped by employing logical instruments, categories, classifications. This being said, objectivist physicalism often goes hand in hand with the positivist proclivity to conceive classifications as mere 'operational' partitions, or as the mechanical recording of breaks or 'objective' discontinuities (as in statistical distributions for instance).

It is no doubt in the work of Alfred Schutz and of the ethnomethodologists that one would find the purest expression of the *subjectivist* vision. Thus Schutz (1962, p. 59) embraces the standpoint exactly opposite to Durkheim's: 'The observational field of the social scientist – social reality – has a specific meaning and relevance structure for the human beings living, acting, and thinking within it. By a series of common-sense constructs, they have pre-selected and pre-interpreted this world which they experience as the reality of their daily life. It is these thought objects of theirs which determine their behavior by motivating it. The thought objects constructed by the social scientist in order to grasp this social reality have to be founded upon the thought objects constructed by the common-sense thinking of men, living their daily life within their social world. Thus, the constructs of the social sciences are, so to speak, constructs of the second degree, that is, constructs of the constructs made by the actors on the social scene.' The opposition is total: in the first instance, scientific knowledge can be obtained only by means of a break with primary representations – called 'prenotions' in Durkheim and 'ideologies' in Marx – leading to unconscious causes. In the second instance, scientific knowledge is in continuity with common sense knowledge, since it is nothing but a 'construct of constructs'.

If I have somewhat belabored this opposition – one of the most harmful of these 'paired concepts' which, as Reinhard Bendix and Bennett Berger (1959) have shown, pervade the social sciences – it is because the most steadfast (and, in my eyes, the most important) intention guiding my work has been to overcome it. At the risk of appearing quite obscure, I could sum up in one phrase the gist of the analysis I am putting forth today: on the one hand, the objective structures that the sociologist constructs, in the objectivist moment, by setting aside the subjective representations of the agents, form the basis for these representations and constitute the structural constraints that bear upon interactions; but, on the other hand, these representations must also be taken into consideration particularly if one wants to account for the daily struggles, individual and collective, which purport to transform or to preserve these structures. This means that the two moments, the objectivist and the subjectivist, stand in a dialectical relationship (Bourdieu 1977) and that, for instance, even if the subjectivist moment seems very close, when taken separately, to interactionist or ethnomethodological analyses, it still differs radically from them: points of view are grasped as such and related to the positions they occupy in the structure of agents under consideration.

In order to transcend the artificial opposition that is thus created between structures and representations, one must also break with the mode of thinking which Cassirer (1923) calls *substantialist* and which inclines one to recognize no reality other than those that are available to direct intuition in ordinary experience, i.e., individuals and groups. The major contribution of what must rightly be called the structuralist revolution consists in having applied to the social world the *relational* mode of thinking which is that of modern mathematics and physics, and which identifies the real not with substances but with relations (Bourdieu 1968). The 'social reality' which Durkheim spoke of is an ensemble of invisible relations, those very relations which constitute a space of positions external to each other and defined by their proximity to, neighborhood with, or distance from each other, and also by their relative position, above or below or yet in between, in the middle. Sociology, in its objectivist moment, is a social topology, an *analysis situs* as they called this new branch of mathematics in Leibniz's time, an analysis of relative positions and of the objective relations between these positions.

This relational mode of thinking is at the point of departure of the construction presented in *Distinction*. It is a fair bet, however, that the space, that is, the system of relations, will go unnoticed by the reader, despite the use of diagrams (and of correspondence analysis, a very sophisticated form of factorial analysis). This is due, first, to the fact that the substantialist mode of thinking is easier to adopt and flows more 'naturally'. Secondly, this is because, as often happens, the means one has to use to construct social space and to exhibit its structure risk concealing the results they enable one to reach. The groups that must be constructed in order to objectivize the positions they occupy hide those positions. Thus the chapter of *Distinction* devoted to the different fractions of the dominant class will be read as a description of the various lifestyles of these fractions, instead of an analysis of locations in the space of positions of power – what I call the field of power.

(Parenthesis: one may see here that changes in vocabulary are at once the condition and the product of a break with the ordinary representation associated with the idea of 'ruling class'.)

At this point of the discussion, we can compare social space to a geographic space within which regions are divided up. But this space is constructed in such a way that the closer the agents, groups or institutions which are situated within this space, the more common properties they have; and the more distant, the fewer. Spatial distances – on paper – coincide with social distances. Such is not the case in real space. It is true that one can observe almost everywhere a tendency toward spatial segregation, people who are close together in social space tending to find themselves, by choice or by necessity, close to one another in geographic space; nevertheless, people who are very distant from each other in social space can encounter one another and interact, if only briefly and intermittently, in physical space. Interactions, which bring immediate gratification to those with empiricist dispositions – they can be observed, recorded, filmed, in sum, they are tangible, one can 'reach out and touch them' – mask the structures that are realized in them. This is one of those cases where the visible, that which is immediately given, hides the invisible which determines it. One thus forgets that the truth of any interaction is never entirely to be found within the interaction as it avails itself for observation. One example will suffice to bring out the difference between structure and interaction and, at the same time, between the structuralist vision I defend as a necessary (but not sufficient) moment of research and the so-called interactionist vision in all its forms (and especially ethnomethodology). I have in mind what I call strategies of condescension, those strategies by which agents who occupy a higher position in one of the hierarchies of objective space symbolically deny the social distance between themselves and others, a distance which does not thereby cease to exist, thus reaping the profits of the recognition granted to a purely symbolic denegation of distance ('she is unaffected', 'he is not highbrow' or 'stand-offish', etc.) which implies a recognition of distances. (The expressions I just quoted always have an implicit rider: 'she is unaffected, for a duchess', 'he is not so highbrow, for a university professor', and so on.) In short, one can use objective distances in such a way as to cumulate the advantages of propinquity and the advantages of distance, that is, distance and the recognition of distance warranted by its symbolic denegation.

How can we concretely grasp these objective relations which are irreducible to the interactions by which they manifest themselves? These objective relations are the relations between positions occupied within the distributions of the resources which are or may become active, effective, like aces in a game of cards, in the competition for the appropriation of scarce goods of which this social universe is the site. According to my empirical investigations, these fundamental powers are economic capital (in its different forms), cultural capital, social capital, and symbolic capital, which is the form that the various species of capital assume when they are perceived and recognized as legitimate (Bourdieu 1986a). Thus agents are distributed in the overall social space, in the first dimension, according to the overall volume of capital they possess and, in the second dimension, according to the structure of their capital, that is, the relative weight of the different species of capital, economic and cultural, in the total volume of their assets.

The misunderstanding that the analyses proposed particularly in *Distinction* elicit are thus due to the fact that classes on paper are liable to being apprehended as real groups. This realist (mis)reading is objectively encouraged by the fact that social space is so constructed that agents who occupy similar or neighboring positions are placed in similar conditions and subjected to similar conditionings, and therefore have every chance of having similar dispositions and interests, and thus of producing practices that are themselves similar. The dispositions acquired in the position occupied imply an adjustment to this position, what Goffman calls the 'sense of one's place'. It is this sense of one's place which, in interactions, leads people whom we call in French *'les gens modestes'*, 'common folks', to keep to their common place, and the others to 'keep their distance', to 'maintain their rank', and to 'not get familiar'. These strategies, it should be noted in passing, may be perfectly unconscious and take the form of what is called timidity or arrogance. In effect, social distances are inscribed in bodies or, more precisely, into the relation to the body, to language and to time – so many structural aspects of practice ignored by the subjectivist vision.

Add to this the fact that this sense of one's place, and the affinities of habitus experienced as sympathy or antipathy, are at the basis of all forms of cooptation, friendships, love affairs, marriages, associations, and so on, thus of all the relationships that are lasting and sometimes sanctioned by law, and you will see that everything leads one to think that classes on paper are real groups – all the more real in that the space is better constructed and the units cut into this space are smaller. If you want to launch a political movement or even an association, you will have a better chance of bringing together people who are in the same sector of social space (for instance, in the northwest region of the diagram, where intellectuals are) than if you want to bring together people situated in regions at the four corners of the diagram.

But just as subjectivism inclines one to reduce structures to visible interactions, objectivism tends to deduce actions and interactions from the structure. So the crucial error, the theoreticist error that you find in Marx, would consist in treating classes on paper as real classes, in concluding from the objective homogeneity of conditions, of conditionings, and thus of dispositions, which flows from the identity of position in social space, that the agents involved exist as a unified group, as a class. The notion of *social space allows us to go beyond the alternative of realism and nominalism* when it comes to social classes (Bourdieu 1985): the political work aimed at producing social classes as *corporate bodies*, permanent groups endowed with permanent organs or representation, acronyms, etc., is all the more likely to succeed when the agents that it seeks to assemble, to unify, to constitute into a group, are closer to each other in social space (and therefore belonging to the same theoretical class). Classes in Marx's sense have to be made through a political work that has all the more chance of succeeding when it is armed with a theory that is well-founded in reality, thus more capable of exerting a *theory effect* – *theorein*, in Greek, means to see – that is, of imposing a vision of divisions.

With the theory effect, we have escaped pure physicalism, but without foresaking the gains of the objectivist phase: groups, such as social classes, are *to be made*. They are not given in 'social reality'. The title of E.P. Thompson's (1963) famous book *The Making of the English Working Class* must be taken quite literally: the working class such as it may appear to us today, through the words meant to designate it, 'working class', 'proletariat', 'workers', 'labor movement', and so on, through the organizations that are supposed to express its will, through the logos, bureaus, locals, flags, etc., is a well-founded historical artefact (in the sense in which Durkheim said that religion is a well-founded illusion). But this in no way means that one can construct anything anyhow, either in theory or in practice.

## II

We have thus moved from social physics to social phenomenology. The 'social reality' objectivists speak about is also an object of perception. And social science must take as its object both this reality and the perception of this reality, the perspectives, the points of view which, by virtue of their position in objective social space, agents have on this reality. The spontaneous visions of the social world, the 'folk theories' ethnomethodologists talk about, or what I call 'spontaneous sociology', but also scientific theories, sociology included, are part of social reality, and, like Marxist theory for instance, can acquire a truly real power of construction.

The objectivist break with pre-notions, ideologies, spontaneous sociology, and 'folk theories', is an inevitable, necessary moment of the scientific enterprise – you cannot do without it, as do interactionism, ethnomethodology, and all these forms of social psychology which rest content with a phenomenal vision of the social world, without exposing yourself to grave mistakes. But it is necessary to effect a *second and more difficult break with objectivism*, by reintroducing, in a second stage, what had to be excluded in order to construct objective reality. Sociology must include a sociology of the perception of the social world, that is, a sociology of the construction of visions of the world which themselves contribute to the construction of this world. But, having constructed social space, we know that these points of view, as the word itself suggests, are views taken from a certain point, that is, from a determinate position within social space. And we also know that there will be different or even antagonistic points of view, since points of view depend on the point from which they are taken, since the vision that every agent has of the space depends on his or her position in that space.

By doing this, we repudiate the universal subject, the transcendental ego of phenomenology that ethnomethodologists have taken over as their own. No doubt agents do have an active apprehension of the world. No doubt they do construct their vision of the world. But this construction is carried out under structural constraints. One may even explain in sociological terms what appears to be a universal property of human experience, namely, the fact that the familiar world tends to be 'taken for granted', perceived as natural. If the social world tends to be perceived as evident and to be grasped, to use Husserl's (1983) expression, in a doxic modality, this is because the dispositions of agents, their habitus, that is, the mental structures through which they apprehend the social world, are essentially the product of the internalization of the structures of that world. As perceptive dispositions tend to be adjusted to position, agents, even the most disadvantaged ones, tend to perceive the world as natural and to accept it much more readily than one might imagine – especially when you look at the situation of the dominated through the social eyes of a dominant.

So the search for invariant forms of perception or of construction of social reality masks different things: firstly, that this construction is not carried out in a social vacuum but subjected to structural constraints; secondly, that structuring structures, cognitive structures, are themselves socially structured because they have a social genesis; thirdly, that the construction of social reality is not only an individual enterprise but may also become a collective enterprise. But the so-called microsociological vision leaves out a good number of other things: as often happens when you look too closely, you cannot see the wood from the tree; and above all, failing to construct the space of positions leaves you no chance of seeing the point from which you see what you see.

Thus the representations of agents vary with their position (and with the interest associated with it) and with their habitus, as a system of schemes of perception and appreciation of practices, cognitive and evaluative structures which are acquired through the lasting experience of a social position. Habitus is both a system of schemes of production of practices and a system of perception and appreciation of practices. And, in both of these dimensions, its operation expresses the social position in which it was elaborated. Consequently, habitus produces practices and representations which are available for classification, which are objectively differentiated; however, they are immediately perceived as such only by those agents who possess the code, the classificatory schemes necessary to understand their social meaning. Habitus thus implies a 'sense of one's place' but also a 'sense of the place of others'. For example, we say of a piece of clothing, a piece of furniture, or a book: 'that looks pretty bourgeois' or 'that's intellectual'. What are the social conditions of possibility of such a judgment? First, it presupposes that taste (or habitus) as a system of schemes of classification, is objectively referred, via the social conditionings that produced it, to a social condition: agents classify themselves, expose themselves to classification, by choosing, in conformity with their taste, different attributes (clothes, types of food, drinks, sports, friends) that go well together and that go well with them or, more exactly, suit their position. To be more precise, they choose, in the space of available goods and services, goods that occupy a position in this space homologous to the position they themselves occupy in social space. This makes for the fact that nothing classifies somebody more than the way he or she classifies. Secondly, a classificatory judgment such as 'that's petty bourgeois' presupposes that, as socialized agents, we are capable of perceiving the relation between practices or representations and positions in social space (as when we guess a person's social position from her accent). Thus, through habitus, we have a world of common sense, a world that seems self-evident.

I have so far adopted the perspective of the perceiving subject and I have mentioned the principal cause of variations in perception, namely, position in social space. But what about variations whose principle is found on the side of the object, in this space itself? It is true that the correspondence that obtains, through habitus (dispositions, taste), between positions and practices, preferences exhibited, opinions expressed, and so on, means that the social world does not present itself as pure chaos, as totally devoid of necessity and liable to being constructed in any way one likes. But this world does not present itself as totally structured either, or as capable of imposing upon every perceiving subject the principles of its own construction. The social world may be uttered and constructed in different ways according to different principles of vision and division – for example, economic divisions and ethnic divisions. If it is true that, in advanced societies, economic and cultural factors have the greatest power of differentiation, the fact remains that the potency of economic and social differences is never so great that one cannot organize agents on the basis of other principles of division – ethnic, religious, or national ones, for instance.

Despite this potential plurality of possible structurings – what Weber called the *Vielseitigkeit* of the given – it remains that the social world presents itself as a highly structured reality. This is because of a simple mechanism, which I want to sketch out briefly. Social space, as I described it above, presents itself in the form of agents endowed with different properties that are systematically linked among themselves: those who drink champagne are opposed to those who drink whiskey, but they are also opposed, in a different way, to those who drink red wine; those who drink champagne, however, have a higher chance than those who drink whiskey, and a far greater chance than those who drink red wine, of having antique furniture, playing golf at select clubs, riding horses or going to see light comedies at the theater. These properties, when they are perceived by agents endowed with the pertinent categories of perception – capable of seeing that playing golf makes you 'look' like a traditional member of the old bourgeoisie – function, in the very reality of social life, as signs: *differences function as distinctive signs* and as signs of distinction, positive or negative, and this happens outside of any intention of distinction, of any conscious search for 'conspicuous consumption'. (This is to say, parenthetically, that my analyses have nothing in common with those of Veblen – all the more so in that distinction as I construe it, from the point of view of indigenous criteria, excludes the deliberate search for distinction). In other words, through the distribution of properties, the social world presents itself, objectively, as a symbolic system which is organized according to the logic of difference, of differential distance. Social space tends to function as a symbolic space, a space of lifestyles and status groups characterized by different lifestyles.

Thus the perception of the social world is the product of a *double structuring*: on the objective side, it is socially structured because the properties attributed to agents or institutions present themselves in combinations that have very unequal probabilities: just as feathered animals are more likely to have wings than furry animals, so the possessors of a sophisticated mastery of language are more likely to be found in a museum than those who do not have this mastery. On the subjective side, it is structured because the schemes of perception and appreciation, especially those inscribed in language itself, express the state of relations of symbolic power. I am thinking for example of pairs of adjectives such as heavy/light, bright/dull, etc., which organize taste in the most diverse domains. Together, these two mechanisms act to produce a common world, a world of commonsense or, at least, a minimum consensus on the social world.

But, as I suggested, the objects of the social world can be perceived and expressed in a variety of ways, since they always include a degree of indeterminacy and vagueness, and, thereby, a certain degree of semantic elasticity. Indeed, even the most constant combinations of properties are always based on statistical connections between interchangeable characteristics; furthermore, they are subject to variations in time so that their meaning, insofar as it depends on the future, is itself held in suspense and relatively indeterminate. This objective element of uncertainty – which is often reinforced by the effect of categorization, since the same word can cover different practices – provides a basis for the plurality of visions of the world which is itself linked to the plurality of points of view. At the same time, it provides a base for symbolic struggles over the power to produce and to impose the legitimate vision of the world. (It is in the intermediate positions of social space, especially in the United States, that the indeterminacy and objective uncertainty of relations between practices and positions is at a maximum, and also, consequently, the intensity of symbolic strategies. It is easy to understand why it is this universe which provides the favorite site of the interactionists and of Goffman in particular.)

Symbolic struggles over the perception of the social world may take two different forms. On the objective side, one may act by actions of representation, individual or collective, meant to display and to throw into relief certain realities: I am thinking for instance of demonstrations whose goal is to exhibit a group, its size, its strength, its cohesiveness, to make it exist visibly (Champagne 1984); and, on the individual level, of all the strategies of presentation of self, so well analyzed by Goffman (1959, 1967), that are designed to manipulate one's self-image and especially – something that Goffman overlooked – the image of one's position in social space. On the subjective side, one may act by trying to transform categories of perception and appreciation of the social world, the cognitive and evaluative structures through which it is constructed. The categories of perception, the schemata of classification, that is, essentially, the words, the names which construct social reality as much as they express it, are the stake par excellence of political struggle, which is a struggle to impose the legitimate principle of vision and division, i.e., a struggle over the legitimate exercise of what I call the 'theory effect'. I have shown elsewhere (Bourdieu 1980, 1986b), in the case of Kabylia, that groups – households, clans, or tribes – and the names that designate them are the instruments and stakes of innumerable strategies and that agents are endlessly occupied in the negotiation of their own identity. They may, for example, manipulate genealogy, just as we, for similar reasons, manipulate the texts of the 'founding fathers' of our discipline. Likewise, on the level of the daily class struggle that social agents wage in an isolated and dispersed state, we have insults (which are a sort of magical attempt at categorization: *kathegorein*, from which our word 'category' comes, originally means to accuse publicly), gossip, rumours, slander, innuendos, and so. On the collective and more properly political level (Bourdieu 1981), we have all the strategies that aim at imposing a new construction of social reality by jettisoning the old political vocabulary, or at preserving the orthodox vision by keeping those words (which are often euphemisms, as in the expression 'common folks' that I just evoked) designed to describe the social world. The most typical of these strategies of construction are those which aim at retrospectively reconstructing a past fitted to the needs of the present – as when General Flemming, disembarking in 1917, exclaimed: 'La Fayette, here we are!' – or at constructing the future, by a creative prediction designed to limit the ever-open sense of the present.

These symbolic struggles, both the individual struggles of everyday life and the collective, organized struggles of political life, have a *specific logic* which endows them with a real autonomy from the structures in which they are rooted. Owing to the fact that symbolic capital is nothing other than economic or cultural capital when it is known and recognized, when it is known through the categories of perception that it imposes, symbolic relations of power tend to reproduce and to reinforce the power relations that constitute the structure of social space. More concretely, legitimation of the social world is not, as some believe, the product of a deliberate and purposive action of propaganda or symbolic imposition; it results, rather, from the fact that agents apply to the objective structures of the social world structures of perception and appreciation which are issued out of these very structures and which tend to picture the world as evident.

Objective relations of power tend to reproduce themselves in relations of symbolic power. In the symbolic struggle for the production of common sense or, more precisely, for the monopoly over legitimate naming, agents put into action the symbolic capital that they have acquired in previous struggles and which may be juridically guaranteed. Thus titles of nobility, like educational credentials, represent true titles of symbolic property which give one a right to share in the profits of recognition. Here again, we must break away from marginalist subjectivism: symbolic order is not formed in the manner of a market price, out of the mere mechanical addition of individual orders. On the other hand, in the determination of the objective classification and of the hierarchy of values granted to individuals and groups, not all judgments have the same weight, and holders of large amounts of symbolic capital, the *nobiles* (etymologically, those who are well-known and recognized), are in a position to impose the scale of values most favorable to their products – notably because, in our societies, they hold a practical *de facto* monopoly over institutions which, like the school system, officially determine and guarantee rank. On the other hand, symbolic capital may be officially sanctioned and guaranteed, and juridically instituted by the effect of official nomination (Bourdieu 1982). Official nomination, that is, the act whereby someone is granted a title, a socially recognized qualification, is one of the most typical expressions of that monopoly over legitimate symbolic violence which belongs to the state or to its representatives. A credential such as a school diploma is a piece of universally recognized and guaranteed symbolic capital, good on all markets. As an official definition of an official identity, it frees its holder from the symbolic struggle of all against all by imposing the universally approved perspective.

The state, which produces the official classification, is in one sense the supreme tribunal to which Kafka (1968) refers in *The Trial* when Block says to the attorney who claims to be one of the 'great attorneys': 'Of course, anybody can say he is "great", if he likes to, but in these matters the question is decided by the practices of the court.' Science need not choose between relativism and absolutism: the truth of the social world is at stake in the struggles between agents who are unequally equipped to reach an absolute, i.e., self-fulfilling vision. The legal consecration of symbolic capital confers upon a perspective an absolute, universal value, thus snatching it from a relativity that is by definition inherent in every point of view, as a view taken from a particular point in social space.

There is an official point of view, which is the point of view of officials and which is expressed in official discourse. This discourse, as Aaron Cicourel has shown, fulfils three functions. First, it performs a diagnostic, that is, an act of knowledge or cognition which begets recognition and which, quite often, tends to assert what a person or a thing is and what it is universally, for every possible person, thus objectively. It is, as Kafka clearly saw, an almost divine discourse which assigns everyone an identity. In the second place, administrative discourse says, through directives, orders, prescriptions, etc., what people have to do, given what they are. Thirdly, it says what people have actually done, as in authorized accounts such as police records. In each case, official discourse imposes a point of view, that of the institution, especially via questionnaires, official forms, and so on. This point of view is instituted as legitimate point of view, that is, a point of view that everyone has to recognize at least within the boundaries of a definite society. The representative of the state is the repository of common sense: official nominations and academic credentials tend to have a universal value on all markets. The most typical effect of the *raison d'Etat* is the effect of codification which is at work in such mundane operations as the granting of a certificate: an expert, physician or jurist, is someone who is appointed to produce a point of view which is recognized as transcendent over particular points of view – in the form of sickness notes, certificates of competence or incompetence – a point of view which confers universally recognized rights on the holder of the certificate. The state thus appears as the central bank which guarantees all certificates. One may say of the state, in the terms Leibniz used about God, that it is the 'geometral locus of all perspectives'. This is why one may generalize Weber's well-known formula and see in the state the holder of the monopoly of legitimate symbolic violence. Or, more precisely, the state is a referee, albeit a powerful one, in struggles over this monopoly.

But in the struggle for the production and imposition of the legitimate vision of the social world, the holders of bureaucratic authority never establish an absolute monopoly, even when they add the authority of science to their bureaucratic authority, as government economists do. In fact, *there are always, in any society, conflicts between symbolic powers that aim at imposing the vision of legitimate divisions*, that is, at constructing groups. Symbolic power, in this sense, is a power of 'world-making'. 'World-making' consists, according to Nelson Goodman (1978), 'in separating and reuniting, often in the same operation', in carrying out a decomposition, an analysis, and a composition, a synthesis, often by the use of labels. Social classifications, as is the case in archaic societies where they often work through dualist oppositions (masculine/feminine, high/low, strong/weak, etc.), organize the perception of the social world and, under certain conditions, can really organize the world itself.

## III

So we can now examine under what conditions a symbolic power can become a *power of constitution*, by taking the term, with Dewey, both in its philosophical sense and in its political sense: that is, a power to preserve or to transform objective principles of union and separation, of marriage and divorce, of association and dissociation, which are at work in the social world; the power to conserve or to transform current classifications in matters of gender, nation, region, age, and social status, and this through the words used to designate or to describe individuals, groups or institutions.

To change the world, one has to change the ways of world-making, that is, the vision of the world and the practical operations by which groups are produced and reproduced. Symbolic power, whose form par excellence is the power to make groups (groups that are already established and have to be consecrated or groups that have yet to be constituted such as the Marxian proletariat), rests on two conditions. Firstly, as any form of performative discourse, symbolic power has to be based on the possession of symbolic capital. The power to impose upon other minds a vision, old or new, of social divisions depends on the social authority acquired in previous struggles. Symbolic capital is a credit; it is the power granted to those who have obtained sufficient recognition to be in a position to impose recognition. In this way, the power of constitution, a power to make a new group, through mobilization, or to make it exist by proxy, by speaking on its behalf as an authorized spokesperson, can be obtained only as the outcome of a long process of institutionalization, at the end of which a representative is instituted, who receives from the group the power to make the group.

Secondly, symbolic efficacy depends on the degree to which the vision proposed is founded in reality. Obviously, the construction of groups cannot be a construction *ex nihilo*. It has all the more chance of succeeding the more it is founded in reality, that is, as I indicated, in the objective affinities between the agents who have to be brought together. The 'theory effect' is all the more powerful the more adequate the theory is. Symbolic power is the power to make things with words. It is only if it is true, that is, adequate to things, that description makes things. In this sense, *symbolic power is a power of consecration or revelation*, the power to consecrate or to reveal things that are already there. Does this mean that it does nothing? In fact, as a constellation which, according to Nelson Goodman (1978), begins to exist only when it is selected and designated as such, a group, a class, a gender, a region, or a nation begins to exist as such, for those who belong to it as well as for the others, only when it is distinguished, according to one principle or another, from other groups, that is, through knowledge and recognition (*connaissance et reconnaissance*).

We can thus, I hope, better understand what is at stake in the struggle over the existence or non-existence of classes. The struggle over classifications is a fundamental dimension of class struggle. The power to impose and to inculcate a vision of divisions, that is, the power to make visible and explicit social divisions that are implicit, is political power par excellence. It is the power to make groups, to manipulate the objective structure of society. As with constellations, the performative power of designation, of naming, brings into existence in an instituted, constituted form (i.e., as a 'corporate body', a *corporatio*, as the medieval canonists studied by Kantorovicz [1981] said), what existed up until then only as a *collectio personarium plurium*, a collection of varied persons, a purely additive series of merely juxtaposed individuals.

Here, if we bear in mind the main problem that I have tried to solve today, that of knowing how one can make things (i.e., groups) with words, we are confronted with one last question, the question of the *mysterium* of the *ministerium*, as the canonists liked to put it (Bourdieu 1984b): how does the spokesperson come to be invested with the full power to act and to speak in the name of the group which he or she produces by the magic of the slogan, the watchword, or the command, and by his mere existence as an incarnation of the collective? As the king in archaic societies, *Rex*, who, according to Benveniste (1969), is entrusted with the task of *regere fines* and *regere sacra*, of tracing out and stating the boundaries between groups and, thereby, of bringing them into existence as such, the leader of a trade union or of a political party, the civil servant or the expert invested with state authority, all are so many personifications of a social fiction to which they give life, in and through their very being, and from which they receive in return their power. The spokesperson is the substitute of the group which fully exists only through this delegation and which acts and speaks through him. He is the group made man, personified. As the canonists said: *status*, the position, is *magistratus*, the magistrate who holds it; or, as Louis XIV proclaimed, '*L'Etat, c'est moi*'; or again, in Robespierre's words, 'I am the People.' The class (or the people, the nation, or any other otherwise elusive social collective) exists if and when there exist agents who can say that they are the class, by the mere fact of speaking publicly, officially, in its place, and of being recognized as entitled to do so by the people who thereby recognize themselves as members of the class, people or nation, or of any other social reality that a realist construction of the world can invent and impose.

I hope that I was able, despite my limited linguistic capabilities, to convince you that complexity lies within social reality and not in a somewhat decadent desire to say complicated things. 'The simple, wrote Bachelard (1985), is never but the simplified.' And he demonstrated that science has never progressed except by questioning simple ideas. It seems to me that such questioning is particularly needed in the social sciences since, for all the reasons I have said, we tend too easily to satisfy ourselves with the commonplaces supplied us by our commonsense experience or by our familiarity with a scholarly tradition.

## References

Bachelard, Gaston. [1934] 1985. *The New Scientific Spirit*. Trans. Arthur Goldhammer. Boston: Beacon Press.

Bendix, Reinhard and Bennett Berger. 1959. 'Images of Society and Problems of Concept Formation in Sociology'. Pp. 92–118 in *Symposium on Sociological Theory*. Edited by Llewelyn Gross. New York: Harper and Row.

Benveniste, Emile. 1969. *Le vocabulaire des institutions indo-européennes*. Vol. II: *Pouvoir, droit, religion*. Paris: Editions de Minuit.

Bourdieu, Pierre. 1968. 'Structuralism and Theory of Sociological Knowledge'. *Social Research* 35 (Winter): 681–706.

——. [1972] 1977. *Outline of a Theory of Practice*. Cambridge: Cambridge University Press.

——. 1980. *Le sens pratique*. Paris: Editions de Minuit.

——. 1981. 'La représentation politique. Eléments pour une théorie du champ politique'. *Actes de la recherche en sciences sociales* 37 (February–March): 3–24.

——. 1982. 'Les rites d'institution'. *Actes de la recherche en sciences sociales* 43 (June): 58–63.

——. [1979] 1984a. *Distinction: A Social Critique of the Judgment of Taste*. Trans. Richard Nice. Cambridge: Harvard University Press.

——. 1984b. 'Delegation and Political Fetishism'. *Thesis Eleven* 10/11 (November): 56–70.

——. [1984] 1985. 'Social Space and the Genesis of Groups'. *Theory and Society* 14 (November): 723–44.

——. [1983] 1986a. 'The Forms of Capital'. Pp. 241–58 in *Handbook of Theory and Research for the Sociology of Education*. Edited by John G. Richardson. New York: Greenwood Press.

——. 1986b. 'From Rules to Strategies'. *Cultural Anthropology* 1–1 (February): 110–20.

Bourdieu, Pierre and Monique de Saint Martin. 1975. 'Les catégories de l'entendement professoral'. *Actes de la recherche en sciences sociales* 3 (May): 68–93. (Reprinted as 'The Categories of Professorial Judgment', in Pierre Bourdieu. [1984] 1988. *Homo Academicus*. Trans. Peter Collier. Cambridge, Polity Press, and Stanford, Stanford University Press, pp. 194–225.)

Bourdieu, Pierre, Jean-Claude Passeron et Monique de Saint Martin. 1965. *Rapport pédagogique et communication*. The Hague: Mouton. (Translated in part as 'Language and Pedagogical Situation', pp. 36–77, and 'Students and the Language of Teaching', pp. 78–124 in *Melbourne Working Papers 1980*, edited by D. McCullum and U. Ozolins, University of Melbourne, Department of Education.)

Bourdieu, Pierre and Jean-Claude Passeron. [1970] 1977. *Reproduction in Education, Society, and Culture*. London: Sage.

Cassirer, Ernst. [1910] 1923. *Substance and Function. Einstein's Theory of Relativity*. Trans. William Curtis Swabey and Marie Collins Swabey. Chicago: Open Court Publishing.

Champagne, Patrick. 1984. 'La manifestation. La production de l'évènement politique'. *Actes de la recherche en sciences sociales* 52/53: 18–41.

Durkheim, Emile. [1897] 1970. 'La conception matérialiste de l'historie'. Pp. 245–52 in *La science sociale et l'action*. Edited by Jean-Francois Filloux. Paris: Presses Universitaires de France.

Goffman, Erving. 1959. *The Presentation of Self in Everyday Life*. Harmondsworth: Pelican.

——. 1967. *Interaction Ritual*. New York: Pantheon.

Goodman, Nelson. 1978. *Ways of Wordmaking*. Indianapolis: Hackett Publishing.

Husserl, Edmund. [1913] 1983. *Ideas Pertaining to a Pure Phenomenology and to a Phenomenological Philosophy, First Book; General Introduction to a Pure Phenomenology*. The Hague: Martinus Nijhoff.

Kafka, Franz. 1968. *The Trial*. New York: Schocken Books.

Kantorowicz, Ernst H. 1981. *The King's Two Bodies: A Study in Medieval Political Theology*. Princeton: Princeton University Press.

Schutz, Alfred. 1962. *Collected Papers*, Vol. I: *The Problem of Social Reality*. The Hague: Martinus Nijhoff.

Thompson, E.P. 1963. *The Making of the English Working Class*. Harmondsworth: Penguin.

# 13 Clegg

## Introduction

Stewart Clegg frames his analysis of power in terms of reference of the modernity/postmodernity debate and, as such, his theoretical perspective is a creative synthesis of contemporary debates on power. He characterizes the modern view of power in terms of a paradigm derived from Hobbes and culminating in Lukes and Giddens, while the postmodern analysis of power has its origins in Machiavelli and has been revived by Nietzsche and Foucault as well as Laclau and Mouffe.

This conceptualization of a division between two traditions of thought is influenced by the Kuhnian view of paradigms. As we saw in the analysis of Barnes' work, for Kuhn advances in science are not characterized by an incremental building of knowledge but, rather, a slow advance broken by discontinuities brought about by scientific revolutions. A scientific revolution is, in essence, a different way of perceiving the world. As with Foucault's *épistémes*, once a new paradigm is entered, the scientific problems of before are not solved – rather, they disappear. It is not that better answers are found, rather that the questions change.

Modern thought is determined by the Enlightenment quest for truth through reason. With the 'death of God' certainty is sought in the idea of undistorted reason. Because of the instrumental success of the physical sciences, the social sciences sought to emulate this model as the path to undistorted truth. In Hobbes the model for this enterprise is mechanical physics. The Leviathan is driven by seventeenth-century laws of mechanics, where Hobbes likened it to a clock which, in turn, he considered an imitation of the universe. Similarly, the machinery of state is constructed from the measurable movements of objects colliding and bouncing against each other. In the work of Dahl and Lukes, these objects of volition – the conceptual equivalent of atoms – are social actors A and B who cause things to happen which would not otherwise have happened. In Lukes, the actor B who suffers from 'false consciousness' is an individual who, because of circumstances of socialization, has internalized knowledge which has been 'corrupted' by power. The only escape for such an actor is to discover truth that transcends the distorting effects of circumstances.

As we have seen in the analysis of Foucault and Bourdieu, science has long been considered a realm which is undistorted by the vicissitudes of culture and 'mere' convention. Hobbes was the first commentator who regarded his work as political science and Marx made similar claims to scientific practice. Scientific method is a way to reveal undistorted truth by sifting power from knowledge, hence transforming false consciousness into true consciousness. While not appealing to science, in contemporary moral philosophy, Habermas's ideal speech situation and Rawl's original position is a modern attempt to find a judgement undistorted by circumstances.

As we saw in the analysis of Foucault (see pp. 181–7), postmodern thought does not concern itself with finding undistorted truth. The world is perceived to be impregnated with ideas and meaning which reflect particular ontologies. To undo this saturation would be to escape from the condition of being itself – an impossibility. The epistemological quest for a secure bridge between the self and the world is replaced by a description of modes of being-in-the-world or subjectivities. Consistent with this view, Machiavelli does not try to construct a scientific model of social order. Rather, he describes society as a pre-existing system of relations and meanings which the individual negotiates through manipulation and strategy. Social order is the effect of a continual flux which is analytically similar to language. As 'would-be adviser' to Lorenzo de'Medici, Machiavelli offers a rich ethnography of power but does not attempt to legislate on what power is or imagine how society would look without it. He simply interprets what power does.

In the work of Foucault, Machiavelli's (pre-modern and yet) postmodern intuitions of power are integrated within a complex descriptive theory of social order which is only implicitly prescriptive. Foucault 'cuts the head off' the modern Leviathan by careful analysis of the constitution of specific subjects through systems of thought. Within this framework truth is a strategy for manipulating meaning and creating subjectivity and the modern Enlightenment question: 'What is the surest path to truth?' is perceived of as a strategy of domination rather than a legitimate question deserving an answer.

While Clegg is clearly sympathetic to the postmodern paradigm, he is careful to find conceptual space for many of the phenomena which informed the modern view of power. Just as Lukes incorporates the work of Dahl and Bachrach and Baratz into his framework, through the idea of dimensions of power, Clegg incorporates many of the observations of the modernists within his new theoretical construct. The image he uses to accomplish this is a postmodern one. Out the door go the metaphorical billiard balls bouncing into each other and they are replaced by an image more redolent of the contemporary age, an electronic image: circuits of power. Dahl's A exercising power over B is the first circuit of power – episodic power. However, this, admittedly economic, circuit is a reflection of a deeper circuit, termed dispositional power. If we return to the image of the police officer directing traffic, of course it is the case that a police officer exercises power over car drivers by making them take turnings which they would not otherwise do but these episodic, momentary, events are only a reflection of a deeper reality: the system of meaning within which such beings as police officers exist. Similarly, if we were to study chess we would not really understand the power of a queen relative to a pawn simply by observing a particular move. Rather, we would understand the power relations of the game by understanding the meaning of 'queen' and 'pawn'.

Dispositional power is a system of meaning and being-in-the-world. When Foucault outlines the creation of disciplinary practices within modernity, he is describing the creation of a specific type of subject who is central to the constitution of industrial/capitalist modes of production. Of course, it is true that a factory boss instructing a worker to stand in front of a particular machine for a particular length of time is exercising power. However, this episodic exercise of power is the manifestation of deeper phenomena, including the creation of a disciplined workforce. Dispositional power works through the creation of specific meaning and modes of subjectification which are internalized in the factory and the school. Because meaning is tied to rules, it is internalized by rule following. Dispositional power is reflected in the 'rules of the game' which constitute reality.

The moment dispositional rules and meanings are reproduced, membership of the system is recreated. Recreation of the rules of the game integrates the individual into society – social integration. Resistance to modes of being is an act of subvertion of the dominant discourse. These resistances find their way into even (or, often, particularly) the strictest of schools and the best supervised factories.

Because dispositional power is always resisted, it has to be reinforced. It does not simply exist. Life is not just a recreational game, the rules have to be fought for and stabilized. In Foucault, we saw how truth performs precisely such a function. It is a view from nowhere which makes the rules of the game simply the way they are. Truth is, of course, not the only strategy for achieving this effect; consequently, Clegg uses a more generalized term. Based upon the work of Laclau and Mouffe, Clegg writes of 'obligatory passage points' which are the rituals and discourses that reify meaning. They are a continual mill through which both speech and action have to be processed before they can be justified.

While dispositional power constitutes the context of episodic power, in itself dispositional power is, in turn, a manifestation of a deeper level of power. This is the overall systemic level which characterizes a particular set of relations of domination. While the disciplined worker is the outcome of dispositional power, these dispositions are a reflection of the capitalist industrial system. The subject who is formed through continual disciplined practice makes sense only within a mode of production where labour power is sold for so much an hour – the disciplined worker would be entirely useless in a world without wage labour. While specific dispositional powers may appear separate and unrelated, they constitute a reflection of a systemic whole. They are a manifestation of system integration which facilitates certain modes of dispositional power while precluding others.

System integration is not self-perpetuating. It is the outcome of continual reinforcement and innovation in techniques resource management. As with Giddens, neither the material nor the authoritative resources are primary. Capitalism is as attributable to the clock as it is to the steam engine. Organizational outflanking is central to systemic change and stability. A dominant group maintains a system by continually organizationally outflanking others while, at the same time, those wishing to change the status quo have to organizationally outflank those who are presently outflanking them. This happens at the systemic level when, for instance, capitalism outflanked feudalism and, arguably, a similar process is currently under way with globalized systems outflanking modern nation-states. However, these macro systemic changes and outflankings are, of course, a reflection of micro outflankings at the local level. When soldiers were for the first time organized according to military discipline which made possible the continuous fire of bullets against the enemy, this resulted in local victories which, no doubt, were important to contemporaries at that time (viz. the Swedish victory in the Thirty Years War). However, what would not have been as immediately obvious to the actors involved was the fact that creation of the disciplined soldier rendered the feudal knight an anachronism – a meaningless, if colourful, piece of flotsam from a bygone epoch, whose superfluity was symptomatic of a new age.

The examples of organizational outflanking cited are agent-specific. Clegg emphasizes that organizational outflanking need not take this form. The transition from feudalism to capitalism was not only a consequence of specific strategies of innovation but was also influenced by exogenous environmental contingencies. In particular, the plague was central to the demise of feudalism. It was not the work of strategists of power but, rather, the humble rat spreading virus across Europe and, similarly, today, global warming is an exogenous force which will have a huge and unpredictable impact upon future relations of domination.

### Further reading

Aside from reading the whole of *Frameworks of Power* (1989) (which is recommended) there are a number of articles and books by Clegg on power, including, 'Power and Authority, Resistance and Legitimacy' in Goverde *et al.* (2000). Since Clegg's work is influenced by Foucault as well as by Laclau and Mouffe (especially 1985), these are recommended for a fuller understanding of his theoretical position.

# From *FRAMEWORKS OF POWER*
## Stewart Clegg

[pp. 198–218]

## Strategic agency

Implicit in the view being developed here is a conception of organizations as locales in which negotiation, contestation and struggle between organizationally divided and linked agencies is a routine occurrence, as Machiavelli saw so clearly. Divisions of labour are to be regarded as both an object and an outcome of struggle. All divisions of labour within any employing organization are necessarily constituted within the context of various contracts of employment. Hence the employment relationship, that of economic domination and subordination, is necessarily an organizational fundamental. It is the underlying sediment through which other organization practices are stratified. Often these will overlap with it in quite complex ways.

The sociological consequences of this view of organizations are evident. Divisions of labour plus their remuneration, as central aspects of the employment contract and effort bargain, will become foci of politics. In these politics, agencies interested in maximizing their strategicality must attempt to transform their point of connection with some other agency or agencies into a 'necessary nodal point': this would be a channel through which traffic between them occurs on terms which privilege the putative strategic agency. Otherwise, strategic inclinations will be unconsummated. Strategic agency will not be successfully achieved. From these observations follow the central points of strategic contingency theory (Hickson et al. [1971]; Hinings et al. [1974]).

To achieve strategic agency requires a disciplining of the discretion of other agencies: at best, from the strategist's point of view, such other agencies will become merely authoritative relays, extensions of strategic agency (Law 1986: 16). Whatever interests such relay-agencies might have would be entirely those that they are represented as having by the strategically subordinating agency. A totally disciplined army squad in the field of battle, obediently subject to higher authority and its commands, would be the extreme example of this evacuation from agency of interests other than those authoritatively attributed to them. The actual agents, in this case the army squad, remain literally non-actors in this process: the only action which is formally allowed is for them to obey unquestioningly, sometimes on penalty of death for mutiny, desertion or insubordination in the field of battle. Ideally, they become agents without interests other than obedience to others' commands. In this respect, the army, as Weber was well aware, represents only the most condensed and concentrated form of much 'normal' organizational power and discipline, at least along the transitive dimension as it applies to low-trust, low-discretion positions. It is expedient if one's military discipline is also buttressed by moral authority, such as a religious vocation: soldiers of God, as Anthony (1977) suggests, historically have been the highest expression of obedient organization membership. Commerce as a moral crusade would be, perhaps, the ultimate cultural evangelist's dream, as Weber (1976), of course, was aware.

High discretionary strategic agency is another matter, for which power will be less prohibitive and more productive, more facilitative of desired outcomes through the disciplined discretion of the agency of empowered authorities. Here the necessity is not so much to forbid or restrict or prohibit but to enable creativity which is imbued with positivity yet still constrained by discipline. The model, of course, is the classical conception of the professional discipline as a vocation, whose testament was so exquisitely conveyed by Weber (1948) in his declaration of faith in 'Science as a Vocation'.

The articulation of interests by strategic agencies is thus the medium and outcome of unique positioning over the discretion of others' positioning in the organization field. It must be reproduced in order for existing structures of power to be reproduced. Indeed, its reproduction is a significant component of the phenomenon of power; its transformation an effective resistance to it. It should be evident that such reproductions are always already structured: they are never flat, one-dimensional topographies. Topography in this instance will always be the result of previous and current contest. In organizational life, such field structure has to be reproduced by strategic agencies or it will be open to transformation.

Agency may be evident in any circuit in a network of practices. Typically, but not necessarily, these circuits will be human, but they may instead be departmental or inanimate. An example of the latter might be the undoubted agency exercised by the complex, highly coupled, computer decision-making systems introduced by the Securities Industry Automation Corporation to Wall Street trading. Some analysts regard these as a contributory factor in the 19 October 1987 stock market crash on Wall Street (Sanger 1987). It is not far-fetched under such circumstances to suggest that agencies need not necessarily be human.

One consequence of the position taken here is that organizational locales will more likely be loci of multivalent powers than monadic sites of total control: contested terrains rather than total institutions. Barnes (1986: 184) puts it thus: 'To retain discretion over a large number of routines requires delegation. But for the maximum retained discretion over any particular routine the requirement is that authority be delegated but not power.'

The theoretically most powerful delegation of authority depends upon the delegated agent acting as one who is 'obedient'. Other than this, there is no way that the delegated routines will be directed without discretion.

'Obedience' cannot be guaranteed, despite the search for a secular equivalent to divinely inspired obeisance, if only because of the complexity and contingency of agency, as a nexus of calculation. Discretion need not entail dissent: it may be organizationally creative, productive, reproductive. None the less, to increase the power of a delegating agency does mean authorizing delegated others and delegated authorities cannot be guaranteed to be loci of wholly predictable and controlled agency, other than if they are dutiful servants. Thus the problematic of 'power in organizations' centres not on the legitimacy or otherwise of subordinates' capacities, as in the conventional view, but on the myriad practices which *inhibit* authorities from becoming powers by restricting action to that which is 'obedient', not only prohibitively but also creatively, productively. Ineluctably, 'ideology', 'expertise' and 'authority', whether 'Systems' or not, are implicated in these practices.

It has been argued thus far that authority is an a posteriori concept to that of power. The enlargement of an agency's power, except in the unlikely event of omnipotence, must be organizationally achieved through delegation. Delegation implies that discretion attaches to delegates.

Important implications flow from the relationship between power and discretion. Power will always be inscribed within contextual 'rules of the game' which both enable and constrain action (Clegg 1975). These rules may be taken to be the underlying rationale of those calculations which agencies routinely make in organizational contexts. Action can only ever be designated as such-and-such an action by reference to rules which identify it as such. Such rules can never be free of surplus or ambiguous meaning: they are always indexical to the context of interpreters and interpretation. Where there are rules there must be indexicality, as has been demonstrated by texts as diverse as Wittgenstein (1968), Garfinkel (1967), Clegg (1975) and Barnes (1986). Rules can never provide for their own interpretation. Issues of interpretation are always implicated in the processes whereby agencies instantiate and signify rules. 'Ruling' is an activity. It is accomplished by some agency as a constitutive sense-making process whereby meaning is fixed. Both rules and games necessarily tend to the subject of contested interpretation, with some players having not only play-moves but also the refereeing of these as power resources. Consequently, where rules are invoked there must be discretion. Thus, resistance is inherent in the regulation of meaning. The embodiment of labour power is also a source of resistance. It is so through the gap between the capacity to labour and its realization. Power and the organization of control is implicated in closing this gap.

Here we confront the central paradox of power: the power of an agency is increased in principle by that agency delegating authority; the delegation of authority can only proceed by rules; rules necessarily entail discretion and discretion potentially empowers delegates. From this arises the tacit and taken-for-granted basis of organizationally negotiated order, and on occasion, its fragility and instability, as has been so well observed by Strauss (1978).

Events and others must be rendered routine and predictable if negotiation is to remain an unusual and out of the ordinary state of affairs. Routines arise not so much by prohibition and intervention into states of affairs, but through the knowledgeable construction of these states of affairs so that subordinate agencies know what is to be done on their part if they are to minimize whatever sanctions might be directed at them by superordinates, or indeed by any others involve in their circuits of power. It is not only power that is premised on knowledge, or its exclusive control or privileged access. It is also subordination: as Barnes (1988: 103) puts it, such agencies 'must recognize that the output of appropriate action which they produce is what minimizes the input of coercion and sanctioning which they receive'. It is for this reason that, wherever questions of time–space extension become necessary for securing organization action, it becomes important that there be some form of rules of practice to which agents can be held. The freedom of discretion requires disciplining if it is to be a reliable relay. Whether this be achieved through what Foucault referred to as 'disciplinary' or some other modes of practice is unimportant. It may be direct surveillance, the interiorized normalizing gaze of professional self-regulation, a standardized reporting scheme, common economic interest or client reports which serve as the rules of practice. In the absence of these, by their evasion or malfunction, organizations are ill-advised to put their trust in agencies, as Machiavelli knew only too well.

Power is implicated in authority and constituted by rules; the interpretation of rules must be disciplined, must be regulated, if new powers are not to be produced and existing powers transformed. In fact, given the inherent indexicality of rule use, things will never be wholly stable; they will usually exhibit tolerance to stress, strain and strife in rule constitution whose limits can only ever be known for sure in their ill-disciplined breach of regulation. By definition, wholly effective discipline admits no breach, no 'disobedience', total rule-boundedness. None of this is far from Weber (1978) or for that matter Foucault (1977), despite protestations to the contrary: see Foucault (1981). What is surprising is that aspects of Weber on 'discipline' (which in themselves echo Durkheim's [1964] stress on 'moral regulation') were not developed in the concern of the sociology of the organizations with power.

Resistance to discipline will be irremediable not because of 'human nature', 'capitalism' or any other putatively essentialist category but because of the power/rule constitution as a nexus of meaning and interpretation which, because of indexicality, is always open to being re-fixed. This is what couples power/knowledge in Foucault's (1977) formulation, because, at its most pervasive, power positions the subject, through the organization of disciplinary practices which constitute the potentialities, incapacities and correlates of specific forms of agency.

Having now established the problematic basis for the expression of organization as agency and agency as organization, we can now move to a formal model for the expression of the dialectic of power and resistance, in terms of a reformed model of episodic power located within a general framework of circuits of power. With this framework, the issue of the relationship between power and structure, which has been at the centre of so much of this book, will be seen to be capable of dissolution in terms which require neither recourse to dualistic formulations of either concept nor reference to alleged attributes of these, such as conceptions of 'real interests'.

## The reformation of power: the contributions of Callon, Latour and colleagues

The relation between power and structure is best approached through an insight which was already present at the onset of modernity. It was developed in Machiavelli's approach to power. In chapter two this was distinguished from and compared with Hobbes' 'sovereign' concept. For Machiavelli, what was most striking about power was its strategic, contingent, extensional nature, a concept of power dependent greatly on alliances, on strategies, for its practical accomplishment. Against the fiction of *Leviathan*, which Hobbes was to engender, the analysis of power in Machiavelli conceptualized it in terms of networks, alliances, points of resistance and instability, using much the same military metaphors that Foucault was later to find congenial. However, not only Foucault has explicitly acknowledged the Machiavellian antecedents of his argument (Foucault 1981: 97); a group of sociologists of science, associated with Michel Callon and Bruno Latour at the Centre de Sociologie de l'Innovation in Paris, have systematically explored the Machiavellian dimension in the analysis of power.

Machiavelli is a conscious model for Callon et al. (1986) in their own ethnographic techniques. Machiavelli presents, they suggest, a method which offers

> a detailed and systematic description of the machinations of princes which flushes out their hidden designs ... (in which) ... he devotes himself, as a participant observer, to what would nowadays be called an ethnography of political action. Establishing his quarters in the palaces of Florence, and following the prince, Machiavelli succeeds in bringing Italian society to life and understanding its history and its conflicts. Paradoxically, in attaching himself to one person, the prince, he reconstitutes the cruel reality of a whole society. To be rigorous in such a project it is necessary to be audacious. In particular, it is vital not to let morality blind oneself in the study of how a society takes shape and is transformed from its strategic loci. (Callon et al. 1986: 5)

In Callon's (1986) work, the debilitation of moral relativism is opposed in practice by several explicit principles. Amongst these are the principles of 'agnosticism' and 'generalized symmetry'. The principle of agnosticism dictates that the power analyst be impartial between actors engaged in controversy while the principle of generalized symmetry demands that where one does encounter conflicting viewpoints one explains them in the same terms. There is a third principle, which is thoroughly consistent with the general realist auspices of this book. The principle of free association requires that one abandon all a priori distinctions between the natural and the social. (This would undermine the enterprise of Giddens at the root of his subjectivism.) These constitutive doctrines can steer a course of interpretation through the hitherto almost unnavigable channel bounded by moral relativism and moral absolutism. They undergird the remainder of this chapter and book.

The general approach which Callon (1986) develops goes by the name of a 'sociology of translation' or, as it is sometimes called, a 'sociology of enrol-ment'. It receives its name through its method. The approach has been devel-oped in empirical studies conducted in the sociology of science. At the focus of its concerns has been an empirical rather than moral approach to those interests which scientists display when doing science and which, at least in terms of some of the so-called 'philosophies' of science, have in the past been represented as if they were 'disinterested'. Such views are no longer sustain-able in the face of empirical investigations of scientists at work. Some em-pirical sociologists of science have been concerned to demonstrates those 'interests' which are implicit in scientific work (see the debates between Woolgar 1981 and Barnes 1981; also see MacKenzie 1978). This is not the position taken by Callon (1986; 1980) and his colleagues (see Callon et al. 1983 and 1986; Callon and Law 1982; Callon and Latour 1981; also see Law and Lodge 1984, part III, in particular).

Rather than imputing interests, on whatever theoretical basis, the ap-proach favoured here is aligned to perspectives which seek to demonstrate how networks of interest are actually constituted and reproduced through conscious strategies and unwitting practices constructed by the actors themselves. Interests appear as 'temporarily stabilized outcomes of previous processes of enrolment' (Callon and Law 1982: 622). These may have been intentionally produced or they may not. Intention is not at all necessary to the model; the 'temporarily stabilized outcomes' may be practices historically encountered in their fixity and facticity which no one necessarily 'intended' in any relevant way. They may be no less real for that, and agents may come to have an interest in them for any number of reasons. Why they should do so is in itself not a necessary part of any explanation. Enrolling others to one's conceptions is a strategy in which formulation of one's own and others' inter-ests may play a strategic role. It is one of the devices whereby we attempt to stamp our agency on others and other things (and especially others treated as reliable other things) through constituting networks of power. Interests thus have no ontological status; they are merely more or less stable devices for achieving relative social order.

The methodological approach which undergirds this position is prefigured in Machiavelli's descriptions which, it is maintained, are made through refer-ence with 'neither fear nor favour of what it is that actors do' (Callon et al.

1986: 5). Without taking sides, without reducing all action to the manifestation of some agencies' putative intentions or interests, or making it the outcrop of some structure, the approach provides an empirical sociology of power, rather than a moral philosophy. By attending to politically engaged agents seeking to constitute agencies, to constitute interests, to constitute structures, the method seeks to map how agents actually do 'translate' phenomena into resources, and resources into organization networks of control, of alliance, of coalition, of antagonism, of interest and of structure. 'Translation' refers to the methods by which these outcomes are accomplished.

Four 'moments' of translation are identified in Callon's (1986: 196) approach. The first of these is *problematization*. Problematization involves the attempt by agents to enrol others to their agency by positing the indispensability of their 'solutions' for (their definition of) the others' 'problems': this is achieved when these others are channelled through the 'obligatory passage points' of practice which the enrolling agency seeks to 'fix'. The traces of post-structuralism are evident. (There is also a hint of the organizational 'garbage-can' approach of Cohen et al. [1972] in which 'solutions' seek 'problems' to which they might attach themselves.) Problematization seeks to construct 'hegemony' by fixing what Laclau and Mouffe (1985) call 'nodal points' of discourse. The term 'nodal points', introduced in the previous chapter, and the term 'obligatory passage points', introduced here from the work of Callon et al. (1986), will henceforth be used interchangeably in this book. They are meant to refer to the construction of a conduit through which traffic must necessarily pass. Power consists in part in the achievement of this positionality.

The second moment in the process of translation is termed *intéressement*. This can be defined as the process of 'interesting' or 'enrolling' another agent to one's own agency: one agency 'attracts a second by coming between that entity and a third. Intéressement is thus a transaction between three entities' (Callon et al. 1986: xvii). It seeks to achieve the 'fixing' or 'locking in' of membership and meaning in certain 'categorization devices'. The 'membership categorization devices' or MCD approach, developed by ethnomethodologists such as Sacks (1972), would be a useful research tool here. How does a universe of categorical possibilities for membership become aligned with a universe of possible members?

The third moment in the process of translation is termed *enrolment*. This is the process whereby agencies seek to construct alliances and coalitions between the memberships and meaning which they have sought to fix. Finally, there is *mobilization* which refers to the set of methods that agencies use to ensure that the representations of interest which other enrolled agencies make are in fact themselves fixed, that the agencies in question do not, as it were, betray or undercut their representatives and representations.

The above is a slight reworking of the terms of the translation approach but it does not undermine its representations. Of the work done under the translation approach, the most easily accessible and interesting study is that conducted by Callon (1986) of the 'domestication of the scallops and the fishermen of St Brieuc Bay'. In this study, a complex interpretation is built up of the relations constituted between three marine biologists, a fishing community at St Brieuc Bay in Brest, and, the major actors in the story, the scallops which are harvested and researched in the bay. The scallop harvest was diminishing; the fishermen's livelihood was threatened. Little local knowledge of the scallop's life-cycle existed. A conference was held in Brest at which the three marine biologists reported on the latest scientific knowledge of the scallop's life-cycle to representatives of the fishing community.

Over the subsequent ten-year period, the marine researchers sought to construct 'obligatory passage points' enrolling the 'interests' of the fishermen, the scallops and their scientific colleagues, in stable representations to form an 'organizational field' in which 'agencies were defined, associated and simultaneously obliged to remain faithful to their alliances' (Callon 1986: 224). It is a fascinating study which repays careful consideration and whose general methodological precepts will be drawn on in the construction of a formal model of 'circuits of power' in this chapter. In the following chapter, the model will be illustrated with reference to the emergence of the circuit of power which is the modern capitalist state.

One insight vital for the reformation of the sociology of power is that strategic emphasis which, it has been argued, was first encountered in Machiavelli and most fully developed as a 'sociology of translation' by Callon and his colleagues. A second important insight, which may be attributed to Foucault (1980), is the distinction between the sovereign conception of power and the notion of disciplinary power. In this chapter the notion of disciplinary power will be conceptualized as a distinct 'circuit of power' in which disciplinary technique, in the broad sense that Foucault suggests, structures the relations of power through its diffusion according to principles of competitive ecological pressure and institutional isomorphism. Although the concept of 'institutional isomorphism' (Meyer and Rowan 1977) appears to be of more recent provenance than the more familiar evolutionist idea of ecological pressure, something very like the process which the concept describes was in fact present in Machiavelli (1958: 49) when he observed that 'Men nearly always follow the tracks made by others and proceed in their affairs by imitation, even though they cannot entirely keep to the tracks of others or emulate the prowess of their models. So a prudent man must always follow in the footsteps of great men and imitate those who have been outstanding. If his own prowess fails to compare with theirs, at least it has an air of greatness about it.' If 'organizations' were to be substituted for 'great men' in this formulation, it would not be unrecognizable to one familiar with modern institutional theory.

The effectiveness of forms of disciplinary power in the nineteenth century, which both Bauman (1982) and Foucault (1977) discuss, had to do with the pressure to innovate techniques of discipline appropriate for more impersonal, large-scale settings in which the *gemeinschaft* conditions whereby each person knew his/her place no longer prevailed. Such localized moral regulation, premised on the transparency of the person to the gaze of the community, was no longer viable. Many new forms of state institution were developed which sought to process categories of surplus population. No grand plan caused these institutions to adopt similar forms of disciplinary technique, which the factory masters belatedly took up. The process is perhaps best seen in terms of the pressures of institutional innovation (Meyer and Rowan 1977). The disciplinary techniques which had been readily available in the monastic milieu of religious vocation had already constituted institutional forms of schooling, poor houses, etc. Their effectiveness in producing soldiers and marines out of peasants had been established during the previous two centuries. Practices of institutional isomorphism would tend to reproduce similar relations of meaning and membership as the basis for social integration in the new institutions of the state (Meyer and Rowan 1977). Because certain forms of technique were already available and known, they had a certain legitimacy which enabled them to be more widely dispersed than they might otherwise have been. One could also, following Aldrich (1979), point to the similarity of 'niche space' of these institutions. In Goffman's (1961) terms they were all 'total institutions'. (Incidentally, although Goffman never made it explicit, it has been suggested that there is an implicit view of power in his writing. Interested readers might refer to Rogers [1977].) Environmental pressures served to structure system integration into a limited range of organizational forms.

## Power and resistance

It has been argued at the outset of this chapter that an appropriate point of departure for an analysis of power would be not agency but the social relations which constitute effective agency, particularly where it is organizational in form. In fact, as we shall see, the relational focus needs to be broader even than this: what is required is a consideration of the relational field of force in which power is configured and in which one aspect of this configuration is the social relations in which agency is constituted. The key to understanding resides in thinking of power as a phenomenon which can be grasped only relationally. It is not a thing nor is it something that people have in a proprietorial sense. They 'possess' power only in so far as they are relationally constituted as doing so. To the extent that the relational conditions which constitute power are reproduced through fixing their obligatory passage points, then possession may be fixed and 'reified' in form.

The greatest achievement of power is its reification. When power is regarded as thinglike, as something solid, real and material, as something an agent has, then this represents power in its most pervasive and concrete mode. It is securely fixed in its representations. However, reified power will rarely if ever occur entirely without resistance. To this extent power is infrequently the complete reification that it is sometimes assumed to be. Reification is rarely achieved in terms of that 'forgetting' of it as even existing as such which, for the classical critical theorists, was the apotheosis of power achieved through the negation of freedom. Resistance to power may be of two kinds. Sometimes, under rare conditions of what will be termed 'organizational outflanking', resistance to power may consolidate itself as a new power and thus constitute a new fixity in the representation of power, with a new relational field of force altogether. On the other hand, it may be resistance to the exercise of power which leaves unquestioned the fixity of the terms in which that power is exercised. It merely resists the exercise not the premises that make that exercise possible. In this respect resistance is compatible with reification and the exercise of power. What is reified is the fixity of powers terms, the representations which constitute it as such, centred on particular obligatory passage points.

Implicit to the conception of episodic agency power is the assumption of resistance. As Wrong (1979: 13) has put it, 'Politics includes both a struggle for power and a struggle to limit, resist and escape *from* power.' Consequently, as power always involves power over another and thus at least two agencies, episodic power will usually call forth resistance because of the power/ knowledge nature of agency. Power and resistance stand in a relationship to each other. One rarely has one without the other. It might be thought that, in the absence of an overt conflict, there will be no resistance to power. This would be to confuse the notion of resistance *per se* with a particularly dramatic expression of it. Excessive politeness in dealing with one to whom one is subject may well ironicize resistance; working to rule may not produce overt conflict with a superior, if one can legitimate one's actions with reference to a rule book governing what one should be doing, but it may well be an effective form of resistance, as many unionists will attest (also see the discussion in Clegg 1987). Barbalet (1985: 531) has characterized that resistance which imposes limits on power as 'frictional' – an absence of interest in the realization of the goals of power – in contrast to intended or direct resistance.

Barbalet's (1985) treatment of 'power and resistance' is the most sustained in the literature, and of particular interest for the clarification it provides of the relation of power and resistance in Weber's (1978: 53) definition of power. It is convincingly argued that these terms stand for distinct but interdependent aspects of phenomena within the power relation, in which resistance should be regarded as a phenomenon in its own right which will be directly implicated in power relations. From this perspective, resistance would be the 'efficacious influence of those subordinate to power' (Barbalet 1985: 542). Some conceptions of resistance are over-extensions of a sweeping concept of power itself, a criticism justifiably made by Dews (1979: 165) when he notes Foucault's (1977) 'tendency to slide from the use of the term "power" to designate one pole of the relation power-resistance, to its use to designate the relations as a whole'. More calibrated conceptions are important because they acknowledge that capacities can never be sure to determine outcomes. Power, as the realization of outcomes, cannot simply be assumed from the capacities of those exercising power, as we have seen in Hindess' (1982) argument. There is always a dialectic to power, always another agency, another set of standing conditions pertinent to the realization of that agency's causal powers against the resistance of another. Consequently, as Barbalet (1985: 539) has suggested, the power of an agent will always be less than the capacities that agent mobilized when attempting to achieve a specific outcome. Rarely will intentions be realized, if we mean by intention the outcome projected by the agency at the outset. Without resistance, we would note either that there is a genuine consensus of wills and thus no antagonistic agency or that there is a capitulation on the part of Bs and their strategic subordination to A. Such a situation would correspond to that relational subordination of B to A routinely secured through dispositional power.

While episodic, one-dimensional conceptions of agency and power may tell us something about the nature of power relations between an already constituted A and B, it can tell us nothing about the constitutive nature of the relational field in which A and B presently are nor how this privileges and handicaps them respectively, in relation to those resources that are constituted as powerful. Contrary to some conventions of power analysis, there is little point in constructing a priori abstract lists of specific resources as power resources. Whether they, whatever they are, are power resources depends entirely on how they are positioned and fixed by the players, the rules, and the game. This point is at the centre of the translation approach.

## Rules and power

Realism would have been greatly facilitated in the past if some conception of structural power had metaphorically skewed and made uneven and fissured that level table on which conceptual billiard balls from Hobbes to Dahl have moved so easily. To skew the table is simultaneously to advantage and disadvantage players dependent upon their relation to the table and the moves they wish to make. It disturbs the equilibrium upon which the rules of the game may fairly be applied, by skewing the rules to the advantage of whomsoever has management of the skewed table. Of course, only in pure games of skill or chance is it ever the case that games are played on a 'level table' or a 'level playing field'. Social games rarely if ever correspond to the ideal conditions of pure games *per se*. The rules will not be as static and idealized as in chess or some other game but will instead be far more fragile, ambiguous, unclear, dependent upon interpretation, and subject either to reproduction or transformation depending on the outcome of struggles to keep them the same or to change them this way or that (see Doyal and Harris 1986: 80–6 for a general discussion of 'rules').

The application of metaphors drawn from an analogy with games to the analysis of power is not uncommon amongst theorists. Hoy (1986: 135), for example, interprets Foucault's (1982) explanation of strategy in terms of a game of chess, an analogy which the present author also introduced in an earlier book on *Power, Rule and Domination* (Clegg 1975). In that text a concern with rules was closely linked to the analysis of power and domination (derived from Wittgenstein's [1968] analysis of 'rules', 'language games' and 'forms of life'), as the title denotes. For instance, following Wittgenstein (1968), the argument was made that behaviour is largely rule-guided: that the fact that policemen or traffic lights can cause traffic to stop makes sense only within reference to a set of explicit and implicit rules with which there is a wide-spread familiarity within a jurisdictional universe. Jurisdiction implies the probability of sanction of its breach in this formulation. Rules are not absolute; they are open to diverse interpretation. Moreover, not all interpretations are equal. One can draw on the analogy with the game of chess. 'Obviously, in an ongoing game, a piece like the queen would start in a more privileged position than a pawn, simply because the extant rules, which are now open to interpretation, enable her to begin the sequence with more potential moves to make' (Clegg 1975: 49). In metaphorical terms, if the power of a queen derives from the 'rules of the game', then the basis of these rules has to be established. In other terms, if the queen's episodic power is greater in scope than that of a pawn, then on what basis are their respective dispositional powers fixed so that their capacity to make their respective moves is rooted and routinized? To raise this question is to move into the circuit of dispositional power.

In fact, the chess analogy employed by Clegg (1975) could and should be extended further, as Saunders (1979: 61) has pointed out: 'it is not simply that powerful actors have greater scope in their permissible actions, but also that they can authoritatively reinterpret (within limits) what the rules mean. In everyday life, queens may begin to move as knights'. Moreover, because of their power, as given by the rules, they are at much greater liberty to make their interpretations of rules stick than those for whom the rules of the game allow only a much more limited set of moves. A recent, though hardly original, example of this was the version of the 'golden rule' by Kerry Packer (one of the richest men in Australia): 'He who has the gold, makes the rules' (quoted in *The Sydney Morning Herald*, 30 July, 1988: 32).

The concept of rules also relates to that of intention. Talk of outcomes in the episodic power model implies that intentions are implicated in power. However, it should be clear that intention is not to be regarded as something interior to private mental states of persons or even as equivalent to what persons tell us comprise their private mental states. For the former we cannot indubitably 'know' another's mind and mental constructs because they remain unarticulated. Nor is our conception of agency at all equivalent with that of another person. When intentions are articulated, they can only be so through whatever forms of discourse are socially available regarding what intentions can sensibly be taken to be, in the forms of language, reasoning and accounting for action. In this respect, talk about intentions that others might have is a reference less to their interior mental states as causal springs of putative action than to currently 'fixed' representations for making sense of what people do. It is to report on the availability and applicability of discursive formulations that are available for identifying behaviours as specific types of social action, to which agents may lay claim with respect to their own actions and which others may judge as 'vocabularies of motive' (Mills 1940; also see Taylor 1972).

In regarding a behaviour as a specific type of social action which can be said to have been intended to be such and such an action, we necessarily make reference to our interpretations of social actions by reference to social rules. That certain types of behaviour can be interpreted as moves in a game of sexual arousal depends upon their being interpreted in terms of the conventions of a game defined as sexual etiquette. Of course, as in many if not most social games, the rules may not be clear and the players may be playing different games unknowingly or unthinkingly. One way of resisting power play is not even to acknowledge the game that one thinks that the other thinks is being played. The point is that an intention to arouse sexually is not necessarily intrinsic to whatever is constituted as sexually arousing action: it resides in the way in which demeanour, appearance, clothes, embodiment, gestures, talk can all be interpreted in terms of available representations and arenas of behaviour. It will be rare indeed that the meaning of these is universally fixed, although, of course, it may be. A major strategy for resistance will always be to try to resist the meaning in which one is being implicated by the other's moves.

If intentionality requires reference to rules on this account, one should have equal recourse to discussion of rules in order to provide an appropriate concept of 'social causality'. Social causality is introduced to distinguish a conception of causality that is different from the implicit model of Humean causality which was found in Dahl's stress on event causation. The stories of the semiotics of traffic lights or of police uniforms and hand signals serve to differentiate this notion of social causality. Neither traffic lights nor policemen are inexorably and infallibly bound by universal causal law in the effects they might produce. These effects are contingent upon a rule being reproduced by being widely obeyed by those who should be subject to it. It is, in this sense, a normative rather than a causal imperative. It will be reproduced for just as long as people choose to obey it. One can easily imagine extraordinary situations of panic or lawlessness in which such rules might not be reproduced: war, a natural disaster such as an earthquake, or widespread social upheaval. Choice is essential to rules, irrelevant to law of a Humean kind (Ball 1976: 207; Harré 1970: 85; Clegg 1979: 39–40).

## Episodic agency power: the 'normal power' of social science

One should conceive of episodic instances of agency power as the most apparent, the most easily accessible and most visible circuit of power. It is the 'normal power' of most social science, that conception which has been identified as stretching from Hobbes right through to the 'dimensional' approach of Lukes (1974). However, it is neither the foundation of the totality of power in the terms that Lukes' dimensional approach suggests nor a free-standing circuit as in the formal model that Dahl (1957) advances. Power, viewed episodically, may move through circuits in which rules, relations and resources that are constitutive of power are translated, fixed and reproduced/transformed. These other circuits of power, which will be termed the circuits of social and system integration in which are implicated dispositional and facilitative power respectively, constitute the field of force in which episodic agency conceptions of power are articulated. Fixing these fields of force is achieved through enrolling other agencies such that they have to traffic through the enrolling agencies' obligatory passage points. Power involves not only securing outcomes, which is achieved in the episodic circuit of power, but also securing or reproducing the 'substantively rational' conditions within which the strategies espoused in the circuit of episodic power make contextual good sense (see Biggart and Hamilton [1987; 1984]; Hamilton and Biggart [1985; 1984] and Hamilton [1986] for complementary discussions of 'substantive rationality').

Different theoretical perspectives diverge on the temporality within which the contextualization of action is conceived. At one level there is the ethnomethodological school which tends to see the reproduction of substantive rationality as occurring within immediate temporal contexts of action; in the least immediate conceptualization of substantive rationality is the concern with long, slow, cyclical and enduring change which characterizes the *Annales* school of historians. It is not a question of which one of these extremes is correct or of the interim point at which one should arrest the temporal flow. In the appropriate empirical context of analysis, any point might be correct. It will depend in part on how efficaciously secured is the substantive rationality which both contextualizes particular strategies of episodic power and undercuts strategic opposition. Some highly structured procedural contexts of action within which questions must elicit accountable answers, such as courtrooms or judicial hearings, have an immediate co-presence of strategy and temporality. Ethnomethodological conversation analysis will thus be a useful research technique for such occasions. Others, such as a particular context of political economy, may show no such strategic returns in the normal course of affairs. Under these conditions, the *longue durée* may well be a more appropriate frame of reference, and the rich narrative, description and data of the *Annales* historian a more apposite technique.

Irrespective of mode of analysis, an adequate framework of power should enable us to sketch a plausible narrative, where plausibility is not brought into question by recourse to devices such as analytical prime movers, or hidden and inexplicable mechanisms of thought control. Episodically, power may be conceived as occurring within a reasonably well delimited framework in which there are systematic relationships between agencies and events. From what has been said beforehand, it should be clear that while this framework may be existentially real, it should also be regarded as the effect of a successful translation in its own right. Thus, it is no eternal set of relations. Systematicity derives from agents' differential control over and interest in events and each other. Interest carries no epistemological baggage in this formulation. It does not refer to an evaluative conception. The reference is only to the representations of interest which agencies make. These are not to be considered as identical to an individual actor's reasons for acting. Such a position brings one too close to a constitutive phenomenology of the subject, premised only on the subject's own discursively available categories. A representational concept of interest, constituted by agency, is clearly not the same thing. It refers to agencies not an actor. Agencies may represent interests precisely as the result of a process of 'translation'. Consequently, reference to interests in this schema is not to be taken as referring either to individual agent's 'reasons' or to their unknown but 'real' interests.

The two defining elements of any power system are agencies and events of interest to these agencies. As a provisional and conventional point of departure for discussion of episodic power in this section we shall begin with some artificial and unrealistic limiting assumptions. The precedents for doing this are obvious. They derive from neo-classical economics, in this instance via the work of Coleman (1977). However, unlike the neo-classical economists we shall progressively drop the unrealistic limiting assumptions as we proceed. At the outset, a 'principle of action' may be specified whereby agencies 'act so as to gain control of those events in which they have an interest. ... The way in which actors gain control of those events that interest them is to give up control of those events over which they have little or no interest' (Coleman 1977: 184). They engage in exchange such that each agency has control over events that interest that agency, subject to the resources with which that agent began: that is, the control over events held as a resource capacity at the outset. This is represented in Figure 1, together with the other circuits of power. It may be useful to refer to this representation subsequently, when the other circuits of power are being discussed.

Power is represented in the circuits framework in a number of ways. (Incidentally, the configuration of this model has a distant lineage in earlier models of 'power, rule and domination' [in Clegg 1975; 1979] although, to be frank, rather more in form than in content.) Power is evidently present as

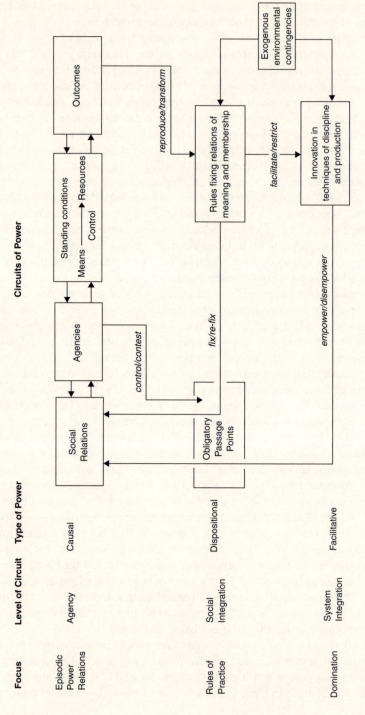

**Focus**  **Level of Circuit**  **Type of Power**  **Circuits of Power**

Episodic
Power
Relations

Agency

Causal

Outcomes

Standing conditions

Means → Resources
← Control

Agencies

Social
Relations

*reproduce/transform*

*control/contest*

*fix/re-fix*

Rules of
Practice

Social
Integration

Dispositional

Obligatory
Passage
Points

Rules fixing relations of
meaning and membership

*facilitate/restrict*

Domination

System
Integration

Facilitative

Innovation in
techniques of discipline
and production

Exogenous
environmental
contingencies

*empower/disempower*

Figure 1

each specified modality of episodic, dispositional and facilitative power. It is also present in the overall flow of action through the circuits of power, the relational articulation which will constitute the calibration of this flow. Empirically, power may be contained within the episodic circuit only or it may flow through the dispositional and facilitative routes. These are properly thought of as aspects of the overall framework of power phenomena and are signified as 'rules' and 'domination' in order to differentiate them from the most frequently conceptualized circuit of power which is so often taken to be power *per se*.

A very brief word on the derivation of the terminology of power, rule and domination may be in order. It is derived from Weber's (1978) discussions of *macht* and *herrschaft*, via Clegg (1975). Where domination is institutionalized through the circuit of dispositional power as a substantive modality of rule, such as patrimonialism or legal rationality, it is conventional to speak of it as authority. It should be clear from the earlier discussion of authority in this chapter that the conventional conception of authority as a legitimating source of power is being dispensed with in favour of a concern with the processes whereby authority may be empowered. Hence the translation of *herrschaft* as 'authority' is displaced in favour of a more accurate rendering as 'domination', leaving open as a matter for investigation whether or not this is accompanied by authority.

In the circuits framework, power is multifarious: it is episodic power; it is also the circuit of power through rules and domination, as well as the overall empirical articulation which configures the theoretical circuits in any application of the model. If this seems complex, one can only submit that the law of 'requisite variety' may well be appropriate here: the complexity of the phenomenon is mirrored in its representation. Certainly, simpler formulations are entirely possible: the earlier chapters of this book bear warrant to that eventuality. They should also have alerted us to some of the drawbacks that such formulations contain.

Existing social relations constitute the identities of agencies, whether individuals or some collective loci of decision-making and action. Agencies' causal powers will be realized through the organization of standing conditions. These require that agencies involved in what Hindess (1982: 501) terms 'arenas of struggle' are capable of utilizing means in order to control resources which have consequential outcomes for the scope of action of these agents. Each agency is operative in a highly complex environment of standing conditions. Each is among many others with strategic interests in each other and in the relations that constitute them as actors in the same system. Agencies possess varying control of resources which they have varying means of effectively utilizing in order to produce consequential outcomes for their own and others' agency. Power at this level will invariably be accompanied by resistance, which is indicated in Figure 1 by pairs of arrows connecting the boxes in the model of episodic power relations. Those pointing to the right-hand side indicate social relations constituting agencies, agencies utilizing standing conditions, and standing conditions utilized by agencies causing outcomes. The arrows which point to the left-hand side indicate resistance. (If it were not that it would have unnecessarily complicated an already complex figure, lines of resistance could have been drawn from outcomes to agencies and social relations, as well as from standing conditions to social relations.) Power which proceeds at the level of these episodic power relations is the most apparent, evident and economical circuit of power. It is 'power over' which, however, necessarily trades off some extant 'fixing' of facilitative and dispositional power. Rules of practice are at the centre of any stabilization or change of the circuitry. Through them, all traffic must pass. However, it is not only as a result of struggles which occur explicitly over relations of meaning and membership that social change occurs. It can also be a function of those changes in the process of innovation which always pose potential transformations for the extant structuring of empowerment and disempowerment, dependent upon extant techniques of production and discipline. The techniques are not only carriers of innovation but almost invariably bearers of domination. Thus, domination is never eternal, never utterly set in time and space: it will invariably be subject to processes of innovation which may as readily subvert as reproduce its functioning. Even in the most closed of systems, where sources of external contingency rarely penetrate (for example, the Japanese empire prior to its forcible opening to the West under the direction of Perry's guns), the domination of particular relations of meaning is not timeless, static nor unchanging.

Let us return to the formal model and some familiar tactics of analysis. Consistent with the artifice of assumptions, imagine an absence of resistance, the economists' rational norm. A situation of non-antagonistic agency would be equivalent to a deal freely entered into by each party to the relationship, where the relationship is a balance of 'inducements' and 'contributions', a fair exchange. In such a situation of fair exchange, the final control of events would leave the two agencies in a similar position of balance vis à vis the 'scope' of their agency. For instance, A may have contracted to provide 100 units of X at $10 per unit cost to B. For A, the loss of 100 Xs would be equivalent for A to the receipt of $1000 while, for B $1000 outlay would secure the balanced satisfaction of 100 units of X. The fiction that economists call a perfect market would prevail.

In this fiction, as Coleman (1977: 184) argues, controlling events would be analogous to 'control over the disposition of a good in a private market'. A price or value of control for each event is negotiated through exchange. Each agency 'can be described as having a certain amount of power, depending on the value of the events', over which control is exerted. There is, as he argues further, 'a simultaneous definition of value and power'. Value is defined by the interest that agents have in an event, weighted by the agents' power. The power of an agent would be equivalent to that agent's control over events, weighted by the value of these events (Coleman 1977: 184). As is clear from the definitions, Coleman's conception of power is developed on an explicit analogy with the conception of wealth in an economic system. It is a neo-classical conception of 'fair exchange'. Adherence to a reality principle requires the abandonment of these limiting assumptions. We shall proceed to do this by first noting the obduracy of resistance as a social phenomenon. Such a 'fair exchange', viewed episodically, would not be consistent with a notion of power ineluctably linked to resistance. If A and B are agencies who freely entered into a relationship with each other (the ideal of this being a spot-market transaction between a buyer and a seller of a good), it is difficult to talk of a relationship of power. The 'perfect market assumptions' ensure that. Beyond a number of highly specific and mostly atypical markets, these conditions do not prevail. They certainly do not prevail on that most important of markets, the labour market. (See the discussion in Clegg et al. [1986: 52–66; 214–49; 259–96]. While this discussion will not be repeated, it is a necessary backdrop to the conception of labour markets which is implicit in this book.) Such exchanges will be more or less unequal. Consideration of power requires consideration of imperfect exchanges under imperfect market conditions. Whether or not an agent's causal powers are realized will depend upon the standing conditions for their utilization of and access to means and resources. These will invariably be distributed unequally.

In an imperfect market, means and resources will be inequitably distributed. Realization of an agency's causal powers will entail gaining an outcome in opposition to the preference of another agency in the exchange. What an agent is able to achieve as an outcome thus depends in part on the causal powers that are constitutive of that actor and, in part, on the standing conditions of access to means and resources which may restrict or enable the achievement of outcomes. Just as in the natural sciences, the arrangement of standing conditions has to be organized experimentally in order to achieve that threshold of action beyond which causal powers can manifest themselves. The difference, of course, is that for social phenomena the agencies who comprise the field of study are also the 'experimentalists', seeking to organize the standing conditions in order to realize their constitutive causal powers.

Where the exchange relationship is unequal, as a result of neither chance nor error but of the constitutive nature of the agencies and the relationships between them, we can say that an A can get a B to do something that B would not otherwise have done. Alternatively we might say that A can get B not to do something that B might reasonably have been expected to do. The important thing is that the episodic conception is now grounded in a less fictional conception of power. Episodic power is seen to derive from the capacities of agents grounded in resource control. The constitutive relations which prevail between agents can be seen to determine the nature of resources. Resources, under the appropriate standing conditions, can empower A vis à vis a specific scope of B's agency, when utilized through means which implement them. The episodic power circuit may thus be conceptualized as both a relatively coherent and an important circuit of power in its own right. Conceptual closure can thus be admitted at this level of power relations. However, closure at this level is not to be taken for closure of consideration of power phenomena *per se*.

A's power attempt and B's resistance to power must have some basis, some resources, which can be activated in the struggle. Moreover, the protagonists must have some means available to them to activate these resources. Such resources are generally deployed not promiscuously but with a target in view. For the protagonist, such a target would be that scope of the other's actions over which the exercise of power is sought. Protagonists may be more or less effective in achieving their target and restricting the scope of the other's actions just as they may be in resisting attempts by others to achieve the same compliance with respect to their own actions. The more successful a protagonist is in achieving means of effective activation of resources, accurately targeted at restricting the extent of options within the scope of another, the more 'integral' the protagonist's power will be. The more successful is resistance to power, the more 'intercursive' or countervailing power will be. (The distinctions between 'integral' and 'intercursive' are made by Wrong [1979: 11; also see 260, ch. 1, n. 28].) The former situation would correspond to the cohesive oligarchic structure of rule which elite theory routinely represents, while the latter would be pluralist. In the pluralist, intercursive situation, both power and resistance may be evident in the same agencies with respect to differing scopes of behaviour of the other agencies.

Resistance to oligarchic or integrative power, when viewed episodically, can take a number of forms. It may seek to exercise countervailing power on the basis of: more effective means of utilization of its existing resources; more precise targeting of the other agencies' more powerful scopes for action and their preferred options within these; enrolling other agencies to its cause and thus making more extensive any episodic attempts at power by the antagonistic agency, and so on.

Terms such as these can be clearly specified. To this extent they do aid us in constructing research into power. However, while some terms, at least, can be quantified, it is doubtful whether quantification is of much use as an end in itself, although it may be a valuable strategy of research which contributes to the overall qualitative picture that investigation into episodic power tries to build up and develop. The quantitative problem is simply that, as we have seen, such terms as 'scope' are difficult to quantify in ways that do not leave the comparative rankings vulnerable to weighty matters of qualitative consideration which cannot be so easily quantified and compared in terms of any single unit of value. None the less, some researchers will always be disposed to counting, since, for many, numbers have their own power. As long as the overall context is considered, so that facile aggregation of inherently and qualitatively non-equivalent phenomena (such as the number of Bs or the number of scopes) is avoided, then no great harm to understanding will be done by this comparative ranking. Indeed, it may well be aided.

[pp. 223–5]

## Social integration and system integration: dispositional and facilitative power respectively

One of those conceptual distinctions which seems to lend itself to constant re-working is that made by Lockwood (1964) in his famous paper on 'Social Integration and System Integration' (for example, see Parkin 1972 and 1976; Habermas 1976; Giddens 1979; Clegg and Dunkerley 1980; Barbalet 1987). As Barbalet (1987: 13) says 'Lockwood's treatment of social and system integration . . . offers a distinctive approach for understanding the relationship between social structural resources and power relations.' However, no single one of these 're-workings' will be adopted here, as it is necessary to conceive of Lockwood's (1964) 'institutional order' in quite specific terms. These conditions will develop a conception of social integration in terms of relations of meaning and membership, as these have been derived from debates about post-structuralism. System integration will be conceptualized in terms of 'material conditions' of techniques of production and discipline, in a conception quite consistent with Lockwood's Weberian formulation:

> Material conditions most obviously include the technological means of control over the physical and social environment and the skills associated with these means. They include not only the material means of production, but also what Weber frequently refers to as the material means of organization and violence. (Lockwood 1964: 251)

Social and system integration can thus be conceptualized as the pathways through which fields of force are fixed and stabilized on 'obligatory passage points' in the circuits of power. What the actual conduits will be cannot be specified in advance but they will be contingent upon what flows through the circuits.

The circuit of social integration is concerned with fixing or refixing relations of meaning and of membership, while the circuit of system integration will be concerned with the empowerment and disempowerment of agencies' capacities, as these become more or less strategic as transformations occur which are incumbent upon changes in techniques of production and discipline. However, the latter circuit cannot, of course, escape relations of meaning and membership. It has to be fixed on obligatory points of passage through these if it is to have any effectiveness. It functions as a potent source of resistance to the stabilization of existing memberships and meanings by generating new techniques of production and new modes of discipline, which, if they are not already present within existing rules of practice, have the capacity to transform these. Existing structures of dominancy are thus in principle always open to subsidence, disruption and innovation, since new techniques may open up new conduits and passages which undermine the presently entrenched structures.

Changes in both social and system integration may be either endogenous or exogenous. If endogenous the changes occur as a result of episodic power outcomes achieving either transformations in the rules that fix relations of meaning and membership or enhancement in the process of innovation of techniques of production and discipline. Exogenous change occurs as a result of environmental contingencies which interrupt and disturb the fixed fields of force of the circuit of either social or system integration. It should be apparent that these circuits may be termed 'integrative' but they should always be viewed as double-edged: they may be disintegrative as well as integrative, particularly where exogenous sources of change are involved. No necessity attaches to exogenous disruption. Whether or not exogenous factors achieve impact will depend upon what Holton (1985: 212) has termed 'a highly complex interrelationship between the exogenous influence of innovations and the receptivity or otherwise of the endogenous unit in question'. Receptivity will always be dependent upon securing conduits through which traffic in the circuit of social integration must pass; hence the centrality to the model of the obligatory passage points and the rules of membership and meaning. Obligatory passage points represent the securing of particular 'indexical' interpretations of what these rules are.

The pathways of these circuits, as fields of force, will be carried by organization. It is for this reason that 'organizational outflanking' is basic to both social control and social change. Hence, each of the circuits of social and system integration will have to reproduce stable relations of episodic power, through fixing obligatory passage points, if they are to reproduce the extant organizational carrying capacity. (This is not represented in Figure 1, in order to avoid unnecessarily confusing detail.) The centrality of organization to the schema suggests that the sources of change therein will be organizational. Indeed, each circuit of social and system integration has a characteristic mode of organization change. For the circuit of social integration in which rules fix relations of meaning and membership, the characteristic device is what Meyer and Rowan (1977) term institutional isomorphism. Certain fixtures of meaning are privileged, certain membership categories are aligned with these meanings (Sacks 1972 on 'membership categorization devices' is relevant here) and, consequently, a specific organizational field (DiMaggio and Powell 1983) or what Callon et al. (1986: xvi) term an 'actor network' is constructed. Indeed, these two labels seem coterminous. An 'actor network' concerns the interrelated set of entities successfully translated by an actor. This book has sought to avoid adopting the actor's perspective, in recognition that agency may well be organizational rather than a human, and so it will deploy the notion of an organization field, somewhat akin to a Foucauldian 'field of force', as a 'recognized area of institutional life' in DiMaggio and Powell's (1983) terms. Such fields exist only to the extent that they are an achievement of episodic power in the institutional field, stabilizing relations of power between organization agencies A, B, . . . N. Episodic power's achievement will consist, first, in constituting a relational field by 'enrolling' other organizations and agencies; second, in the 'stabilizing' of a network of power centrality, alliance and coalition among agencies within the field; third, in the 'fixing' of common relations of meaning and membership among the agencies within that field, such that they are reflexively aware of their constitution as a field.

## References

Aldrich, H. (1979) *Organizations and Environments*. Englewood Cliffs NJ: Prentice Hall.

Anthony, P.D. (1977) *The Ideology of Work*. London: Tavistock.

Ball, T. (1976) 'Power, Causation and Explanation', *Polity*, Winter: 189–214.

Barbalet, J.M. (1985) 'Power and Resistance', *British Journal of Sociology*, 36(1): 521–48.

Barbalet, J.M. (1987) 'Power, Structural Resources and Agency', *Perspectives in Social Theory*, 8: 1–24.

Barnes, B. (1981) 'On the "Hows" and "Whys" of Cultural Change', *Social Studies of Science*, 11: 491–8.

Barnes, B. (1986) 'On Authority and its Relationship to Power', pp. 180–95 in J. Law (ed.), *Power, Action and Belief: A New Sociology of Knowledge?* Sociological Review Monograph 32, London: Routledge and Kegan Paul.

Barnes, B. (1988) *The Nature of Power*. Cambridge: Polity Press.

Bauman, Z. (1982) *Memories of Class: The Pre-History and After-Life of Class*. London: Routledge and Kegan Paul.

Biggart, N.W. and G.G. Hamilton (1984) 'The Power of Obedience', *Administrative Science Quarterly*, 29(4): 540–9.

Callon, M. (1980) 'Struggles and Negotiations to Define What is Problematic and What is Not: The Socio-logic of Translation', pp. 197–219 in K.D. Knorr-Cetina, R. Krohn and R.D. Whitley (eds), *The Social Processes of Scientific Investigation*. Sociology of the Sciences Yearbook, Vol. 4. Dordrecht: Reidel.

Callon, M. (1986) 'Some Elements of a Sociology of Translation: Domestication of the Scallops and the Fishermen of St Brieuc Bay', in J. Law (ed.), *Power, Action and Belief: A New Sociology of Knowledge?* Sociological Review Monograph 32. London: Routledge and Kegan Paul.

Callon, M. and B. Latour (1981) 'Unscrewing the Big Leviathan: How Actors Macrostructure Reality and Sociologists Help Them to Do So', pp. 227–303 in K.D. Knorr-Cetina and A. Cicourel (eds), *Advances in Social Theory and Methodology: Towards an Integration of Micro- and Macro-Sociologies*. London: Routledge and Kegan Paul.

Callon, M. and J. Law (1982) 'On Interests and their Transformation', *Social Studies of Science*, 1: 615–25.

Callon, M., J.P. Courtial, W.A. Turner and S. Bauin (1983) 'From Translations to Problematic Networks: An Introduction to Co-Word Analysis', *Social Science Information*, 22: 199–235.

Callon, M., J. Law and A. Rip (eds) (1986) *Mapping out the Dynamics of Science and Technology: Sociology of Science in the Real World*. London: Macmillan.

Clegg, S.R. (1975) *Power, Rule and Domination: A Critical and Empirical Understanding of Power in Sociological Theory and Organizational Life*. London: Routledge and Kegan Paul.

Clegg, S.R. (1979) *The Theory of Power and Organization*. London: Routledge and Kegan Paul.

Clegg, S.R. (1987) 'The Power of Language, the Language of Power', *Organization Studies*, 8(1): 60–70.

Clegg, S.R. and D. Dunkerley (1980) *Organization, Class and Control*. London: Routledge and Kegan Paul.

Clegg, S.R., P. Boreham and G. Dow (1983) 'Politics and Crisis: The State of the Recession', pp. 1–50 in S.R. Clegg, G. Dow and P. Boreham (eds), *The State, Class and the Recession*. London: Croom Helm.

Clegg, S.R., P. Boreham and G. Dow (1986) *Class, Politics and the Economy*. London: Routledge and Kegan Paul.

Cohen, M.D., J.G. March and J. Olsen (1972) 'A Garbage-Can Model of Organizational Choice', *Administrative Science Quarterly*, 17(1): 1–25.

Coleman, J. (1977) 'Notes on the Study of Power', pp. 183–98 in R.J. Liebert and A.W. Imerskein (eds), *Power, Paradigms and Community Research*. London: Sage Publications.

Dahl, R.A. (1957) 'The Concept of Power', *Behavioural Science*, 2: 201–5.

Dews, P. (1979) 'The Nouvelle Philosophie and Foucault', *Economy and Society*, 8(2): 127–71.

DiMaggio, P. and W. Powell (1983) 'The Iron Cage Revisited: Institutional Isomorphism and Collective Rationality in Organizational fields', *American Sociological Review*, 48(2): 147–60.

Doyal, L. and R. Harris (1986) *Empiricism, Explanation and Rationality: An Introduction to the Philosophy of the Social Sciences*. London: Routledge and Kegan Paul.

Durkheim, E. (1964) *The Division of Labour*. New York: Free Press.

Foucault, M. (1977) *Discipline and Punish: The Birth of the Prison*. Harmondsworth: Penguin.

Foucault, M. (1980) *Power/Knowledge: Selected Interviews and Other Writings 1972–1977*, ed. C. Gordon. Brighton: Harvester Press.

Foucault, M. (1981) 'Questions of Method: An Interview with Michel Foucault', *Ideology and Consciousness*, 8: 1–14.

Foucault, M. (1984) *The History of Sexuality: An Introduction*. Harmondsworth: Peregrine.

Garfinkel, H. (1967) *Studies in Ethnomethodology*. Englewood Cliffs, NJ: Prentice Hall.

Giddens, A. (1979) *Central Problems in Social Theory*. London: Macmillan.

Goffman, E. (1961) *Asylums*. Harmondsworth: Penguin.

Habermas, J. (1976) *Legitimation Crisis*. London: Heinemann Educational Books.

Hamilton, G.G. (1986) 'Patriarchalism in Imperial China and Western Europe: A Revision of Weber's Sociology of Domination', *Theory and Society*, 13(3): 393–425.

Hamilton, G.G. and N.W. Biggart (1984) *Governor Reagan, Governor Brown: A Sociology of Executive Power*. New York: Columbia University Press.

Hamilton, G.G and N.W. Biggart (1985) 'Why People Obey: Theoretical Observations on Power and Obedience in Complex Organizations', *Sociological Perspectives*, 28(1): 3–28.

Harré, R. (1970) 'Powers', *British Journal for the Philosophy of Science*, 21: 81–101.

Hickson, D.J., C.R. Hinings, C.A. Lee, R.E. Schneck and J.M. Pennings (1971) 'A Strategic Contingencies Theory of Intra-Organizational Power', *Administrative Science Quarterly*, 16: 216–29.

Hindess, B. (1982) 'Power, Interests and the Outcomes of Struggles', *Sociology*, 16(4): 498–511.

Hinings, C.R., D.J. Hickson, J.M. Pennings and R.E. Schneck (1974) 'Structural Conditions of Intra-Organizational Power', *Administrative Science Quarterly*, 9(1): 22–44.

Holton, R.J. (1985) *The Transition from Feudalism to Capitalism*. London: Macmillan.

Hoy, D.C. (1986) 'Power, Repression, Progress: Foucault, Lukes and the Frankfurt School', pp. 123–48 in D.C. Hoy (ed.), *Foucault: A Critical Reader*. Oxford: Blackwell.

Laclau, E. and C. Mouffe (1985) *Hegemony and Socialist Strategy*. London: Verso.

Law, J. (1986) 'Editor's Introduction: Power/Knowledge and the Dissolution of the Sociology of Knowledge', pp. 1–19 in J. Law (ed.), *Power, Action and Belief: A New Sociology of Knowledge?* Sociological Review Monograph 32. London: Routledge and Kegan Paul.

Law, J. and P. Lodge (1984) *Science for Social Scientists*. London: Macmillan.

Lockwood, D. (1964) 'Social Integration and System Integration', pp. 244–57 in G.K. Zollschan and W. Hirsch (eds), *Explorations in Social Change*. London: Routledge and Kegan Paul.

Lukes, S. (1974) *Power: A Radical View*. London: Macmillan.

Machiavelli, N. (1958) *The Prince*. London: Everyman.

MacKenzie, D. (1978) 'Statistical Theory and Social Interests: A Case Study', *Social Studies of Science*, 8: 35–83.

Meyer, J. and B. Rowan (1977) Institutionalized Organizations: Formal Structure as Myth and Ceremony', *American Journal of Sociology*, 83: 340–63.

Mills, C.W. (1940) 'Situated Actions and Vocabularies of Motive', *American Sociological Review*, 5: 904–13.

Parkin, F. (1972) *Class Inequality and Political Order: Social Stratification in Capitalist and Communist Societies*. London: McGibbon and Kee.

Parkin, F. (1976) 'System Contradiction and Political Transformation: The Comparative Study of Industrial Societies', *European Journal of Sociology*, 13: 45–62.

Rogers, M. (1977) 'Goffman on Power', *American Sociologist,* 12: 88–95.

Sacks, H. (1972) 'An Initial Investigation of the Usability of Conversational Data for Doing Sociology', pp. 31–74 in D. Sudnow (ed.), *Studies in Social Interaction*. New York: Free Press.

Sanger, D.E. (1987) 'High Tech as Villain: On Wall Street, Computer Programs came to Replace Individual Judgement', *International Herald Tribune*, Singapore, 16 December: 1, 6.

Saunders, P. (1979) *Urban Politics*. Harmondsworth: Penguin.

Strauss, A. (1978) *Negotiations: Varieties, Contexts, Processes and Social Order*. London: Jossey-Bass.

Taylor, L. (1972) 'The Significance and Interpretation of Replies to Motivational Questions: The Case of Sex Offenders'. *Sociology*, 6(1): 23–40.

Weber, M. (1948) *From Max Weber: Essays in Social Theory*. London: Routledge and Kegan Paul.

Weber, M. (1976) *The Protestant Ethic and the Spirit of Capitalism*. London: Allen and Unwin.

Weber, M. (1978) *Economy and Society: An Outline of Interpretive Sociology* (2 Vols), ed. G. Roth and C. Wittich. Berkeley: University of California Press.

Wittgenstein, L. (1968) *Philosophical Investigations*, tr. G.E.M. Anscombe. Oxford: Blackwell.

Woolgar, S. (1981) Interests and Explanation in the Social Study of Science', *Social Studies of Science*, 11: 365–94.

Wrong, D. (1979) *Power: Its Forms, Bases and Uses*. Oxford: Blackwell.

# 14 Morriss

## Introduction

In the general introduction it was argued that power is a family resemblance concept and, consequently, that there exists no one 'entity' which constitutes power. Rather, there are different concepts (plural) of power and each usage is shaped by a specific context. As Morriss is an analytic philosopher and this is an analytic point, I think it appropriate, now that we have analysed a number of different thinkers, to revisit this theme again by way of introduction to his work.

As we have seen in the analysis of Giddens and Foucault, the meaning of words is essentially systemic. This entails the conclusion that there is intrinsic incommensurability between languages, thus translation is always a question of reinterpretation and approximation – which is why translators will never be replaced by computers. The academic literature on power may be regarded as comprising many micro-languages or language games. Within each game there are local uses which are shaped by the nature of the local language game as a whole. Two elements determine the types of concepts used: 1) the aims and objectives of the language game and 2) the internal structure of the language game.

To take the first point: if, for instance, the object of the language game is morally evaluative then the concept of responsibility, hence intention, looms large. Among other things, complex and sophisticated analysis about whether or not power should be defined in terms of its exercise or as a disposition is also appropriate. These debates are normatively significant because, in that context, the definition of power defines the parameters of moral responsibility but they are not, necessarily, pertinent within other language games – such as social theory. Concepts are 'tools' and just as carpenters and plumbers are entitled to use different tools so, too, academics engaged in different intellectual exercises choose the concepts appropriate to the task they have embarked upon.

The second point (2), follows on from the first: conceptual tools are shaped not only by objectives but, also, by the totality of the tools in the box. To take the example of Parsons' concept of power: it was shaped by his sociology and, thus, is far removed from the concept of power used by moral philosophers. However, from the perspective of local language games, Parsons' concept of power should be deemed inadequate only if, either: a) it was a hindrance rather than a help to understanding his sociological theory (a poorly constructed conceptual tool) or b) if he made the mistake of claiming that he was talking about the same thing as moral philosophers (he did make this mistake but, I would argue, that the real problem with Parsons' theory of power is not so much his concept of power as his sociology!).

Morriss' conceptualization of power falls within the realm of analytical political philosophy. The objective is to aid our ability to construct political theory through an approach to power, which involves building upon what we know tacitly about the usage of the concept, and, following that, to make our uses theoretically consistent. If one were to use sociological terminology derived from Giddens (a vocabulary Morriss does not employ), the aim is to turn practical consciousness into discursive consciousness knowledge and systematizing discursive consciousness into logical coherence. The object of the exercise is to clarify concepts so as to prevent philosophical errors through inconsistency. It is a task succinctly summarized by John Selden (quoted approvingly by Morriss at the beginning of the book): 'The not distinguishing where things should be distinguished, and the not confounding where things should be confounded, is the cause of all the mistakes in the world.'

Conceptual tools have the capacity to shape our perception of our work. By definition, theory building entails generalizing from different instances of the 'same concept'; consequently, if we misrecognize what constitutes the 'same concept' this can determine our philosophical position. The primary source of this error derives from the fact that words shift from concept to concept – the same word can stand for many concepts.

A paradigmatic instance of how clarifying concepts can fundamentally alter theory building is Isaiah Berlin's famous distinction between positive liberty (liberty to) and negative liberty (liberty from). Berlin's article made discursive a distinction which fundamentally altered the course of political thought. It rendered it obvious that, for instance, libertarians and Marxists simply were not talking about the same thing when they used the word 'liberty'. Another instance of the same phenomenon is the belief held by naive egalitarians to the effect that their intellectual adversaries on the right do not value equality. Actually, libertarians may feel passionately about equality; indeed, so passionate that they cannot countenance any redistribution of resources. The equality which the left-wing egalitarian is concerned about is equality of resources while, in contrast, the libertarian is thinking of equality of opportunity or desert.

Once differences in usage are recognized then the next task is to identify which is the inconsistent usage and/or which usage presupposes what type of normative political theory. There are many ways of accomplishing this task. It is possible to construct a stipulative (specifically constructed) definition which is defended as 'the best' because of terminological succinctness or analytical neatness. However, the method more commonly used by analytical philosophers is to move back and forth between concepts and theory and, in so doing, to reveal inconsistencies of thought. This is theoretically parallel to the process captured by Rawls' felicitous phrase 'reflective equilibrium' (1971, p. 21).

Reflective equilibrium is a process whereby we move back and forth between theoretical constructs and our intuitions. When students are first introduced to Rawls' thought experiment – the original position – they often find it difficult to make sense of how this peculiar, almost quaint, otherworldly imagining could inform us about justice in the world of politics (in the original position we are to imagine a position where, among others things, we are not ignorant of our position in society, our natural endowments (both physical and mental) and our concept of what constitutes the good). However, the idea of such an act of imagination is not to tell us *on its own* what justice should be or should not be but, rather, it functions as a sounding-board which systematizes our intuitions – organizes what we already know in a coherent way.

While Rawls was not engaged in political theory as a form of conceptual analysis, the process used by Morriss is not dissimilar to 'reflective equilibrium'. Ordinary language takes the place of intuitions. It is not that ordinary language is the last word but, rather, a point of departure. In order to capture the essence of these usages, hypothetical situations are constructed and by a careful process of sifting between usage and thought experiment, conceptual clarity is given to the concept of power. Just as students are bemused by the status of the original position, so too, with regard to the analytical power literature, the novice is frequently bemused by the fact that theorists who claim to concern themselves with politics (it is political philosophy after all!) expend endless ink and mental energy pondering complex thought experiments. Such a hypothetical construction does not tell us directly what we mean by political power. Rather, the object of such a thought experiment is to function as a regulatory device for distilling the essence of the concept of power. This will enable us to know what we mean when we claim that 'Democracy entails an equal distribution of power'. Without definitional conceptual clarity, an assertion such as this is virtually meaningless. While the process starts from ordinary usage the position is finally reached where we know when ordinary usage is misleading and which uses of the concept of power are appropriate to a particular theory.

A useful way to understand the distinctiveness of this approach is to compare how Parsons, Barnes and Morriss deal with the question of whether or not power is zero-sum. All three agree that it is not zero-sum. However, while Barnes and Parsons disagree on the reason, their arguments are of the same type, whereas Morriss' takes an entirely different form from theirs.

As we have seen, Parsons argues that power is not zero-sum because it can be produced with greater or lesser efficiency by the polity. Barnes argues that power can be increased through reinforcing and increasing a ring of self-validating social knowledge. Parsons and Barnes disagree on the source of fluctuations in social power but they both approach the problem by building a model of how power is produced through the creation of social order.

Morriss approaches the zero-sum problem through the construction of a thought experiment and a conceptual analysis of what is meant by asserting that God is 'omnipotent'.

Morriss devises a thought experiment where he enters a local beauty competition and wins. At first sight this might appear as a paradigmatic example of zero-sum power – if Morriss wins everyone else who enters the competition loses. However, this is a misreading. In this instance winning may have been zero-sum but the 'power to win' was not necessarily so. It may be the case that there are millions of people out there who could have beaten Morriss in the beauty competition but who, for whatever reason, chose not to enter. Morriss' 'ableness' (ableness is a form of power) was not at the expense of those millions of individuals and, as a consequence, their capacity to win (power) was not decreased by Morriss' act of winning (Morriss 1987, pp. 91–2).

It is central to Christian religious belief that God is all-powerful, which raises the age-old problem of explaining how it is that there is any power left over for 'the likes of you and me' (Morriss does not mention the devil). However, the perception of the problem in these terms is, in fact, premised upon a tacit perception of power as constant-sum. Although God could do anything he wanted – he has power as an infinite capacity – this does not entail that he actually chooses always to exercise it. If God is all-powerful, 'whether I can walk across the room now or not is up to God; He has it in His power to prevent me or make me. But, also, it *is* in my power to walk across the room because we know that God will not intervene . . .' (Morriss 1987, p. 92). The omnipotence of God is not necessarily at the expense of Morriss' power and from this we can infer that power is not necessarily zero-sum.

The tradition of normative conceptual analysis of power is rich with debate and Morriss is one of its most sophisticated exponents. In the extract which follows he shows us the distinction between power and influence and demonstrates that power is a 'capacity' concept. The former is theoretically significant because political theorists frequently elide power and influence. The latter is rendered particularly significant because Dahl is inconsistent on whether power is an 'exercise' or 'capacity' concept – a confusion which has implications for his theorization of pluralist democracy.

Following the extract given below, Morriss makes many insightful conceptual clarifications including an account of conditionals, 'ability' and 'ableness' and constructs a sophisticated argument for the idea of 'passive power'. Building upon these conceptual clarifications, the book concludes with mathematical models.

**Further reading**

A second edition of *Morriss' Power: A Philosophical Analysis* is shortly to be published and contains an extended introduction dealing with some of the more significant debates in this area of power analysis since the first edition of 1987. Reviews and commentaries on Morriss (1987) include Barry (1988), Benton (1988) and Ledyaev (1997).

After Morriss, the reader should look at Keith Dowding's *Power* (1996) (a clearly explained analytical conceptual account of power which also makes use of rational choice theory) and Barry (1991). Other important texts include Dowding (1991), Wrong (1995) and Connolly (1983).

# From POWER:
# A PHILOSOPHICAL ANALYSIS
## Peter Morriss

### 2 Power and influence contrasted

In this Part, I shall be concerned with explicating ordinary usage and with understanding the reasons why our language is as it is. It is true that we cannot discover the purpose of a word just by looking it up in a dictionary. But we can gain an insight into the point of a word by contrasting it with near-synonyms, particularly near-synonyms that cannot be substituted for it without either changing the sense or – as often happens – changing sense into nonsense. We must be sensitive to the nuances of language. (My thinking here has been confirmed and much improved by Fowler's *Modern English Usage*, which I stumbled across when writing the final version of this book. Fowler should be essential reading for anyone trying to philosophize about language and concepts.)

I start this Part by contrasting the near-synonyms 'power' and 'influence'. My approach here is thus the complete opposite of that adopted by the early and influential behaviouralists, who cavalierly collapsed terms such as 'power', 'influence', 'control' and 'coercion' into one category, and then endeavoured to find the one definition that 'lay behind' all of these terms.[1]

Reprinted by kind permission of Manchester University Press from *Power: A Philosophical Analysis* (pp. 8–35). Copyright © 1987.

This single-minded, and simple-minded, attitude to concepts has had disastrously stultifying results over the last thirty years or so. I hope to show how much more fruitful it is to take note of the considerable differences between 'power' and 'influence', rather than deliberately to overlook them. For 'power' and 'influence' are not interchangeable; there are good conceptual reasons for this; and clarity demands that we do not blur these conceptual distinctions.

I shall start with three different sorts of evidence about the words 'power' and 'influence': their grammar, their derivations, and their current meanings as given by a dictionary.

The most obvious fact about the words is that 'influence' is both a noun and a verb, whilst 'power' is primarily a noun. (The verb 'to power' does exist, meaning 'to provide power' or 'empower'. It is certainly common to form verbs from nouns in this way – for instance 'to house' – but the verb only has meaning through the noun, as it were. 'To influence', on the other hand, does not mean 'to provide influence'; it counts as a verb in its own right.) This grammatical difference between 'influence' and 'power' is not something to be shrugged off as a peculiarity of the English language (as Dahl tries to do in Dahl, 1957a: p. 80), for it may turn out that 'power' refers to something that cannot be expressed by a verb. Verbs describe happenings, actions, events, occurrences and the like; but 'power', I shall suggest, is in an entirely different logical category. It would indeed be odd if 'power' and 'influence' were synonyms, and yet one of them had a verb form that the other lacked; the oddity would disappear if they were not synonyms after all.

A second difference between the two words is shown by their derivations. 'Power' came from the Latin *potere*, which meant 'to be able'. Influence', however, derived from the Latin *influere*, 'to flow in', and referred to an astrological belief that a substance emanated from the stars and flowed into people in the sublunary world, changing their behaviour or at least affecting them in some way. Hence 'under the influence', and also 'influenza'.

So 'power' and 'influence' started out in their linguistic life as expressions of completely different ideas: for being able and being affected by occult fluids are not exactly similar. But the meanings of words change, and maybe 'power' and 'influence' are now indistinguishable. That this is not the case is easily shown by looking at the entries in the *Oxford English Dictionary*, which is the most authoritative source of twentieth-century linguistic usage. The *OED* confirms the suspicion that the meanings of the words have changed so that there is now a considerable amount of overlap, but demonstrates conclusively that there also remain several differences. The best way of showing the range of meanings of the words is by quoting all the non-obsolete entries in the *OED*.

*Influence* (noun)
2. (Specifically in Astrology) The supposed flowing or streaming from the stars or heavens of an etherial fluid acting upon the character and destiny of men, and

affecting sublunary things generally. In later times gradually viewed less literally, as an exercise of power or 'virtue', or of an occult force, and in late use chiefly a poetical or humorous reflex of earlier notions.

  b. (transferred sense) The exercise of personal power by human beings, figured as something of the same nature as astral influence. (Now only poetic.)

4. The exertion of action of which the operation is unseen or insensible (or perceptible only in its effects), by one person or thing upon another; the action thus exercised.

5. The capacity or faculty of producing effects by insensible or invisible means, without the employment of material force, or the exercise of formal authority; ascendancy of a person or social group; moral power over or with a person; ascendancy, sway, control, or authority, not formally or overtly expressed.

6. A thing (or person) that exercises action or power of a non-material or unexpressed kind.

*Influence* (verb)

1. (transitive) To exert influence upon, to affect by influence.

  a. To affect the mind or action of; to move or induce by influence; sometimes especially to move by improper or undue influence.

  b. To affect the condition of, to have an effect on.

*Power* (noun)

1. Ability to do or effect something or anything, or to act upon a person or thing.

2. Ability to act or affect something strongly; physical or mental strength; might; vigour, energy; force of character; telling force, effect.

  b. Political or national strength.

3. Of inanimate things: Active property; capacity of producing some effect; the active principle of a herb, etc.

4. Possession of control or command over others; dominion, rule; government, domination, sway, command; control, influence, authority. Often followed by *over*.

  b. Authority given or committed; hence, sometimes, liberty or permission to act.

  d. Personal or social ascendancy, influence.

  e. Political ascendancy or influence in the government of a country or state.

5. Legal ability, capacity, or authority to act; especially delegated authority; authorization, commission, faculty; specifically legal authority vested in a person or persons in a particular capacity.

6. One who or that which is possessed of or exercises power, influence, or government; an influential or governing person, body or thing; in early use, one in authority, a ruler, governor.

  b. In late use, a state or nation regarded from the point of view of its international authority or influence.[2]

That there is an overlap, an area of synonymity, is clear: we only have to compare Influence$_5$ with Power$_4$ to see that. But that there is not complete synonymity should also be clear.

Indeed, a closer analysis reveals (at least) six different ideas present in these definitions of the two words: two of these ideas are common to both words, a further two are restricted to 'influence', and the remaining two are restricted to 'power'. The range of senses can be most clearly shown, I think, by starting with the senses that 'influence' alone has, moving into the area of overlap, and ending by looking at the senses peculiar to 'power'. I shall make free use of the awe-inspiring scholarship of the *OED*'s editors by using their illustrative examples.

1. 'Influence' as a verb describes an event in which something is affected in a certain manner: 'the Pope influences all the Powers and all the Princes of Europe [on this matter]'. This is the sense closest to the original derivation: altering by imperceptible means.

We can start to understand the nuances of this verb by considering how the illustrative sentence is altered if various possible alternatives are substituted for 'influences'. First, 'powers' is not even a possible alternative, since the verb form cannot be used in this context. Second, 'causes' would make the sentence grammatically correct but meaningless: the Pope causes the Princes – to do *what* on this matter? So 'cause' and 'influence' are not synonyms: the former requires a description of an event as its object, whilst 'influence' takes as object the thing or person affected. Nevertheless, 'influence' and 'cause' are clearly related: when the Pope influences the Princes he causes *something* to happen. Third, 'affects' could be substituted for 'influences', though with a loss of meaning. Influencing is a *specific* form of affecting, to be contrasted, for instance, with bribing or coercing. Since we are now less impressed with the power of occult forces, we tend to mean by 'influencing' any process in which someone's views or ideas are altered by some non-obvious mechanism, such as rational argument or an ill-understood working of the psyche.

It follows from this that anything could be the subject of the verb 'influence': a person, a thing, or an abstract quality like an idea. Similarly, anything can be the object of the verb that is capable of being affected in the appropriate way. To influence, then, is to affect in some hidden, unclear or unknown way.

2. 'Influence' is also the noun describing an act of influencing, as in Influence$_4$: 'the land tax would . . . have comparatively little influence in preventing or retarding improvements'.

3. It is perhaps a natural step to move from Influence$_4$ to Influence$_5$: from an influence as an *action* that influences, to an influence as a *capacity* to influence. Hence 'this position gave him a vast amount of influence which he continued to use for his own advantage'. Here 'power' *can* be substituted for 'influence', with only a slight change in nuance; indeed, the *OED* gives an almost identical example under Power$_{4e}$ – 'they employed the power which they possessed in the state for the purpose of making their king mighty and honoured'.

4. The move from Influence$_5$ to Influence$_6$ (and Power$_4$ to Power$_6$) is another understandable one: 'an Influence' is extended to describe the person (or thing) that has influence or that influences. Thus: 'He was an influence in the Dominion Legislature.' Again the *OED* provides a parallel example for 'power': 'Bell was a power in the house in Upper Parchment Street.'

5. Whilst Influence$_5$ is control that is 'not formally or overtly expressed', power has no such limitation; Power$_5$ refers specifically to control that *is* formally or overtly expressed: *de jure* power. 'He was careful not to assume any of those powers which the Constitution had placed in other hands' has no counterpart for 'influence', precisely because constitutions do not allocate influences: there is no such thing as *de jure* influence.[3]

6. Whilst the operation of influence is invisible, no such limitation is placed on the operation of power; hence a power is *any* capacity to produce effects, whatever the method of production. Power$_1$ is no more than a description of a (any) dispositional property. 'They were ready to afford any information in their power' means nothing more specific than that they would provide any information they could. This sense of 'power' – the 'ability to ... effect ... anything' – is not an idea that can be expressed using 'influence'; we have now left that word far behind.

It would seem from this survey that 'power' and 'influence' do overlap; but that at their cores are very different ideas, and that therefore neither is a subcategory of the other or can be replaced by it.

The first difference between 'power' and 'influence' that I want to draw attention to is that 'power' always refers to a *capacity* to do things, whilst 'influence' sometimes (and typically) does not. Thus *all* the definitions of 'power' refer to the ability to do something or the possession of control (or the person possessing such an ability); there is no meaning of 'power' comparable to Influence$_4$. This is brought out clearly in Influence$_2$ and Influence$_6$, which both refer to influence as an *exercise* of power, but not as the *possession* of power.

Indeed, this difference is so obvious that even those who claim that 'power' and 'influence' are synonyms recognize it, subconsciously, even when their 'official' analysis denies it. For instance, two of the definitions that Dahl offered of the allegedly identical 'power' and 'influence' were:

> My intuitive idea of power, then, is something like this: A *has power* over B to the extent that he *can* get B to do something that B would not otherwise do. (Dahl, 1957a: p. 80; my emphases)

> Our common-sense notion, then, goes something like this: A *influences* B to the extent that he *gets* B to do something that B would not otherwise do. (Dahl, 1963: p. 40; my emphases)

It is a great pity that Dahl did not draw from these different definitions the conclusion that power might be a dispositional form of influence – for even though that would not have been quite right, it would at least have moved the discussion in the right direction.

Dahl also sometimes uses 'power' in the pure dispositional sense – the one at the furthest extreme from 'influence':

> When one says that the President has more *power to influence* foreign policy than I have, then I think one means that the President *can cause* behaviour in the State

Department or Congress or in Germany or elsewhere that I *cannot* cause. (Dahl, 1965: p. 93; my emphases)

Quite so; but it is *influence* here that carries the causal weight, whilst *power* is simply a stand-in for 'can': the sentence has the same meaning as 'the President can influence foreign policy more than I can'. And, of course, if 'power' and 'influence' *are* synonyms, then the phrase 'power to influence' becomes nonsense.

It is easy to find other examples that amply support Hannah Pitkin's complaint that 'the social scientist who purports to use 'power' and 'influence' interchangeably does not really do so. He has simply abdicated from the task of noticing the patterns in accord with which he uses now one term, now the other' (Pitkin, 1972: pp. 277–8). Dahl himself *uses* language quite acutely; it is when he tries to write about it that his acuteness evaporates.[4]

'Power', then, I claim, is always a concept referring to an ability, capacity or dispositional property. Since this claim underlies everything in this book, perhaps a brief account of dispositional concepts would not be inappropriate at this point. In the next chapter I shall describe them, stress their importance, and look quickly at how to treat them – and how not to treat them. By the end of this slight detour I hope that any unease you may feel at my description of 'power' as a dispositional concept will have disappeared.

## 3 Dispositional concepts

### 3.1 – Dispositionals introduced

In both everyday language and scientific discourse constant reference is made to events and happenings: things that, put crudely, we can observe. We look to see whether it is raining, whether the window is open, or if the litmus paper is turning red. But this is not all we talk about; we constantly find it necessary to 'go behind' the changing flux of events, by referring to relatively unchanging underlying conditions, called the dispositional properties of the world.

A standard dispositional term, such as 'soluble', is different from a term like 'dissolving' which describes an event, since to state that a sugar lump is soluble in water is not to describe any episode, occurrence or event, but is to describe a property of the object. So dispositional concepts do different work from episodic ones in our conceptual vocabulary: episodic concepts report happenings or events, whilst dispositionals refer to relatively enduring capacities of objects. We must always make sure that we do not confuse these two quite different ideas.

We can understand the nature of dispositional concepts better by exposing two fallacies often committed in interpreting them. These involve confusing the existence of a disposition with its *exercise*, on the one hand, and its *vehicle*, on the other. These fallacies have been well summarised by Kenny:

Consider the capacity of whisky to intoxicate. The possession of this capacity is clearly distinct from its exercise: the whisky possesses the capacity while it is standing harmlessly in the bottle, but it only begins to exercise it after being imbibed. The vehicle of this capacity to intoxicate is the alcohol that the whisky contains: it is the ingredient in virtue of which the whisky has the power to intoxicate. The vehicle of a power need not be a substantial ingredient like alcohol which can be physically separated from the possessor of the power. . . . The connection between the power and its vehicle may be a necessary or a contingent one. It is a contingent matter, discovered by experiment, that alcohol is the vehicle of intoxication; but it is a conceptual truth that a round peg has the power to fit into a round hole.

Throughout the history of philosophy there has been a tendency for philosophers – especially scientifically-minded philosophers – to attempt to reduce potentialities to actualities. But there have been two different forms of reductionism, often combined and often confused, depending on whether the attempt was to reduce a power to its exercise or to its vehicle. Hume when he said that the distinction between a power and its exercise was wholly frivolous wanted to reduce powers to their exercises. Descartes when he attempted to identify all the powers of bodies with their geometrical properties wanted to reduce powers to their vehicles. (Kenny, 1975: p. 10. See also his ch. VII)

The former fallacy – reducing a power to its exercise – has been more prevalent in political science, perhaps mainly because operationalism (an extreme form of this fallacy) has had no little influence on the thinking of recent political scientists. I shall discuss this fallacy first, and then the vehicle fallacy.

### 3.2 – The exercise fallacy

The exercise fallacy is the claim that the power to do something is nothing more than the doing of it: that talking of your *having* power is imply a metaphysically illegitimate way of saying that you are *exercising* that power. This view is present in Hobbes and Hume, and was revived during the post-war behavioural revolution by social scientists impressed by pre-war positivism. A typical expression of this view is Dahl's: 'for the assertion "C has power over R", one can substitute the assertion, "C's behavior causes R's behavior".[5]

But that there is a difference between a disposition and its exercise was noticed by Aristotle over two thousand years ago, so one might have hoped that it would not still be regularly overlooked. Yet it is, and there seem to be two reasons why many recent social scientists have refused to recognise the dispositional nature of power: either they have adopted a mistaken view of science or they have striven too hard to avoid falling into the other trap and committing the vehicle fallacy.

The reliance on a hopelessly oversimplified view of science is well demonstrated by Nelson Polsby's claim that:

the assertion that any group 'potentially' could exercise significant, or decisive, or any influence in community affairs is not easy to discuss in a scientific manner. How can one tell, after all, whether or not an actor is powerful unless some sequence of events, competently observed, attests to his power? If these events take place, then the power of the actor is not 'potential' but actual. If these events do not occur, then what grounds have we to suppose that the actor is powerful? There appear to be no scientific grounds for such a supposition. . . . [It is] impossible to confirm or disprove *in principle*. (Polsby, 1963/1980: pp. 60, 68)

Unfortunately for Polsby's argument, all philosophers of science have accepted for many years that all sciences are chock-full of statements that are impossible to confirm or disprove in principle, and that these sciences are none the worse for that. Indeed, science would disappear altogether if such statements were dismissed as meaningless. For compare Polsby's passage with the following:

How can one tell, after all, whether or not a sugar lump is soluble unless some sequence of events, competently observed, attests to its solubility? If these events take place, then the solubility of the sugar lump is not 'potential' but actual [i.e., presumably, the sugar lump dissolves]. If these events do not occur, then what grounds have we to suppose that the sugar lump is soluble?

The answer, of course, is innumerable observations of sugar lumps, together with well-confirmed low-level generalizations about them.

As well as being confused about science, Polsby's logic is confused. It is, of course, true that one cannot tell whether an actor is powerful unless *some* set of observations 'attests to' his power. But there is no reason whatsoever why these observations should be of the actualization of that power. When I go to a zoo, I can see that a lion is powerful enough to eat me up by observing its jaws, teeth and muscles, and combining these observations with my general knowledge of animals' masticatory performances. If I am still in doubt, I can observe what the lion does to a hunk of meat, and induce. Not even the most dogmatic positivist would declare that he couldn't know if the lion could eat him up until it had actually done so.

But dispositions do go beyond the evidence of our senses – and beyond the possible evidence of our senses. Whilst actualities can be observed, potentialities cannot be; we can therefore never *observe* a disposition, but only manifestations of it. Therefore it is incoherent to apply an operationalist approach to evidence to dispositional terms. Operationalism demands that the only terms that can be used are those which refer to direct or indirect observations, but this is simply not what dispositional concepts are concerned with. Gilbert Ryle, in his discussion of dispositions in *The Concept of Mind*, is particularly concerned to nail this fallacy, and open up a space for dispositions.

Naturally, the addicts of the superstition that all true indicative sentences either describe existents or report occurrences will demand that sentences such as 'this wire conducts electricity', or 'John Doe knows French', shall be construed as conveying factual information of the same type as that conveyed by 'this wire is conducting electricity' and 'John Doe is speaking French'. How could the statements be true unless there were something now going on, even though going on, unfortunately, behind the scenes? Yet they have to agree that we do often know that a wire conducts electricity and that individuals know French, without having first discovered any undiscoverable goings on. (Ryle, 1949: p. 124)

Indeed, dispositions can remain forever unmanifested: a fragile cup remains fragile throughout its existence, even if it never breaks; a sample of sulphuric acid has the power to dissolve zinc, even though none is ever put into it; the Congress has the power to pass bills vetoed by the President (by passing them with a two-thirds majority), even if the President vetoes no bills. So a dispositional property can exist and yet never give rise to anything that actually occurs. A sentence about a dispositional property, as we shall see, often refers to a hypothetical event – and hypothetical events are by definition unobservable.

An operationalist approach to power thus solves the problem at a stroke – but the stroke is that of a guillotine. For a consistent radical operationalism demands that we no longer talk about powers; that is, it 'solves' the problem by killing it.

This would be a loss. Whilst it is possible to devise a vocabulary which does not contain dispositional concepts, it would be a very impoverished one. For the world viewed through this linguistic framework would contain only a series of more of less unrelated events or happenings. A.J. Ayer has said how in his younger, more harshly positivist, days he lost a favourite fountain pen, and tried to persuade himself that all that had happened was the cessation of a stream of favourable sensations, rather than the disappearance of an *object*. Even at that time, when his ontology did not admit anything as far removed from sense-data as ordinary objects, he was not convinced by his description of what had happened – and rightly so. For if we ignore its dispositional properties, the world must appear just a buzzing, bewildering confusion of haphazard events: indeed it is unlikely that anybody could view the world in that way for very long without going mad.

*3.3 – The vehicle fallacy*

Unlike the exercise fallacy, the vehicle fallacy tends to be committed by philosophers rather than by political scientists. Quine, for example, advances a realist interpretation of dispositions, considering that when we say that something is soluble at a given time, we are intruding a 'stabilizing factor' of

> a theory of subvisible structure. What we have seen dissolve in water had, according to the theory, a structure suited to dissolving; and when now we speak of some new dry sugar lump as soluble, we may be considered merely to be saying that it, whether destined for water or not, is similarly structured. (Quine, 1960: p. 223)

But there is no reason why dispositionals should refer to 'subvisible structures'. They may; but we can talk perfectly sensibly about the dispositional properties of an object without bothering our heads about its structure, visible or otherwise. For, as Stanley Benn has commented, 'the power to extinguish a flame is possessed alike by a bucket of water, a cold wind, or a quantity of pyrene foam, each possessing the same power by virtue of quite different [structural] properties' (Benn, 1972: pp. 191–2). To ask *why* a substance has a property (by virtue of *what?*) is different from, and not necessary for, asserting that it *does* have this property.

When we come to consider the dispositional properties of *people* it becomes obvious that talk of 'subvisible structure' is simply no help at all. It is either false or empty to claim that someone who can speak French has a different subvisible structure from someone who cannot.

## 3.4 – Conclusion

One obvious way to start studying power is by cataloguing the actors' resources. Doubtless some sociologists who have tried this have carelessly claimed or implied that resources themselves were power, thus falling into the vehicle fallacy. On the other hand, part of the reason why behaviouralists have refused to infer power from resources has been a laudable desire to avoid this fallacy (see, e.g., Dahl, 1984: pp. 21–2). Wealth is not political power, they have said, since, whilst some people use their wealth to collect politicians, others can only collect paintings. Even position in a formal hierarchy is not, in itself, power: the President may be too incompetent to use the resources of office, or the *real* power may lie elsewhere. How can we know where the power is, then, unless we see it exercised?

But there is a big difference between committing the vehicle fallacy by *identifying* power with the resources that give rise to it and acknowledging that resources can be useful *evidence* in reaching assessments of power. Using such evidence is not easy, but that it is certainly possible I try to show in Chapter 19. All I am concerned to argue here is that there is, logically, a third alternative, so that we need not identify power with its exercise in order to avoid identifying it with resources.

So power, as a dispositional concept, is neither a *thing* (a resource or vehicle) nor an *event* (an exercise of power): it is a *capacity*. And dispositional concepts are perfectly respectable ones that we do not need to replace by concepts of some other sort. On the contrary we clearly need such dispositional concepts in our conceptual vocabulary. We need not feel ashamed that 'power' is such a dispositional concept.

## 4 Power as a dispositional concept

I hope that I have now established that a power is a disposition of some sort. In this chapter I will expand on the significance of this, and examine further exactly what the dispositional nature of power is.

### 4.1 – Power and its exercise

When power is *exercised*, something happens: for instance, the United States overthrows the government in Grenada. Such an event could be described in many different ways, of course – you may prefer talking about the liberation of Grenada from communist tyranny, perhaps. But in this section I want to contrast two possible types of description of this event: the description of the event as the overthrow of a government or the liberation of a country, on the one hand, and the description of the same event as the United States *exercising its power* to overthrow a government or liberate a country. I shall suggest that the fact that we can rephrase many descriptions of events into statements about the exercise of power has led many social scientists (and philosophers) to misunderstand the significance of power, and to think that we are interested in the acts that people do *because* they are exercises of power, and not simply because they are acts of a certain sort.

A good example of what can happen if one doesn't exercise care is the following gaffe made by Quentin Gibson. Gibson refers to Stanley Benn's (Benn, 1967: p. 426) example:

> of the careless smoker who constantly causes fires but never achieves anything he intends. Such a person, says Benn, could not be called powerful. But this, it seems to me, is to misjudge normal usage. The man is clearly able to cause fires, whether he actually intends to or not, and *it is precisely in this that the regrettable power of such people lies*. (Gibson, 1971: p. 103; my emphasis)

But this is just wrong. What is regrettable about careless smokers is not that they are *able* to cause fires, but that they *do* cause fires. It is not the *power* to cause fires that we regret in this case since you also have this power and no one regrets *that* – unless, of course, you are a careless smoker or a pyromaniac. We are typically interested simply in who *does* set fire to things.

A similar mistake vitiates the analysis of power that William Connolly provides in his chapter on Power and Responsibility in *The Terms of Political Discourse* (Connolly, 1974/1983: ch. 3). Most commentators have concentrated on exposing weaknesses in the way Connolly talks about responsibility,[6] but have not noticed that Connolly is not really talking about power at all in this chapter, despite his frequent use of the word. Instead, Connolly has fallen into the trap of thinking that because something can be *described* as an exercise of power we must be interested in it *as* an exercise of power. It is instructive to see how he makes this mistake.

Connolly draws up a 'paradigm' of power which 'briefly stated' is that 'A exercises power over B when he is responsible for some X that increases the costs, risks, or difficulties to B in promoting B's desires or in recognizing or promoting B's interests or obligations' (pp. 102–3). But Connolly recognizes that the locution '*having* power' is 'basic' (p. 101), and so he recasts his paradigm so that someone *has* power, but does not exercise it, 'when he could, but does not, limit B in the ways specified' (p. 103). This is Connolly's definition, or paradigm, of 'A *has* power over B'.

What Connolly completely overlooks is that this move destroys the main thesis of his chapter, which is 'that there is a particularly intimate connection between alleging that A has power over B and concluding that A is properly held responsible to some degree for B's conduct or situation' (p. 95). For if A could, *but does not*, 'limit' B in some way, then there is nothing in B's conduct or situation for which A can be held responsible: ex hypothesi, A has *not* contributed to the situation that B faces. It is only when A *does* act that he can be held responsible for the act's consequences. So it is not *power* that Connolly tries to link with responsibility, but various sorts of *acts*.[7]

What Connolly is doing in his chapter, then, is discussing which types of action are always permissible (persuasion is one such, he thinks), and which types of action have a 'moral presumption' against them (p. 95). This is certainly a very important subject, and one which involves our whole moral outlook on personal interaction – but it does not refer to power, and it only obscures the issue to include 'power' in it. When it comes to holding people morally responsible – praising and blaming them – it is invariably their actions (and omissions) that we look at, not their powers. One is not censured for having the *power* to start forest fires or the *power* to coerce people to do one's bidding, but only for actually doing such things. When discussing the rightness or wrongness of someone's actions, we require a morally appropriate vocabulary for describing these actions, and a set of moral beliefs for judging them; we do not require a redrawn concept of power.[8]

The message of this section is that, whilst many events can be described as an exercise of power, we should only use the vocabulary of power if we are interested specifically in the *capacity* for producing events of this sort, and not if we are just interested in the events themselves.

## 4.2 – Habitual and conditional dispositions

But the capacity for producing events may mean two different things, for there are two different sorts of disposition. This distinction is of considerable importance for understanding 'power', and yet it has not received the attention due to it.

We can understand this distinction by analysing the following passage by Gilbert Ryle, in which he describes dispositional properties.

> To possess a dispositional property is not to be in a particular state, or to undergo a particular change; it is to be bound or liable to be in a particular state, or to undergo a particular change, when a particular condition is realised. The same is true about specifically human dispositions such as qualities of character. My being an habitual smoker does not entail that I am at this or that moment smoking; it is my permanent proneness to smoke when I am not eating, sleeping, lecturing or attending funerals, and have not quite recently been smoking. (Ryle, 1949: p. 43)

But that someone is a smoker is a different sort of property from a standard dispositional one such as a sugar lump being soluble – for the latter involves *conditionals* whilst the former does not. To say that a sugar lump is soluble is to say that *if* it were to be placed in water, it would dissolve. The conditional clause here states an activating condition: a circumstance necessary for the dispositional property to be actualized. But to say that Samantha is a smoker does not mean that, if the present conditions were different from what they are, she would be smoking; rather it is to assert that in a relatively short amount of time from now she will be smoking, and that a relatively short amount of time ago she was smoking (barring the sort of exceptions that Ryle mentions). And *these* are straightforward future and past indicative sentences, without conditional elements.

Attempts at introducing sensible conditionals all fail. Thus we can try, as a translation of 'Samantha is a smoker', 'if Samantha experienced the relevant sort of cravings for a smoke now, she would smoke'. This differentiates between the smoker and the person who, giving up, successfully fights against her occasional desires for a smoke; but a true non-smoker never experiences these cravings, and whether she would succumb to them if she did is not the relevant issue. Thus to distinguish the smoker from the non-smoker we have to add to the conditional some such codicil as 'and Samantha frequently experiences such cravings' – which is a straightforward descriptive statement. One could, I suppose, try some such formula as 'if it were two hours later than it is now, Samantha would have smoked in the last two hours', or 'if Samantha had not smoked in the last two hours, she would be smoking now', but these seem unnecessarily tortuous. Ryle's comment about the smoker's 'permanent proneness' to smoke seems little help indeed – and it is precisely such sorts of account that Ryle is attacking in *The Concept of Mind*.

It is worth noting that my suggested analysis of 'Samantha smokes' would be different if, for some reason, cigarettes were in short supply: *then* the dispositional term 'smoker' *could* be used conditionally, meaning 'if Samantha could have obtained some cigarettes today, she would have smoked them'. This could well occur to someone who smokes dope – if cannabis becomes unusually difficult to obtain, we would still say of someone that she smokes it even if she hasn't touched the stuff for months because she has been unable to get hold of any.

I will call this the distinction between habitual dispositions and true or conditional dispositions. We would recognise, I think, that it is a distinction we draw in ordinary language, particularly if we change the example from smoking to drinking (alcohol). A habitual drinker is one who drinks regularly (and frequently) regardless of circumstances; we normally want to distinguish such a person from one who drinks only in certain circumstances (e.g. a 'social' drinker); and differentiate the latter from a person who is tee-total. The habits of the habitual drinker and of the teetotaller will accurately be described by a suitable non-conditional sentence, whilst the moderate or occasional drinker will require some suitable conditional to describe his drinking.

I think we can now see why treating influence as a special sort of power (as do, for instance, Partridge [1963] and Oppenheim [1981]) immediately gives rise to odd consequences. We readily talk of the influence of Cézanne on painting or Joyce on literature (Partridge's examples: p. 111); hence, if influence is a sort of power, a less specific way of saying much the same thing would be to talk of the *power* of Cézanne on (over?) painting. But we rarely attribute powers to people after they are dead.

It is my feeling that 'influence', used in its capacity sense, refers to a habitual disposition, whilst 'power' most usually indicates a conditional disposition. To say that someone is an influence is of a similar logical form to saying that someone is a smoker: it is to say that they *do* influence (smoke), and not just once but often. The episodes of influencing take place so frequently that, rather than enumerating them, we roll them all together and talk of the person's influence extending continuously over time. This is the sense in which we talk of the influence of Cézanne on painting.

A power, however, is a disposition that may or may not be activated: TNT is explosive because it explodes *when the conditions are right*, not because it explodes frequently. A person is powerful if she can do things *when she wants to* – not only if she does do things frequently. From this it is fairly clear why the dead have no powers of this sort: whilst they can still influence, they do not have a disposition to influence that they can activate.

This is why we do not say that someone had influence, or was influential, but never bothered to influence anyone; we do say that people have power, or are powerful, but do not bother to use it. An influence, then, is a capacity in the sense of a continuing influence; not a capacity in the sense of a potential influence. If we want to describe someone as having the capacity to influence in this latter sense, we have to say that they have the *power* to influence.

### 4.3 – Dispositional properties and abilities

In this section I shall consider the logic of *our* dispositional properties – that is, of human powers. Let us start by returning to Aristotle,

who drew a sharp distinction between rational powers, such as the ability to speak Greek, and natural powers like the power of fire to burn. If all the necessary conditions for the exercise of a natural power were present, then, he maintained, the power was necessarily exercised: put the wood, appropriately dry, on the fire, and the fire will burn it; there are no two ways about it. Rational powers, however, are essentially, he argued, two-way powers, powers which can be exercised at will: a rational agent, presented with all the necessary external conditions for exercising a power, may choose not to do so. (Kenny, 1975: pp. 52–3, citing Aristotle, c. 330 BC: Theta 1046a–1048a)

But this distinction is not quite correct; for, as Kenny points out, 'Aristotle was surely wrong to identify rational powers and two-way powers. If someone speaks a language I know in my hearing it isn't in my power not to understand it' (Kenny, 1975: p. 53).

It seems, then, that people have ordinary dispositional powers and also powers which can be exercised at will, and that these two are very different. I shall call the latter *abilities*. The difference between a human ability and a mere disposition is that the ability involves, in some way, an act of will, a choice or a decision. Abilities refer not to things which happen to us, but to things which we do.[9] So abilities are conditional dispositional properties that depend on the actor activating them: one of the necessary conditions for exercising an ability is that the actor must choose to do so.

### 4.4 – Power and intention

Whilst many writers have defined power as the ability to affect people in accordance with one's intentions,[10] some have denied any connection at all between power and intentions. Those who have resisted the suggestion that 'power' makes some reference to the intentions of the power-holder have advanced three sorts of arguments against it. The first 'argument' is that intention is such a difficult concept that we are better off without it.[11] This is not worth the trouble of taking seriously: if it turns out that an analysis of 'power' requires us to include intentions, then we have to make the best of it. I hope to show, in any case, that we can cope with all the terrors that the concept of intention can produce for us.

The second sort of argument consists of producing examples that are allegedly self-evident examples of power but which contain no intentional element. The trouble with this method is that most such examples are clearly cases of influence, not power, and often are even described as such. The plausibility of these examples depends on the prior identification of 'influence' and 'power', which is, of course, something I am at pains to deny. Hence Oppenheim invites us to 'take the pollsters who predicted that Truman would lose the presidential election of 1948, and thereby quite unintentionally *influenced* voters – to disconfirm that prediction. Did they not *exercise power* over voters who voted for Truman because of these polls?' (Oppenheim, 1981: pp. 44–5; my emphases). Oppenheim has many more such examples, all equally unconvincing. 'We are inclined to regard', he says, people who prevent others from doing things, without intending to do so, as 'thereby acquiring power' over them – for instance, 'the winner in an athletic competition has power over the losers' (p, 45). Conceptual arguments that rely on ordinary usage are, by themselves, never convincing – but they are even less convincing when they so clearly get ordinary usage wrong.

Connolly and Lukes adopt a rather more sophisticated version of this approach. They have already defined an exercise of power as an action (or failure to act) for which the actor is responsible and which adversely affects someone in some way, and they then point out, rightly, that we can all adversely affect people without intending to do so, and we can then even (sometimes) be held morally responsible for adversely affecting them.[12] According to their definitions, we have thereby exercised power unintentionally. But all this only follows, of course, if we accept the link between responsibility and power that Lukes and Connolly claimed – and I have already shown that the arguments for this link fail to hold because of the confusion between power and its exercise (see above, pp. 21–2). The examples they offer, then, will fail to convince a disbeliever that power can be exercised unintentionally.

The third, and most interesting, way of trying to separate power from intention has been suggested by Quentin Gibson.[13] Gibson considers that 'intentions are irrelevant', for:

> to insist on intentionality has one extremely odd result. It prevents us, at one stroke, from attributing power to inanimate things. That a stormy sea has the power to wreck a ship or an engine the power to turn the wheels is surely something which no one should feel hesitant about maintaining. It may be said that this is anthropomorphism, and that in the literal sense only people have power. But this would be to confuse the origin of the concept with its nature. It may well be that in earlier and more animistic days, power, like causal efficacy, was attributable only to human or other spiritual agencies with wills. But generalization of the concept has taken place long since, certainly by the time of Hobbes and Locke. The move from human power to horse power, and from horse power to engine power is a matter of history. (Gibson, 1971: pp. 103–4)

What Gibson here is missing is that the 'move' from human power to engine power is not a generalization, but a change in meaning. When we assert that a stormy sea has the power to wreck a ship, what we are referring to is either a dispositional property, pure and simple (Power$_1$), or Power$_2$ ('the ability to . . . affect something strongly; vigour, energy'). The word 'power' is undoubtedly used in both these senses. But when we talk about, for instance, the Prime Minister's power to dissolve Parliament, it is quite clear that neither of these senses are being employed. For whilst 'the sulphuric acid has the power to dissolve zinc' means (more or less) that if zinc is placed in sulphuric acid it will dissolve, the corresponding power of the British Prime Minister is to dissolve Parliament *when she wants to*.

Gibson's argument fails, then, because he does not realize that 'power' can refer to a variety of different dispositional properties, each of which may have a slightly different logic. Intentions are *sometimes* irrelevant to an actor's powers, but Gibson's examples do not show that intentions are *always* irrelevant. Intentions are usually not relevant when we are considering powers that are not abilities; but an intention is usually part of the definition of any power that is an ability – for abilities are things we can do *when we want*.[15]

To explore further the nature of this distinction, I would like to consider an interesting passage of Danto's in which he discusses sexual impotence. It seems that, if Danto is right, our use of 'impotence' in this context is in accord with the sense of power as a mere dispositional, and not as an ability.

Danto starts with a passage from Hume: 'We are not able to move all the organs of the body with like authority, though we cannot assign any reason besides experience, for so remarkable a difference between one and the other.' He then quotes St Augustine, who agreed with Hume that:

> We *could* have been framed with our authority differently seated: 'God could early have made us with all our members subjected to the will', he [Augustine] writes, adding the possibility which obviously haunted him as a man, as we might recall from the *Confessions*, 'even those which *now* are moved by lust'. I italicize the word 'now', which occurs twice in this passage. For it was Augustine's curious view that Adam, in paradise, indeed was so framed that he could perform what I term basic actions with his sexual organ, and hence achieve the sexual act immune from the contaminations of sin. . . .
>
> I am not at all certain that it is a merely contingent matter that voluntary erection lies outside the boundaries of direct action. For curiously enough, a man who were able to erect at will might in fact be impotent in the received sense, which is an incapacity for genuine sexual *response*; where *response* implies precisely the absence of that order of control Augustine supposes our first parent to have exemplified. A man who had direct control, or who was obliged to exercise direct control, would be a man without *feeling*, erection being the common *expression* of male sexual feeling. And it is in some measure a logical truth that if erection were an action it would not be an expression, and the entire meaning of sexuality would be altered were tumescence something over which we had 'authority'. (Danto, 1973: pp. 116–17)[16]

It would seem, then, that the power which those who are impotent lack is a power in the purely dispositional sense of the term, and not the ability sense. For if erection (in the appropriate situations) is not an *action*, then we cannot have (or lack) the ability to perform it. Erection as a response is like the knee-jerk reflex or laughing: something that happens to our bodies rather than something we do. Danto's discussion of such responses, how they differ from actions done at will, and how important they are in our social lives is, I think, very well done, and could form the basis of some important work. If Danto is right, then, it seems that our natural powers, which we do not exercise at will, are very important to us in our social interactions.

And these natural powers are very different from our abilities. The lesson to be drawn from this discussion is that we must not confuse abilities with natural powers, and think that because they are both powers they must have an identical analysis. There is a crucial difference here, which Gibson overlooked.

If Gibson's argument fails, he is nevertheless quite right to suggest that power is not influence with some added intentions. The difference between power and influence runs deeper than this. I shall argue in the next chapter that most accounts of 'power' are defective because they have been modelled too closely on 'influence'.

## 5 Power and influence: the differences concluded

### 5.1 – Affecting and effecting

The most common account of 'power' in the social science literature is one that involves somehow *affecting* others. Hence Steven Lukes claims as (almost) uncontroversial that 'the absolutely basic common core to, or primitive notion lying behind, all talk of power is the notion that A in some way affects B' (Lukes, 1974: p. 26).[17] And this 'primitive notion' certainly does lie behind almost all recent analyses of power.

Yet several writers have pointed out that simply *affecting* someone is not what we understand by power. For if it were, then the victim who incautiously displays a well-filled wallet would exercise power over the thief who robs him (Wormuth, 1967: p. 817); a person who overturned their car and burdened the insurance company with the bill would, likewise, have thereby exercised power (Young, 1978: p. 643); and so would the bankrupt financier whose fall ruined thousands of people who had invested their savings with him (Benn, 1967: p. 426).

I want to suggest that we cannot get rid of these anomalies by putting restrictions on the sorts of affecting that are to 'count' as an exercise of power, as Lukes and others want to do. The error runs deeper: 'power' is not concerned at all with affecting, though 'influence' is. 'Power' is concerned with *effecting*, which is a very different idea.

To *affect* something is to alter it or impinge on it in some way (*any* way); to *effect* something is to bring about or accomplish it. For example, 'a single glass of brandy may affect [i.e. alter for better or worse the prospects of] his recovery' is very different from 'a single glass of brandy may effect [i.e. bring about] his recovery'.[18]

It follows from this difference in meaning that the verbs 'affect' and 'effect' take different objects: you can affect something if you can alter it in some way; you can effect something if you can accomplish it. Hence you can affect, but not effect, a person; and you can effect, but not affect, a state of affairs that does not now exist.

The subjects of the verbs sometimes differ as well. Only beings that are in some (perhaps metaphorical) sense conscious and active can effect anything because only these beings can bring about or accomplish something whilst a much wider range of entities can affect. Hence books and idea can affect but not effect, and so can famous but dead people, like Cézanne.

I hope that by now 'affects' is beginning to look very similar to 'influences', and 'effects' rather like 'exercises power'. This is not surprising since, if you glance back at the definitions given on pp. 279–80, you will see that 'influence' is defined as *affecting* (in a certain way), whilst 'power' is usually defined as the ability to *effect*. The examples given in the second paragraph of this section seem so clearly not to be examples of power precisely because no effecting is going on in them: those who affect others without effecting anything are rightly seen not as powerful but merely as nuisances. Benn's bankrupt financier had a certain amount of power *before* his fall, which he lost when his empire collapsed; although his fall possibly affected people more drastically than any of his previous actions, he did not thereby exercise power.

To affect something (or somebody) but not effect (accomplish) anything seems, then, not to be an exercise of power.

### 5.2 – Power without affecting

I have suggested that simply affecting something or somebody is not an exercise of power unless the actor thereby effects something, and that correspondingly, the capacity to affect is not power unless the capacity to effect is also present. I now want to go one step further, and argue that someone may be powerful when they have the capacity to *effect* something even when they cannot *affect* anything.

Let us look a bit closer at the idea that power involves the capacity to affect an existing state of affairs (or person). Here is an example (an adaptation of one of Alvin Goldman's). You have a rain-making machine. On clear sunny days (all clear sunny days, and only clear sunny days) you can crank up your machine, and within six hours a gentle drizzle will be falling from the heavens. It never fails. Sometimes, of course, it would have rained anyway, and then you can't take much credit for the rain (you don't make it rain any harder); but often it would not have rained, and then you have made it rain. You have the power to make rain (on clear sunny days). But do you have the power to make rain on all clear sunny days *including* those when it would have rained anyway; or only on those clear sunny days when it would *not* have rained? It would seem that when it would have rained anyway you are impotent to do anything about the weather with your rain-making machine (you don't have a rain-*preventing* machine): your machine can make no difference at all. So, since it rains whatever you do, you don't have any powers or abilities with respect to the issue of whether it rains or not on these necessarily rainy occasions.

This is, more or less, how Goldman argues.[19] I think he is wrong to do so. I think that one can have the power or ability to do something even if it would have been brought about in any case. It is true that, on days when it would have rained, your machine cannot affect the weather: it rains whether or not you set your machine to work. If it is power to affect the weather that we are interested in, then Goldman's approach is the right one: you lack this power on rainy days. But you *do* still have the power to *ensure rain*. Your power (or your machine's power) to produce rain does not somehow disappear when rain-clouds are gathering unseen beyond the horizon. Your machine ensures that you can have rain whenever you want it: that you do indeed have the power to produce rain.

At this point we need to ask exactly what it is that we want to know. I have assumed that we are interested in whether your machine can ensure that it will rain whenever you set it going, and this seems to me a not unreasonable interpretation. (That is what a gardener, for instance, would want to know when wondering whether to buy your machine.) But we might be interested, I suppose, in whether your machine could *make* it rain (perhaps on a given occasion), and by this mean that the rain must be created by the machine rather than by any other means. If this is what we want to know, then we are inquiring whether the machine can both effect rain and affect the weather, and your machine, which cannot do both of these if the weather would have been wet anyway, must be judged powerless. So the power to *make* rain, unlike the power to *ensure* rain, requires both effecting and affecting.[20]

From this it should be clear that it is crucial to specify very carefully the exact power which we are interested in. Goldman goes wrong, I think, in choosing to analyse the cumbersome formulation 'power with respect to the issue of whether or not it rains' and not the more straightforward (and informative) 'power to make (it) rain' or 'power to ensure rain'. This seems difficult to defend: doctors and would-be assassins both have power with respect to the issue of whether we live or die, yet the power to prevent a chronically ill person dying is one that we usually wish to distinguish from the power to kill a healthy person.

Clearly, if the phrase we are trying to analyse is 'power with respect to an issue', then we will be led to an account of power that involves affecting and not effecting; for one can *affect* whether or not it rains, whilst one cannot *effect* whether or not it rains. Yet, as I have suggested, it is more likely than not that it is the power to effect rain that really interests us. If so we must look at power to effect *outcomes* (states of affairs) and not power over *issues*.[21] It is, therefore, very important which phrase, containing the word 'power', we choose to employ. This will be the topic of the next section.

## 5.3 – Power-to or power-over?

'A has power' is incomplete: it tells us that A has *some* dispositional property or capacity or ability, but it does not say *which*. Since all objects, of whatever sort, have dispositional properties, 'A has power' is a singularly unhelpful utterance. We clearly need to specify the power in some way. This has been widely recognised in the literature, and most writers have felt that, in the social sciences, we must immediately go on to specify *over whom* A has power. For instance:

> I do not 'have power – period'. I have (perhaps) power over my students as [the author's abbreviation for 'with respect to'] their reading *Leviathan*: Such expressions are elliptical. (Oppenheim, 1981: p. 6)

Thus Oppenheim's chosen definiendum is 'P has power over R wrt his not doing X' (p. 21), and any statement about power that doesn't specify the person that the power is over – and 'with respect to' which of their actions – is considered by Oppenheim to be incomplete.

This move is a mistake, and we can now see why so many people have been led to make it. If 'power' is thought of as involving affecting, then a full statement of the power must state what is affected. When we are concerned with *social* power, it is natural to suppose that a *person* (rather than a thing) must be affected by the power. The only way that the English language allows 'power' to be followed by a word for a person is by talking of the power being *over* the person. Ergo, it seems, all social power becomes power over someone.

Now anyone with an ear for language, or knowledge of English usage would find this conclusion very odd. It is far more common to say that someone has the power *to do something* than it is to say that they have power *over someone*.[22] We readily contrast the Prime Minister's power to dissolve Parliament with the American President's lack of such power; we talk (as even Dahl does) of the President having more power to influence foreign policy than we do; we lament that we do not have the power to paint our council house the colour of our choice, or we rejoice that we do have the power to make our views known to our elected representatives – and, periodically, the power to dismiss them. None of these powers can be expressed adequately using 'power over'; these are all powers to obtain some specified *outcome*, and whilst affecting others *may* be the desired outcome (I paint my council house crimson to annoy the neighbours), it is more likely not to be.

Further, when we do say that A has power over a person B – or that B is in A's power – we do so when A can get B to do a large number of things, not just one. A blackmailer has power over his victim if there is a wide range of things that the victim will do readily rather than have his guilty secret revealed; we would say that a Congressperson who owes another a favour is within her power if the latter can call in this debt at a time and in a manner of her own choosing.[23] So the locution 'power over' has a specific use of its own; it is not the general, and certainly not the main, way we talk of power.

This emphasis on power as affecting others has had serious repercussions, which have stemmed from the loose way that 'power over' has been used. Mostly the phrase 'A has power over B' was meant in a wide sense, to mean that B is the object of A's power (that is, B is the person *through* whom A attains his ends, or who is affected *by* A attaining his ends). But the more natural reading of the phrase is the much narrower one that the subordination of B is the *objective* of A's power.[24] Concentration on 'power over' has had the deplorable tendency of emphasizing this latter sort of power, so that Dahl, Lukes and many others have defined power in terms of someone's ability to affect others in various nasty ways. But our ability to kick others around (or to harm their interests, or get them to do things they don't want to do) can scarcely encompass *everything* we understand as power in social contexts.[25] Frequently we value power simply because it enables us to do things we want to do: to have more control over our own lives.

This distortion has, I think, had worse results than just causing academic confusion: it has had pernicious political consequences. The reception of the slogan 'Black Power' is a case in point. 'Black Power' encapsulated a platform aimed at giving blacks the power to run their own lives; it represented a demand for autonomy. The originators of the movement never intended the slogan to imply that black people should have disproportionate power *over* non-blacks – should somehow dominate them.[26] Indeed, one strand of the movement sought to eliminate as much contact between white and black people as they could: it advocated setting up black enclaves which were as self-governing as possible. White supremacists, however, by equating power-to with power-over, were able to portray the legitimate demands of black people for equality as equivalent to a desire for black domination. It is regrettable that reputable, and liberal, academics, by considering power over others as the only sort of power, may have unwittingly encouraged such distortions.

How, then, have social scientists defended their near exclusive emphasis on power *over* people? I think it is fair to say that this really crucial decision has never been adequately considered in the literature: either the matter is ignored entirely; or (spurious) considerations of ordinary language are adduced; or the author simply declares that power to do things is not what he is interested in.[27] The one argument that has been tried is the claim that talking about power *to* do things 'cannot bring out what seems to me the important distinguishing feature of *social* power; namely, that it refers to an interaction relation, a relationship between some action y of P and some possible *action* x of R' (Oppenheim, 1981: p. 31). Or, from a more self-consciously radical perspective, the locution 'power to' 'indicates a "capacity", a "facility", an "ability", not a relationship. Accordingly, the conflictual aspect of power – the fact [sic] that it is exercised *over* people – disappears altogether from view' (Lukes, 1974: p. 31).

But this talk of power as a relationship is not particularly enlightening. As Hannah Pitkin points out: 'one may . . . "have" a "relationship", but always "with" someone else. . . . And one does not "exercise" a "relationship" at all. What the social scientists mean by calling power relational, if I understand them, is that the phenomena of power go on among people' (Pitkin, 1972: p. 276). If we are interested in the 'conflictual aspect' of power, we can very easily look at someone's power *to* kick others around, or their power *to* win conflicts. Everything that needs to be said about power can be said using the idea of the capacity to effect outcomes – unless we are mesmerised by a desire to get the notion of *affecting* into 'power' at all costs.

There is a further dubious aspect to Lukes's argument, since what he seems to be doing is cramming into his chosen *concept* of power claims which ought to be considered as empirical. Thus even if Lukes is correct, and if it *is* a fact that power is always exercised over people, this is not a reason for defining power so that it can *only* be exercised over people. If conflict is indeed omnipresent within society, then a neutral definition will surely discover it.[28]

It may be worth noting that no empirical researcher has taken such a limited attitude to power in their research. Even Dahl, whose conceptual writings stress repeatedly that power is exercised over someone, forgets this in his empirical work, in which he equates a person's power with their success on matters of key importance (Dahl, 1961: p. 333).

### 5.4 – Conclusion

Oppenheim's definiendum is so contorted and clumsy because of his misunderstanding of our use of 'power': he wants to use the word 'power'; he wants to use a notion of power as affecting; and he wants the thing affected to be a person. But these three desires do not fit naturally together. If I want to say that I have the power to get my students to read *Leviathan*, I can say just that; I don't have to say that I have power over my students with respect to their reading *Leviathan*; nor is it natural to do so. Oppenheim, Goldman and many others are pushed into the position of talking about power 'with respect to' someone's action, or 'with respect to' some issue, because of their reliance on the model of power as a form of affecting.[29] But, as I have already suggested, it is both more natural and more informative to fill out the content of our powers by describing the outcomes that we are capable of effecting. This is invariably what we do say (when we are not captivated by an erroneous theory), and it enables us to say what we want to say neatly and accurately.

In the next chapter I shall look somewhat more closely at what sorts of things we *do* want to say when we use this concept of power.

### Notes

1 See, for instance, Simon (1953: n. 3) or Dahl (1957a: p. 80).
2 The dictionary goes on to give many other technical senses.
3 Bagehot states that the British monarch has 'the right to be consulted, the right to encourage, the right to warn' (1867: p. 111). These rights give the monarch considerable influence. But no constitution, even an unwritten one, could give such influence explicitly.
4 In recent editions of his *Modern Political Analysis*, Dahl refers to Pitkin's 'interesting attempt to clarify the meaning of various influence terms' (Dahl, 1984: p. 20 n. 2) but in his text he completely ignores her complaint quoted here.
5 The quotation from Dahl is from his (1968: p. 410), in which he follows Simon (1957: p. 5). For Hobbes see his (1655: ch. 10). Hume, in *A Treatise of Human Nature*, states baldly that 'the distinction, which we often make betwixt *power* and the *exercise* of it, is . . . without foundation' (Hume, 1739: p. 171); but later he comments that 'tho' this be strictly true in a just and philosophical way of thinking, 'tis certain it is not the philosophy of our passions' (p. 311), and he

then modifies his account, considering 'it may justly be concluded, that power has always a reference to its exercise, *either actual or probable*, and that we consider a person as endow'd with any ability when we find from past experience, that 'tis probable, *or at least possible* he may exert it' (p. 313: my emphases). Such equivocation is not uncommon amongst those who equate power and its exercise whilst knowing intuitively that they are wrong to do so.

6  See, for example, the careful analysis by Reeve (1982).

7  And omissions. Connolly considers that someone can *exercise* power by *refraining* from helping others when he could do so, provided that he could reasonably be expected to understand the harm he was causing by not acting (pp. 102, 106). Connolly also includes as an *exercise* of power that sense of 'having power' in which the powerholder does not need to act because his actions are anticipated, and he is given what he wants without needing to bestir himself (pp. 101–2).

8  In sections 6.2 and 6.3 I shall discuss how power and responsibility *do* connect.

9  This has the odd-sounding consequence that understanding Greek or English does not count as a human ability – although it is a human dispositional power (and certainly is not a *non-human ability*). This apparent difficulty is resolved in section 13.2.

10  Wrong (1979: p. 4) defines power as intended influence, as do many others.

11  See Oppenheim (1981: p. 46), Georgiou (1977), and, to an extent, White (1971).

12  See Connolly (1974/1983: pp. 104–6) and Lukes (1974: pp. 51–2).

13  Gibson offers two arguments; the second has already been considered and dismissed on pp. 20–1.

14  *De facto* power; not the *de jure* power of Powers, which the Prime Minister possibly lacks.

15  This idea is explored further and in greater detail in chapter 8.

16  The quotations are from Hume's *Treatise of Human Nature*, section vii, part I, and St Augustine, *The City of God* XIV, ch. 24. For Danto's discussion see (Danto, 1973: pp. 116–19; also the rest of ch. 5 and pp. 151–3).

17  But compare Lukes's more recent version, in an excellent survey article: 'The absolutely basic common core to all conceptions of power is the notion of the bringing about of consequences, with no restriction on what the consequences might be or what brings them about' (Lukes, 1979: pp. 634–5).

18  I owe this example to Fowler (1968: p. 13). The ease with which people confuse 'affect' and 'effect' is partly explained by an unfortunate oddity in the English language: the noun corresponding to the verb 'to affect' is 'an *effect*', and there is no noun 'an affect'. So 'the brandy has an effect on his recovery' does not mean that it *effects* it, but that it *affects* it. Hence *an effect* is something caused; it is not restricted to something accomplished. Perhaps this muddle has added to the confusion over the two very different verbs.

19  See Goldman (1972: section I and p. 241, and, particularly, n. 4).

20  For a further discussion of effecting and affecting see Appendix 3.3 (p. 221).

21  Goldman, in his (1974: p. 233), does talk of power being over *outcomes* (and *control* over issues), but he does not investigate the difference this makes, apparently considering it merely a different terminological decision.

22  The *OED* gives seventeen different senses of 'power', of which at least four can be considered senses of social power (senses 1, 4, 5 and 6); only one of these senses can be followed by 'over' (sense 4). The *OED* gives thirty different quotations to illustrate the usage of this one sense of power, and in only *one* of these is the phrase 'power over' employed. If 'power' *was* normally followed by 'over' in our discussions of politics, the compilers of the *OED* would assuredly have noticed.

23  Perhaps this form of horse-trading (doing favours for people to put them in your power) is what American politicians have in mind when they contrast being powerful with being influential. See, for instance, Manley's discussion in his (1970: pp. 121–35).

24  This way of drawing the contrast is Ted Benton's: see Benton (1981: p. 174).
    Stanley Benn has found an equivocation of this sort in Hobbes, who 'seems to oscillate between two conceptions of confrontations of powers. In the first place, there is the simple competition for a common objective, the success of one contender implying simply failure for the rest. . . . By contrast, there is a contention that arises from the effort of one man to control another, to win power over *his* power. . . . In the first case, the powers that are matched are the powers to gain primary objectives, like desired objects, jobs, or sweethearts, [and thereby the

powerful indirectly affect those who fail to gain such objectives]; in the second, they are powers *against* each other, the power to inflict harm or confer benefits, used to induce compliance' (Benn, 1972: pp. 210–11).

25 *Why* this very limited conception of power has proved so congenial I leave to the future sociologist – or psychologist – of social science. Maybe a suggestion is that seeing power as harming others is characteristic of men at the third stage of the Freudians' four-stage personality typology (the phallic stage), whilst women, and men at other stages, conceptualize power very differently (see McClelland, 1975). It may be that when people rely on their intuitions about power they tell us less about power than they realise; but more about themselves.

26 See Carmichael and Hamilton (1968), and cf. Aberback and Walker (1970). Of course, achieving black power would have involved *affecting* people in ways they might not have liked, since it would have meant reducing the power of many whites. But the goal desired was that of giving black people more power over their own lives, *not* more power over other (white) people.

27 Connolly is someone who takes this last tack (Connolly, 1974/1983: pp. 86–8), overlooking that it is unclear why what he *is* interested in should be labelled 'power'.

28 Richard Peters has claimed that Hobbes's theory of power rests on a similar suppressed empirical claim that is hidden because he uses two definitions of power (a narrow one and a wide one) and fails to distinguish between them. The wide sense is an ability to obtain something; the narrow sense assumes the inevitability of conflict (Peters, 1956: p. 139).

29 I agree with Fowler that 'the compound preposition "with respect to" . . . should be used not as often, but as seldom, as possible' (Fowler, 1968: p. 521). It needs treating with great care and suspicion if muddled thinking is to be avoided. See also Fowler's strictures on those who misuse the word 'relationship' (pp. 514–15).

# References

Aberback, J.D. and Walker, J.L. (1970): 'The meanings of black power: a comparison of white and black interpretations of a political slogan', *American Political Science Review* 64: pp. 367–88.

Ayers, M.R. (1968): *The Refutation of Determinism* (London: Methuen).

Bagehot, W. (1867): *The English Constitution* (Glasgow: Collins, 1963).

Bell, R., Edwards, D.V. and Wagner, R.H., eds (1969): *Political Power: A Reader in Theory and Research* (New York: Free Press).

Benn, S. (1967): 'Power', in *The Encyclopaedia of Philosophy*, ed. P. Edwards (New York: Macmillan) vol. 6, pp. 424–7.

Benn, S. (1972): 'Hobbes on power', in M. Cranston and R.S. Peters, eds, *Hobbes and Rousseau* (New York: Anchor Books) pp. 184–212.

Benton, T. (1981): 'Objective interests and the sociology of power', *Sociology* 15: pp. 161–84.

Carmichael, S. and Hamilton, C.V. (1968): *Black Power: The Politics of Liberation in America* (Harmondsworth: Penguin).

Connolly, W.E. (1974/1983): *The Terms of Political Discourse* (first edition: Lexington, Mass.: D.C. Heath; second edition: Oxford: Martin Robertson).

Dahl, R.A. (1957a): 'The concept of power', *Behavioral Science* 2: pp. 201–15. Reprinted in Bell (1969).

Dahl, R.A. (1957b): 'A rejoinder', *American Political Science Review* 51: pp. 1053–61.

Dahl, R.A. (1961): *Who Governs? Democracy and Power in an American City* (New Haven: Yale University Press).

Dahl, R.A. (1963): *Modern Political Analysis* (first edition; Englewood Cliffs, New Jersey: Prentice Hall).

Dahl, R.A. (1965): 'Cause and effect in the study of politics', in D. Lerner, ed., *Cause and Effect: The Hayden Colloquium on Scientific Method and Concept* (New York: Free Press) pp. 75–98.

Dahl, R.A. (1968): 'Power', in *International Encyclopaedia of the Social Sciences*, ed. D.L. Sills (New York: Free Press) vol. 12, pp. 405–15.

Dahl, R.A. (1984): *Modem Political Analysis* (fourth edition; Englewood Cliffs, New Jersey: Prentice Hall).

Danto, A.C. (1973): *Analytical Philosophy of Action* (Cambridge: Cambridge University Press).

Fowler, H.W. (1968): *A Dictionary of Modern English Usage* (second edition, revised by Sir E. Gowers; Oxford: Oxford University Press).

Georgiou, P. (1977): 'The concept of power: a critique and an alternative', *Australian Journal of Politics and History* 23: pp. 252–67.

Gibson, Q. (1971): 'Power', *Philosophy of the Social Sciences* 1: pp. 101–12.

Goldman, A.I. (1972): 'Toward a theory of social power'. *Philosophical Studies* 23: pp. 221–68.

Goldman, A.I. (1974): 'On the measurement of power', *Journal of Philosophy* 71: pp. 231–52.

Hobbes, T. (1651): *Leviathan*, ed. J. Plamenatz (London: Fontana, 1962).

Hobbes, T. (1655): *De Corpore*, in *English Works* vol. 1 (London: John Bohn, 1839).

Hume, D. (1739): *A Treatise of Human Nature*, ed. L.A. Selby-Bigge (Oxford: Oxford University Press, 1888).

Kenny, A. (1975): *Will, Freedom and Power* (Oxford: Blackwell).

Lukes, S. (1974): *Power: A Radical View* (London: Macmillan).

Lukes, S. (1979): 'Power and authority', in T. Bottomore and R. Nisbet, eds, *A History of Sociological Analysis* (London: Heinemann) pp. 633–76.

McClelland, D.C. (1975): *Power: The Inner Experience* (New York: Irvington).

Manley, J.F. (1970): *The Politics of Finance: The House Committee on Ways and Means* (Boston: Little Brown).

Oppenheim, F. (1981): *Political Concepts: A Reconstruction* (Oxford: Blackwell).

Partridge, P.H. (1963): 'Some notes on the concept of power', *Political Studies* 11: pp. 107–25.

Peters, R.S. (1956): *Hobbes* (Harmondsworth: Penguin, 1967).

Pitkin, H.F. (1972): *Wittgenstein and Justice* (Berkeley: University of California Press).

Polsby, N.W. (1963/1980): *Community Power and Political Theory* (New Haven: Yale University Press).

Quine, W.V.O. (1960): *Word and Object* (New York: Wiley).

Reeve, A. (1982): 'Power without responsibility', *Political Studies* 30: pp. 379–92.

Ryle, G. (1949): *The Concept of Mind* (London: Hutchinson).

Simon, H.A. (1953): 'Notes on the observation and measurement of political power', *Journal of Politics* 15: pp. 500–16. Reprinted in Bell (1969).

Simon, H.A. (1957): *Models of Man* (New York: Wiley).

White, A.R. (1975): 'Power and intention', *American Political Science Review* 65: pp. 749–59.

Wormuth, F.D. (1967): 'Matched-dependent behavioralism: the cargo cult in political science', *Western Political Quarterly* 20: pp. 809–40.

Wrong, D.H. (1979): *Power: Its Forms, Bases and Uses* (Oxford: Blackwell).

Young, R.A. (1978): 'Steven Lukes's radical view of power', *Canadian Journal of Political Science* 11: pp. 639–49.

# 15  Haugaard

## Introduction

*The Constitution of Power* is divided into two parts. The first is devoted to a fairly extensive analysis of Dahl, Lukes, Barnes, Giddens and Foucault. These perspectives are used as an agenda-setting device to frame the analysis of power which follows in Part Two. It is a theory of power which is presented as part of a general theory of social order.

Consistent with Dahl's agency-based concept of power, it is held that, at its most fundamental, power entails the capacity of one actor to make another actor do something which they would not otherwise do – in the form A has power over B to the extent that he can get B to do something that B would not otherwise have done (see chapter 1). However, in contrast to Dahl, account is also taken of the structural conditions and the systems of knowledge which make such an exercise of power possible.

Social structure is the basic unit of social order. If we say that an aspect of social life is structured, this assertion means that it is ordered. This is what Giddens meant by arguing that, at its most fundamental, social structure consists of an ordering or binding of time-space (see chapter 8). Structure is an ordering of social life by social actors which has the aggregate consequence of contributing to the creation of social order as a whole.

As was argued by Barry Barnes (chapter 6), social order is inherently beneficial to social actors. If the actions of other actors were chaotic or random, this would render all collaborative endeavours impossible. If natural power is a capacity of action which actors gain from the predictability of nature, then social power can be conceptualized as a capacity for action which actors gain by virtue of their membership of society. Social power is derivable from predictability in the behaviour of others. The success of A's ability to make B do things that they would not otherwise do is premised upon the predictability of B's behaviour. In a random social world, A would not be able to exercise power over B. Social power presupposes social structure by making the actions of others predictable. As a consequence of this distinction between goals and structures, social action should be deemed to consist of two parts: goals pursued and structures reproduced. The structural element of action entails order and order presupposes sameness of meaning. To take a simple instance, if I put a tick in a box next to a person's name in an election the structuredness of this act is the meaning reproduced, not the goal pursued. I may vote entirely differently from everyone else but this does not alter the fact that I am exercising my vote and, as an unintended consequence, thus contributing to the reproduction of a democratic system.

While voting is a structured act which we are fairly conscious of on a discursive level, the majority of structural reproduction is routine – in Giddens' terminology, it is practical consciousness knowledge. Since practical consciousness knowledge is tacit, actors frequently fail critically to evaluate much of the implied content of their acts of structural reproduction. In Haugaard (1997) it is argued that this contributes to the observed phenomenon which underpins the idea of three-dimensional power – that the dominated have internalized ideas which contribute to their own domination. However, in contrast to the Marxist position, this is not regarded as 'false consciousness' but, rather, theorized in terms of practical consciousness knowledge. Social critique, as the undermining of three-dimensional power, takes place through the conversion of practical consciousness knowledge into discursive consciousness knowledge. For instance, when the reader encounters Foucault's description of the Panopticon contained in this volume, they do not learn about their 'real interests' but, rather, may recognize structural practices with which they are familiar in the workplace or, as a child, in school. In this moment of recognition, practical consciousness knowledge becomes discursive; consequently compliance in the reproduction of relations of domination become subject to scrutiny.

In the selection from *The Constitution of Power* which follows below, the distinction between structures and goals is used to argue that there are two types of conflict in social life. The first are conflicts over specific goals which reproduce existing structures, hence meanings. In a later part of the book it is argued that these conflicts correspond to Foucault's idea of shallow conflict. The second type of conflict is over structure and represents a deeper conflict because the existing social order itself is up for negotiation. Because structure entails meaning, structural conflict concerns conflict over meaning.

In the chapters which follow the extract reproduced below, the role which truth plays in the stabilization of relations of domination is analysed. Foucault's observations are theorized within the language of goals and structures, and it is argued that truth is used to reify social structures by placing them beyond convention – I made partial use of this analysis in the introductions to Foucault and Bourdieu (also briefly in Davis). Even if actors are discursively aware that specific structures entail relations of domination which disadvantage them, they may well reproduce those structures if they perceive of them as representing a view from 'nowhere' – truth, nature or (more usually in the past) tradition and the word of God are perceived of as solid rock beyond the vicissitudes of the merely conventional, hence arbitrary, world of cultural constructs. Actors will not be complicit in the reproduction of structures of domination of which they are discursively conscious if they believe those structures to be mere 'local custom'. In that case they will have to be physically coerced. In contrast, if those same structures can be reified this is not the case. After all, in certain contexts, denying the truth, nature, tradition or the word of God are manifestations of pure 'irrationality', and for most people relative powerlessness is preferable to being classified of as 'the conceptual equivalent of "mad"'. One of the contributions of modernity is the attempt to move beyond the mere coercion of the 'delinquent' by placing them in institutional contexts where they learn to structure their behaviour predictably through discipline. In this theorization, Foucault's Panopticon is a resocialization machine where actors learn how to structure with predictability – as observed by Giddens, at their most fundamental, structures are a recursive binding of time-space.

Most actors structure predictably because their interpretative horizon has been constituted in a way which is similar to those of others. This horizon is the way in which they make sense of the world and, simultaneously, constitutes their very being-in-the-world. By teaching them to structure 'appropriately', the Panopticon creates a new ontology – a new being – and, thus, a new and predictable subject who 'fits' within existing structural relations.

While this analysis contains many references to postmodern authors, it does not represent a postmodern position, in the sense that there is still a centred-self and the observation that truth is used to reify relations of domination is not taken to imply that there is no such thing as truth. The self is not centred upon a single essentialist human nature but, rather, a self who has the capacity to be a self by distancing themselves from 'local' systems of meaning through a process of moving between interpretative horizons. This self is central to the ability of agents to practise social critique by transcending local realities. With regard to truth, the sociological observation that actors make use of truth in certain ways does not actually tell us anything concerning the epistemological status of truth – if there are philosophical or scientific truths or not. Furthermore, the use of reification to ensure predictable structuration is not entirely negative either – as observed by Barry Barnes, chaos does not benefit anyone. Without the routine reproduction of structure we would descend into pure meaninglessness, become ontologically insecure and unable to make use of any of the collaborative, consensual, social power which gives us the capacity to do things which we could not otherwise accomplish.

These observations are also used to re-analyse Bourdieu's concept of capital and, in so doing, provide a synthesis between some of his and Foucault's observations – albeit, within a theoretical framework which differs from those used by both theorists.

## Further reading

*The Constitution of Power* is an accessible work and covers and develops further many of the themes which have been touched upon in this Reader. Clegg analyses this work in Clegg (2000b). The issue of the relationship between conflict, consensus and democracy – which is analysed in the extract below – has been the subject of debate between Haugaard and Jane Mansbridge in *Constellations* (Haugaard 1997b and Mansbridge 1997). An overview of some of some of the main theories of power are given in Haugaard (1999).

# From *THE CONSTITUTION OF POWER*
## Mark Haugaard

### 6 Conflict and consensus

In the previous chapter we distinguished between goals and structures. We will now deepen this analysis by looking at the differences in conflict which arise from this division. We shall argue that there is conflict in terms of actors prevailing over one another with regard to specific goals and, alternatively, that there is conflict with regard to the structural and institutional machinery of power which confers differentials of power upon actors. In terms of emphasis, the analysis which follows balances conflict and consensus equally against each other with regard to goals and structures.

On the level of thematic development, this chapter is divided into nine sections: the first is introductory, concerning social conflict and consensus as scalar phenomena; this is followed by an analysis of structural conflict in the second section; the third consists of a list of combinations and permutations of conflict and consensus; each of sections four to ten, respectively, constitutes an individual analysis of the various combinations of consensus and conflict delineated in section three.

### Conflict and consensus as scalar phenomena

As we have seen in the first four chapters, the relationship between conflict and consensus has been a major source of debate in literature on power over the years. It has taken the form of an insistence by some that power is primarily conflictual and others that it is mostly consensual. The prime representatives of the conflict side of the debate include Max Weber (for example, 1978, p. 53),[1] Robert Dahl, Peter Bachrach and Morton Baratz, and Steven

Lukes. The most important consensual theorists are Talcott Parsons, Barry Barnes and Hannah Arendt (1970, p. 52). Generally those of the consensual school tend to provide more conceptual space for conflict than those of the conflictual perspective do for consensus. Aside from these opposing positions, there is also a middle ground which provides relatively more balance between conflict and consensus, the primary representatives of which are Foucault, Stewart Clegg (1989) and Giddens.

In this chapter we shall hold a middle position: sometimes there is consensus, sometimes conflict and, most frequently, there is both. This is not some form of theoretical compromise but, rather, the argument that conflict and consensus exist as scalar phenomena. At one end of the scale there is pure conflict as an ideal type. At the other, there exists an equally idealized consensus. Whilst there is always some social interaction which falls at one end of the spectrum or the other, most social relations take place in the space between these extremes.

There are two primary reasons why most interaction is neither purely consensual nor conflictual. The first and most obvious reason is the complexity of people's motives. Most frequently people are neither completely in favour of something nor completely opposed to it. Furthermore, in the course of carrying out an action they often change their perception of what it is that they are doing. In the case of conflict, when they are made to do something which they do not really wish to do, they frequently convince themselves that it is indeed what they really wanted. This conviction can be either a form of stoic compliance: I want whatever fate decrees for me' attitude; or 'sour grapes' – 'I don't really want what I can't get.' In short, the reason for an absence of either pure consensus or conflict has to do with an ambiguous attitude towards specific goals.

The second reason for the frequent blend of conflict and consensus in interaction is because of the dual nature of all social action whereby it has both a goal-oriented and a structural aspect. Frequently, there is a mismatch between goals and structures where one is consensual and the other conflictual. This opposition of goals and structures is frequently stable and/or mutually compatible. Compatibility on different levels is not necessarily mutually negating – it actually makes sense, for example, to combine conflict with regard to goals with consensus on structures. Even when such a combination is in some sense contradictory, stability may derive from a disjuncture between practical and discursive consciousness. In order to explain these assertions we will, in the next section, look at the concept of structural conflict and its relationship to social consciousness.

## Structural conflict

In the previous chapter, structure was described as an integral element in the production of power to realize specific goals. What is left unsaid was the fact that structures do not confer power equally across the system. Structures and institutions confer large amounts of power upon some individuals and none upon others and/or some goals are privileged over others.

Social structures/institutions enable actors to realize predictable outcomes through the reproduction of meaning. However, one aspect of structures and institutions is that they are neither generalized in their productive capacity, nor are they available to all. Structures and institutions are always goal-specific and frequently actor-specific.

The goal-specific nature of structures and institutions means large areas of goal powerlessness. Sometimes these areas of powerlessness are of no consequence to anyone. However, frequently they are of consequence when they include goals which are of interest to specific groups. Indeed, this is what lies at the heart of Bachrach and Baratz's second dimension of power. Organization is the mobilization of bias whereby some issues are organized into politics, whereas others are organized out.

One of the primary aims of democracy has to be the construction of a set of institutional procedures which do not arbitrarily privilege some goals over others. However, even if it is accepted that democratic institutions should be neutral between goals, this still leaves the issue of how far democracy should extend. One of the hallmarks of a liberal-democratic position is the perception of a clear division between public and private and the insistence that only the public should be democratic. Traditionally, Marxists and, more recently, communitarians and feminists have questioned this division, arguing that this confining of the democratic process is a method of legitimating capitalist (in the case of the Marxists), liberal (communitarians) or male (feminists) domination. This takes us back to Lukes' contention that power is an essentially contested concept. When, and if, everyone agrees that democracy involves the equal distribution of political power, the definition of power becomes the point of conflict. If a narrow definition is adopted then the institutional scope of democracy becomes limited. On the other hand, if a wide 'radical' definition of power is adopted then democratic institutions have a much wider scope. What is at issue in the definition of power is a conflict over the nature and extent of democratic institutions.

Not only do structures and institutions privilege some goals over others but they also privilege some actors over others. Authoritative power structures give specific powers to some which are denied to others. While many structures and institutions do not specifically privilege certain actors in the explicit way that authoritative structures/institutions do, the consequence of particular structural and institutional configurations frequently results in highly unequal distributions of power resources. Take the structures and institutions which are central to the constitution of private property as a resource. In principle, within modern capitalism everyone is equally entitled to private property. This is in contrast to authoritative power and, also, property rights found in pre-capitalist relations of production. In many forms of feudalism only certain individuals were entitled to own property. The principle that every person has an equal right to the possession of property is part of the arsenal of the legitimacy of capitalism. However, while property is not actor-specific in the way in which authority is, it still has to be accepted that, in practice, the principle of the equal right to property does not translate into the equal ownership of property.

The fact that structures and institutions do not confer power equally means that it makes strategic sense for those who do not hold property to engage in conflict over the structures and institutions which are central to the constitution of private property within the capitalist system.

The conflict over structure can be conceptualized through contrast with chess. In chess there are rules of the game which privilege the goals of each player equally and each player begins the game with the same number of pieces. In social life there are rules of the game – structural constraints and frameworks of meaning – which, in complete contrast, privilege goals and players unequally. Some goals are privileged over others and the players start with an unequal number of pieces – unequal resources.

The challenge to the existing social order is what we mean by structural and institutional conflict. Those who are disadvantaged with regard to the achievement of their aspirations have good reason to challenge the existing social order and those who benefit from the existing order have good reason to defend it and/or, if they are sufficiently pragmatic, to change the institutional procedures so that they are in an even more privileged position.

This perception that structure defines relations of relative empowerment and disempowerment is consistent with many of the points made by Stewart Clegg (1989) in his argument for a second circuit of power. In Clegg the first circuit of power is the equivalent of actors pursuing goals and the second circuit of power is the rules of the game which define meaning, membership and generally provide the structural context within which actors pursue their purposive behaviour (Clegg 1989, pp. 186–240). Where I would disagree with Clegg is in his perception that structural inequality is beyond agency. This is not only a postmodernist abandonment of the importance of agency but it is an acceptance of a view which we find in Lukes (1977) that structure belongs to some realm over and beyond individuals in conflict. While Foucault did not perceive it because of his death of the subject hypothesis, one of the lessons of his work is precisely that structures and meaning are continually contested terrain for individuals in interaction.

Structural and institutional conflict do not necessarily presuppose conflict with regard to goals and vice versa. In politics actors frequently agree with regard to structures and are in conflict over goals. It is not, as might intuitively be expected that conflict at one level automatically translates into conflict at the other level. Actors are frequently able to let conflict at one level be overridden by a consensus at another level.

The existence of a mismatch between goals and structures is frequently made easier by the discursive practical consciousness split of social knowledge. If the consensus which we are talking of is at a practical consciousness level, it is only tacit consent. As long as something is practical consciousness an actor does not critically reflect upon it and it is critical reflection which makes conflict manifest to the actor. If structures are kept at the level of practical consciousness there will not be conflict over them. Hence, an actor who reproduces social order primarily from practical consciousness knowledge is an actor who only tacitly consents to structural reproduction and it may well be the case that if this very same actor were called upon to give discursive consciousness consent to particular forms of structural reproduction that the consent would not be forthcoming.

The idea of tacit consent is problematic because consent is frequently thought of as the base line for legitimacy. Structures or institutions are considered legitimate if they receive discursive consent, but it is matter of debate whether tacit consent is sufficient to confer legitimacy (see Beetham 1991, p. 12).

With regard to this question, we must distinguish between political philosophy and social theory. For the social theorist, the concept of tacit consent is a description of part of social reality. For the political philosopher the issue of consent has to do with the link between consent and normative legitimacy. In the work of many political philosophers, such as that of Locke (Locke 1924), the idea of tacit consent is used to legitimate highly unequal social relations. This is not the conceptual move which is being made here. The arguments contained in this chapter are social theory. When we speak of actors giving practical consciousness consent to various form of structural reproduction we are simply making an empirical claim about consent rather than a normative one concerning legitimacy.

If we return to Lukes' three-dimensional power argument, I would argue that part of the whole process of 'radical' politics is not necessarily to tell actors what their real interests are but to explain to actors the way in which their structured practices feed into the reinforcement of a regime of domination which is contrary to their interests – interests which are already known them. What is at issue is not true and false interests but an understanding of structural and institutional relations of domination.[2] If we understand autonomy as a capacity for self-reflection, the maintenance of large bodies of knowledge as practical consciousness is inextricably bound up with the reproduction of certain relations of domination. Once an actor reflects upon his or her practical consciousness knowledge then he or she is realizing relative autonomy. I say relative autonomy because there is no such thing as autonomy which is entirely independent of social context. When an actor transfers practical consciousness knowledge into discursive consciousness, they have not moved outside society into nowhere but they have evaluated the full implications of structural practice. To refer back to the issue of normative legitimacy, it seems to me that consent can confer moral legitimacy only when it comes from a relatively autonomous individual. In other words, from an individual who is discursively, rather than tacitly, consenting to reproduce structures and institutions. This is consistent with Hyland's argument that the issue concerning three-dimensional power is not true or false interests but one of autonomy (Hyland 1995, pp. 193–221).

It is the capacity for self-reflection as linked to autonomy – the care of the self – which Foucault attempts to develop in his Histories. He exposes our tacit knowledge to a history of social relations which demonstrates that exist-ing structural relations need not be as they are. In so doing, Foucault stimu-lates a process whereby we translate much of our practical consciousness knowledge into discursive consciousness and, thus, we realize that our past social actions involved tacit knowledge consent to structural practices of which we were previously unaware. When, for instance, Foucault presents us with the image of the Panopticon he stimulates a process whereby his readers are called upon to translate their practical consciousness knowledge of the office, the classroom and many other power containers into discursive con-sciousness knowledge. What they come to see is not their true interests but the actual content of their practical consciousness knowledge, i.e. what they consent to in everyday structural practice.

## Combinations and permutations of conflict and consensus

In an interactive context the dual aspect of social action gives two possible potential sources of conflict and consent. On one level actors may agree or disagree on goals or, alternatively, they may agree or disagree on the struc-tured practices necessary for the realization of those goals.

When we analyse conflict and consensus at the level of structure and goals, the focus of attention is upon the person who responds in the particular inter-action because success or failure in an interaction is measured by the reaction of that person. For instance, imagine that an actor A is the holder of author-ity which is traditionally based. Imagine that A tells B to 'X' and, further, that B does not particularly want to do 'X' – 'X' is not one of their goals. If B does indeed do 'X', we can explain this by postulating that B is a traditionally minded person whereby they are willing to let their conflict with regard to goals be overridden by a consensus on traditional structures. Frequently, the consent to tradition will be a tacit practical consciousness consent. Alter-natively, B may be compliant because they perceive of the coercive resources of A as sufficient to make compliance with A's wishes the best option. The success or otherwise of this interaction has nothing to do with A's percep-tions. For all we know, A may simply be *aware* of tradition as a power resource but this does not mean that A is a supporter of tradition. It may well be the case A is an instrumentally rational actor who thinks post-traditionally but is exploiting the traditional beliefs of B in order to realize certain goals. The

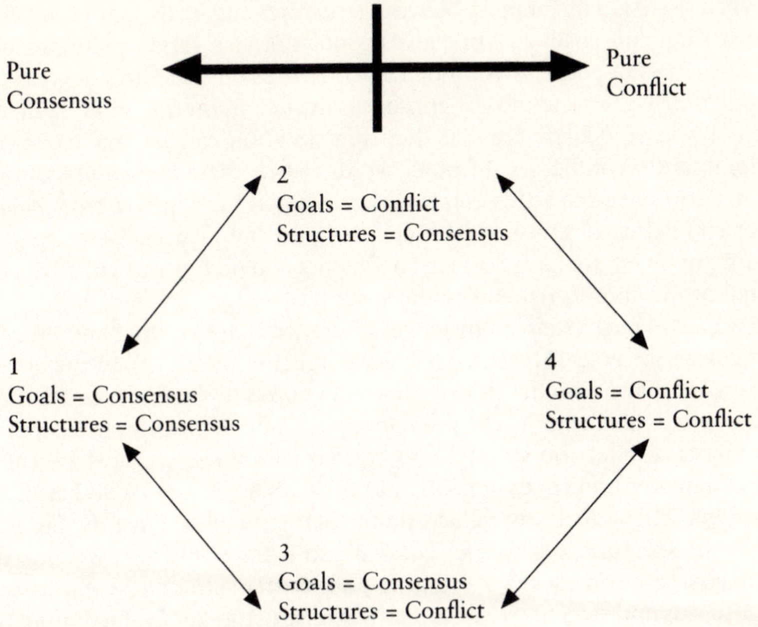

Pure
Consensus

Pure
Conflict

2
Goals = Conflict
Structures = Consensus

1
Goals = Consensus
Structures = Consensus

4
Goals = Conflict
Structures = Conflict

3
Goals = Consensus
Structures = Conflict

Figure 1 Scalar opposition of conflict and consensus

same point can be brought out by reversing the example: let us imagine that A is a believer in the sacred authority of tradition and that this tradition confers upon them the authority to command B to do 'X'. Assuming that B does not desire 'X' and that A does not have some other resources at their disposal, what is crucial to the ability of A to command B is belief in the importance of traditional structures. If B is a post-traditional rational actor who does not consent to traditional authority A will have lost their power to realize goal 'X' irrespective of A's own belief in the sacredness of tradition.

So, if we are interested in the success or otherwise of an exercise of power what is of interest is the position of this second actor vis a vis the goals and structures which the exercise of power involves. If A wishes to exercise power over B with regard to issue 'X', what is important to the success of the inter-action is the reaction of actor B. B will either find the goals and/or structures to their liking or dislike. From the perspective of B this gives four possible combinations of agreement and disagreement with A. These are as follows: (1) goals as consensus and structures as consensus; (2) goals as conflict and structures as consensus; (3) goals as consensus and structures as conflict; or (4) goals as conflict and structures as conflict (see Figure 1). Numbers 1 and 4 represent opposite ends of the spectrum – consensual power and conflict-ual power in their pure form. Numbers 2 and 3 fall between these extremes.

When there is a disjuncture between structures and goals, actors will either let structural consensus override goals conflict or vice versa. If either conflict over structures or goals is overridden by consensus on structures or goals then the outcome is characterized by consensus overall. If, on the other hand, consensus is overridden by conflict then the situation can be characterized as predominantly conflictual. In other words, when there is a combination of conflict and consensus this can result in a reaction which is *predominantly* either conflictual or consensual. Depending on the relative intensity of the feelings involved, we have a situation which will tend towards either the conflictual or the consensual end of the spectrum.

If we distinguish between instances of predominant conflict and predominant consensus where the structures have a higher priority than the goals or where goals have a higher priority than structures, divisions 2 and 3 can be further subdivided into 4. On the consensual side of the spectrum there is: (a) goals as conflict and structures as consensus where structures are considered of a higher priority than goals; and (b) goals as consensus and structures as conflict where goals are valued more than structures. On the conflictual side of the spectrum there is: (c) goals as conflict and structure as consensus where goals are considered of a higher priority than structures; and (d) goals as consensus and structures as conflict where structures are valued more than goals.

When the fourfold subdivision is combined with the two pure forms of conflict and consensus this gives a sixfold typology of levels of conflict and consensus: On the consensual side of the spectrum: (1) double consensus; (2) consensus on structure and conflict with regard to goals, where structures override goals; and (3) conflict over structure and consensus with regard to goals, where goals override structures. One the conflictual side of the spectrum: (4) consensus on structure and conflict with regard to goals, where goals override structure; (5) consensus over goals and conflict with respect to structures, where structures override goals; and (6) double conflict (see Figure 2). Beginning at the consensual end of the spectrum, in what follows we shall analyse the implications of these six typologies.

*1 Pure consensus* In this combination there is overall consensus on both goals and structured practices. All conflict is absent. This is consensus, as an ideal type, as it exists at the opposite end of the spectrum from pure conflict.

With regard to power this is pure consensual power. If an actor A is engaged in social interaction with B for the purpose of pursuing goal X, A and B will evaluate their interaction relative to the pursuit of this goal. At another level, they may also realize that the actualization of this goal necessitates the reproduction of certain shared social structures a, b, and c. If there is consensus both with respect to X and a, b, and c, this is the situation of pure consensus which we are describing.

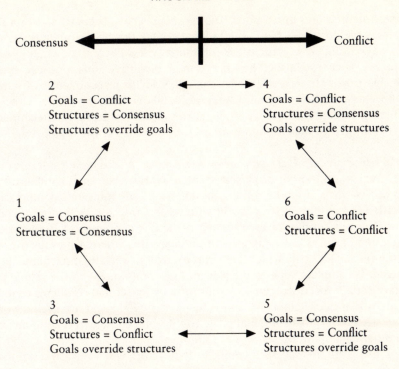

Figure 2 Combinations of goals and structure

If Arendt's definition of power were rephrased, the concept of idealized consensual power would read as follows: consensual power is an ability to act in concert in the pursuit of common goals through the mobilization of practices which meet the approval of all (see Arendt 1970, p. 44). Reformulating Dahl's conflictual definition of power to take account of consensus: A and B have consensual power to the extent that they can realize common goals, which they could not otherwise do, through shared consensually constituted structured practices (see Dahl 1957, pp. 202–3).

While consensus on goals and structures may be a double discursive consciousness phenomenon, in many cases of social interaction the structures reproduced are so taken for granted that actors do not evaluate them. In other words, they exist as practical consciousness knowledge. If this is the situation, once actors perceive a shared goal, consensual power will automatically follow. In this instance, consensual power does not necessitate any discursively conscious agreement on institutions. Consensus on structural reproduction is a purely tacit reflection of practical consciousness knowledge.

In a long established political system procedures become so taken for granted that political actors, by and large, would not consider questioning these structures and institutions. The procedures have become, so to speak, 'the way we do things here'. When practices are practical consciousness in this way, conflict over structure is substantially less likely than when procedures are newly established and hence more discursive consciousness – presumably this is the reason that Machiavelli's advice to conquerors of states with well-established political custom was to take control, if possible, without initiating institutional change while, at the same time, using the machinery of government to maximum advantage (Machiavelli 1974, p. 176).

*2 Consensus overall, where structure overrides goals*   At the broadest level conflict involves opposition of perceived interests. However, such conflict need not necessarily presuppose conflict overall. As already indicated, conflict can be either at the level of structure or with respect to goals. One form of consensual power conflict takes place when there is consensus at the level of structured practices but disagreement on goals. It is where A prevails over B in the pursuit of goals which are contrary to B's expressed preferences but where B is compliant due to their overriding commitment to the reproduction of certain social structures. As this form of consensual conflict is central to the workings of democracy and is frequently overlooked, we shall devote more attention to this combination of conflict and consensus than to any of the other combinations.

At first sight it may seem unlikely that actors will value structures so highly that they will consent to reproduce them even if they know that such reproduction contributes to the realization of goals which they do not support.

Contrary to what might appear at first glance, this form of consensual power is immensely common and central to political procedure. As will be explained, it is power which is generated by the 'rules of the game' which enable one actor to prevail over another by virtue of the second actor's commitment to those rules. It represents a form of structured conflict which prevents conflict from escaping certain well-defined parameters. As institutionalized political procedure, it is a way of preventing conflict from turning into coercion or violence.

As the phrase 'rules of the game' suggests, the workings of conflictual power operate in its *idealized* form in games. In a game of chess there is a conflict of interest: both actors desire different outcomes. Yet, actors prevail over each other without threats of coercion. What enables them to do this is a shared commitment to the rules of the game. When actor A reaches a position of checkmate, it is assumed that A will accept defeat. At the moment of checkmate, when the loser concedes defeat they are, in effect, allowing themselves to be prevailed upon on the basis of an overriding commitment to the rules of the game. In this sense, a commitment to the rules of the game entails a tacit acceptance of the possibility of defeat. Chess players are not forced into defeat, they consent to it.

It is the overriding commitment to the rules of the game which makes the continued existence of chess, over time, possible. While it is true that, at times, players do attempt to cheat, the general point still remains that the existence of chess is dependent upon a player being committed to certain practices by and large. The cheat, who does not allow the rules of the game to override their desire to win, is the exception. Such a person is a free-rider who is parasitic upon others.

The *raison d'etre* for playing according to the rules, even when the application of those rules entails defeat, is a long-term one. As an assembled set of rules the game of chess is a miniature system for generation of consensual power in a situation of conflict. It can be conceptualized as a power machine which produces the power necessary for one actor to prevail over the other. The maintenance of the rules of the game, in essence, means the maintenance of a particular power machine. If we assume that everyone enjoys winning, in the long term it makes sense to contribute to the recreation and maintenance of the game as an assembled set of practices. The loser consents to defeat on the understanding that, at some future date, they can win. They consent to defeat in the interest of maintaining a set of assembled structured practices which, potentially at least, can be used to realize an outcome which they desire.

In politics, institutions and the structures in which those institutions float constitute the 'rules of the game'. These political institutions and structures enable actors to prevail over one another without having recourse to threats or coercion. In modern parliamentary democracies political parties are not coerced into defeat, by and large, they consent to being defeated.

The political procedure whereby parties consent to defeat can either be tacitly or explicitly agreed upon in immediate advance of the conflict. In other words, the rules of the game can either be practical or discursive consciousness. As a given procedure becomes more established the more practical consciousness it becomes and, with it, the more stable it is. In other words, even if the rules of the game begin as discursive consciousness – as political institutions – over time they become practical consciousness. In this sense the rules of politics are no different from the example of rules of language given in the second example of language acquisition. Within a well-established democracy, the democratic game is taken for granted and, with the growth of levels of tacit knowledge, it becomes less and less likely for losers to refuse defeat or question the rules of the game. This is possibly the reason why modern democracies show remarkable stability once established over time. In countries where democratic institutions have existed for as long as twenty years the breakdown of democracy to non-democratic forms of decision-making is extremely rare (Dahl 1989, p. 315).

In politics, and in a democracy in particular, there are at least four discursive consciousness *raisons d'etre* for accepting defeat – four reasons why actors might value practice over goal attainment. The first is exactly the same as that found in chess, the other three are not. As in chess, actors have a long-term interest in maintaining the rules of the game: I consent to my present defeat on the understanding that, at some time in the future, you will similarly accept your defeat. Hence, if I wish to win at some time in the future, I will reproduce the rules of the game now, even if this contributes to the realization of outcomes which I consider undesirable in the short term.

It is precisely the absence of the possibility of ever winning which makes minorities in divided societies withdraw their consent to majority rule democracy. In pluralist societies the presence of a multiplicity of competing parties gives even the smallest parties the possibility of winning at some time or other. Even with majority rule, minorities are in a position to influence outcomes – realize their particular goals. A small political party always has the hope of 'winning' – implementing aspects of its agenda – by increasing its electoral support, by holding the balance of power, or by forming part of a coalition government. In a divided society these options will be closed to the permanent minority. When a society is divided into two stable monolithic groups, the minority group will always be the loser according to the institutional practices of majority rule. The consequence of never having the possibility of winning through institutional practice will, over time, lead to an inevitable withdrawal of consent from the democratic process. Northern Ireland is a classic example of a society where there is permanent division between traditions over a single issue. The consequence of this division of society into two permanent blocks means that democracy, as majority rule, in essence means inevitable and continual defeat for about a third of the population. The consequence of this has been been an erosion of the willingness to consent to defeat by the Nationalist minority.

Following from the long-term *raison d'etre*, there is a second reason for playing according to the rules. Politics is unlike chess in that consensual conflict is not the only form of conflict. If conflict over goals results in the withdrawal of consent with regard to structures the level of conflict deepens – social interaction has moved from the consensual to the conflictual end of the spectrum. As will be discussed later in this chapter, one of the costs of moving from the consensual to the conflictual end of the spectrum is that the realization of outcomes necessitates coercion. If we take it as given that coercion is frequently considered intrinsically undesirable, the mutual fear of escalation of conflict gives actors a shared interest in the acceptance of the rules of the game.

In politics there is a third normative *raison d'etre* for accepting structured practice (also one which is not found in games of chess). Political parties that have been in opposition for years may continue to reproduce the practices whereby they are defeated out of a normative commitment to the process. Obviously, in such a situation, the longer the experience of defeat, the more altruistic a party would have to be in order to continue valuing structures over goals.

This normative commitment is, in essence, linked to the issue of institutional legitimacy. There is nothing intrinsically legitimate about the rules of chess. However, the rules of a political system are often considered intrinsically worthy of normative support because they are either considered fair or just in themselves. In a system where democracy is well established the normative commitment which actors have to the principles of democracy often makes it morally unthinkable for them not to accept defeat.

A fourth *raison d'etre* is the idea that structures have acquired qualities which makes them more than simple convention. Once social structures are not seen as conventional but as having some form of intrinsic value or validity which transcends local cultural practices, structures gain a binding force which makes consent virtually inevitable. The most obvious example of this is tradition. If a certain structural practice acquires the force of tradition, it gains solidity which, to the actors involved, makes the structural practice more than a contingent local way of life.

While we shall not detail the exact workings of this fourth *raison d'etre* at this moment, the reader should note that this is an important theme to which we shall later return.[3]

As a qualification upon these four *raisons d'etre* it has to be observed that, like most of the concepts dealt with so far, they are ideal types. In real life these *raisons d'etre* do not usually occur singly or in their pure form. For instance, in most democracies political parties consent to defeat from a combination of the four *raisons d'etre*. Also, as we shall see, at the conflictual end of the spectrum these *raisons d'etre* may still be operative but they may be augmented by coercion.

A commitment to structure allows a modern political system to manage conflict without *continual* recourse to the threat of violence. This applies not only to conflicts within the political system, such as conflicts between parties, but is also true for conflict between citizens and the state. While Weber's definition of the state as having the monopoly of violence would still hold empirically, recourse to this monopoly of violence is not sufficient to explain the total quantities of power within a political system. As was observed by Arendt (1970, p. 50) Parsons (1963) and Barnes, the total quantity of power in a political system vastly outstrips the quantity of coercive resources available to the state. In a political system neither the ability of the state to prevail over others nor the relative containment of the cut and thrust of politics can be reduced to threats and coercion.

The idea that power conflict can be consensual and, hence, not necessitate coercion is one that is frequently missed. Only recently an article by Jane Mansbridge began 'In democracies we must use power to get things done. By power I mean coercion – getting people to do what they would not otherwise do by the threat of sanction or the use of force' (Mansbridge 1994, p. 53). The article then goes on to criticize, among others, Hannah Arendt, Sheldon

Wolin, Michael Walzer and Jürgen Habermas for failing to take account of the necessity for coercion, within democracies, once there is a conflict of interests (Mansbridge 1994, p. 57). According to Mansbridge, when deliberation does not yield consensus a democracy has only two choices: either to maintain the status quo or to coerce the minority (Mansbridge 1994, p. 56). This misses the important third alternative: consensual conflict where consent with regard to structures overrides conflict with regard to goals. As has already been asserted, in most democracies minorities are not coerced into defeat, frequently they consent to it.

It could be argued that Habermas fails to take account of the consensual basis of conflict in democracy when he argues that the consensual basis of communicative interaction presupposes convergence. Part of that argument is linked to a move from Mead's analysis of the consensual basis of symbolic interaction to the presupposition that this base consensus implies a long-term commitment to consensual outcomes. As we have seen here, structural consensus does not necessarily have anything to do with consensus on outcomes or goals.[4]

The idea of consenting to defeat throws light upon a plausible sympathetic interpretation of Rousseau's idea of being forced to be free. According to Rousseau, the social contract should be decided on the basis of unanimity. However, once the contract is in place then a simple majority is sufficient for decision-making. Despite the absence of unanimity, while conforming to the wills of others, the minority would be free – they would be forced to be free (Rousseau 1973, p. 250).

If the social contract is interpreted as the rules of the game, agreed in advance of specific outcomes, and conflict is taken to be conflict over goals, then, in agreeing to the social contract, all parties have, in principle, implicitly given consent to the possibility of their own future defeat. When they find themselves defeated according to the rules of the game that defeat is an actualization of their own commitment to certain structured practices. Consequently, when an actor is prevailed upon according to the principles of the initial contract (is prevailed upon by the majority) that actor is free. If they were to win in spite of the will of the majority (contrary to the rules of the game), the outcome would be one which was contrary to their own structural commitments. In this sense, it is not entirely contradictory to say that 'If my particular opinion had carried the day I should have achieved the opposite of what was my will; and it is in that case that I should not have been free' (Rousseau 1973, p. 250).

Whether this is Rousseau's intended meaning is a moot point. However, it is still true to say that the concept of being forced to be free, if interpreted in this sense, is central to the idea of political procedure both in theory and in practice. To the extent to which democratic politics is aimed at the management of conflict without coercion, democratic political procedure is premised upon the idea of consenting (to being free) to one's own defeat.

As has been argued convincingly by Dahl in his more recent work, given the scale and plurality of most modern states, overall agreement on common goals is unlikely, hence, conflict is inherent to modern society. However, this should not cause us to abandon the idea of a common good. Rather, in a contemporary context, the appropriate conceptualization for the idea of the common good is in terms of process and institutions: 'Our common good, then – the good and interests we share with others – rarely consists of specific objects, activities and relations: ordinarily it consists of the practices, arrangements, institutions and processes' (Dahl 1989, p. 307). In this sense the idea of common good as structured political practice is commensurable with conflict.

It could also be argued that it is this form of consensual conflict which Arendt had in mind when she developed her theory of power. In her analysis of the distinction between violence and power, Arendt observes that 'no government exclusively based on the means of violence has ever existed' (Arendt 1970, p. 50). Then she goes on to argue that 'power is indeed the essence of all government, but violence is not' (Arendt 1970, p. 51). By this she means that 'government is essentially institutionalized power' (Arendt 1970, p. 51) which is an end in itself. By this she does not

> deny that governments pursue policies and employ their power to achieve prescribed goals. But the power structure itself precedes and outlasts all aims, so that power, far from being the means to an end, is actually the very condition enabling a group of people to think and act in terms of the means-end category. (Arendt 1970, p. 51)

In other words, she reduces power to consensus on structure which overrides the pursuit of specific goals. To return to the third and fourth *raison d'etre* for affirming practice over goal attainment and also to the idea of the social contract defining the initial rules of the game, Arendt argues that power is inherently linked to legitimacy which is constituted through the initial act of getting together rather than any goals which are realized thereafter (Arendt 1970, p. 52).

Building upon this, I would argue that the commitment to consenting to defeat is crucial to the difference between being a player and not being a player in a particular political game. If the political game is a form of institutionalized democracy, a lack of commitment to accepting defeat places the player outside the democratic game. A non-democratic party is one which is not willing to consent to its own defeat. To borrow the language of Rousseau, a non-democratic party is not willing to let itself be 'forced to be free'. To take an example from Irish politics, before the beginning of the peace process in 1994, one of the factors which distinguished Sinn Fein from other minority parties was that they were unwilling to accept the idea that 10 per cent electoral support in Northern Ireland (Northern Ireland general election 9 April 1992 (Marsh *et al.* 1993, p. 186)) and 1.7 per cent in the Republic of

Ireland (Irish general election 25 November 1992 (Gallagher and Laver 1993, p. 194)) made it impossible to realize their political agenda according to the rules of the game as they were constituted. It is because of this inability to consent to defeat that it can be argued that they were a fundamentally undemocratic political party. The whole of point of the peace process is precisely for Sinn Fein to enter into a negotiating situation where they will let institutional procedure override their interest in a united Ireland, at least in the short term.

*3 Overall consensus, where goals override structures*   The second form of consensual conflict is where there is conflict over structure and consensus on goals, with the latter overriding the former.

In this form of consensual conflict there is a trade-off between goals and structures: an actor so desires a certain goal that they consent to reproducing structures which they find undesirable. In the previous form of consensual conflict there was not this type of direct trade-off.

Because structural conflict presupposes discursive consciousness knowledge, in this type of consensual conflict structures is always a form of discursive consciousness knowledge. This is unlike the previous form of conflict where structures were frequently carried at the level of practical consciousness.

The purely discursive consciousness nature of structural conflict can be illustrated by the example of the twin Marxist concepts of a class-for-itself (a class with class consciousness) and a class-in-itself (economically speaking a class but without class identity). By virtue of class consciousness, the class-for-itself, knows that the structures which it reproduces, through its social practices, are contrary to its interests. In contrast to this, the class-in-itself is not discursively aware of the structures of the system of which it forms a part. In this context, becoming conscious, gaining class-consciousness, implies becoming discursively aware of the insidious nature of the structured practices whereby the capitalist system is reproduced. In other words, when a class-in-itself transforms itself into a class-for-itself, part of that act of transformation includes the translation of practical consciousness knowledge of structures into discursive consciousness. It is this act of translation which is responsible for the development of structural conflict. It is almost a truism to say that a class-in-itself, which is not discursively aware of the structures of capitalism, is not capable of engaging in structural conflict. This argument relates back to our discussion of Foucault's work as a form of radical critique.

Benevolent dictatorship is the classic instance where goals override practice. What we have in mind here is a dictatorship with the following type of characteristics: it is made up of subjects who are committed democrats but ruled by a dictator who, by virtue of economic wizardry, gives the state a higher standard of living than equivalent democratic states and, because of this higher standard of living, the subjects are willing to accept a trade-off between their democratic principles and their high standard of living. These are subjects who do not really approve of the institutional practices of government but, despite this, are willingly compliant.

*4 Overall conflict, where goals override structures*  This is the form of interaction where there is consensus on structured practice, conflict over goals and where goals override structures. It is a predominantly conflictual situation. In terms of the scalar opposition between consensus and conflict, we have moved from the consensual to the conflictual side of the spectrum.

Whatever the type of conflict or consensus, on the consensual side of the spectrum outcomes are always realized unless the resources are lacking. The fact that consensus overrides conflict means that it is in every person's perceived interests that outcomes should be realized so, presumably, they are. However, in a situation where conflict overrides consensus this is not the case. In this situation the balance between consensus and conflict must artificially be tipped in favour of consensus or compliance.

Coercion works by making non-compliance in some way costly. It does so in the form of a threat. This threat means artificially adding a consequence to certain outcomes which is not actually intrinsic to those outcomes. What I mean by extrinsic can be illustrated by the following assertion: 'If you do not pay your taxes then you will go to gaol.' Going to gaol and paying taxes are not in any respect intrinsically linked outcomes. It is not like the statement: 'If you do not sow then you will not reap.' Sowing and reaping are intrinsically linked activities. Going to gaol is an outcome which has been artificially linked to taxes to ensure compliance by making non-compliance inherently costly.

When we are a situation where rules are consensual but goals conflictual, coercion works by making the cost of rule-breaking potentially higher than the potential benefits from non-compliance. In other words, it artificially tops up the balance between conflict and consensus in favour of consensus.

It is important to note that coercion is uncertain in a way in which consensus is not. Coercion is always potentially open to being neutralized or destroyed by equal or greater coercive resources. Furthermore, coercion will always be ineffective against the actor who is willing to die for a cause. If we recall Giddens' example of the prison hunger strike, this is an excellent example of the limits of coercion. When an actor or organization possesses overwhelming coercive resources, as does the state relative to an individual, the realization of outcomes is never guaranteed unless what is the desired outcome is the death of the individual. However, in most instances, killing an individual is a second preference choice. When actor A says to actor B 'Don't move or I shoot', B moves and A shoots B, this does not represent A's first preference option.

When do actors affirm structural practices but let conflict with respect to goals override that consent? The two most obvious types of situation where this takes place are the following: firstly, the free-rider; and, secondly, where consensual practice delivers deeply objectionable outcomes.

The free-rider is the political equivalent to the person who cheats at chess. Usually, the person who cheats at chess does not do so because of disagreement with the rules. Rather, they are driven by a strong desire to win. Similarly, the person who fails to pay income tax or the party that rigs a ballot may consider the rules of the game perfectly legitimate but, nevertheless, violates them because they value a specific outcome more than the rules themselves. This is, by and large, an essentially inaltruistic position where there is a discursive knowledge of the legitimacy or validity of certain practices but the desire to 'win' is so great that it overrides everything else.

The existence of the free-rider is one of the primary factors which legitimates the state's monopoly of violence. Part of the principle of 'legitimate' coercion is the idea that the threat of violence is used only to induce actors to comply with common commitments. In other words, the recalcitrant are 'coerced to be free'.

The second version of this scenario would be the example of an actor who fully accepts the legitimacy of the rules of the game but is unable to consent to defeat because of a deeply felt opposition to the outcome. Unlike the previous highly inaltruistic instance of rule breaking, in this case there is likely to be a high level of cognitive dissonance. On the one hand, the actor accepts that certain structured practices are inherently valid. Yet, on the other, they find that structured practices throw up outcomes which to them are unacceptable. In this situation the actor may be conscious of the four *raisons d'etre* which make the actor in the consensually equivalent situation (where a commitment to structures overrides the pursuit of goals) affirm practices but, at the same time, they are overwhelmingly driven by the perception that the outcomes which they are asked to affirm contribute to the realization of goals which are deeply contrary to their interests or aspirations.

An idealized example of such a situation is raised by the issue of stability with regard to Rawls' original position. The fundamental organizing principle of the original position is the idea of justice as fairness (see Rawls 1993, p. 15). For Rawls, justice as fairness is operationalized by drawing upon a commitment to free and equal citizenship which we all share qua democrats (Rawls 1993, p. 23). All democrats share this commitment as part of their comprehensive world view. In addition to this, depending upon the contingencies of our life story (religious belief, economic background etc.), our comprehensive doctrines are made up of an assembled set of beliefs and commitments which are unique to us as individuals. However, for Rawls being a democrat implies a prior commitment to the idea of allowing those aspects of our comprehensive doctrine which are particular to our world view to be overridden by the shared democratic commitment to free and equal citizenship. In other words, when aspects which are particular to the world view of Jews and Muslims, rich and poor, gay and straight come into conflict with their shared commitment to free and equal citizenship and all that is entailed by that principle, then the former gives way to the latter.

If one were to imagine a society organized according to Rawlsian principles, it is not at all improbable that actors would affirm the principles of the original position as inherently fair, yet, in practice, when it came to the crunch, would be unwilling to let principle override outcomes. In real life Jews and Muslims, rich and poor, gay and straight may agree to being democrats first and Jewish, Muslim, rich, poor, gay or straight second. A devout Catholic might well be convinced of the inherent legitimacy of Rawlsian principles, be further persuaded that Rawlsian liberalism entailed the legalization of divorce and yet, in contradiction to all this, resist the introduction of divorce. In essence, while affirming the legitimacy of certain principles they would not be willing to allow their structural commitments to override the pursuit or non-pursuit of specific outcomes. They do not consent to being forced to be free.

Lukes gives an interesting example of this type of mismatch between practice and outcome. He theorizes it in terms of Gramsci's concept of the disjuncture of theory and practice. The example he gives is taken from Sriniva's analysis of the Indian caste system, a hierarchy which, in principle – according to the rules of the game – does not allow for upward mobility. It is also a system which, rather surprisingly, has, in principle at least, the wide support of even the lowest castes. In other words, it would appear that even the lower castes affirm the principles of caste immobility. Yet, despite this institutional consensus, almost invariably, lower caste members seize opportunities to rise up the caste system (Lukes 1974, p. 49). In short, it would appear that, on the one hand, members of the caste system discursively consent to the idea of a rigid caste system yet, on the other, they do not fully accept the consequences or outcomes of living according to the principles which they affirm.

While Lukes' example would appear to indicate that actors are capable of living their lives overriding structured practice which they affirm, it has to be said that this must inherently be a less stable situation than the consensual equivalent. If practices continually throw up outcomes which actors find sufficiently undesirable that they continually wish to subvert them, it would appear unlikely that, over time, consensus at the level of practice would not be replaced by conflict. The cognitive dissonance implicit in disconfirmation of 'legitimate' structures would *tend*[5] to make the situation inherently unstable. The overall tendency would be for conflict and consensus to be replaced by double conflict. To return to the example of the devout Catholic: over time, there would be an innate tendency for them to find reason to reject Rawlsian principles or, alternatively, to insist upon a new interpretation of them which would be consistent with the Catholic particulars of their comprehensive doctrine.

5 *Overall conflict, where structure override goals*   This is the form of interaction where there is consensus on goals, conflict over structures and where a commitment to structure overrides goals. Again, it is a predominantly conflictual situation.

Here the commitment to practices is so great that actors would prefer to affirm structured practices even when such affirmation results in the realization of inherently desirable goals. To put it the other way, even though a certain goal might be intrinsically desirable in itself, an actor considers that desirability insufficient to compensate for the perceived negative attributes associated with the reproduction of the structures necessary for the realization of those goals. Given that conflict over structure always implies discursive consciousness knowledge, it is an instance where, when allowed a free choice, discursive consciousness knowledge of practices would lead actors to refrain from the pursuit of common goals. Consequently, as in the other two forms of predominantly conflictual interaction, coercion is necessary to make up the consensual deficit if goals are to be realized.

The most common reason actors have for not wishing to affirm certain structures is that they do not wish to legitimate them. Governments often share goals with terrorist organizations but refrain from pursuing them for fear of legitimating certain norms. Women may refrain from pursuing a common goal with men if the pursuit of these goals involves the reproduction of patriarchal social practices. To return to the example of benevolent dictatorship once more, an actor may desire the higher standard of living which the dictator offers, yet, despite this, they may resist compliance because of an overriding commitment to democracy. If this is so, the benevolent dictator will need coercive resources to ensure compliance, in which case, of course, the dictator is no longer quite so benevolent.

Another instance of this conflict is to be found in the labour process in the instance when it involves individuals who do not consider the capitalist system legitimate but who, nonetheless, sell their labour because they have nothing other than their labour power to sell. In this situation they reproduce the capitalist relations of production only because they are coerced into it by circumstances.[6]

Meaning is created through structure and, as a consequence, conflict over meaning is a form of structural conflict. When a conflict arises solely out of disagreement over meaning, it is a form of conflict which is not open to conflict resolution. Even if the conflict is removed by one stage and a set of procedures and norms are agreed for the purpose of resolving the conflict, the conflict will not be resolvable because of the arbitrary nature of meaning. Let us take the instance of Habermas' 'ideal speech situation' – a set of institutional procedures which is intended to create the basis for conflict resolution without coercion. In the 'ideal speech situation' actors enter into an open discursive debate where they agree that the better argument will win. It is a procedural situation where structures are intended to override goals. If the conflict is purely over goals as outcomes (i.e. there is no difference of meaning) the conflict is resolved when the better argument wins. However, in the special case when the conflict is over meaning, it will not be resolved because meaning is arbitrary and, as such, is not open to reason. If we return to the example of games, in a chess match there is resolution of the conflict when one of the players is in check-mate. However, setting up an ideal speech situation for the resolution of a conflict which is rooted in meaning is the theoretical equivalent of agreeing to the rules of chess but using pieces that are unalike. Even if both sides are willing to give overriding consent to the institutions of the ideal speech situation, the fact that each side sees the pieces as carriers of different meaning implies that the conflict is inherently irresolvable except through coercion. Possibly the best illustration of this form of conflict is the abortion debate. If one side views the object of the dispute as a fetus while the other sees it as an unborn baby, there is no reason to suppose that either side will ever agree, even if there is total agreement upon what constitutes a better argument according to procedural criteria.

Conflicts over meaning are integral to conflict which is ultimately rooted in culture. These are typical of the conflicts within pluralist societies and, globally, conflicts between states of different cultural traditions.

*6 Pure conflict*   This is the pure form of conflict where there is conflict both with respect to goals and with regard to structure.

Unlike the other forms of conflict examined, in pure conflict there is no consensus to build upon. Hence, if structures are to be reproduced or goals attained, coercion is the sole source of compliance. Compliance is not, as in the other two forms of non-consensual conflict, simply a matter of compensating for a consensual deficit. If one actor is to prevail over the other, it is entirely through coercion.

This form of conflict can be described as 'primitive' in the sense that there is no Leviathan. In other words, there is no assembled set of structures generating power. There is no machinery of power. If we take it that politics is about institutions and procedures, it is, in this sense, a form of non-political conflict. This is partly what Foucault had in mind when he argued that power is not the same as violence and that politics is the continuation of war by other means. In a situation of pure conflict (war), there are no rules which will allow one actor to prevail over the other. Structures and institutions, on the other hand, encode the conflict of war by proceduralizing conflict.

### Notes

1 In this context references are given only to authors who are not discussed in part one.
2 See Beetham 1991 p. 111 for the use of a similar argument concerning the relationship between social science and normative theory.
3 Chapter ten.

**4** See Habermas 1987 pp. 1–113 and Cooke 1994. Kertzer makes a similar point with regard to Durkheim's analysis of the relationship between social cohesion and ritual (Kertzer 1988 pp. 57–76).

**5** As we shall see in chapter eight, actors can live with surprisingly inconsistent ideas and perceptions.

**6** It could be argued that this is an instance of three – goals as consensus and structures as conflict, where goals override structures.

## References

Arendt, Hannah (1970) *On Violence*, London, Allen Lane.

Beetham, David (1991) *The Legitimation of Power*, London, Macmillan.

Clegg, Stewart R. (1989) *Frameworks of Power*, London, Sage.

Cooke, Maeve (1994) *Language and Reason: A Study of Habermas' Pragmatics*, Cambridge, Mass., MIT Press.

Dahl, Robert A. (1957) 'The Concept of Power', *Behavioural Science*, Vol. 2.

Dahl, Robert A. (1989) *Democracy and Its Critics*, New Haven, Yale University Press.

Gallagher, Michael and Michael Laver (1993) *How Ireland Voted*, Dublin and Limerick, Folens and PSAI Press.

Habermas, Jürgen (1987) *The Theory of Communicative Action*, Vol. 2, *The Critique of Functionalist Reason*, Cambridge, Polity Press.

Hyland, James L. (1995) *Democratic Theory: The Philosophical Foundations*, Manchester, Manchester University Press.

Locke, John (1924) *Two Treatises of Government*, London, Dent.

Lukes, Steven (1974) *Power: A Radical View*, London, Macmillan.

Lukes, Steven (1977) *Essays in Social Theory*, London, Macmillan.

Machiavelli, Niccolò (1974) *The Discourses*, Harmondsworth, Penguin Books.

Mansbridge, Jane (1994) 'Using Power/Fighting Power', *Constellations*, Vol. 1.

Marsh, Michael, Rick Wilford and Rona Fitzgerald (1993) 'Irish Political Data', *Irish Political Studies*, Vol. 8.

Parsons, Talcott (1963) 'On the Concept of Political Power', *Proceedings of the American Philosophical Society*, Vol. 107.

Rousseau, Jean-Jacques (1973) *The Social Contract and Discourses*, London, J.M. Dent & Sons.

Weber, Max (1978) *Economy and Society*, Vol. 1, *An Outline of Interpretive Sociology*, Berkeley, University of California Press.

# Bibliography

This is the bibliography to any references contained in the introductions. Additionally, it constitutes a list some of some of the most significant publications on power in recent years and, also, by the fifteen authors included in this volume.

Adams, Richard N. (1975) *Energy and Structure: A Theory of Social Power*, University of Texas Press, Austin.

Ahmed, Sarah (1998) *Differences That Matter: Feminist Theory and Postmodernism*, Cambridge University Press, Cambridge.

Allen, Amy (1998) 'Rethinking Power', *Hyptia*, vol. 13.

Allen, Amy (1999) *The Power of Feminist Theory: Domination, Resistance, Solidarity*, Westview Press, Boulder CO.

Althusser, Louis and Etienne Balibar (1970) *Reading Capital*, trans. B. Brewster, New Left Books, London.

Anderson, Perry (1974) *Lineages of the Absolutist State*, Verso, London.

Archer, Margaret S. (1988) *Culture and Agency: The Place of Culture in Social Theory*, Cambridge University Press, Cambridge.

Arendt, Hannah (1958) *The Human Condition*, University of Chicago Press, Chicago.

Arendt, Hannah (1959) *The Origins of Totalitarianism*, Allen and Unwin, London.

Arendt, Hannah (1970) *On Violence*, Penguin, London.

Aristotle (1941) *The Basic Works of Aristotle*, ed. Richard McKeon, Random House, New York.

Aron, Raymond (1986) 'Macht, Power, Puissance', *European Journal of Sociology*, vol. 5. Reprinted in Steven Lukes (ed.) (1986).

Bachrach, Peter (1962) 'Elite Consensus and Democracy', *Journal of Politics*, vol. 24.

Bachrach, Peter (1967) *The Theory of Democratic Elitism*, Little, Brown, Boston.

Bachrach, Peter (1971) (ed.) *Political Elites in a Democracy*, Atherton Press, New York.

Bachrach, Peter and Morton S. Baratz (1962) 'The Two Faces of Power', *American Political Science Review*, vol. 56.

Bachrach, Peter and Morton S. Baratz (1963) 'Decisions and Nondecisions', *American Political Science Review*, vol. 57.

Bachrach, Peter and Morton S. Baratz (1970) *Power and Poverty: Theory and Practice*, Oxford University Press, Oxford.

Bachrach, Peter and Morton S. Baratz (1975) 'Power and Its Two Faces Revisited: A Reply to Geoffrey Debnam', *American Political Science Review*, vol. 69. Also in Scott (ed.) (1994).

Baechler, Jean, John A. Hall and Michael Mann (1988) (eds) *Europe and the Rise of Capitalism*, Blackwell, Oxford.

Balbus, Isaac (1986) 'Disciplining Women: Michel Foucault and the Power of Feminist Discourse', *Paxis International*, vol. 5.

Baldwin, David (1989) *Paradoxes of Power*, Blackwell, Oxford.

Ball, Terence (1976) 'Power, Causation and Explanation', *Polity*, Winter.

Ball, Terence (1978) 'Power Revisited', *The Journal of Politics*, vol. 40.

Ball, Terence (1988) *Transforming Political Discourse*, Basil Blackwell, Oxford.

Ball, Terence (1993) 'Power', in R.E. Goodin and Philip Pettit (eds) *A Companion to Contemporary Political Philosophy*.

Barbalet, J.M. (1985) 'Power and Resistance', *British Journal of Sociology*, vol. 36.

Barbalet, J.M. (1987) 'Power, Structural Resources, and Agency', *Current Perspectives in Social Theory*, vol. 8.

Barker, Philip (1993) *Michel Foucault: Subversions of the Subject*, St. Martin's Press, New York.

Barnes, Barry (1974) *Scientific Knowledge and Sociological Theory*, Routledge, London.

Barnes, Barry (1977) *Interest and the Growth of Knowledge*, Routledge, London.

Barnes, Barry (1982) *T.S. Kuhn and Social Science*, Macmillan, London.

Barnes, Barry (1986) 'On Authority and its Relationship to Power', in John Law (ed.), *Power, Action and Belief: A New Sociology of Knowledge?*, Sociological Review Monograph 32, Routledge and Kegan Paul, London.

Barnes, Barry (1988) *The Nature of Power*, Polity, Cambridge.

Barnes, Barry (1995) *The Elements of Social Theory*, UCL, London.

Barnes, Barry (2000) *Understanding Agency: Social Theory and Responsible Action*, Sage, London.

Barnes, Barry, David Bloor and John Henry (1996) *Scientific Knowledge: A Sociological Analysis*, Athlone, London.

Barry, Brian (1976) *Power and Political Theory: Some European Perspectives*, John Wiley, London.

Barry, Brian (1988) 'The Uses of "Power" ' *Government and Opposition*, vol. 23. Also in Barry (1991).

Barry, Brian (1991) *Democracy and Power: Essays in Political Theory*, vol. 1, Oxford University Press, Oxford.

Baumann, Zygmunt (1989) *Modernity and the Holocaust*, Polity, Cambridge.

Baumann, Zygmunt (1991) *Modernity and Ambivalence*, Polity, Cambridge.

de Beauvoir, Simone (1973) *The Second Sex*, Vintage, New York.

Beck, Ulrich (1992) *Risk Society: Towards a New Modernity*, Sage, London.

Beetham, David (1991) *The Legitimation of Power*, Macmillan, London.

Benhabib, Seyla (1988) 'Judgement and the Moral Foundations of Politics in Arendt's thought', *Political Theory*, vol. 16.

Benton, Ted (1981) ' "Objective" Interests and the Outcomes of Struggles', *Sociology*, vol. 15. Also in Scott (1994).

Benton, Ted (1988) 'Review of P. Morriss, *Power*', *Sociology*, vol. 22.

Betts, Katharine (1986) 'The Conditions of Action, Power and the Problem of Interests', *Sociological Review*, vol. 34. Also in Scott (ed.) (1994).

Bird, J.F. (1989) 'Foucault: Power and Politics', in Peter Lassman (ed.), *Politics and Social Theory*, Routledge, London.

Blau, Peter (1964) *Exchange and Power in Social Life*, Wiley, New York.

Boulding, Kenneth E. (1990) *Three Faces of Power*, Sage, London.

Bourdieu, Pierre (1979) *Algeria 1960: The Disenchantment of the World*, Cambridge University Press, Cambridge.

Bourdieu, Pierre (1979) *The Inheritors: French Students and Their Relation to Culture*, University of Chicago Press, Chicago.

Bourdieu, Pierre (1984) *Distinction: A Social Critique of the Judgement of Taste*, Routledge, London.

Bourdieu, Pierre (1986) 'The Forms of Capital', in John G. Richardson (ed.), *Handbook of Theory and Research for the Sociology of Education*, Greedwood, New York.

Bourdieu, Pierre (1988) *Homo Academicus*, Polity, Cambridge.

Bourdieu, Pierre (1989) 'Social Space and Symbolic Power', *Sociological Theory*, vol. 7.

Bourdieu, Pierre (1990a) *The Logic of Practice*, Polity, Cambridge.

Bourdieu, Pierre (1990b) *In Other Words: Essays Towards a Reflexive Sociology*, Polity, Cambridge.

Bourdieu, Pierre (1991a) *The Political Ontology of Martin Heidegger*, Polity, Cambridge.

Bourdieu, Pierre (1991b) *Language and Symbolic Power: The Economy of Linguistic Exchanges*, Polity, Cambridge.

Bourdieu, Pierre (1993) *Sociology in Question*, Polity, Cambridge.

Bourdieu, Pierre (1993) *The Field of Cultural Production: Essays on Art and Literature*, Polity, Cambridge.

Bourdieu, Pierre (1994) *Academic Discourse: Linguistic Misunderstanding and Professorial Power*, Polity, Cambridge.

Bourdieu, Pierre (1996) *The State Nobility: Elite Schools in the Field of Power*, Polity, Cambridge.

Bourdieu, Pierre (1996) *The Rules of Art*, Polity, Cambridge.

Bourdieu, Pierre (1998) *Practical Reason: On the Theory of Action*, Polity, Cambridge.

Bourdieu, Pierre and Loic J.D. Wacquant (1992) *An Invitation to Reflexive Sociology*, Polity, Cambridge.

Bradshaw, Alan (1976) 'A Critique of Steven Lukes' "Power: A Radical View" ' *Sociology*, vol. 10.

Bradshaw, Leah (1989) *Acting and Thinking: The Political Thought of Hannah Arendt*, University of Toronto Press, Toronto.

Brown, Wendy (1995) *States of Inquiry: Power and Freedom in Late Modernity*, Princeton University Press, Princeton, NJ.

Bryant G.A. and David Jary (1991) (eds) *Giddens' Theory of Structuration: A Critical Appreciation*, Routledge, London.

Butler, Judith (1990) *Gender Trouble: Feminism and the Subversion of Identity*, Routledge, New York.

Butler, Judith (1997) *The Psychic Life of Power: Theories in Subjection*, Stanford University Press, Stanford.

Calhoun, Craig, Edward LiPuma and Moishe Postone (1993) (eds) *Bourdieu: Critical Perspectives*, Polity, Cambridge.

Calhoun, Craig, Marshall W. Meyer and W. Richard Scott (1990) (eds) *Structures of Power and Constraint: Papers in Honor of Peter M. Blau*, Cambridge University Press, Cambridge.

Callinicos, Alex (1985) 'Anthony Giddens: A Contemporary Critique', *Theory and Society*, vol. 14.

Canovan, Margaret (1974) *The Political Thought of Hannah Arendt*, J.M. Dent, London.

Canovan, Margaret (1992) *Hannah Arendt: A Reinterpretation of Her Political Thought*, Cambridge University Press, Cambridge.

Cassell, Philip (1993) *The Giddens Reader*, Macmillan, London.

Cerny, Philip (1990) *The Changing Architecture of Politics*, Sage, London.

Cerny, Philip (2000) 'Globalization and the Disarticulation of Power: Towards a New Middle Ages', in Henri Goverde *et al.* (eds), *Power in Contemporary Politics*, Sage, London.

Clegg, Stewart (1975) *Power, Rule, Domination*, Routledge, London.

Clegg, Stewart (1979) *The Theory of Power and Organization*, Routledge, London.

Clegg, S.R. (1987) 'The Power of Language and the Language of Power', *Organizational Studies*, vol. 8.

Clegg, Stewart (1989) *Frameworks of Power*, Sage, London.

Clegg, Stewart (1990) *Modern Organizations: Organization Studies in the Postmodern World*, Sage, London.

Clegg, Stewart (2000a) 'Power and Authority, Resistance and Legitimacy', in Henri Goverde *et al.* (eds), *Power in Contemporary Politics*, Sage, London.

Clegg, Stewart (2000b) 'Theories of Power', *Theory Culture and Society*, vol. 17.

Clegg, Stewart R. and Gill Palmer (1996) (eds) *The Politics of Management Knowledge*, Sage, London.

Cohen, Ira (1989) *Structuration Theory: Anthony Giddens and the Constitution of Social Life*, Macmillan, London.

Connell, R.W. (1987) *Gender and Power*, Routledge, London.

Connolly, William (1983) *The Terms of Political Discourse*, 2nd edn, Princeton University Press, Princeton, NJ.

Cook, Karen (1977) 'Exchange and Power in Networks of Interorganizational Relations', *The Sociological Quarterly*, vol. 18. Also in Scott (ed.) (1994).

Cook, Karen, Richard Emerson, Mary Gillmore and Toshio Yamagishi (1983) 'The Distribution of Power in Exchange Networks: Theory and Experimental Results', *American Journal of Sociology*, vol. 89. Also in Scott (ed.) (1994).

Craib, Ian (1992) *Anthony Giddens*, Routledge, London.

Crenson, Matthew A. (1971) *The Un-Politics of Air Pollution*, Johns Hopkins Press, Baltimore.

Crenson, Matthew (1978) 'Social Networks and Political Process in Urban Networks', *American Journal of Political Science*, vol. 22. Also in Scott (ed.) (1994).

Crespi, Franco (1992) *Social Action and Power*, Blackwell, Oxford.

Dahl, Robert A. (1957) 'The Concept of Power', *Behavioural Science*, vol. 2.

Dahl, Robert A. (1958) 'A Critique of this Ruling-Elite Model', *American Political Science Review*, vol. 52.

Dahl, Robert A. (1961) *Who Governs? Democracy and Power in an American City*, Yale University Press, New Haven.

Dahl, Robert A. (1968) 'Power', in David L. Shills (1968), *International Encyclopedia of the Social Sciences*, vol. 12, Macmillan, New York.

Dahl, Robert A. (1984) *Modern Political Analysis*, Prentice Hall, Englewood Cliffs, NJ.

Dahl, Robert A. (1985) *A Preface to Economic Democracy*, Polity, Cambridge.

Dahl, Robert A. (1989) *Democracy and Its Critics*, Yale University Press, New Haven.

Dallmayr, Fred (1984) 'Pluralism Old and New: Foucault on Power', in *Polis and Praxis*, MIT Press, Cambridge, MA.

Davis, Kathy (1988) *Power Under the Microscope: Toward a Grounded Theory of Gender Relations in Medical Encounters*, Foris Publications, Dordrecht.

Davis, Kathy (1995) *Reshaping the Female Body: The Dilemma of Cosmetic Surgery*, Routledge, London.

Davis, Kathy (1997) (ed.) *Embodied Practices: Feminist Perspectives on the Body*, Sage, London.

Davis, Kathy, Monique Leijenaar and Jantine Oldersma (1991) *The Gender of Power*, Sage, London.

Dean, Mitchell (1999) *Governmentality: Power and Rule in Modern Society*, Sage, London.

Debnam, Geoffrey (1975a) 'Nondecisions and Power: The Two Faces of Bachrach and Baratz', *American Political Science Review*, vol. 69. Also in Scott (ed.) (1994).

Debnam, Geoffrey (1975b) 'Rejoinder to "Comment" by Peter Bachrach and Morton Baratz', *American Political Science Review*, vol. 69. Also in Scott (ed.) (1994).

Digeser, Peter (1992) 'The Fourth Face of Power', *Journal of Politics*, vol. 54.

Dowding, Keith (1991) *Rational Choice and Political Power*, Edward Elgar, Aldershot.

Dowding, Keith (1996) *Power*, Open University Press, Buckingham.

Dreyfus, Hubert L. and Paul Rabinow (1982) *Michel Foucault: Beyond Structuralism and Hermeneutics*, Harvester Wheatsheaf, London.

Dyrberg, Torben Bech (1997) *The Circular Structure of Power: Politics, Identity, Community*, Verso, London.

Elias, Norbert (2000) *The Civilizing Process*, Basil Blackwell, Oxford.

Fanon, Frantz (1967) *The Wretched of the Earth*, Penguin, Harmondsworth.

Faubion, James D. (2000) (ed.) *Michel Foucault: Power*, The New Press, New York.

Felsenthal, D.S. and M. Machover (1998) *The Measurement of Voting Power: Theory and Practice, Problems and Paradoxes*, Edward Elgar, Cheltenham.

Flammang, Janet (1994) 'Feminist Theory: The Question of Power', *Current Perspectives in Social Theory*, vol. 4. Also in Scott (1994).

Flyvbjerg, Bent (1998) *Rationality and Power: Democracy in Practice*, University of Chicago Press, Chicago.

Foucault, Michel (1970) *The Order of Things*, Routledge, London.

Foucault, Michel (1971) *Madness and Civilization: A History of Insanity in the Age of Reason*, Tavistock, London.

Foucault, Michel (1975) (ed.) *I, Pierre Riviere, having slaughtered my mother, my sister and my brother . . . a case of parricide in the 19th century*, Penguin, Harmondsworth.

Foucault, Michel (1977) *Language, Counter-memory, Practice: Selected Essays and Interviews*, ed. Donald F. Bouchard, Cornell University Press, New York.

Foucault, Michel (1979) *Discipline and Punish: The Birth of the Prison*, Penguin, Harmondsworth.

Foucault, Michel (1980) *Power/Knowledge: Selected Interviews and Other Writings 1972–1977*, ed. Colin Gordon, Harvester Press, Brighton.

Foucault, Michel (1981) *The History of Sexuality Volume 1: An Introduction*, Penguin, Harmondsworth.

Foucault, Michel (1982) 'The Subject and Power', in Hubert L. Dreyfus and Paul Rabinow, *Michel Foucault: Beyond Structuralism and Hermeneutics*, Harvester Wheatsheaf, London.

Foucault, Michel (1986) *The Use of Pleasure: The History of Sexuality Volume 2*, Penguin, Harmondsworth.

Foucault, Michel (1987) in *The Final Foucault*, ed. James Bernauer and David Rasmussen, MIT Press, Cambridge MA.

Foucault, Michel (1988) in *Michel Foucault: Politics, Philosophy, Culture*, ed. Lawrence D. Kritzman, Routledge, London.

Foucault, Michel (1989) *The Birth of the Clinic: An Archaeology of Medical Perception*, Routledge, London.

Foucault, Michel (1989) *The Archaeology of Knowledge*, Routledge, London.

Foucault, Michel (1990) *The Care of the Self: The History of Sexuality Volume 3*, Penguin, Harmondsworth.

Foucault, Michel (1991) *The Foucault Reader: An Introduction to His Thought*, ed. Paul Rabinow, Penguin, Harmondsworth.

Foucault, Michel (2000) *Michel Foucault: Power*, ed. James D. Faubion, The New Press, New York.

Fowler, Bridget (1997) *Pierre Bourdieu and Cultural Theory: Critical Investigations*, Sage, London.

Fraser, Nancy (1981) 'Foucault on Modern Power: Empirical Insights and Normative Confusions', *Praxis International*, vol. 1.

Fraser, Nancy (1985) 'Michel Foucault: A "Young Conservative"?', *Ethics*, vol. 96.

Fraser, Nancy (1989) *Unruly Practices: Power, Discourse and Gender in Contemporary Social Theory*, Polity Press, Cambridge.

French, John (1956) 'A Formal Theory of Social Power', *Psychological Review*, vol. 63. Also in Scott (1994).

Frey, Frederick (1971) 'Comment: On Issues and Nonissues in the Study of Power', *American Political Science Review*, vol. 65. Also in Scott (ed.) (1994).

Friedkin, Noah (1986) 'A Formal Theory of Social Power', *Journal of Mathematical Sociology*, vol. 12. Also in Scott (ed.) (1994).

Fyfe, Gordon and John Law (1988) *Picturing Power: Visual Depiction and Social Relations*, Sociological Review Monographs, Routledge, London.

Galbraith, John Kenneth (1983) *The Anatomy of Power*, Hamish Hamilton, London.

Gallie, W.B. (1955) 'Essentially Contested Concepts', *Proceedings of the Aristotelian Society*, vol. 56.

Gane, Mike (1986) (ed.) *Towards a Critique of Foucault*, Routledge and Kegan Paul, London.

Garfinkel, Harold (1984) *Studies in Ethnomethodology*, Polity, Cambridge.

Gaventa, John (1980) *Power and Powerlessness: Quiescence and Rebellion in an Appalachian Valley*, Clarendon Press, Oxford.

Giddens, Anthony (1968) ' "Power" in the Recent Writings of Talcott Parsons', *Sociology*, vol. 2.

Giddens, Anthony (1971) *Capitalism and Modern Social Theory: An Analysis of the Writings of Marx, Durkheim and Max Weber*, Cambridge University Press, Cambridge.

Giddens, Anthony (1976) *New Rules of Sociological Method*, Hutchinson, London.

Giddens, Anthony (1977) *Studies in Social and Political Theory*, Hutchinson, London.

Giddens, Anthony (1979) *Central Problems in Social Theory: Action, Structure and Contradiction in Social Analysis*, Macmillan, London.

Giddens, Anthony (1981) *A Contemporary Critique of Historical Materialism: Vol. I, Power, Property and the State*, Macmillan, London.

Giddens, Anthony (1984) *The Constitution of Society*, Polity, Cambridge.

Giddens, Anthony (1985) *The Nation-State and Violence: Vol. II of A Contemporary Critique of Historical Materialism*, Polity, Cambridge.

Giddens, Anthony (1993) *The Giddens Reader*, ed. Philip Cassell, Macmillan, London.

Giddens, Anthony and David Held (1982) (eds) *Classes, Power and Conflict*, Macmillan, London.

Giddens, Anthony and Jonathan H. Turner (1987) (eds) *Social Theory Today*, Polity, Cambridge.

Gledhill, John (1994) *Power and Its Disguises*, Pluto, London.

Goehler, Gehard (2000) 'Constitution and Use of Power', in Henri Goverde *et al.* (eds), *Power in Contemporary Politics*, Sage, London.

Goffman, Erving (1961) *Asylums*, Pelican, Harmondsworth.

Goffman, Erving (1971) *The Presentation of Self in Everyday Life*, Pelican, Harmondsworth.

Goodin, Robert E. and Philip Pettit (1993) *Contemporary Political Philosophy: an Anthology*, Blackwell, Oxford.

Goverde, Henri, Philip Cerny, Mark Haugaard and Howard Lentner (2000) *Power in Contemporary Politics*, Sage, London.

Gramsci, Antonio (1971) *Selections from the Prison Notebooks of Antonio Gramsci* (ed.) Quintin Hoare and Geoffrey Nowell-Smith, Lawrence and Wishart, London.

Grenfell, Michael and David James (1998) (eds) *Bourdieu and Education: Acts of Practical Theory*, Falmer Press, London.

Habermas, Jürgen (1977) 'Hannah Arendt's Communications Concept of Power', *Social Research*, vol. 44. Also in Lukes (ed.) (1977).

Habermas, Jürgen (1984) *The Theory of Communicative Action: Vol. I, Reason and the Rationalization of Society*, Polity, Cambridge.

Habermas, Jürgen (1986) 'The Genealogical Writing of History: On Some Aprorias in Foucault's Theory of Power', *Canadian Journal of Political and Social Theory*, vol. 10.

Habermas, Jürgen (1987) *The Theory of Communicative Action: Vol. II, The Critique of Functionalist Reason*, Polity, Cambridge.

Hall, John A. (1994) *Coercion and Consent: Studies on the Modern State*, Polity, Cambridge.

Hamilton, Gary and Nicole Biggart (1985) 'Theoretical Observations on Power and Obedience in Complex Organizations', *Sociological Perspectives*, vol. 28. Also in Scott (ed.) (1994).

Hansen, Phillip (1993) *Hannah Arendt: Politics History and Citizenship*, Polity, Cambridge.

Harker, Richard, Cheleen Mahar and Chris Wilkes (1990) *An Introduction to the Work of Pierre Bourdieu: The Practice of Theory*, Macmillan, Basingstoke.

Harré, Rom (1970) 'Powers', *British Journal for the Philosophy of Science*, vol. 21.

Harré, Rom and E.H. Madden (1975) 'Causal Powers: A Theory of Natural Necessity', Rowan and Littlefield, Totowa, NJ.

Hartsock, Nancy (1985) *Money, Sex and Power: Toward a Feminist Historical Materialism*, Northeastern University Press, Boston.

Hartsock, Nancy (1990) 'Foucault on Power: A Theory for Women?', in Linda Nicholson (ed.), *Feminism/Postmodernism*, Routledge, London.

Haugaard, Mark (1992) *Structures, Restructuration and Social Power*, Avebury, Aldershot.

Haugaard, Mark (1997a) *The Constitution of Power*, Manchester University Press, Manchester.

Haugaard, Mark (1997b) 'The Consensual Basis of Conflictual Power', *Constellations*, vol. 3.

Haugaard, Mark (1999) 'Power: Social and Political Theories of', in *Encyclopaedia of Violence, Peace and Conflict*, Vol. 3, Academic Press, San Diego.

Haugaard, Mark (2000) 'Power, Ideology and Legitimacy', in Henri Goverde *et al.* (eds), *Power in Contemporary Politics*, Sage, London.

Haugaard, Mark (2002) 'Foucault and the Birth of the Subject', in Iain MacKenzie and Sinisa Malesevic (eds), *Ideology after Post-Structuralism*, Pluto, London.

Hayward, Clarissa Rile (2000) *De-facing Power*, Cambridge University Press, Cambridge.

Heidegger, Martin (1962) *Being and Time*, Basil Blackwell, Oxford.

Held, David and John Thompson (1989) *Social Theory of Modern Societies: Anthony Giddens and His Critics*, Cambridge University Press, Cambridge.

Hiley, David (1984) 'Foucault and the Analysis of Power', *Praxis International*, vol. 4.

Hindess, Barry (1982) 'Power, Interests and the Outcome of Struggles', *Sociology*, vol. 16.

Hindess, Barry (1996) *Discourses of Power: From Hobbes to Foucault*, Blackwell, Oxford.

Hobbes, Thomas (1914) *Leviathan*, Everyman Library, J.M. Dent & Sons, London.

Honneth, Axel (1991) *The Critique of Power: Reflective Stages in a Critical Social Theory*, MIT Press, Cambridge, MA.

Hooke, Alexander (1987) 'Is Foucault's Antihumanism Against Human Action?', *Political Theory*, vol. 15.

Hoy, David Couzens (1986) *Foucault: A Critical Reader*, Basil Blackwell, Oxford.

Hunter, Floyd (1953) *Community Power Structure: A Study of Decision-makers*, North Carolina Press, Chapel Hill.

Hyland, James (1995) *Democratic Theory: The Philosophical Foundations*, Manchester University Press, Manchester.

Ingram, David (1986) 'Foucault and the Frankfurt School: A Discourse on Nietzsche, Power and Knowledge', *Praxis International*, vol. 6.

Isaac, Jeffrey (1987a) *Power and Marxist Theory: A Realist View*, Cornell University Press, Ithaca.

Isaac, Jeffrey (1987b) 'Beyond the Three Faces of Power', *Polity*, vol. 20.

Jenkins, Richard (1992) *Pierre Bourdieu*, Routledge, London.

Jessop, Bob (1982) *The Capitalist State*, Robertson, Oxford.

Jessop, Bob (1985) *Nicos Poulantzas: Marxist Theory and Political Strategy*, Macmillan Basingstoke.

Jessop, Bob (1990) *State Theory: Putting the Capitalist State in its Place*, Polity, Cambridge.

Jessop, R.D. (1969) 'Exchange and Power in Structural Analysis', *Sociological Review*, vol. 17. Also in Scott (ed.) (1994).

Jenkins, Richard (1992) *Pierre Bourdieu*, Routledge, London.

Keenan, Tom (1987) 'The Paradox of Knowledge and Power: Reading Foucault on a Bias', *Political Theory*, vol. 15.

Kelly, Michael (1994) *Critique and Power: Recasting the Foucault/Habermas Debate*, MIT Press, Cambridge, MA.

Kenny, Anthony (1975) *Will, Freedom and Power*, Blackwell, London.

Kertzer, David (1988) *Ritual, Politics and Power*, Yale University Press, New Haven.

Knights, David and John Roberts (1982) 'The Power of Organization or the Organization of Power', *Organizational Studies*, vol. 3. Also in Scott (ed.) (1994).

Knights, David and Hugh Willmott (1982) 'Power, Values and Relations: A Comment on Benton', *Sociology*, vol. 16. Also in Scott (ed.) (1994).

Kreisberg, Seth (1992) *Transforming Power: Domination, Empowerment, and Education*, State University of New York Press, Albany.

Kuhn, Thomas S. (1970) *The Structure of Scientific Revolutions*, The University of Chicago Press, Chicago.

Kuhn, Thomas S. (1977) *The Essential Tension: Selected Studies in Scientific Thought and Change*, The University of Chicago Press, Chicago.

Laclau, Ernesto and Chantal Mouffe (1985) *Hegemony and Socialist Strategy*, Verso, London.

Lasswell, Harold (1958) *Politics: Who Gets What, When, and How*, Whittlesey Books, New York.

Lasswell, Harold and Abraham Kaplan (1950) *Power and Society*, Yale University Press, New Haven.

Law, John (1986) (ed.) *Power, Action and Belief: A New Sociology of Knowledge?*, Sociological Review Monograph 32, Routledge and Kegan Paul, London.

Layder, Derek (1985) 'Power, Structure and Agency', *Journal for the Theory of Social Behaviour*, vol. 15.

Layder, Derek (1987) 'Key Issues in Structuration Theory: Some Critical Remarks', *Current Perspectives in Social Theory*, vol. 8.

Ledyaev, V.G. (1997) *Power: A Conceptual Analysis*, Nova Science Publishers, Commack, NY.

Lentner, Howard (2000) 'Politics, Power and States in Globalization', in Henri Goverde *et al.* (eds), *Power in Contemporary Politics*, Sage, London.

Liebert R.J. and A.W. Imerskein (eds) *Power, Paradigms and Community Research*, Sage, London.

Lipset, Seymour Martin (1960) *Political Man*, Heinemann, London.

Locke, John (1924) *Two Treatises of Government*, Dent, Everyman's Library, London.

Luke, Timothy W. (1989) *Screens of Power: Ideology, Domination, and Resistance in Informational Society*, University of Illinois Press.

Luhmann, Niklas (1979) *Trust and Power*, John Wiley, London.

Lukács, Georg (1971) *History and Class Consciousness*, Merlin, London.

Lukes, Steven (1972) *Emile Durkheim: His Life and Work*, Allen Lane, London.

Lukes, Steven (1973) *Individualism*, Blackwell, Oxford.

Lukes, Steven (1974) *Power: A Radical View*, Macmillan, London.

Lukes, Steven (1976) 'Reply to Bradshaw', *Sociology*, vol. 10.

Lukes, Steven (1977) *Essays in Social Theory*, Macmillan, London (also (1994) Gregg Revivals, Aldershot).

Lukes, Steven (1979a) 'On the Relativity of Power', in S.C. Brown (ed.), *Philosophical Disputes in the Social Sciences*, Harvester Press, Sussex.

Lukes, Steven (1979b) 'Power and Authority', in Tom Bottomore and Robert Nisbet (eds), *A History of Sociological Analysis*, Heinemann, London.

Lukes, Steven (1985) *Marxism and Morality*, Oxford University Press, Oxford.

Lukes, Steven (1986) (ed.) *Power*, Basil Blackwell, Oxford.

Lukes, Steven (1991a) 'Equality and Liberty: Must They Conflict?', in David Held (ed.), *Political Theory Today*, Stanford University Press, Stanford.

Lukes, Steven (1991b) *Moral Conflict and Politics*, Clarendon, Oxford.

Machiavelli, Niccolò (1958) *The Prince*, Everyman, London.

Machiavelli, Niccolò (1974) *The Discourses*, Penguin Books, Harmondsworth.

MacPherson, C.B. (1962) *The Political Theory of Possessive Individualism: Hobbes to Locke*, Oxford University Press, Oxford.

Markovsky, Barry, Travis Patton and David Miller (1988) 'Power Relations in Exchange Networks, *American Sociological Review*, vol. 53. Also in Scott (ed.) (1994).

Mann, Michael (1984) 'The Autonomous Power of the State: Its Origins, Mechanisms and Results', *European Journal of Sociology*, vol. 25.

Mann, Michael (1986) *The Sources of Social Power, Vol. 1: A History of Power From the Beginning to A.D. 1760*, Cambridge University Press, Cambridge.

Mann, Michael (1988) *States War and Capitalism: Studies in Political Sociology*, Blackwell, Oxford.

Mann, Michael (1990) *The Rise and Decline of the Nation-State*, Blackwell, Oxford.

Mann, Michael (1993) *The Sources of Social Power, Vol. II: The Rise of Classes and Nation-states, 1760–1914*, Cambridge University Press, Cambridge.

Mansbridge, Jane (1994) 'Using Power/Fighting Power', *Constellations*, vol. 1.

Mansbridge, Jane (1997) 'Taking Coercion Seriously', *Constellations*, vol. 3.

March, James (1955) "An Introduction to the Theory and Measurement of Influence', *American Political Science Review*, vol. 59.

Martin, Robert 'The Concept of Power: A Critical Defence', *British Journal of Sociology*, vol. 22. Also in Scott (ed.) (1994).

Mayfield, Sue (1988) *Women and Power*, Dryad, London.

McIntosh, Ian (1997) *Classical Sociological Theory: A Reader*, Edinburgh University Press, Edinburgh.

McLachlan Hugh V. (1981) 'Is "Power" an Evaluative Concept?' *British Journal of Sociology*, vol. 32. Also in Scott (ed.) (1994).

McNay, Lois (1994) *Foucault: A Critical Introduction*, Polity, Cambridge.

Mészáros, István (1989) *The Power of Ideology*, Harvester Wheatsheaf, London.

Merquior, J.G. (1991) *Foucault*, Fontana, London.

Michels, Robert (1915) *Political Parties*, The Free Press, Glencoe.

Miles, Rosalind (1985) *Women and Power*, Futura, London.

Miliband, Ralph (1969) *The State in Capitalist Society*, Quartet, London.

Miliband, Ralph (1970) 'The Capitalist State – Reply to Nicos Poulantzas', *New Left Review*, vol. 59.

Miller, Peter (1987) *Domination and Power*, Routledge, London.

Mills, C. Wright (1956) *The Power Elite*, Oxford University Press, Oxford.

Mills, C. Wright (1958) 'The Structure of Power in American Society', *British Journal of Sociology*, vol. 9.

Mills, C. Wright (1959) *The Sociological Imagination*, Oxford University Press, Oxford.

Mills, C. Wright (1963) *Power, Politics and People*, Oxford University Press, Oxford.

Molm, Linda (1986) 'Gender, Power and Legitimation: A Test of Three Theories', *American Journal of Sociology*, vol. 91. Also in Scott (ed.) (1994).

Morriss, Peter (1972) 'Power in New Haven: A Reassessment of "Who Governs"', *British Journal of Political Science*, vol. 2. Also in Scott (ed.) (1994).

Morriss, Peter (1975) 'The Pluralist Case Not Proven: Hewitt on Britain', *British Journal of Political Science*, vol. 5.

Morriss, Peter (1986) 'Being Discriminating About Discrimination', *Politics*, vol. 6.

Morriss, Peter (1987) *Power: A Philosophical Analysis*, Manchester University Press, Manchester, 2nd edn with a new introduction by the author, forthcoming.

Mosca, Gaetano (1939) *The Ruling Class*, McGraw-Hill, New York.

Nagel, Jack (1975) *The Descriptive Analysis of Power*, Yale University Press, New Haven.

Newton, Kenneth (1969) 'A Critique of the Ruling Elite Model', *Acta Sociologica*, vol. 12. Also in Scott (ed.).

Nietzsche, Friedrich (1956) *The Birth of Tragedy and The Genealogy of Morals*, Doubleday, New York.

Nietzsche, Friedrich (1968) *The Will to Power*, Vintage, New York.

Olsen, Marvin E. and Martin N. Marger (1993) *Power in Modern Societies*, Westview Press, Boulder CO.

O'Neill, John (1987) 'The Disciplinary Society: From Weber to Foucault', *British Journal of Sociology*, vol. 37.

Parenti, Michael (1978) *Power and the Powerless*, St Martin's Press, New York.

Parsons, Talcott (1957) 'The Distribution of Power in American Society', *World Politics*, vol. 10.

Parsons, Talcott (1960) *Structure and Process in Modern Societies* (Includes: 'Authority, Legitimation and Political Action' and 'The Distribution of Power in America'), Free Press, New York.

Parsons, Talcott (1963a) 'On the Concept of Political Power', *Proceedings of the American Philosophical Society*, vol. 107.

Parsons, Talcott (1963b) 'On the Concept of Influence', *Public Opinion Quarterly*, vol. 27.

Parsons, Talcott (1967) *Sociological Theory and Modern Society* (Essays include: 'On The Concept of Political Power', 'Some Reflections on the Place of Force in Social Process' and 'On the Concept of Influence'), Free Press, New York.

Parsons, Talcott (1967) 'The Political Aspects of Social Structure and Process', in David Easton (ed.) *Varieties of Political Theory*, Prentice Hall, Englewood Cliffs, NJ.

Parsons, Talcott (1968) *The Structure of Social Action*, Free Press, New York.

Parsons, Talcott (1991) *The Social System*, Routledge, London.

Parsons, Talcott and Edward Shils (eds) (1961) *Toward a General Theory of Action*, Harvard University Press, Cambridge, MA.

Patton, Paul (1989) 'Taylor and Foucault on Power and Freedom', *Political Studies*, vol. 37.

Pettit, Philip (1996) 'Freedom as Antipower', *Ethics*, vol. 106.

Philp, Mark (1983) 'Foucault on Power: A Problem in Radical Translation?', *Political Theory*, vol. 11.

Pitkin, Hanna F. (1972) *Wittgenstein and Justice*, University of California Press, Berkeley.

Poggi, Gianfranco (1978) *The Development of the Modern State*, Stanford University Press, Stanford.

Poggi, Gianfranco (2000) *Forms of Power*, Polity Press, Cambridge.

Polsby, N.W. (1960) 'How to Study Community Power: The Pluralist Alternative', *Journal of Politics*, vol. 22.

Polsby, Nelson (1979) 'Empirical Investigation of the Mobilization of Bias in Community Power Research', *Political Studies*, vol. 27. Also in Scott (ed.) (1994).

Polby, Nelson W. (1963 and 1980 (2nd edn)) *Community Power and Political Theory*, Yale University Press, London.

Poulantzas, Nicos (1969) 'The Problem of the Capitalist State', *New Left Review*, vol. 58.

Poulantzas, Nicos (1973) *Political Power and Social Classes*, NLB, London.

Poulantzas, Nicos (1976) *The Crisis of the Dictatorships: Portugal, Greece, Spain*, NLB, London.

Poulantzas, Nicos (1978) *State Power Socialism*, Verso, London.

Poulantzas, Nicos (1979) *Class in Contemporary Capitalism*, Verso, London.

Rabinow, Paul (1984) (ed.) *The Foucault Reader: An Introduction to His Thought*, Penguin, Harmondsworth.

Radtke, Lorraine and Henderikus Stam (eds) (1994) *Power/Gender*, Sage, London.

Rawls, John (1971) *A Theory of Justice*, Oxford University Press, Oxford.

Rawls, John (1993) *Political Liberalism*, Columbia University Press, New York.

Robbins, Derek (1991) *The Work of Pierre Bourdieu*, Open University Press, Milton Keynes.

Robbins, Derek (1999) (ed.) *Pierre Bourdieu*, Sage, London.

Robbins, Derek (2000) *Bourdieu and Culture*, Sage, London.

Rose, Nikolas (1989) *Governing the Soul: The Shaping of the Private Self*, Routledge, London.

Rose, Nikolas (1996) *Inventing Our Selves: Psychology, Power and Personhood*, Cambridge University Press, Cambridge.

Rose, Nikolas (1999) *Power of Liberty*, Cambridge University Press, Cambridge.

Rosinski, Herbert (1965) *Power and Human Destiny*, New York, Praeger.

Rueschemeyer, Dietrich (1986) *Power and the Division of Labour*, Polity, Cambridge.

Russell, Bertrand (1975) *Power: A New Social Analysis*, Unwin, London.

de Saussure, Ferdinand (1960) *Course in General Linguistics*, Peter Owen Ltd, London.

Sawicki, Jena (1991) *Disciplining Foucault: Feminism, Power and the Body*, Routledge, London.

Schneck, Stephen (1987) 'Michel Foucault on Power/Discourse, Theory and Practice', *Human Studies*, vol. 10.

Schumpeter, Joseph A. (1976) *Capitalism, Socialism and Democracy* (5th edn), Allen and Unwin, London.

Scott, James C. (1987) *Weapons of the Weak: Everyday Forms of Peasant Resistance*, Yale University Press, New Haven.

Scott, John (1994) (ed.) *Power: Critical Concepts*, 3 vols, Routledge, London.

Sewell, William (1992) 'A Theory of Structure: Duality, Agency, and Transformation', *American Journal of Sociology*, vol. 98.

Sheridan, Alan (1980) *Michel Foucault: The Will to Truth*, Tavistock, London.

Shumway, David R. (1989) *Michel Foucault*, The University Press of Virginia, Charlottesville.

Simon, Herbert (1953) 'Notes on the Observation and Measurement of Political Power', *Journal of Politics*, vol. 15. Also in Scott (ed.) (1994).

Smart, Barry (1983) *Foucault, Marxism and Critique*, Routledge, London.

Smart, Barry (1985) *Michel Foucault*, Routledge, London.

Smith, Anna Maria (1998) *Laclau and Mouffe*, Routledge, London.

Sorel, Georges (1914) *Reflections on Violence*, B.W. Huebsch, New York.

Spivak, Gayatri C. (1996) *The Spivak Reader: Selected Works of Gayatri Chakravorty Spivak*, ed. Donna Landry and Gerald MacLean, Routledge, New York, 1996.

Spruyt, Hendrik (1994) *The Sovereign State and its Competitors: An Analysis of Systems Change*, Princeton University Press, Princeton, NJ.

Swartz, David (1997) *Culture & Power: The Sociology of Pierre Bourdieu*, University of Chicago Press, Chicago.

Taylor, Charles (1984) 'Foucault on Freedom and Truth', *Political Theory*, vol. 12.

Taylor, Charles (1985) 'Connolly, Foucault and Truth', *Political Theory*, vol. 13.

Taylor, Charles (1989) 'Taylor and Foucault on Power and Freedom: A Reply', *Political Studies*, vol. 37.

Therborn, Göran (1978) *What Does the Ruling Class do When it Rules?*, Verso, London.

Therborn, Göran (1999) *The Ideology of Power and Power of Ideology*, Verso, London.

Thiele, Leslie (1990) 'The Agony of Politics: The Nietzschean Roots of Foucault's Thought', *American Political Science Review*, vol. 84.

Tilly, Charles (1990) *Coercion, Capital, and European States*, Cambridge University Press, Cambridge.

Urry, John (1982) 'The Duality of Structure: Some Critical Issues', *Theory, Culture and Society*, vol. 1.

Ward, Hugh (1987) 'Structural Power: A Contradiction in Terms', *Political Studies*, vol. 35.

Warren, Mark (1991) *Nietzsche and Political Thought*, The MIT Press, Cambridge, MA.

Wartenberg, Thomas E. (1988) 'The Concept of Power in Feminist Theory', *Praxis International*, vol. 8.

Wartenberg, Thomas E. (1990) *The Forms of Power: From Domination to Transformation*, Temple University Press, Philadelphia.

Wartenberg, Thomas E. (1992) (ed.) *Rethinking Power*, State University of New York Press, Albany.

Waste, Robert J. (1986) (ed.) *Community Power: Directions for Future Research*, Sage, London.

Weber, Max (1948) *From Max Weber: Essays in Sociology*, ed. H.H. Gerth and C. Wright Mills, Routledge, London.

Weber, Max (1976) *The Protestant Ethic and the Spirit of Capitalism*, Allen and Unwin, London.

Weber, Max (1978) *Economy and Society* (2 vols), *An Outline of Interpretive Sociology*, University of California Press, Berkeley.

West, David (1987) 'Power and Formation: New Foundations For a Radical Concept of Power', *Inquiry*, vol. 30.

White, D.M. (1971) 'Power and Intention', *American Political Science Review*, vol. 65.

Willis, Paul (1977) *Learning to Labour*, Saxon House, Farnborough.

Wittgenstein, Ludwig (1967) *Philosophical Investigations*, Oxford University Press, Oxford.

Wittig, Monique (1981) 'One is Not Born a Woman', *Feminist Issues*, vol. 1.

Wolfinger, Raymond (1960) 'Reputation and Reality in the Study of "Community Power"', *American Sociological Review*, vol. 25. Also in Scott (ed.) (1994).

Wolfinger, Raymond (1971a) 'Nondecisions and the Study of Local Politics', *American Political Science Review*, vol. 65. Also in Scott (ed.) (1994).

Wolfinger, Raymond (1971b) 'Rejoinder to Frey's "Comments"', *American Political Science Review*, vol. 65. Also in Scott (ed.) (1994).

Wrong, Denis (1967) 'Some problems in Defining Social Power', *American Journal of Sociology*, vol. 73.

Wrong, Denis ([1979] 1995) *Power: Its Forms Bases and Uses* (with a new introduction by the author), Transaction Publishers, New Brunswick, NJ.

# Index